THE ULTIMATE ACCOUNT OF THE GREATEST POLITICAL DRAMA OF OUR TIME—RIGHT THROUGH THE LAST DESPERATE HOURS

Less than two years before, Richard Nixon had been overwhelmingly elected President. Now, in the inmost circles of the White House, his aides, led by former General Alexander Haig, desperately sought a way to communicate to him, to persuade him to resign, to avoid the fearful catastrophe bearing down upon him and the nation. How had this happened? What had gone wrong? Now Theodore White has written a book not to accuse, not to apologize, but to reveal the whole intensely complex, immensely important, unforgettably compelling story.

"A story for the ages. In the hands of Theodore White, Watergate becomes a compassionate, terrifying Greek-style tragedy" —**Robert Ardley**

"A triumph . . . a fast-moving narrative that illuminates who Nixon is, who we all are, and what our country has become" —*Saturday Review*

"This is not just another book about Watergate—it is *the other* book" —**Eugene J. McCarthy**

"Not only Theodore White's best book, but also the best book written about Watergate" —*Washington Monthly*

THEODORE H. WHITE

Breach of Faith

THE FALL OF RICHARD NIXON

A DELL BOOK

Published by
DELL PUBLISHING CO., INC.
1 Dag Hammarskjold Plaza
New York, New York 10017

For
GEORGE BACKER
(1902 - 1974)

CONTENTS

Breach of Faith

1

LET JUSTICE BE DONE

Wednesday dawned with an overcast in Washington—hot, sticky, threatening to rain—July 24th, 1974. And the flag over the Supreme Court was at half-staff, in memory of Earl Warren.

Inside the Court was hush. Breaking tradition, the Court had called the White House the day before, suggesting the President's counsel be at hand this morning.

The chamber soaked up sound now, as those who came to listen filed in, the double rows of four pillars on each side of the square hall making an echoless chamber in which murmuring hummed below the threshold of hearing. At five minutes of eleven Leon Jaworski, Special Prosecutor, entered, flanked by two younger lawyers, to take their seats before the bar to the right. Then came three young White House lawyers, in summer suits, seating themselves to the left. From above, the light fell from white porcelain ceiling rosettes to the throng crowding seats and galleries.

Then the voice of the marshal, "Oyez! Oyez! Oyez! All-persons-having-business-before-the-Honorable-the-Supreme-Court-of-the-United-States-are-admonished-to-draw-near-and-give-their-attention-for-the-Court-is-now-sitting. God-save-the-United-States-and-this-Honorable-Court!"

Oyez, Oyez, Oyez—the words echoed out of the medieval French and the particular system of justice the Normans imposed almost a thousand years ago on conquered England, from which had developed that common law which still governs Americans and Englishmen. This system of justice holds that the law must act on evidence; to get at that evidence, all the power of the state may be mobilized. What was at issue this day was whether those close associates of Richard Nixon, President of the United States, under indictment at that moment, could be fairly judged in court without necessary facts; and the highest court in the land had been summoned to judge the President's authority to withhold those facts. Oyez, Oyez, Oyez—Give Ear, Give Ear, Give Ear. Listen! And then the Justices, eight out of nine (Justice Rehnquist had disqualified himself from hearing this case), silently materialized from behind the wine-red velvet drapes to take their seats on the bench.

The Chief Justice, Warren Burger, leaned forward in his black leather chair and spoke for a moment of his predecessor, Earl Warren, who had just died. Earl Warren had enlarged the power of this Court more than any other Justice of the twentieth century. Now, Burger was to enlarge that power yet further as he proceeded to speak to Case No. 73–1766, United States against Nixon, and the cross-petition, Case No. 73–1834, Nixon against the United States.

Holding his notes steady in hand, expressionless, Burger read.

He dismissed first the petition of Nixon against the United States; reviewed the authority of the President's Special Prosecutor, who had brought suit; demolished at once the President's contention that this was a dispute within the Executive Branch of government, to be decided by the President alone. "His [the Special Prosecutor's] authority," said Burger, "is to represent the United States as a sovereign, and it includes express authority to contest any privilege asserted by the Executive Branch." Then to the central question as the Court saw it: Who decides what the law is? "We . . . reaffirm . . . emphatically the province and the duty of this Court to say what the law is with respect to a claim of privilege such as presented in this case."

The others on the bench listened without expression. They were old men, one saw, very old, their reach going back through thirty-five years of American politics. Justice Douglas, oldest, an appointee of Franklin Roosevelt, a frail man now, appeared bored. Stewart, an Eisenhower choice, was expressionless. Powell, a Nixon choice, was intent, drawn and pale. Marshall, a choice of Lyndon Johnson, only a few years earlier a burly, vigorous man, listened head down—old, too. Only Byron White, a Kennedy choice, seemed in full vigor, at times leaning back, then cupping his chin in his hand, and then again, drumming his fingers noiselessly on the bench as Burger continued to define the power and privileges to which the Chief Executive was entitled.

There were indeed, said Burger, executive privileges of secrecy that were implicit in the President's power to govern, but "here the claim of privilege rests simply on the generalized undifferentiated claim of the need to keep all presidential communications private and confidential. . . . [Yet] the constitutional need for production of relevant evidence in a criminal proceeding is specific and central to the fair adjudication of a particular criminal case in the administration of justice."

An intake of breath, and Burger proceeded to his conclusion. In the case at instance, a Federal judge, John J. Sirica, had ordered Richard Nixon to produce those taped recordings of the President's private conversations which might contain evidence of crime. The President had said no, and appealed for review of Sirica's ruling. Concluding, Burger said, "The generalized assertion of privilege must yield to the demonstrated specific need for the evidence in a pending criminal trial. Accordingly the judgment under review is affirmed. . . ."

Silence. Then the clack of a gavel. And then the Justices swiveled in their chairs, rose and, like ghosts of an olden drama, disappeared through the burgundy drapes behind them, the thwack of the gavel still echoing. It was 11:20 in the morning in Washington, only 8:20 in San Clemente, California, where Richard Nixon had secluded himself. Eight hours later would come the next thwack of a gavel, as Peter Rodino, chairman of the Judiciary Committee of the House of Representatives, would call to order in Room 2141 of the Rayburn House Office Building those members of his committee who, for the next six days, must act to define power—theirs, the people's and the President's—in rolling, vivid and brilliant debate for all the world to see and hear.

"*Fiat justitia, ruat coelum,*" the Roman lawmakers had said. "Let Justice be done, though the heavens fall." Justice, at every level of American power, was now under way: in two weeks a President would fall.

*   *   *

I had lunch within an hour of the decision with Leon Jaworski, whose authority as Special Prosecutor Chief Justice Burger had just affirmed as sovereign. But as Jaworski sat at table, breaking his custom in order to celebrate with a carafe of white wine, there was little of sovereign manner about him. He was an old man, today weary, tufts of white hair above the face of a friendly goblin, the voice firm, now precise, then again grandfatherly. And no elation in his voice about the victory.

Jaworski recalled that over a year ago he had first been approached to become Special Prosecutor. He had insisted on complete independence and been told he would have to operate within guidelines set by the Department of Justice, and the matter was dropped. Later his name had been suggested to Nixon as chief counsel *for* the President's defense. But nothing came of that. Six months after the first approach he had finally accepted the role of Special Prosecutor only because the President's Chief of Staff, General Alexander Haig, had specifically promised, "If necessary, you can take the President to court." He was, Jaworski insisted, "not after the President; I just want all the facts out . . . we're in search of the truth. Wherever the truth leads, we're going to prosecute them." Unless he was dissembling, it seemed to this reporter that Jaworski had no inkling, no fore-echo of what it was that Richard Nixon had been concealing, what the subpoenaed tapes would soon reveal.

Mostly, Jaworski was in a reminiscent mood, reminiscences going back to Texas, his boyhood in Waco, trials in local courts, the upward life of a successful lawyer. But through the recollections ran his underlying cause, in phrases which on any other day and occasion would have sounded trite, but now carried meaning.

"What happened this morning," said the tired man, "proved what we teach in schools, it proved what we teach in colleges, it proved everything we've been trying to get across—that no man is above the law." Jaworski was living now in a two-room-and-dinette suite at the Jefferson Hotel, his wife cooking for him, far from the comforts and pleasant estate of his life in Texas. But he intended to go through with this to the end, he said, he had to, not for reward nor for fame, but simply because of the young people. This case, said Jaworski, would shape what the young of

America would think or say or do in this system for all of the next generation. Unless the young people believed, really believed in our insitutions, the system simply would not work. He quoted Disraeli; according to his recall, Disraeli had said, "The youth of the nation are the trustees of posterity." His clients were the youth of the nation, his prosecution a defense of the system.

At about the same time, a few blocks away in the exclusive White House Executive Dining Room, at a table spread with stiff napery and shining silver, four other men, whose client was the President of the United States, were also sitting down to lunch. They were Dean Burch, coordinator of the President's political defense; William Timmons, the President's liaison chief and advocate on Capitol Hill; Leonard Garment, who had withdrawn from the post of Watergate counsel at the end of 1973 but still remained the house conscience of the White House; and Fred Buzhardt, special counsel in charge of the tapes.

They were gloomy. Loyalists all, devoted to what they thought best in the Nixon Presidency, they were like German officers on the firing line in 1918 who knew long before the Kaiser that the time for surrender had come. Timmons and Burch felt that this morning's Court ruling had been decisive; it was time for the President to pack it in. All the previous week, Timmons' reporting of Congressional votes had shown persistent, accelerating erosion of Richard Nixon's support. Now, argued Timmons, a moment of principle had come that would let the President resign with honor—this decision would undermine all future Presidents' authority and thus, in defense of future Presidents, Richard Nixon should, at this moment, resign. (After lunch, Timmons would speak to General Haig in San Clemente and ask that this advice be brought, in his name, immediately to the President.) Burch concurred with Timmons. Garment, a romantic with a fondness for losing causes, felt disaster was inevitable, too; the President must resign—but not that day; they ought to at least still consider the route of going to the floor of the House.

Buzhardt listened to their conversation, saying little. Buzhardt knew more about the tapes on which the court's decision had turned than any of them—insofar as Richard Nixon permitted any man to be his surrogate in this area of his inner privacy. Only by specific permission of the President, and generally only after the President had listened first, could copies of tapes be brought to Buzhardt's office in Room 106 of the Executive Office Building, where he would listen and transcribe the portions suggested. At their lunch, Buzhardt, usually a sparkling talker, was strangely silent. He would mutter quietly, "It's all over, it's all over now."

What his lunch companions did not know was that Buzhardt had already listened to the critical tapes subpoenaed that morning; and had discovered that the man, the President, he had defended for so long, to his own exhaustion and heart attack, was a liar. Buzhardt had spoken to the President in San Clemente very early that morning, before the opening of the Court in Washington, and given his opinion that the decision would be adverse; and that they, out there in California, should be giving serious thought to their reaction. The President himself had responded and said Buzhardt ought to listen to the June 23rd tapes— "there may be a problem there." Buzhardt had found the tapes quickly. The first morning conversation of the President, as the tape had caught it on June 23rd, 1972, was full of gobbledygook and silences; then came the discussion of routine business—but in between was five minutes of what Buzhardt would later call "this horrible thing."

The horrible thing was quite simple: there was the voice of the President on June 23rd, 1972, directing the CIA to halt an FBI investigation which would be politically embarrassing to his re-election—an obstruction of justice. To Buzhardt it was personally devastating. More than a year before, he had prepared the final draft of the President's public statement of May 22nd, 1973, denying any use of the CIA for domestic political purposes. Buzhardt at that time had wanted to get out the story of the Nixon administration surveillances, *in toto*, and fast. He had taken the CIA passage of that statement to Nixon personally, admonishing, "We have got to be right, we've got to be precisely accurate." He had been assured that what was written was so. "I thought," said Buzhardt, "that statement would stand for all time." Now it could not stand.

Buzhardt listened to the tape a second time and decided

that "school was out." He telephoned General Alexander Haig and Presidential counsel James St. Clair immediately in California and reported that "the smoking pistol" had been found. To which he added, to Haig, that the time had come for the President to concentrate on how he should leave office—now. For the story had to be disclosed. Haig agreed to relay the message to the President.

All this had happened before Buzhardt joined his friends for lunch, but he told them none of it. The problem was out there in California, with the President; that was where decision must be made.

At San Clemente that morning, the first news flash of the Court decision had been carried over the tickers to the West Coast White House, a rambling, one-story, stucco building, with redwood trim, at about 8:25. One of General Haig's aides—Charles Wardell, a Vietnam combat veteran and a Harvard graduate in political science—was monitoring the news, and sped the flash to his chief: "We lost, eight to nothing." Haig asked for the ticker copy itself and took that to the President.

Haig remains absolutely resistant to quotation of any conversation with Richard Nixon ("It's his story, he'll write it his way when he gets round to it"). But it is quite certain that, at the first news flash, the President did not feel it was mandatory to obey the decision; it still seemed to him that he might be able to stonewall a defense and let the impeachment process start—until it was pointed out to him that the country simply would not stand for such defiance; nor would his staff. The tapes would have to be released.

It was thus not until early afternoon in Washington that Haig's response was received—to start transcription immediately, and from duplicate tapes, not the originals. It would take days to duplicate the tapes of the sixty-four conversations subpoenaed, and Haig did not want to chance mangling or mutilating any of the tapes. There must be no further mysterious erasures.

The Western White House would be silent for almost eight hours. Before any statement could be made, they must wait for the full, reasoned text of the decision—all thirty-one pages—to be wired to the President's attendant defense counsel, St. Clair. Response on this issue was too important to be based on a news flash.

While they waited, the President worked on the text of a major economics speech with Ray Price, his favorite speechwriter. Inflation was the corrosive peril of America in 1974, and if Nixon could turn America's attention from the drama of impeachment to the common danger of inflation, the President would not only be doing his duty but might score points in headlines for leadership. Price remembers the President, working with him on the economics speech, as cool and composed. But Price was one of the few men who could see the President, who had become increasingly inaccessible since spring.

Paperwork had been congesting and congealing for months—indeed, since late January, when the President had first listened privately to the June 23rd tapes. The work of the Presidency had gone on, but not the President. Since some time in February, Haig had been more than deputy President—from his desk, appointments, legislation, bills all moved to proper channels, sometimes with and sometimes without the consideration of the President. "Nixon was a haunted man," said a member of his staff, "able to focus stiffly only on foreign affairs, which both intrigued and distracted him." He was able that last week in San Clemente to focus on the war in Cyprus, to overrule an agitated American ambassador who insisted that the Sixth Fleet must land a force there immediately to avert massacre. But his behavior in San Clemente had become increasingly erratic. He would, for example, call urgently to have the Secretary of Housing and Urban Development, James T. Lynn, and the chief of the Domestic Council, Kenneth R. Cole, come out to San Clemente on a Thursday—then receive them for ten minutes on Saturday and send them back. This day, so far as is known, the President saw only St. Clair, Price, Haig and Press Secretary Ronald Ziegler. Both Haig and Price report him as cool.

Not so the other men of the Presidential party scattered at various inns and motels near the San Clemente estate. The President had told Haig that Fred Buzhardt was still sick, still not well after his heart attack, and that he had misread the tapes. But the young men knew that Buzhardt had also spoken to St. Clair and St. Clair was thoroughly upset. Whatever was on the tapes Buzhardt had just listened to in Washington was very bad.

The nation was waiting for response, however. The television audience was about to tune in for Peter Rodino's Judiciary Committee debate on impeachment, and so, shortly before the gavel fell in Washington (seven o'clock Eastern time, four o'clock Pacific time), St. Clair stood before the cameras at the Surf-and-Sand Hotel and stated that the President would turn over all subpoenaed tapes to Judge Sirica as soon as they could be made ready; he would, said St. Clair, "comply with [the Court's] decision." "That's news?" muttered a TV cameraman waiting to enter Rodino's Judiciary chamber.

At that point only two senior men in government knew the President was about to be caught in a great big lie—Fred Buzhardt and Richard Nixon. So, too, did several others no longer in government—Bob Haldeman, John Mitchell, John Dean.

The President himself, with Haig and Ziegler, did not return from California until four days later, Sunday evening, July 28th. But others of the Presidential party had been returning earlier; and by Saturday and early Sunday all were struck by the contrast in moods. At San Clemente the mood had been one of combat and confrontation. They would fight; they had set up three task forces, one for each article of expected impeachment, to prepare for full defense in House and Senate. Now, rejoining their comrades at the White House, they were startled by the mood of defeat, the sense of those on the scene that it was all over, all battles lost. They did not know yet what lay on the June 23rd tapes—nor did James St. Clair in any detail. St. Clair had come back on Firday, for he was required to appear before Judge Sirica to arrange compliance with the Supreme Court order; and there he had been chided by the Judge for not having listened to the tapes in person. But St. Clair was exhausted, and so flew off to Boston, his home, that Friday afternoon, for a weekend of rest, not returning to Washington until Monday, not listening to the tapes until Tuesday.

By Tuesday, the White House had begun to ripple in a tight but widening vortex of internal turmoil that would spread, grow, suck in the entire nation and all its politics in the next seven days. On Saturday, the House Judiciary Committee had voted to recommend impeachment of the President on Article I—Obstruction of Justice. On Monday, it had voted to recommend Article II—Abuse of Power; on Tuesday, it had voted to recommend Article III—Defiance of Committee Subpoenas.

It was that day, Tuesday, that the President himself listened to the questionable June 23rd tapes again—all three tapes of that date—and summoned Buzhardt to his office. The President was still convinced he had done nothing wrong, even after listening to the tapes, and insisted that Buzhardt go back to his office and listen once more—then return and admit that he was mistaken in thinking they marked the end of the fight. Buzhardt went back and listened again, this time with St. Clair—and, in Buzhardt's opinion, the two afternoon tapes only compounded and made worse the crime defined in the morning tape; he so reported to the President at 6:30 in the evening. The President was furious—and for a week he would not talk to Buzhardt.

"He still didn't believe he made that decision," said Buzhardt later. "It was obvious that he had. But he really believed what he was saying, it was pathetic. . . . He could have passed a lie-detector test."

St. Clair passed his Rubicon that afternoon, too. An overworked man for months, he had not enjoyed listening to the scratchy sounds of the tapes. His ear for electronic recordings of such poor quality was bad, and he had been unable to afford hours and hours of listening. An agreement had been worked out by St. Clair and Buzhardt: whatever the President made available to Buzhardt, Buzhardt would make available to St. Clair—if St. Clair chose to listen. This Tuesday afternoon, Buzhardt insisted St. Clair listen. A young aide of St. Clair's remembers tiptoeing into Buzhardt's office that day while both senior lawyers were listening, earphones over their heads, to the playing of the reels. The young aide remembers St. Clair saying to Buzhardt, "Did you hear that, Fred? I can't believe he said that." The aide walked out without disturbing them.

It was Tuesday also that Buzhardt told Haig precisely what lay on the tapes. Haig is described by one White House lawyer that day as more than disgusted—"Al was sick, plain sick." Stiff-lipped to a fault, Haig refuses to discuss his reaction and describes himself only as "shocked, just shocked." So shocked he would not take Buzhardt's word for what had been said; he wanted a transcript, an accurate transcript, and one of his own secretaries, Pat McKee, would listen and transcribe.

On Wednesday, July 31st, with the rough transcripts on his desk, Alexander Haig knew he must act. Read the conversations however one would, there was no doubt that on June 23rd, six days after the Watergate burglary of the Democratic Party's headquarters, the President had been told that his former Attorney General and dear friend John Mitchell was involved in that burglary. And worse: on the advice of said John Mitchell, relayed by John Dean to Bob Haldeman, Richard Nixon had used the Federal machinery —namely, the CIA—to obstruct and halt the FBI investigation of the break-in. Nixon had been lying, therefore, for more than two years, lying to the public, lying to Congress, lying to his own staff, at times probably lying to himself. The matter was intolerable. Unless he, Haig, acted immediately, then he, St. Clair, Garment, Burch, Timmons and other honorable men who had served the President unflinchingly would themselves become party to crime.

There could be no cover-up any longer. The first twenty of the sixty-four subpoenaed conversations had already been delivered to Judge Sirica's office on Monday, and, sooner or later, they must leak and become public.

Haig, normally a debonair, cheerful man, ready with quip or smile for civilian visitors, can transform himself to snap-tempered, full four-star-general grimness at will. Wednesday afternoon, thus, he was full four-star grim. Ziegler felt it when Haig screamed at him on the telephone. Timmons knew it quickly, too. Timmons asked Haig that day to get him an early transcript of the tapes, for he, Timmons, had an obligation to the stalwarts on the Judiciary Committee and to the entire Republican minority; he must let them know the worst so a defense could be fashioned. Haig curtly replied that these tapes were very bothersome —Timmons would have to wait. His secretary Muriel Hartley asked him about the tapes; Haig snapped back, "Worst ever," and went on.

Haig was busy that Wednesday. First he must tell Henry Kissinger. Kissinger had already decided two weeks earlier that there was no way out for the President except to resign. Kissinger could sense the erosion in foreign affairs; the President had lost his authority abroad; he was unwelcome in Europe. Now Kissinger counseled that however Haig handled the situation, there must be no panic, no collapse of government; whatever exit was planned must be a dignified one and the government must stay on course. Kissinger and Haig would be on the telephone to each other three or four times a day, all the next week. Kissinger had been Haig's mentor and chief for four years of the first Nixon term, in the National Security office of the Presidency. But now the burden lay on Haig—*he*, not Kissinger, was Chief of Staff to the President; and this President could not long remain President.

Haig was a military man, still an amateur in politics, but he had learned much. A West Point graduate, he had been assigned to General MacArthur's staff in Toyko in 1947 and watched the American military there rewrite Japanese politics. He had served in combat in the Korean War, returned to Washington and come swiftly to the attention of one of Robert McNamara's favorites at the Pentagon, Democrat Joseph Califano. Detailed to work with Robert Kennedy during the Cuban missile crisis, Haig had seen the White House from the inside. In Vietnam he had commanded a battalion in action, and then, at Califano's suggestion, had become aide to Henry Kissinger in Richard Nixon's White House, rising swiftly in rank from colonel to four-star general—his last promotion earning him the quiet rancor of 240 senior generals over whom he had been jumped to eminence. He had replaced Haldeman as Nixon's Chief of Staff, and still thought of himself as a non-political man. "I learned to be an observer in politics, not an advocate," he told writer Nick Thimmesch once. "I made value judgments and kept them to myself. But that's changing. I have strong views—I'm not a eunuch or a whore—but it's not an excessive burden to restrain them."

That day, July 31st, the combination of Haig's military and political backgrounds came together. The Presidency needed a leader; Haig could sense dissolution and consternation all about him, as men questioned their own loyalties, their own risks, their own futures.

As, for example, St. Clair's evening visit to Leonard Garment. St. Clair wandered down the empty corridors of the Executive Office Building and settled down on Garment's couch. Without telling Garment exactly what was on the tapes, St. Clair asked what he should do. A lawyer has to stick by his client, does he not? But were there other superior considerations? Garment answered that, professionally, St. Clair had no other way—he had an obligation to Richard Nixon to continue as his lawyer. Garment added that he himself was not going to run out on the President *in extremis* at this moment. But he admitted that he was approaching the point where there might be a contradiction between his lawyer's duty and the national interest; and that St. Clair, too, might soon have to insert his own values of national need into interpretation of the law. Only not right then.

Thursday, August 1st, was the day Haig became acting President of the United States.

In his search for guidance, he had begun with an early-morning visit to the office of Vice-President Ford on the second floor of the Executive Office Building, telling Ford only that there was new evidence on its way to Judge Sirica which might sway the House to vote impeachment. He followed with several lawyers' conferences at the White House. Sometime during the day, Haig thought of sounding out Senator James O. Eastland, one of the President's absolute loyalists on the Hill. He told Eastland of the nature of the new evidence—and Eastland replied that with such evidence the Senate would certainly convict. And then, at 3:30 in the afternoon, still troubled by uncertainties, Haig crossed to the EOB once more to brief Ford in fuller detail on what was on the tapes, which he called "devastating, even catastrophic." Haig reviewed all the options under discussion in the divided White House—full fight, resignation, pledges of pardon—and asked Ford's advice. "I told him," said Ford later, "that I had to have some time to think. . . ."

There was no guidance there; there could be none from Nixon's Constitutional successor—a political fact of life which Ford nailed down firmly in a call to Haig. He had, said Ford, "no intention of recommending what President Nixon should do about resigning or not resigning."

And thus, by Thursday afternoon, since Ford could or would not lead, Haig was on his own. There was no parallel in all American history for the episode over which Haig presided for the next seven days. Action had to be taken, and he had to take it. Other countries had known such moments, episodes where the chief-of-state had been forced from office either by those he loved or by a cabal which hated him, but not America. It was quite clear in Haig's mind how he must go about relieving Richard Nixon of his command. First, the government had to be kept turning and functioning, no matter what. Second, there could be no air of panic. The President must be sheltered against the unbearable pressures already building up so he could think. And third, in order to let him think, he must be given the facts, in the most precise, accurate and realistic terms—in short, in Haig's words, "all of this to help keep his analytical processes going."

What the men in the White House were involved in, without ever admitting it to themselves, was the management of an unstable personality.

In seclusion with his children, his wife and Bebe Rebozo, Richard Nixon was seeing from outside almost no one but Ronald Ziegler and Alexander Haig. But Haig was a channel of fact and cold reporting; no advocate any longer of Richard Nixon, Haig was an advocate for the Presidency. If he could get the facts before the President clearly, he was certain that the President would act beyond himself in the national interest and resign. Yet—with too much pressure, something might trigger the combat instinct in Richard Nixon to follow the trail through to the Congress, through to the Senate trial for months that might keep the country leaderless in time of crisis at home and abroad. Haig was dealing with a time bomb which, if not defused in just the right way, might blow the course of American history apart.

Early in the evening, Haig was off on his own track. He called in speechwriter Ray Price, whom everyone trusted, and telling him specifically, but briefly, what the new tapes contained, informed Price that there was no question, even in the President's mind, about disclosure of the tapes; the only question was how, and when; and relayed the information that the President was considering the idea of a television address to the nation to accompany their revelation. After which, Haig offered a thought of his own: he urged Price to do something more, to start drafting a statement of resignation for the President, to be ready when necessary. Haig was setting up the prime option.

By Friday, August 2nd, Haig, still Chief of Staff to the President, was nonetheless pursuing the course that only he could lead—the course that would bring the President to resignation without forcing his hand. And that required the triggering of political realities which the President would be unable to ignore.

Most important, thus, was the afternoon visit of Congressman Charles Wiggins. An unkown Southern California Congressman two weeks earlier, Wiggins had become a national figure. His defense of the President's case before the Judiciary Committee on television had been no less than brilliant; with an eloquence few lawyers achieve, with stubbornness and a grasp of sequential facts, Wiggins had in good faith become the public leader of the Nixon cause. Now he must be undeceived. At the moment, Friday morning, Wiggins was organizing Nixon's House loyalists for defense on the floor of Congress, listing names for debates, reaching for allies, drafting the minority report of the Judiciary Committee which he would take to the House, against the majority report for impeachment. For Haig to let Wiggins go forward with an uninformed and misleading minority report would be to let down all the loyalists on the Judiciary Committee.

At 1:15 St. Clair tried to reach Wiggins at his office; at 2:00 Wiggins called back; at 2:30 Wiggins was ushered into Alexander Haig's office, where St. Clair was also waiting. Haig thanked Wiggins for his defense of the President, remarked that only in the last few days had he and St. Clair, for the first time, come across portions of a conversation on June 23rd, 1972, between the President and H. R. Haldeman, which were of "evil significance." Haig thrust across the table a few sheets of transcript and Wiggins began to read. "I began with no sense of foreboding," recalled Wiggins. "During the last two weeks I'd gotten my adversary hat on. I was ready to do battle with the whole damned Congress. I was looking at it as Nixon's attorney, not as a member of Congress." Wiggins read the pages quickly once; and then a second time, slowly; and then it came over him, the full extent of the disaster.

"What do you intend to do with this information?" he asked; then, answering his own question, said, "It seems to me you've either got to claim the Fifth Amendment or let it out." They told him the material had been sent to Judge Sirica; that it would also be turned over to Congress; and they asked him what the effect there would be. Wiggins replied, "Devastating." He asked what more was to come, and St. Clair replied that they didn't know—every time a secretary sat down to transcribe, they were on tenterhooks about what might come out of the tapes. Wiggins read the pages a third time and then, thinking aloud, said that the question of impeachment and conviction was no longer in doubt; for the President's sake, for the sake of the country and the party, the President should be urged to consider resignation immediately. "It came right out of me," recalled Wiggins. "Always I'd been saying no to resignation."

There was no protest from the lawyer and the General; they acquiesced. But St. Clair observed that as the President's legal counsel he could not raise that matter; and Haig observed that as Chief of Staff his duty was to be supportive of the President in the crisis; not urge resignation. Wiggins observed dryly, as a lawyer, that even from Nixon's personal standpoint it should be a resignation—that if he were impeached and convicted, Nixon wouldn't be able to afford even to live in San Clemente. The conversation lasted an hour; and when Wiggins left, driving back to his office with growing anger, he left behind two men who knew they had triggered reality, a reality which would soon become apparent to Richard Nixon, too.

Haig pulled a second trigger immediately after Wiggins had left—this time with a call to Senator Robert P. Griffin of Michigan. Griffin, too, was a loyalist—Nixon had exerted himself to the utmost in 1972 to ensure Griffin's re-election. Haig caught Griffin as he was about to fly back to Michigan for the weekend; he told Griffin, too, the story. The next morning, after a sleepless night, Griffin called his Washington office and dictated a note to the President, to be delivered immediately. Not revealing what Haig had told him of the tapes, Griffin concluded his letter on an insurrectionary note. The President, said Griffin, had barely enough votes to survive a Senate trial; the Senate would have to subpoena his tapes for that trial; "If you should defy such a subpoena," Griffin concluded, "I shall regard that as an impeachable offense and vote accordingly."

There was still more for Haig to do that Friday evening. The President had asked that Haig seek the reaction of the slim and diminishing group he trusted most, the group that next gathered in Haig's office at seven o'clock. In addition to Buzhardt, St. Clair, Haig and Price, a true believer was added: speechwriter Patrick Buchanan, conservative, eloquent, faithful to the cause. Now for the first time both Price and Buchanan read the transcripts, and there was no doubt in the mind of either. They were bitterly angry. If the President wanted their reaction, their reaction was unanimous: the President should resign.

Buchanan and Price were upset not only on principle, but personally. After all, they too had labored far into the nights a year ago, in May, 1973, when the President had pledged the nation in a public statement that "At no time did I attempt, or did I authorize others to attempt, to implicate the CIA in the Watergate matter." One night over a year ago, as they began their defense of the President, Price and Buchanan had had before them the private memoranda of Lieutenant General Vernon Walters of the CIA, stating that the President's staff had requested the CIA to move in and call off the FBI; Buchanan remembers Walters characterizing the request as "100% political." Trying to write an honest statement a year ago, Buchanan and Price had asked the President whether such an approach had indeed been made to the CIA for political purposes; the President had assured them that simply was not so. Now, reading the transcripts in Haig's office, Buchanan was outraged. Price was of a milder mood ("The President had done me a favor by deceiving me," he said later. "It meant that I'd been able to write for him honestly").

The news of Buchanan's defection must have disturbed the President most. He had chosen Buchanan as a twenty-five-year-old eight years earlier, from the editorial desk of the St. Louis *Globe-Democrat*, attracted by the flair of a writer of a quality uncommon among young conservatives. If Nixon could not count on Buchanan, he could count on no man of quality. The thought must have been expressed at the family dinner table that night, for about midnight, when Buchanan remembers he was "stoning myself with dry martinis," the President's daughter Julie was on the telephone to him—she must see him the next morning.

All of Richard Nixon's power now was reduced to this —a family circle, plus Bebe Rebozo, Rose Mary Woods and Ronald Ziegler—and they, the family, must reach out through the corridors of the White House to private telephone numbers seeking potential loyalists, appealing to people like Pat Buchanan. Armies and fleets, Secret Service and Cabinet members, party zealots and White House staff all alike were servants, some of the Republic, some of the party, some of the Presidency. But the instruments of Nixon's personal authority had vanished, and with them his power; those he trusted most would no longer march for him; or rather, they would march only one way—to his resignation from office. And so his daughter was telephoning at midnight, chief lieutenant of a cause already lost.

Buchanan met early the next morning, Saturday, in the solarium of the White House, with the two daughters of the President and Bebe Rebozo. What they were seeking was one staff member, just one, to lead the President's guard to the last battle. Would Buchanan do it? They wanted to carry the fight right down to the Senate floor. Buchanan argued against—they had only one choice: either their father would be the first President of the United States to resign, or he would be the first President to be impeached and convicted. Which did they want? If they fought, Buchanan said, they would drag the whole party down with them; it simply wasn't right to take the country through this debate for another three or four months with no hope for victory. The daughters disagreed. Buchanan countered again: if we had known about this mess fifteen months ago, we could have gone to the nation, made a confession of it like the Bay of Pigs. But there had been a year of "ongoing deception." They insisted that Buchanan must lead the fight. Pat compromised—let us wait, wait just a few days, wait to see what the nation's reaction would be.

By noon, back in his office, Buchanan learned that he had lost the argument. Ziegler was spreading the word from the White House across the street: the President had decided to fight, to go all the way through to the Senate, come what may.

In the afternoon, Haig, St. Clair and Price gathered to consider the President's wish. Nixon had decided to make a television speech to the nation on Monday evening, simultaneously with the release of the latest transcripts. He would admit he had deceived the nation, but state that nonetheless he felt it his duty to continue, his duty to let the Constitutional process run its course; that, whatever his mistakes, they did not reach the level that justified removal of a President from office. None liked the decision. But to march in a group to force the President's hand would be dangerously close to a *coup d'état*, unprecedented in American history; and to resign singly would leave Richard Nixon dependent for advice on two daughters, their two young husbands, Bebe Rebozo and Ronald Ziegler.

They would have to handle this outburst of Richard Nixon's combat reflex some other way. Already, that Saturday afternoon, the President had taken off for Camp David, where, the next day, he wanted the innermost staff to join him for a "working session" on the television speech he was to make to the nation on Monday evening.

That night, late, Price called Buchanan and they reinforced each other's conviction. They had known Richard Nixon longer than anyone else of the working group; these two had come to Richard Nixon's service, Buchanan in 1966, Price in 1967, as young writers, balancing each other, one a devout conservative, the other a decided liberal. Now finally they were in total agreement on purpose and tactics: Nixon must resign, yet resignation could not be forced on him. Whatever they worked out together the next day at Camp David, the speech or statement must not lock the President into a specific course of action—neither a declaration of combat nor a decision of immediate resignation. It had been agreed that the transcripts would be published on Monday; then would come the reaction of both Congress and the public; events must convince the President, not their pressure. They were dealing now with a hollow man whose perimeters of dignity must be preserved so that he could think.

Sunday, August 4th, was again cloudy, the sky low, and the working party at the White House was not at all sure that the helicopter could make it through such weather to the Camp David rendezvous. Tense, they waited until 12:30, when the sky cleared enough for flying, and the White House party drove to the Pentagon helicopter pad to be air-lifted to Camp David at 1:30. The party waited in Laurel Lodge while Haig strolled over to see the President, who sat alone in Aspen Lodge.

Haig was back shortly: the President had changed his mind once more. He was not resigning—but neither was he taking his fight to the people on television at this point. The transcripts would be released tomorrow—but with only an explanatory statement by the President. Price would go off and write the statement—a brisk 500-word message—while the rest counseled in the main dining room at Laurel Lodge.

While Price drafted, the others conferred, Ziegler and Haig occasionally talking to the President. St. Clair felt the resignation should come tomorrow, Monday, along with the statement, flat. The others moved that thought around and disagreed. The President could not be forced, it was not their job to force him; it would take time to prepare the country for what the tapes would show, and then the country's reaction would become a fact the President could not escape.

They worked the record over again. Was any defense possible? Was it possible that the President had, at some time in the past turbulent year, forgotten that it was he himself who had given instructions to thwart the FBI, a slip of memory, tragic but explainable? From Camp David they called the White House and asked that the logs of the tapes and the President's movements be examined once more. They recalled that on May 5th, three months earlier, Haig had met Prosecutor Jaworski in the White House map room at 2:55 P.M. Jaworski had offered a compromise—release seventeen of the tapes, not all sixty-four, and he would be content. And implicit in Jaworski's offer, they felt, had been the understanding the President would not be named an unindicted co-conspirator in the Watergate cover-up. The logs, read back to the Camp David group from the White House, now showed that on May 6th the critical tapes had been checked out to the President personally, who had listened to them alone in his Executive Office Building hideaway. The President, recalled Haig, had said, "I haven't got the time to go on listening to tapes." Now it was clear: the President had not forgotten the critical conversations; as an old poker player, he had simply decided to bluff it out; the Supreme Court had called his hand, and it was, in the memory of one of those present, a "busted flush." There was no defense possible, then, of any kind; it made no difference what their draft statement would rea

"He was doomed," said Buchanan; only it was vital that he come to see this himself.

By the time Price came back with his draft, there were other matters to be included and the Presidential statement grew. St. Clair and Haig wanted it clearly stated that they, too, had been deceived. So the phrases were shaped: "Although I recognized that these [the June 23rd tapes] presented potential problems, I did not inform my staff or my counsel of it, or those arguing my case, nor did I amend my submission to the Judiciary Committee in order to include and reflect it." At the President's own insistence, two closing sentences were added: "I am firmly convinced that the record, in its entirety, does not justify the extreme step of impeachment and removal of a President. I trust that as the Constitutional process goes forward, this perspective will prevail."

And with a rough draft, the party left Camp David for Washington at 7:00 P.M., Price to write the final draft in time for presentation to the President in the morning, the President to ruminate with his family about the options still left open, the others to set in motion the events that would close the President in the vise of reality.

By Monday, August 5th, such events were in motion. In the Executive Office Building, the lawyers were in session, earphones on their heads, checking and rechecking phrases against the recordings. Price was laboring over a final draft of the statement, consulting with the President, working against a deadline of 2:30 in the afternoon. Garment, having finally seen the transcript, was urging immediate resignation that very day—a flat, short statement with no gloss of rhetoric. Price and Buchanan had to explain to Garment the President's mood and the Camp David decision to make the resignation a two-step affair—first the release and the reaction to it, and then, it was hoped, the President's resignation would come after the reaction.

Upstairs, at 9:00 the defense group met in Dean Burch's office, second floor, West Wing, for their daily session of planning, co-ordinating the political front in Congress and in the press—Burch, Timmons, Ken Clawson, Jerry Jones, Buchanan. Buchanan briefed the group and distributed copies of the transcript, raw, mistyped, penciled over with corrections. They read it and Burch broke the meeting up —"Get the ice," he said, "pour the Scotch." Timmons proposed a toast to the President and it was over; and they were being asked down to Haig's office.

For months, for over a year actually, the President's defense had been a completely unco-ordinated one—fragmented, compartmentalized, at cross-purposes, secrets within secrets. It had to be so: its leader, the President, sat with a lie. But no strategy based on concealment could work. Now Haig took over. "For fifteen months," said Haig, recalling, "I'd been watching this. Now, for once it had to be pulled together as it should have been fifteen months ago, with people knowing what they should do, meeting dates set, the Cabinet informed, the contacts set for whom to see. I took over." Congress, the party, the public, the Cabinet, the staff all had to be brought together. There must be no panic.

First, the Hill. In Congress, the key character had to be the House Minority Leader, John Rhodes; Buzhardt and Burch would be sent to Rhodes's home to brief him at lunch, and George Bush, Republican National Chairman, would be asked to join them to hear the news at the same time. Rhodes described the transcript as "cataclysmic"; the President had just plain lied. He would vote for impeachment.

At 3:30 another deputation, led by St. Clair and Timmons, convened nine of the ten Republican stalwarts of the Judiciary Committee in the office of Minority Whip Leslie Arends, and St. Clair did the briefing. Wiggins averred that he had read the transcripts himself on Friday and St. Clair's report was accurate: the President had lied. He would be making his own statement that afternoon. Briefly, they discussed whether to issue a joint statement repudiating the President or use Wiggins' prepared statement, and then decided that at this moment it was every man for himself. And they left to prepare their own farewells, each to his typewriter, then to the mimeograph machines that posted their statements in the House press gallery, then to the television cameras—evening news time was drawing on.

From Arends' office St. Clair and Timmons proceeded across the marble corridors from the House wing to the Senate wing of the Capital, to the office of Hugh Scott, Senate Minority Leader, where a group of Senate Republican leaders was assembled. There, again the same story, except with a larger, more vivid reaction.

Meanwhile, Haig had taken the authority to hold the White House staff together and functioning in crisis. A hastily assembled *ad hoc* list of names running from Cabinet officers to secretaries had been put together starting at noon; those reached were invited to convene in the Executive Office Building conference room, Number 450 on the fourth floor, at 3:15. About 150 people were gathered when, choking, his jaw set, his eyes unfocused, Haig went to the platform to tell what was about to happen. He read the President's statement, which Price had just finished, and then went on—if they could not give their loyalty to the President, they must now give their loyalty to the country. It was, said one of the listeners, as if a pitcher of cold water had been thrown on them. Haig praised them for their devotion, saying in an emotion choked voice that he, "as a man not unfamiliar with combat," was as proud of this White House staff as of any men he had served with in combat. A few secretaries cried—not for sadness for Richard Nixon, said one of them, but for themselves, because it was the end of the fight, the final defeat. Then all clapped for Haig and dispersed to read the statement. One young man remembers lying on his couch in his office and thinking, "Oh, those bastards, those sons of bitches out there who've been saying all these things about the President all year— those bastards I hated, they were right." Another of the young men remarked, "Reading it was like reading a document and discovering that your own father was not your father."

There was still another base to be touched—the hard core of defense in the Senate. At 4:30 a White House emissary summoned Barry Goldwater off the floor of the Senate to hand him a copy of statement and transcripts. Goldwater had an appointment at 5:00 in his office with Dean Burch of the White House damage-assessment group, where Senator Carl Curtis of Nebraska would join them. Goldwater walked slowly from the Senate to his office building, reading the statement as he went, rising to rage as he read. "I was mad," he said. "I was mad as hell. I was goddamned mad when I got to the office." At the office, Burch sounded out Curtis and Goldwater. Curtis mournfully said that he was too far committed to the defense to pull out now; he would hang in. But Goldwater, the voice of all old virtues, had made up his mind: the President must resign now. Or else be impeached and convicted. Would the President resign now? Goldwater asked. Burch replied that it was touchy, the President's mind was balanced on a needle point, it could go either way: the big problem was that the family had just been told and no one could measure their advice. By now, recalls Goldwater, that "phone son-of-a-bitch was ringing, every light was on," they were trying to get at him. And he went home to brood, answering no calls for the rest of the evening. Goldwater was still furious— what that man had done to those two wonderful girls of his; he had put them out on a limb, and their husbands, too. "He lied to his family," Goldwater repeated over and over again, days later. And Goldwater decided that night that on Article II of the impeachment, Abuse of Power, he would have to vote to convict.

Since mid-morning the press room of the White House had been moiling. The normal 11:00 briefing had been postponed once, then again, then again; the networks were calling men back from vacation; the stars of the Washington press corps were assembling. Shortly after 4:00 the statement and transcripts were in their hands, and from 6:00, when the early ABC evening newscast is piped by special line to the White House from Baltimore, until 7:30, when the CBS evening news is finished, the defense crumbled as the television nets fed out to the nation the White

House story. The network broadcasters played it clinically; they had no need to dramatize either the President's statement or the transcripts. Said John Chancellor, leading off for NBC in the flattest tone he could command, "Good evening. President Nixon stunned the country today by admitting that he held back evidence from the House judiciary Committee, keeping it a secret from his lawyers, and not disclosing it in public statements. The news has caused a storm in Washington, and some of Mr. Nixon's most loyal supporters are calling for his resignation. . . ." And from there the networks let the situation speak for itself—Senator Griffin calling for resignation; Wiggins, whose image of supreme loyalist had been engraved by television on the nation's mind, choking back tears, calling for resignation; Charles Sandman of New Jersey, whose snarl of defiance at Nixon's enemies had been his distinguishing characteristic on the Judiciary Committee, now snarling defiance at the President himself; man-in-the-street interviews from Iowa to New York. The voices were all the same—bearing hurt, anger, contempt, incomprehension all through the night.

The President was boating that evening; he had gone off with his family and Rose Mary Woods for his last evening cruise down the Potomac on the Presidential yacht, the *Sequoia,* through the lovely Virginia countryside to Mount Vernon. Haig telephoned him on the yacht and suggested an early Cabinet meeting the next day. The President agreed, and that night the Cabinet was summoned to meet for the last time with Richard Nixon the next morning, August 6th.

The jolting of the United States government in the eleven years since the Kennedy assassination has given it a resilience in absorbing shock.

It goes on.

The Pentagon is an action agency, first line of defense, always ready. This week the Pentagon was watching the situation in Cyprus, the Mediterranean fleet on alert. For the instant, that night, it was alert internally, too—by order of Defense Secretary James Schlesinger, all military commands had been warned to accept no direct orders either from the White House or from any source without the counter-signature of the Defense Secretary himself.

Other agencies were moving of themselves on a reach of problems that ranged from the narrowly technical to the ultimate far-off limits of future civilization. The Treasury may have been pleased that the stock market was going up (by 13.38 points). But it must have been disturbed by the rush of citizens at Federal Reserve banks, jostling to buy Treasury bills at 9 percent, the highest yield ever, thus draining the stability of ordinary savings banks by their withdrawals.

At HEW, matters were smoother. The staff had been slowly, for months, compromising and shaping a landmark pension-reform bill that would be the largest change in Social Security since Franklin Roosevelt's original measure of 1936; and the r   act was moving nicely through the machinery. Inde a, it would pass on August 22nd, as the last of t' ʳ ᵒr Nixon legislation, one of the more beneficial use   . his power.

At Commerce, there were yet longer-range matters to consider. For weeks Dr. Robert M. White, the head of the National Oceanic and Atmospheric Administration, had been urging on Secretary Dent, his chief, the matter of climate, hoping that if he could engage ʰe Secretary's concern, the Secretary might engage the co. ᵉrn of the President. The 1974 drought in the Midwest, some American scientists thought, might conceivably be only a cyclical phenomenon, but they had other reasons to believe that it might be a harbinger of a longer cycle, one of those millennial changes that transform deserts to gardens, forests to deserts, dooming ports to become landlocked cities, or changing coastal plains into underwater fish warrens. That matter, though, was still stalled in the clotted chanels of access to the beleaguered President.

The morning meeting of the President's Cabinet considered none of these matters.

Nixon was fighting for his political life and leadership; his purpose was to keep his government together at a moment of disaster until he learned whether disaster was irrevocable. He rambled as he opened the Cabinet meeting, a loose discourse on his purpose: he would not resign, he said, it was his Constitutional duty to remain. Staff members who usually line the wall in back seats were excluded; only Cabinet Secretaries, General Haig and Republican

Chairman George Bush attended; none applauded. They sat silent as the President went on to discuss the inflation problem, enemy number one, proposing an economic summit conference; but there came from him no real thinking on inflation, either. That crisis, as much psychological as real, could be mastered only by a President of authority; and the authority of this one was fading hourly. Attorney General Saxbe said aloud that the President ought to take a week to see if he could govern—for the crisis of the inflation was confidence. There was no response to Saxbe's remark. Vice-President Ford sat through the meeting, said little, departed shortly to meet the Republicans on the Hill. The atmosphere, said George Bush of the last Cabinet meeting, was entirely "unreal," and the Cabinet members broke up into little knots after the President left, discussing his performance. Bush approached Haig and asked, "What are we going to do?" Haig told Bush to calm down, explained, "We get him up to the mountaintop, then he comes down again, then we get him up again."

When the Cabinet dispersed, the Secretaries dutifully carried the Nixon message: the President wanted his government to know he was not resigning, and at each staff meeting in each department, as the Secretaries reconvened their own staffs, they passed that message as they were supposed to do.

Except that within two hours of the Cabinet's departure the resolution of the President had begun to fade. There was, first, Henry Kissinger, who lingered after the others' departure: now, for the first time, Kissinger offered his opinion directly to the President—that he should resign, and resign with dignity, not in bitterness. Kissinger was followed at noon, at the President's request, by William Timmons. Timmons' five liaison officers on the Hill were the President's eyes and ears on Congress. All the previous week the staff had been bringing tidings of disaster to Timmons from the House—one by one, hard-rock Republicans, party loyalists, personal friends of the President had been dropping off. "It hurt to tell him," said Timmons. "I'd give him names, one by one, as we checked, and he'd wince, he'd say nothing." Timmons had already reported to the President that he would be impeached by the House. But the President, sitting alone with Timmons, now wanted to know about the Senate—the likely vote if it came to trial. The week before, Timmons had still held out hope in the Senate—twenty-two sure Nixon votes, by name count and commitment; ten votes uncommitted, but leaning to acquit the President; eight possibles, depending on evidence, defense and pressure. But today, Tuesday—Timmons reported that the count for acquittal, if the vote were held today, would come to no more than twenty; and if the vote were held weeks or months hence, perhaps less. The President asked him to check five specific names that afternoon.

At noon, on the Hill, Vice-President Ford was visiting with Minority Leader Scott and other key Republican Senators. Ford reported the Cabinet meeting to the Senators, and Goldwater, speaking fir , snapped out, "He ought to resign now." The meeting g ew wild; Ford left, then Goldwater. By 3:30 an inner group had been reconvened by Scott—the Senate Rep lican Policy Committee (Scott, Griffin, Wallace Bennett, Norris Cotton, Bill Brock, John Tower) joined by Goldwater and Jacob Javits. It was now not a question of whether the President should resign, but of how he could be caused to resign. They considered: should all eight go as a group? But Cotton and Bennett refused to join in such a *putsch*. Should they choose a special committee to wait on the President? That suggestion was rejected as too much pressure. Then, finally, they turned to Goldwater—would he, the arch-conservative, bell the cat? I'll try, said Goldwater, and left to call up his friend at the White House, Dean Burch—requesting an audience not with the President, but with Burch and Haig to convey a message.

It was now late afternoon of Tuesday, August 6th, a bad day at the White House. All ten stalwarts of the Republican House Judiciary contingent had now, one by one, publicly abandoned the President they had defended for so long. On the Hill, Minority Leader Rhodes had announced he would support impeachment. From California, Governor Ronald Reagan had just issued a call for resignation. And Haig, gently but firmly, was adjusting the controls for the final descent, careful not to jog, push or pressure the uncertain pilot of state, not to provoke the explosion of personality he feared.

The President was on downslope. Timmons had been on

the phone to the President several times that afternoon, answering his calls, or phoning in the reports on the individual Senate names the President had requested he check. The President's "base of power," at each call, was eroding. By late afternoon Timmons had written and passed on to the President, via Haig, a scenario of resignation which he wanted brought to the President's immediate attention as an option paper. It suggested that the departure should take place after three meetings: first with a Senate Republican delegation headed by Goldwater to give Nixon the final facts; next a meeting of a farewell with the constituted Congressional leadership of five—Speaker of the House, and Majority and Minority Leaders in both House and Senate; and then a final Napoleonic farewell to the thirty or forty friends who had remained loyal to him to the end.

The President was moving toward the only conclusion possible, held back from it only by the family guard. Julie Nixon Eisenhower was its leader; now she insisted on an appointment with Haig for her husband, David Eisenhower, to press on Haig her father's plea. The President had lied to her, as well as to everyone else, but he was her father; and she could see in him not only his anguish but what she felt was his greatness. Haig listened, not commenting, recognizing that the only resistance left came from the family.

That evening, Haig sent for Price and gave him guidance from the President: the President had *not* yet decided to resign, but wanted nonetheless to have a resignation speech ready; there was no *fait accompli* yet, Haig insisted. But if there were to be a speech of resignation, the President wanted to go out with his head held high, with no admission of guilt. Mark Twain is reported to have said, "Confession may be good for the soul, but it's bad for my reputation." Nixon acted in that spirit. He wanted it made clear that what mistakes he had made, he had made in the best interests of the country, that those mistakes had been made only because he had felt that what would destroy the Nixon Presidency would also destroy the chance for the peace he sought for the world. A difficult assignment. And Price took it from there, working all through the night on a draft which he must get to Haig at eight Wednesday morning, ready for the President to scan at ten. Price agreed there need be no confession of guilt. He, too, had been burned in the war between President and press. Said Price, "The Washington *Post* would have loved a guilty statement. But even a guilty statement wouldn't have satisfied them. What they wanted was a ceremony on the South Lawn, with the President incinerating himself, and Ben Bradlee toasting marshmallows in the flames."

On Wednesday, the Haig orchestration reached its climax.

There was, first, the Vice-President to be informed. The Vice-President, if Haig's plans worked, would become President on Friday after a Thursday speech of resignation. Haig so informed Ford, by a visit to Ford's office on the second floor of the Executive Office Building, early. Within half an hour Ford's own machinery, on standby for days, was working, reaching as far as San Francisco by 10:00 Washington time (7:00 Pacific time) to summon William Scranton, former candidate for the Presidency and once Governor of Pennsylvania, to rush East and join a transition task force.

There was, next, the choreography of the confrontations that must reinforce the President's desire to depart. Haig would have lunch with Barry Goldwater at Dean Burch's house to explain personally the delicate, almost psychiatric problem, for it must be Goldwater who would explain to the President what was involved.

And there was, finally, the neutralization of the President's last inner guard, the family. At Buzhardt's office in the EOB, Haig met with Buchanan and asked Buchanan to undertake that thankless chore.

Trying to reinforce the impact of the Goldwater visit, Haig deputized Timmons to fold in two other Republican stalwarts, Hugh Scott and John Rhodes, to accompany Goldwater to the President's office, and then he was off to lunch with Goldwater.

Haig wore his cool at lunch at Dean Burch's house. Goldwater, a man of impeccable honesty and self-igniting rage, has a habit of candor that cuts like a razor. What Haig wanted of Goldwater was restraint in the afternoon visit, at that time scheduled for four o'clock. He begged Goldwater to use discretion; Haig was not sure of the President's intent—the President had either already decided on resignation or was on the verge of deciding, and the whole matter was so "seesaw" in the President's mind that one wrong move could swing it to full fight, all the way through impeachment and a Senate floor trial to the very end, four, six, eight months hence.

Thus, on the afternoon of Wednesday, as the world fell in around him, only two tracks were open to the President's mind.

The first was a family track. The loyalty of his daughters and their husbands was the last genuine base of support he commanded. Deputized to receive them, Buchanan listened in his EOB office to the last plea of Edward Cox and David Eisenhower, at three o'clock. "They were eloquent," said Buchanan; they were as familiar with every detail of the transcript as Buzhardt himself, and they knew the dangers to both the party and the country. But they were appealing to Buchanan as a man of the conservative cause. For the sake of history, the record ought to show how much good had been done for the country by Richard Nixon; the record should demonstrate by trial in the Senate the precise reason why he had been removed. The two young men made no attempt to justify the "trivial" crime of which Nixon was guilty. But, they argued, the fight must be made all the way to the Senate floor, because Constitutionally it was important that a President not be removed by a wave of public opinion; he must be removed only by clear Constitutional judgment of his responsibility and its abuse. The offense, the impeachable offense, must be focused sharply.

To which Buchanan could only reply: the course they sought could not balance the danger to the President himself, vulnerable to every penalty of law if he were found guilty by the Senate. Nor could it balance the danger to the country—months more of controversy in a lost cause until the vote came on the floor of the Senate, with the country unable to strain the clear and narrow perspectives of crime from the turmoil. There was no purpose to such a fight at such a cost. At about four, the two young men left and, said Buchanan, "I felt no minds had been changed."

What message the sons-in-law carried back to the President from Buchanan must have been a melancholy one. But the messages coming in to him from his party via the Haig track were worse.

The previous day, Senator Stennis of Mississippi had re-layed his message that the President must resign. The pre-vious evening George Bush, National Chairman of the Re-publican Party, a close personal friend, almost a protégé of the President's, had pondered his loyalties, personal and partisan, and on Wednesday morning had delivered to the White House his final judgment as party leader. "Dear Mr. President," read the Bush letter, "It is my considered judg-ment that you should now resign. I expect in your lonely embattled position this would seem to you as an act of dis-loyalty from one you have supported and helped in so many ways. My own view is that I would now ill serve a President, whose massive accomplishments I will always re-spect and whose family I love, if I did not now give you my judgment. Until this moment resignation has been no answer at all, but given the impact of the latest development, and it will be a lasting one, I now firmly feel resignation is best for this country, best for this Pesident. I believe this view is held by most Republican leaders across the country. This letter is much more difficult because of the gratitude I will always have for you. If you do leave office history will properly record your achievements with a lasting respect."

And the most punishing blow of all was yet to come in late afternoon when the President received, in his Oval Of-fice, the Congressional leaders of his party—Barry Goldwa-ter, Hugh Scott, John Rhodes. The accounts of all three co-incide.

They arrived at 5:00 and all remember the President as serene, with his feet on the desk in the Oval Office. "He looked like a man who had just made a hole-in-one," said Goldwater. Rhodes remembers the President as calm, com-posed, but tired and gray. A few minutes of chatter about times past, about campaigns when the President had put himself out for Barry Goldwater, about campaigns in sup-port of Hugh Scott, the reminiscences which are obligatory courtesies of political conversation. Then, abruptly, the President asked for an assessment of the situation. The three had agreed that Goldwater would be their spokesman; they had agreed, also, that they would only report the situa-tion, not recommend any options.

Goldwater averred that there were not more than fifteen votes left in his support in the Senate: Cotton of New

Hampshire, Bennett of Utah, Curtis of Nebraska, and a handful of Southern Democrats. Scott affirmed Goldwater's count, added that the vote might be as few as twelve, and mentioned names. "I helped some of those people," said Richard Nixon, showing little emotion.

He turned to Rhodes, who was mostly silent. He offered Rhodes the thought that he doubted whether he could count more than ten on the floor of the House either. Rodes, privately, still felt the President's supporters might muster fifty out of the 435 in the House, but would not give a count. I don't have many alternatives, do I? said the President to Rhodes; and Rhodes countered, When I come out of here, Mr. President, I don't want to say to anybody that I talked about alternatives to you. And Barry Goldwater put in the last punishing blow. He offered the thought that a good smart lawyer might still be able to beat Articles I and III (Obstruction of Justice and Defiance of Committee Subpoenas) in a Senate trial. How about Article II? asked the President. And Goldwater replied, according to his recollection, "I'm leaning that way myself, Mr. President."

The session lasted less than thirty minutes. And there was no one left, no major American political figure to support the man who had been elected by the largest free majority in American history. Those closest to him had all left, or abandoned him, or been cut off. Haig had issued instructions to the White House switchboard that no calls from either Haldeman or Ehrlichman be put through to the President without passing through Haig. Haldeman had called and been switched to Haig that day; Haldeman asked that the President grant him a pardon; Haig curtly told him it was "just not possible." Ehrlichman had tried a different track, calling via Rose Mary Woods for the same purpose. She relayed the message to Haig the next morning and that message, too, was blocked.[1]

It is not a long walk from the Oval Office to the home quarters of the White House, and the final decision was tak-

[1] Haldeman was still trying to reach the President across the Haig barrier on Friday. One of his calls reached the Nixon plane in its flight to California before the Presidency had officially passed from Nixon. Ziegler took that call on the plane, but he, too, refused to let his former superior speak to the President.

en some time about 7:30, just before the President walked home. He called Haig about then, and at the Haig end of the conversation an observer remembers Haig comforting the President, "Yes . . . yes . . . yes . . . I think it is the right decision." Then Richard Nixon went home, and told his family just before they sat down to dinner; and forbade them to open the matter again while they ate.

There was another call to Haig at 8:30, a last bubble of resentment, described as "bitter," the President complaining that his lawyers had not been "the best in the world." And then he summoned Henry Kissinger to the family quarters and the partners spent two hours together, not talking about foreign policy but about what had gone wrong at home. Kissinger, reserving the conversation for his memoirs, drops his head and says, "Heart-rending, heart-rending." When Kissinger left, the President was on the phone to Ray Price, who was working on the final, final draft of the resignation speech he had begun one week before. Price was to have little sleep that night. The President was recomposing the draft in almost consecutive phone calls until two in the morning, when Price was finally off to bed; at 4:15 he was awakened again with another call and more thoughts from the President, and the calls went on until he dressed and went to the White House to continue work.

The final decision had thus been made Wednesday night, as Haig had wanted it. At 9:00 on Thursday morning, Haig informed the White House staff meeting that the resignation would come in a nationwide speech at nine in the evening. To Timmons' request that the Congressional leaders be informed first, Haig consented—and at noon Timmons informed the official leadership that they would see the President in the Executive Office Building at 7:30 before the speech; and told a group of the Nixon loyalists that they would meet their hero in the Cabinet Room at 8:00.

All was now proceeding smoothly. From the White House, furnishings, mementoes, clothes, souvenirs were being trundled to the elevator, down the elevator to the basement, and from there by truck to two planes waiting to take the President's personal belongings to San Clemente.

At 10:50 Nixon received Price in absolute composure, his mind at its editorial best, pointing out redundancies of phrase in the farewell address, marking possible contractions, circling and tracking flow points.

At 11:00 he received Vice-President Ford. The meeting, with Ford sitting beside the President, hung awkwardly in silence in the Oval Office for a few moments, and then Nixon broke the silence by saying he knew Ford would be a good President; then they were off on a ramble of slightly more than an hour, about the nation and world affairs, which remains still secret.

At about noon the President received Buzhardt, with whom he had been quite cross since they had disagreed about the tapes nine days earlier. The President, remembers Buzhardt, was in remarkably calm control of himself; people had been in and out to see him for the past several days, said Nixon, and a lot of them were crying. "It ought to be me that's doing the crying," said Nixon, trying a joke. But now he was talking to Buzhardt as client to a lawyer, not as President—exploring with Buzhardt what "they" were likely to do to him, how far the Prosecutor was likely to go.

Ford had just left. The President told Buzhardt he anticipated no pardon; he was fatalistic; and with some show of bravado even discussed the possibility of a jail sentence— some of the best political writing of this century, he said, had been written from jail by men like Gandhi and Lenin. And in his somber conversation there was a religious undertone which Buzhardt refuses to discuss; it concerned the value of prayer and contrition.

By 2:00 in the afternoon Nixon had had his last conversation with Ray Price about his speech, a last few literary glosses on his record in foreign affairs, and then a personal sentimental break with Price about what might have been, what great affairs in the world they might have brought to conclusion had not this happened. But by now the decision was irrevocable, and the news was public.

Ziegler had announced shortly after noon that the President would request television time for a national address at 9:00 in the evening. By afternoon the press room of the White House was thronged, reporters and photographers pressed together. By evening the crowd at the gate was thick, thicker than it had been on the night of the Kennedy assassination. "Jail to the Chief," shouted some. Automobiles honked. Police cleared passageways.

The five Congressional leaders—Carl Albert, James Eastland, Mike Mansfield for the Democrats, Rhodes and Scott for the Republicans—gathered in Bill Timmons' office shortly after 7:00. Timmons poured them each a drink, and then together they walked across the street to the President's Executive Office Building hideaway and sat down. Nixon was brief and thoroughly professional in his farewell. He had decided that his political base had eroded, he said. There was a lot to be said for fighting on, but he could foresee a Senate trial that might drag on for months. In the name of future Presidents it might have been worth fighting the battle to the end. But, on the other hand, he could not leave foreign policy in the air for months to come. So it was best that he go. He would not be back in Washington again for a long time, he concluded, and wanted to thank them for being honorable fighters all these years. He was grateful particularly to Carl (Albert) and Mike (Mansfield) for their support on his trips to Moscow; then he remarked, "I'll miss our breakfasts, Mike"; then to Albert, "I'll miss our breakfasts, too, Carl." He rose, shook hands with each; they mumbled courtesies, and departed for their cars in the driveway.

It took a few minutes for the President to compose himself again, and he asked that the White House grounds be sealed for his last stroll across from the hideaway to the Oval Office and the scheduled visit with his loyalists waiting in the Diplomatic Reception Room. Dean Burch had invited forty-six Congressmen and Senators to say farewell, and had been pouring them drinks before they were invited to the Cabinet Room. The President entered almost immediately after they were seated; some were already crying when the President came in, but he launched directly into what he had to say. It was brief and not coherent—he talked about his family; talked about his mother; talked about how he would have preferred to fight this one out. But he could not—there would be a trial that would take at least six months, he said, foreign policy would not stand still that long. There was the national interest to consider. No one spoke but the President. None urged a last-minute stay of decision; "I just hope," the President closed as he reached for the arms of his chair—and then his composure gave way entirely, his breath sucking into a sob which he controlled long enough to continue, "I just hope . . . I haven't let you down," and then he broke, tears streaming down his face. He tried to get up, missed the arm of the chair, could not rise, then found the chair arm and rose. Goldwater hugged him as he passed; others tried to do the same; and several aides intervened to clear his way back to the Oval Office, where in twenty minutes he would face the nation. Now almost all were crying, as if at a death in the family. Congressman Earl Landgrebe pressed a Nixon-for-President button into Timmons' hand, asking him to pass it to the President as his keepsake; Joe Waggonner of Louisiana was beating on the wall of the Cabinet Room with his fist; John Tower of Texas had held himself in to the end—then he, too, broke down, sobbing.

Then the President was alone in the Oval Office—no staff, no family, none of the customary circle of aides, just the TV technicians as he began,

"Good evening."

He was dressed in a customary dark blue suit, the American flag pin in his lapel as so often before, his television blue necktie making color harmony with the light blue drapes behind him.

". . . In all the decisions I have made in my public life, I have always tried to do what was best for the Nation . . . ," he began.

His eyes were pouched, the lines of his cheeks sharper than ever, his jowls puffy.

"In the past few days . . . it has become evident to me that I no longer have a strong enough political base in the Congress to justify continuing that effort. . . ."

His voice was firm, the underquaver rarely surfacing.

"Therefore, I shall resign the Presidency effective at noon tomorrow. . . ." [2]

He dined that evening alone with his family; received a farewell visit from Henry Kissinger; and then, until well after midnight, was on the telephone making outgoing calls.

What he was doing on his last night in the White House was calling people to whom he thought he owed apologies, repeating the same message, "I hope I didn't let you down, I hope I didn't let you down."

---

[2] See Appendix B for full text of the President's farewell.

Garment received one of the last calls, long after the lights were out in his bedroom. Again an apology. The President said he hoped he had not let down fellows like Price and Garment. Garment consoled the President, and the President continued, melancholy but with a touch of gallows humor. Maybe, he said to Garment, they could all go out to California and found a new law firm, Nixon, Cox, Garment and Eisenhower. Garment chuckled, and the President added that the firm might do fine until they found out it was the wrong Cox—Eddie, not Archibald. Garment added that it was the right thing the President had done— now perhaps there might be some healing, the bitterness might go, the kind of venom of the *New York Times* editorial that morning might pass. The President had read the editorial, too, and observed that going to jail might not be so bad. He wanted to write again; so long as he had a sturdy table, a reasonably adequate library nearby, and the goddamned phone didn't keep ringing, he might get some good writing done. Then, with a brisk "Give my love to Grace and the children," he hung up.

The staff choreographed him to the end; the last script of the last day started with his arrival in the East Room.

"9:30 A.M.," read the President's official schedule for August 9, 1974, "You and the First Family pause in the Grand Hallway for Honors and announcement. You enter to 'Hail To The Chief' and move directly to the platform along the center of the East wall and take your positions (stage right to left) as follows: Ed. Tricia. Mrs. Nixon. THE PRESIDENT (behind podium). Julie. David.

"NOTE: There will be tape on the platform indicating where each family member should stand. There will be a slight separation between Mrs. Nixon and Tricia so that Mrs. Nixon will be closer to you as you speak."

And so on, finishing with, "12:00 Noon PDT. Arrive El Toro MCAS. Board helicopter and depart en route Western White House. 12:25 P.M. Arrive Western White House."

But when he stood to speak and the television cameras zoomed in, it was a personal farewell. It was the Nixon of the stump, the Nixon who used to talk to rallies in the rain, the Nixon who had so often campaigned through Middle America, full of his hurts, his pride, his resentments, who

used to be able to twinge Middle American hearts as he re-
minisced of his childhood, of his mother and father, of
quitters and fighters, the Nixon who had walked across
American politics for twenty-five years and changed it. He
had not been invited to the swearing in of Vice-President
Ford, which would follow at noon; Ford's advisers had decided that they did not want Richard Nixon present; but
Nixon was too sensitive to invite the rebuff, and so they had
no need of turning him away. His staff sat in little gold-
backed chairs up front, close to the speaker, who spoke
with tears glistening on his cheeks.

Almost every television set in Washington was tuned in
for the farewell, for Washington is a town of government,
and no crisis of government like this had eve~ ' ~~ned to
Americans before. Even those most remote fror. _ 'tics
watched. In the Department of Commerce, the weather scientists were preparing for an afternoon meeting with other
executive agencies, trying to devise some plan that might
bring the long-range problems of climatic change to the attention of the new President. But the next President, or the
next few Presidents, might have a fifty-year span in which
to make ready this civilization for the changes that climate
might force on mankind—so they paused at the suggestion
of their chief, Dr. Robert White, to watch the President's
farewell. And as the television set showed the helicopter
lifting, they could see simultaneously from their corner
window the actual plane lifting off from the lawn and fading into the distance. The scientists watched, crying, and
White remembers himself sobbing with the rest as it disappeared.

Television caught Richard Nixon once more, fifteen minutes later, as he arrived at Andrews Air Force Base. Mrs.
Nixon, Tricia, Eddie Cox preceded him up the staircase to
the plane. He marched up the stairs briskly, then turned in
the black cutout of the plane's doorway and gave the familiar arms-uplifted double wave of good cheer that had been
one of the signatures of his many campaigns. Then the door
closed.

Command, however, still rested with the departing President. For this special day the Department of Defense had
prepared two "footballs"—those dark briefcases that give a
President his nuclear strike options. The "football" is never

more than a few paces away from a President wherever he travels, and this morning one was ready for Gerald Ford, another to accompany Richard Nixon on his journey. If American radar picks up the trace of incoming nuclear rockets, a President has at most fifteen minutes to choose our form of retaliation before enemy bombs hit. Until Gerald Ford became President, it was still Nixon's duty to scan the options in the "football" for response, and the Pentagon must obey. With the receipt of the resignation by Secretary of State Kissinger, the "football" on the plane was inoperative. From that moment on, it was Gerald Ford's football —his decision on response in a moment of annihilation; and the time was 11:35 A.M.

Officially and Constitutionally, however, the Presidency did not pass from Richard Nixon until noon, somewhere over Illinois or Missouri, as he flew over the heart of Middle America, which had always been his base, which he had betrayed. Middle America had been without a great leader for generations, and in Richard Nixon it had elevated a man of talent and ability, a President so powerful as to change the world, so powerful that Richard Nixon alone had been able to destroy Richard Nixon. All the other actors in the drama were clear-cut, a panel of heroes that ran from Sam Ervin to Mike Mansfield, from Peter Rodino to Archibald Cox, from Leon Jaworski to John Doar, from John Sirica to the Justices of the Supreme Court, from Benjamin Bradlee to the concerted editorial voices of the country. So, too, were the villains clear-cut—Haldeman and Mitchell and Magruder and Dean, and the lesser hustlers of the underground.

But neither heroes nor villains had written Richard Nixon's destruction; neither the law, nor Congress, nor the press had driven him from office. He had done so himself —for his perception of power, at which he thought himself a master, was flawed, as his character was flawed.

He would perhaps write his story someday, at San Clemente, his Elba on the Pacific. Others, too, for generations would be rewriting that story, as drama, as fiction, as scholarship, or as a study in psychiatric imbalance. For it was certain the story would not end there in his silence by the ocean, just as it was certain the story had not begun in the week that the Judiciary Committee moved to begin its hearings; nor the week that Archibald Cox had demanded the facts; nor the week the President had first lied; nor the week that his agents had broken into Democratic national headquarters.

To understand the story of Richard Nixon's Presidency, which is the story of this book, one would have to go back to the simplest definition of history—that it is the tale of the great forces that bear down on solitary men who accidentally stand at their junction. And it is the reactions of such men to the pressures on them that shape decisions, history and lives.

For at least twenty years before Richard Nixon's departure, the American Presidential system had been coming under growing pressure as the American party system on which it once rested had continued to come apart. At some point in that twenty-year span these grinding pressures would have become too much for a weak man to bear they would intersect in a personality whose flaws of character, whether small or great, would crack. They would crack that man, as surely as a bearing in a giant machine cracks under strains for which it was not designed. When such forces and strains intersected in Richard Nixon—his character did crack.

But the forces had been there long before August 9th, 1974; the forces are as important as the man. This story is thus, first, a story of the forces operating in American politics; and, next, of the President and his men confronting them.

Perhaps 1952 is as useful a date as any to start with; and Chicago in that year was probably the best place to listen to the first groaning of the hinges, as the world turned and America changed.

2

THE POLITICS OF MANIPULATION

Chicago in 1952 seems far away now, a monochrome fading in the album of early postwar America.

The city by the lake, raddled by the vacant lots and dingy buildings left by the Depression, was the unchallenged turf of the old Cook County machine, then approaching zenith. Autocrat Richard Daley's new city was yet to be built; the towers of its present lake front were not yet even a dream. No new buildings had been built in downtown Chicago since the Depression year of 1932, and its old hotels presented a façade as familiar to politicians and convention-goers as the invisible but equally permanent Cook County machine. Blacks were still only 14 percent of Chicago's population, docile participants in the machine's operation, an offstage presence. Politics was still the business of men who met behind closed doors; indeed, the phrase "smoke-filled room," which covered an era of politics, had been born in Chicago in Room 408 of the old Blackstone Hotel, where Harding had been chosen by the bosses in 1920. Eighteen national conventions had been held in this pivot city of American politics since Abraham Lincoln was first nominated there in 1860. But American life was changing; and now, in 1952, Chicago was to house both the Republican and Democratic conventions in the same month.

Few of those who gathered that July in hot and muggy Chicago were aware that they were ushering in a new chapter of American politics—the age of manipulation.

The last time the Democrats met there had been in 1944, when they named Franklin Roosevelt for the fourth time and, for the first time, Harry Truman. In retrospect, we can see that Harry Truman offered old politics at its best. A graduate of the Kansas City machine, he was trusted by the bosses of all the other big-city machines. He had proved an excellent President when he succeeded Roosevelt and by 1948 had become a peerless campaigner. That campaign of 1948 can best be remembered as the end of a passage in the ancient politics of balancing blocs and interests. From the back of his train, crisscrossing the country, Truman, in staccato, was voicing the chant of all Presidents in their permanent war with Congress—he was "giving 'em hell." In 1948, Truman was still able to talk, as Presidential campaigners had for generations, about things Americans could understand, of matters they were competent to judge. He could talk of the price of corn and wheat, of wages and labor and the Taft-Hartley Act, of roads and cities and veterans' benefits and civil rights. Opinion polling was still a crude art; a successful campaigner could, and Truman did, ignore what the polls said. Television news coverage was a bubble of experiment, groping its way out of the old newsreel style, local stations reaching fragmented regions. The nation was at peace; politics stopped at the coastline; and the last war was a fresh and splendid memory.

By 1952, war had become once more the dominant present fact of American politics, but this time the nation hated it. Wars are ideological, they warp American politics out of bent, they crush with their passions all bread-and-butter issues. What was new and important in 1952 was that war, or the threat of war, was about to become permanent, overriding almost all domestic issues. Choice of Presidents would henceforth come by the feel people got of a candidate's ability to manage war and peace, matters too complicated for them to judge by themselves. War and the flag had always been the unifying symbols of America's diverse peoples. In Dwight D. Eisenhower the Republicans were about to offer a tested war hero; he promised, "I shall go to Korea"; the people trusted his ability to stop the killing there, and they chose him.

But his nomination was not easy, and might not have come about at all, had it not been for other conditions of the new politics. And, of these new conditions, television was the foremost.

Gathering the first week in July, the Republicans found the familiar city festooned with cables; vines of wire dangled in hotel rooms and convention hall, cameras staked out the doors of candidates and committees. The politics of Presidential nomination were about to go public, for a revolution of communications had taken place between this national convention and those of 1948.

One year before the convention opened, an event had exploded in American life comparable in impact to the driving of the Golden Spike which, in 1869, tied America by one railway net from coast to coast. In September of 1951, engineers had succeeded in splicing together by microwave relay and coaxial cable a national television network; and two months later, late on a Sunday afternoon, November 18th, 1951, Edward R. Murrow, sitting in a swivel chair in CBS Studio 41, had swung about, back to audience, and invited his handful of viewers (3,000,000 of them) to look. There before him were two television monitors, one showing the Golden Gate Bridge in San Francisco, the other showing the Brooklyn Bridge in New York. The cameras flicked again—there was the Statue of Liberty in New York and Telegraph Hill in San Francisco. Both at the same time. Live. The nation was collected as one, seeing itself in a new mirror, on a twelve-inch television tube. Murrow then swiveled back to the audience and lifted his dark eyebrows in amusement, as if he were a magician performing a trick. He followed with a sequence on Fox Company, 2nd Platoon, United States 19th Infantry, tucked away in the hills of Korea, going about its war.

And one realized this was no trick. On that tube, orchestrated by producers in New York, the battles of American politics would take place with ever increasing intensity; on its stage the emotions of America would be manipulated. Not even Murrow could foresee the influence that would eventually spread through that tube to change America's view of itself, of war and of the world.

But even then the networks were preparing to cover the Chicago conventions of 1952—2,000 radio and television men being mobilized, more electronic men than delegates —$10 million set aside in their budgets, new equipment being rushed to completion by technicians for an audience that was expected to be larger than any political assembly in all history.

It was Robert Taft who first realized at Chicago what television could do to the old politics. Senator Taft, the front runner for the Republican nomination, was a regular, of the bone and gristle of his party. 604 delegates were needed to nominate and Taft's managers boasted between 603 and 607 delegates pledged, leaning or lurable on the first ballot. Of these, however, they counted 17 in dispute from Georgia and 38 from Texas—and the Eisenhower managers claimed that these delegates had been stolen at state conventions behind closed doors.

Ordinarily, contests over credentials would have been quickly settled by whoever controlled the convention's machinery—and Taft's regulars controlled the convention machinery from sergeant-at-arms to choice of keynote speaker, General Douglas MacArthur, whose appearance would produce a first-night television audience of 21,000,000 Americans. But television wanted to show more than podium presence, it wanted to be inside. And the next afternoon the Taft regulars made the men of television their enemies. In a wild, shoving, shouting melee outside the Boulevard Room at the Conrad Hilton Hotel, the regulars of the National Committee locked the cameras out. Now the newborn television networks had a real story—the regulars were trying to steal delegates behind closed doors, closed to cameras and thus to the public. Delegates, buttonholed on the convention floor, exposed on camera, had to come out either for "fair play," or for "the steal."

Until then the senior personalities of American radio news had disdained television as a sideshow, not a news medium. And the young and untried men assigned to television coverage in Chicago had no idea of the impact of their performance until the telegrams of protest came flooding back in protest against "the steal"—as many as 10,000 in a single day. Commentators deplored, editorialists screamed, common citizens telephoned their indignation to their delegates. "Up until then," said Donald Hewitt, the thirty-year-old director of the CBS convention show, "we'd thought of television as a conduit, that what we were doing was interesting only to political buffs. We were learning how to serve it up, how to make it more dramatic, more exciting. We were dealing with something called the attention span; my job was to capture and hold the attention of the American public by putting on the best show, like putting a frame around a picture. Only it wasn't a picture of the convention, it was a picture of Cronkite."

The term "anchor man" had just been invented by a CBS vice-president to describe what role the young Cronkite would play, which he did superbly. Cronkite thought of himself then, however, not as a TV personality but as a managing editor—as he still does. One of his literary heroes was Walter Burns, mythical managing editor of *The Front Page*—and Cronkite felt it was his job to sequence and arrange the events and episodes of the convention as a managing editor would. From his experience would develop the governing tradition of television news—and the nightmare of Richard Nixon, sleepless, years later, at television's power to rearrange images and shape the nation's thinking. But that week in Chicago, Nixon played to television's tune. When California caucused, its junior Senator, Richard Nixon, led the fight for "fair play" and the California delegation threw enough votes *against* the seating of the Texas and Georgia regulars and *for* the seating of Eisenhower delegates to give the General the nomination—and earn the young Senator consideration for Vice-President.

Days later, Taft privately jotted down for his friends a bitter memorandum. He ascribed his defeat to three forces —Eastern financial interests, the internationalist press and the impact of television. Of these three, television had done the most to wreck his hopes. His bitterness sounded the first note of a theme that would become familiar in both parties, and a favorite of Republicans. Years later, Eisenhower would rouse the largest cheers of the 1964 Republican convention by denouncing "the divisive efforts of those outside our family, including sensation-seeking columnists and commentators . . ."; the convention exploded to hear the news system denounced by so respected an authority, and one delegate from North Dakota was seen jumping up and down shrieking, "Down with Walter Lippmann! Down with Walter Lippmann!" Barry Goldwater, nominated at that convention, would later ascribe his defeat above all to what television did to his campaign from New Hampshire through San Francisco. Ultimately, Spiro T. Agnew would shape this visceral hate of the old politics for television into a dogma, describing its luminaries as "A small group of men, numbering perhaps no more than a dozen anchormen, commentators and executive producers. . . . To a man these commentators . . . live and work in the geographical and intellectual confines of Washington, D.C., or New York City, the latter of which James Reston terms the most unrepresentative community in the entire United States. . . . They draw their political and social views from the same sources. Worse, they talk constantly to one another, thereby providing artificial reinforcement to their shared viewpoints . . . we'd never trust such power . . . over public opinion in the hands of an elected Government. It's time we questioned it in the hands of a small and unelected elite. . . ."

The men of television were to outlast Agnew as they outlasted Taft and Eisenhower, Kennedy and Johnson, Goldwater and Nixon. In the twenty-two years between 1952 and 1974, their electronic magic would change American politics. Television would free national candidates more and more from dependence on, or discipline by, their parties; the tube could sway more swing votes than any party organization. A candidate's hopes could be destroyed by television in a single unguarded moment, as George Romney's were to be in 1967. Or a man could use it to appeal over his party, over its managers, even over the head of the ticket. One must mark 1952 as the date that Richard Nixon discovered how spectacular the influence of television could be, when, with his masterful and era-marking "Checkers speech," he reached for the first time, nationally, to stir the emotions of Middle America and override the decision of the party masters for his dismissal.

The Checkers speech was a primitive one, in modern terms—hastily produced, amateurishly assembled—but its success scored the mind of every realistic politician. Television would change the mechanics of all future American campaigning, inviting in the manipulators. The new system would require new professionals, image merchants, market analysts, psephologists, artist-producers in a managerial enterprise divorced from party structure, responsible to one man only—the candidate. To use television effectively would require huge sums of money, an extravagance of campaign financing unimagined in 1952. But the Cain-and-Abel brotherhood of television and politics began there in Chicago, in 1952, on July 8th.

Eight days later, in the same Conrad Hilton Hotel that had housed Robert Taft's headquarters, another political revolution began—this time with the Democratic convention as background. There, on the fifteenth floor, a group called the Draft Stevenson Committee rented three rooms in a completely unauthorized attempt to draft Adlai E. Stevenson of Illinois as Democratic candidate for the Presidency of the United States. All campaigns had customarily set up front groups called "Citizens For . . ." Hitherto such committees had always been party-created, window dressing for candidates the bosses themselves had privately chosen. But this citizens' group proposed to make the bosses do what it wanted.

There are, really, very few experts at national politics; national campaigns follow each other at intervals of four years;   nvention is a two-week exercise; earnest and dedicate amateurs can quickly study up and master the complicated rules of national conventions. A professor—Walter Johnson of the University of Chicago—led the Draft Stevenson "amateurs." But his associates were lawyers, businessmen, a community-newspaper publisher and others who were bound together by a common conviction that Adlai Stevenson stood for peace and decency, and that their professional skills could press the big-city bosses to accept the candidate who, to them, symbolized what was best in the Democratic Party.

Their three rooms grew to six rooms in less than a week; a week later, they had expanded to fourteen rooms filled with student volunteers who could swiftly learn the practical mechanics they had heard about in political-science courses: to identify delegates, card-file and index them. Above all, these newcomers had an intuitive understanding of the press and the news system, its need for copy, the appetite of its changing members for headline-making novelties. Their press releases broke gracefully away from the prose of the old-pol handout—they were readable. And the newcomers were on to a good thing: the party pros needed a candidate to match Eisenhower in the peace appeal, and their candidate, Stevenson, Governor of Illinois, would have to be supported by Dick Daley, boss of the Cook County machine.

The feat of the Johnson committee in drafting Adlai Stevenson, and convincing both Stevenson and the convention (on the third ballot) that the Democratic Party needed him, is of record. More important was the resonance of the act. If Stevenson's amateurs could perform in Chicago, as they had, to snatch a nomination from the bosses, then other amateurs, other citizen groups, other student and professorial types could do the same at home. Out of the Stevenson nomination came the fundamental stimulus to power for various local citizen associations that hitherto had seen themselves only as "reformers." They now had a national candidate in their own image, one who talked their language. In New York, in Illinois, in Wisconsin, in California, in Massachusetts entirely new types were called to action in the campaign of 1952. They were styled "eggheads" in the phrase of the time—amateurs, goody-goodies, thinkers, intellectuals. But they would go their way over the next twenty years, some becoming corrupt and battle-hardened mercenaries—and others going on to become "issue" men who could enlist, by their appeal to conscience, hordes of students, housewives, academics. The issue men, in their way, became a new breed of professionals who could organize volunteer efforts as efficiently as public-relations men and then cap their action with the street insurgency of 1968 or the McGovern coup of 1972. It was a long road from Stevenson in 1952 to Kennedy in 1960, to McCarthy in 1968, to McGovern in 1972—but it began there in Chicago.

From the Stevenson nomination on, certain terms became hallowed—"open conventions," "participatory democracy"—which meant simply that Democratic politics was to become a game that any group could enter. The bosses' monopoly over nominations had been broken.

For both Republican and Democratic parties, 1952 marked the beginning of a new era. Both would be split for years to come, each in its own way—on the one hand by professional management men, the manipulators of voter moods and perceptions, on the other hand by hot-issue men who could call up waves of national indignation and morality. The old parties might still control local nominations and elections. But in a national campaign the new breed, whether of managerial manipulators or the ideological moralists, could master the leaders of the old parties.

It was not the root idea of American politics that was changing—the idea that free men have the right to vote into power their choice of leaders without fear of reprisal. But the techniques of old politics were becoming obsolete. Old-fashioned party politics was textbook simple: you had to identify your voters, name by name or group by group; then you needed an idea or, preferably, a candidate who could penetrate voter apathy by appeal to greed, fear or hope; and then you had to pull your identified voters to the polls on Election Day. Identify them. Heat them up. Pull them out. That was the way party leaders had worked from the days of Martin Van Buren to Harry Truman.

Now better professional ways of identifying voters and computerizing such names were approaching; newer ways of stirring them; newer ways of manipulating images and motions; or fashionable ideological causes which could do the same thing. These newer techniques could no more be resisted by candidates for power than a householder in the 1920's could have resisted substituting for his gas mantle an electric bulb. Except that a fundamental contradiction was to be built into these newer technologies of politics—they required translating increasingly complicated issues of state into increasingly simplified slogans.

The old political system, whereby established party leaders chose the candidate and let him define the issues, did not fit the realities of life any longer. But then—neither did the new breed of manipulators or "hot-issue men" understand how complicated these realities were.

There were two central facts about American politics in the twenty-year span from 1952 to 1972.

The first, of course, was war or threat of war. That issue was the one that separated generations—most leaders of the governing generation, having fought the last good war, believed that all must be subordinated to national security and survival. Most of the vocal, younger, incoming generation believed that loyalties ran to humankind, not to defense or survival. The leaders of the two generations would come to regard each other variously as traitors or Neanderthals, killers or cowards, inhumans or wild radicals.

But the second fact, mocking the first, was American prosperity. For all their upheavals and blood, the two decades brought to America a time of unrivaled and extravagant prosperity. No period in human history, anywhere, has known so swift a reach toward universal well-being. Economists and statisticians, who had just taught politicians to talk of billions of dollars as manageable figures, began themselves to talk in trillions. The Gross National Product was to go from 211 billion dollars at the end of the war to just over one trillion dollars by the time Richard Nixon won his second Presidency in 1972.

All planning, both public and private, was bottomed on this assumption of limitless, ever-growing prosperity. The prosperity invited fancies, dreams, ideas that had seemed unreal only a few years earlier. Economic growth incubated a mood of experiment, and so, in all forms of life—social, governmental, corporate, private—experiment began. Few of the experimenters could foresee the consequences of their planning and successes. Success is harder to absorb than failure. Failure leaves things as they are; success changes the conditions of life and brings new, undreamed-of problems—above all, in politics.

Looking backward, one could pick up the thread of experiment–success–new-crisis almost anywhere in the early 1950's, and each thread interwove with another.

Take, for example, the thread that began with the Eisenhower Highway Act of 1955–56. The idea was breathtaking —over $33 billion to be spent on the largest system of road-building ever undertaken anywhere, to be paid for democratically by simple taxes on gasoline and tires. The revenues would accumulate in a Federal trust fund and be used for the best and safest system of roads ever engineered —concrete or asphalt ribbons stretching from coast to coast, no red lights, no dangerous curves, built to last forever. The simple tax would compound automatically—like an Arab sheik's oil royalties—until by now it has become a swollen sack of money in Washington, a bursting bladder of funds that no one knows how to use for good purpose.

The railways protested the act. One of their spokesmen likened the railways to a chicken that had been plucked over by every Congress for eighty years until now the scrawny chicken had only a handful of tail feathers left and was being chased around the barnyard by people who wanted to pluck those last few tail feathers as well. The railways squawked, but no one paid mind—railways had squawked at every bit of legislation that might hurt them ever since Congress, a hundred years ago, had tried to curb their then-despotic power over American life. But twenty years after the Highway Act was passed, as the roads rolled out over the meadows and the airlines chewed away at passenger transport, most of the Northeast railways were close to bankruptcy and rail passenger transportation had become a Federal burden. Meanwhile, the nation, invited by the new highways to become guzzlers of gasoline, had learned to drive five miles for a six-pack of beer or a pound of butter. Twenty years later, their appetite for driving had become the Energy Crisis. An entire civilization of shopping centers, drive-in theaters, chain motels, trailer camps, flatland drive-to-work factories rested on the new highways and cheap gasoline. Consumption of motor fuel had risen from 40 billion gallons in 1950 to 105 billion gallons in 1972; America was dependent on imported fuel—and more vulnerable to economic warfare than ever before in her history.

One can follow the thread of this single Highway Act on to politics: the reasoning behind the Federal Highway Act was so seductive as to melt resistance. It ran thus: the entries to and exits from big cities were so congested that a way had to be created for people to move into and out of such cities easily and go wherever they wanted to. But where more and more Americans wanted to go was the suburbs; and suburbia was to change American politics just as much as the opening of the West a century before.

The new highways became not simply holiday routes for Fourth of July and Labor Day weekends, or highball expressways to bring food and supplies into the hearts of the cities. They were arteries of a new way of American life. In the twenty years covered by the census from 1950 to 1970, the growth of the suburbs was the growth of America. In the first decade of the span, 61 percent of all American population growth happened in the suburbs; in the second decade, ending in 1970, 70 percent of its growth.

Suburbia had a new kind of politics, and only word of mouth to explain it. Most suburban communities knew little or nothing about how they were governed. Most suburbs cannot support good newspapers or sustain local television stations subjecting local government to daily scrutiny. Suburbia has thus replaced the big city as the heartland of petty corruption. Suburban politics revolve around land—the home-owners' use of land; where new expressways will go; where new factories will go; zoning ordinances and land-use variances that politicians broker among themselves for money. In suburbia, schools are generally good, police are usually polite to white people, the old big-city graft from prostitution, gambling, ticket-fixing is minimal. But the graft that comes from real-estate deals, zoning fixes and highway construction is maximal. It was in suburbia—Baltimore County in Maryland—that Spiro T. Agnew began his political career in the late 1950's; on the take by 1962 from engineering firms, he remained on the take all the way through his career, until it was learned in 1973 that he was on the take still, even as he sat as Vice-President across the street from the White House. Suburbia had no tools, no mirrors, no way of finding out about itself except in such rare enclaves as Suffolk and Nassau counties in New York, where Long Island's *Newsday* makes an attempt to explain. Suburbia is captive to ignorance locally—and captive nationally to the big-city press and television, which tell it what is going on outside and parade the symbols that stir national politics. It is in suburbia that professional manipulators and "hot-issue" men alike find their easiest loot of votes.

The changing pattern of politics enlarged even further as one took a longer perspective than the radial and cross-country highways, a larger frame than the suburban girdles, and went back to look at the big cities within the girdle. As the whites left, the black and Spanish-speaking arrived, and the big cities began to tip. In 1950, not a single big city in the Union had a black majority. By 1970, Newark, Gary, Atlanta, Washington, D.C., all had black majorities and it was inevitable that more would follow. In 1950, New York counted 10 percent blacks, Los Angeles 9 percent, Chicago 14 percent. By 1970 those figures read New York 21 percent, Chicago 33 percent, Los Angeles 18 percent. But St. Louis (41 percent), Baltimore (46 percent), Detroit (44 percent) all seemed destined for black majorities by the census of 1980.

The black migration was, of course, an expression of the prosperity of the times—jobs drew blacks North, jobs at living wages in the heavy industries, farm jobs in New Jersey, Pennsylvania, Michigan, Indiana, from which it was easy to slip into settled jobs in the cities. Prosperity sustained blacks in the big cities. In the big city, the rural family life of the Southern black, as well as the village life of the Spanish-speaking, broke down—but the big city shouldered the burden. In New York City alone, welfare clients were to go from 324,000 in 1960 to 1,265,000 in 1972; and with such clients the city assumed the expense of new kinds of schools, new kinds of policing, new demands on health and hospital systems.

Nor was there any way of reversing such trends. Blacks were no longer voiceless. Twenty years earlier, blacks counted only two Congressmen in the House—William L. Dawson of Chicago and the flamboyant Adam Clayton Powell of New York, who for six of his twenty-two years in Congress served as chairman of the House Committee on Education and Labor, doing almost nothing with his leverage to help his people, and ending his career in disgrace, a refugee on the sun-buttered island of Bimini. Year by year in the decades of change, the numbers of black Congressmen grew as big-city ghettoes filled formerly white seats with their own kind, until in 1972 there were fifteen black Congressmen and one black Senator, of a passion and conviction completely different from those of Adam Clayton Powell. They wanted their share of the prosperity for their people—and their say in the course of experiment.

The prosperity had created another community in America almost as significant as the suburban communities or the black communities—the student and academic community. To be a college student in pre-World War II America was the way to earn a ticket of admission to the life of the elite. One went to college to get a whack at a better job—either supported by parents who were comfortable enough to send one there, or because a craving for knowledge was so insatiable that the student would make any sacrifice to win a scholarship and get his learning. In all, only 1,350,000 Americans were in college in 1939, before World War II. By 1974 college students numbered 10,137,065, a multiplication of eight times. Learning was the largest single industry in America, and the student proletariat outnumbered steel workers, coal miners, automobile workers, needle workers *and* farmers all combined. When, by 1971, all young people eighteen years old or over were empowered to vote by the 26th Amendment, they became potentially the largest single bloc in the nation's politics—moved more easily by symbols than by self-interest or ethnic heritage.

The students and their teachers, with their intellectual fashions, fancies and occasional creative insights, their tastes in rhetoric, were to press on every single American political decision from the 1960's on—for they had ideas, and their ideas had style. Much of their style appalled an older America—the style of their hair, longer and longer as the years wore on; the style of their sex life, freer and freer as the years wore on; the style of their escape, and their trips into the unknown as their experimental drug culture spread. They were creating a new culture, a counter-culture, in American life—but their ideas were as important as their style, and chief among their ideas was the one which held the central American government in Washington responsible for the total behavior of the American state. Like their teachers, the young students wanted a strong President.

It was not an idea confined to students. Black leaders were carrying their cause to Washington, too—both to the Congress and to the Supreme Court. So also were big-city politicians—clamoring for more school funds, more transportation funds, more welfare funds. So also were the spokesmen of suburbia, who wanted more cheap mortgage credit from Federal agencies as well as more heavily subsidized roads such as the Highway Act was giving them; they wanted, too, cleaner and better air, more and stricter environment controls which only the Federal government could give them, to keep the green grass green as it was when they came to suburbia.

Prosperity was giving everyone more freedom to experiment, to plan, to hope, to seek the promises the future held. But the promises could be redeemed nowhere else but in Washington. The local party politicians could do little more for the citizen than grant a petty favor. Only Washington could change the rules of the game.

What was happening in the decades between 1932 and

1972 was the end of an old American myth—the myth that began with the meeting in town hall, where independent men came together and discussed the town taxes or where the town roads should run. The problems now were too complicated to be discussed in town hall; the parties were too arthritic, too stiff at the joints to flex with the changing needs of America. The press described what was happening on the broad horizon; and television translated what the press reported into emotional symbols that stimulated shock, concern, alarm, sorrow, pride. Assassinations, inaugurations, the dusty moon, the riotous conventions, the violence in the streets, the pollution of shore, stream, lake, the upheaval of the blacks, above all, the war in Vietnam— each passed into political emotion via the tube of television, and there on the tube was transformed into supercharged symbols of Good and Bad.

But whoever ran the government of the United States would be dealing not only with symbols; not simply with the traditional clash of blocs and interests; not simply with the news system that capsulized complicated realities into ninety-second visuals or 1,200-word dispatches. He would be dealing with facts—not least the brutal facts of demography.

Americans were living longer than ever; the number of those over sixty-five was to rise from 12,300,000 in 1950 to 20,900,000 in 1972. These people needed health services, Medicare, shelter. Rising expectations created a crisis in medicine, but the number of hospitals did not rise with the needs—and even declined slightly; the number of hospital beds dropped more sharply. It was up to the Federal government, the President, to do something. Demographically, the most startling bulge on the historic graphs of population were the young. In 1960 there had been only 27,000,000 Americans between the ages of fourteen and twenty-four; by 1970 the postwar baby boom had pushed that figure to 40,000,000. Not only did the thrust of such young people add a dynamic, sometimes irrational, new element to politics, but physically they had to be cared for with funds for universities, dormitories, student loans. And as brutal as the home realities pushed on any President by demography were the realities of the outer world. The great domestic prosperity rested on America's management and control of the trading world which it had created when American arms dominated the globe. But the globe was growing more restless every year, the cost of arms rising exponentially, and the sickening wars needed to maintain that trading world were ever more intolerable for the young required to fight them.

All such problems locked on the President's desk.

By the 1950's the nation had, for twenty years already, tucked away into its back memory the original purpose of the Republic—to preserve liberty at home and defend the land against foreign enemies, the original theory having held that each man determined the condition of his own life, by striving. Government was now, however, held to a higher standard: it was there to improve the condition of *your* life; and government meant Federal government, since local governments were thought too small, too corrupt, too inefficient to meet the needs of a people who had seen and felt the collapse of the old industrial system in the 1930's.

The experience of those twenty years between 1932 and 1952 had taught millions of Americans that when they talked of power, power meant Washington. Workers competed for scarce jobs or hungered in breadlines in 1932, and when they tried to organize, thugs and cops beat them up. Only the Federal government could protect them and their unions; thus by 1935 the Federal government had passed the first National Labor Relations Act; and by 1938 had set the minimum wage at 25 cents an hour. Administration by administration, that minimum wage would grow, reaching $1.60 an hour under Lyndon Johnson and $2.00 an hour under Richard Nixon, with a promise of a rise to $2.30 in 1976. If Washington had the power to set wages, then the unions had to organize to influence Washington; and in a generation the AFL/CIO had become the powerhouse of Democratic party politics, brass-knuckling its way through every closed door, punishing its enemies at the polls, financing candidates of its choice in every state of the Union.

The farmers, disorganized and bankrupted by the collapse of their world markets in the Depression, were brought under Federal control by the Agricultural Adjustment Act of 1938. The AAA began with price supports for

only three crops—wheat, corn and cotton. But, Congress by
Congress, the government enlarged its embrace, fixing
acreage allotments, supporting peanuts, tobacco, soybeans,
milk. So the farmers organized as naturally as did labor. If
the price of milk was to be fixed in Washington, they reasoned, they had every inducement to contribute to politicians willing to fix milk prices their way, just as labor contributed to fix wages its way. And so the milk men entered
politics, slipping cash to Democrats and Republicans alike,
from Humphrey to Nixon, until finally their effort ruptured
in scandal.

Like so many other controls, controls of food and farm-
ing almost inevitably intertwined with foreign affairs in the
postwar world. If there was a Marshall Plan, the Federal
farm surplus was a costless instrument of diplomacy. If India's new democracy tottered in near-starvation, surplus-
food programs could handle that crisis—with an almost un-
noticed $2.75 billion in food. Controls brought lobbyists
from around the world to apply pressure in Washington. In
1934, to protect the American sugar growers from low-
price world competition, 55 percent of all America's sugar
market was reserved for domestic growers. Thus for thirty
years sugar cost American consumers billions more than it
should have, while foreign nations hired Washington lobbyists to plead for their "traditional" share of the rich American sugar market.

Controls multiplied, then multiplied again. Controls over
securities exchanges and investments. Controls over saving
banks. Mortgages had been guaranteed by government, first
for Depression-squeezed farmers, then for returning veterans, then for millions more in the booming suburbs. The
Federal government moved into the big city—with a first
billion-dollar authorization for slum clearance under Truman, then more under Eisenhower, then with its reach enlarged under Johnson by the acts of Model Cities and Urban
Renewal. And under Federal housing programs, new projects
became the scourge of the poor and the ravagers of old
communities.

Through Republican and Democratic administrations
alike, the process ran on—and by the 1950's, the Supreme
Court, previously a brake on centralization, had become
one of its accelerating forces. Once the Supreme Court

sanctioned any step forward in any system of controls, the subsequent steps seemed inevitable. In 1954 the Supreme Court ruled that segregation of schoolchildren because their color was black was not only a national abomination but illegal, and in 1957 Eisenhower sent Federal paratroopers into Arkansas to enforce the law. By 1971 the issue had been transmuted from "desegregation" to "integration," and schoolchildren could now be excluded from certain schools and sent to other schools because their color was white.

Democrats generally cheered Federal action. Republicans generally protested, but both parties were under the same pressure—a nation with so explosive a prosperity at home, with such far-ranging world interests abroad, required a central order. When world oil surpluses threatened to wipe out high-cost domestic oil production, an Eisenhower set up rigid quotas on oil imports which later, in the energy crisis, proved salvation. When prosperity's rubbish burst nature's limits of containment, a Nixon set up environmental controls that reached from automobile tailpipes to the topmost tip of utility smokestacks.

By the early 1970's, without ever pausing to analyze the problems of a totally centralized industrial society, America had become a totally centralized industrial society. If the terms of debate—"busing," "national security," "slave labor," "right to work," "freedom of speech," "equal rights," "clean air," "reverse discrimination," "quotas"—were symbolic, the political realities were not.

Every group had to press its leverage in Washington, by fair means or foul, to thrive—or sometimes simply to survive. Money poured into national politics just to open doors. The airlines wheedled billions out of Washington and, for a while, thrived. The railways could not learn the new language of politics and began to wither. The American shipping industry learned the ways of Washington late—but when Nixon's ship-building subsidies began to flow from Washington, it rose from creeping decay to flourishing good health. Almost 2,000,000 people worked in the American arms industry at its 1968 peak—their jobs depended not only on the national defense program but also on the skill of their Congressmen and lobbyists to keep Seattle, or Fort Worth, or Santa Monica, or Long Island at the top of the Pentagon's procurement list. Scholarships and fellowships;

symphony orchestras and art museums; savings-and-loan societies; magazines with large or small circulations; private universities and public school systems; environmentalists and paper mills—all of them, and too many more to catalogue, depended for their well-being on the amount of pressure they could bring to bear in Washington. And the maximum pressure point was the desk of the President. The Presidency, said John F. Kennedy the night before his election in 1960, had become the "center of action"—the center of action for the price of your milk, meat and bread, for the decision to snatch your son for war, for the protection of your child from the "school-busers," for decisions affecting every ethnic, corporate, idealistic, commercial or regional group interest in the country.

The Presidency had become a job of paralyzing complexity and bloated power. It was infinitely difficult for one man to control the office—but it was even more difficult to control that man. The old parties had long since lost their control or influence over the Presidents who spoke in their name, and no new disciplinary force had risen to replace the old parties except the courts and the news system. With the election of Dwight D. Eisenhower, Presidents had broken free into a world of their own, guided by little more than their own instinct and character, responding to conflicting pressures that defied easy compromise, dependent more and more on men who braced their personal philosophies and style.

Of these, in many ways the most representative President of the twenty-year span was Richard M. Nixon—he understood the politics of the times; he understood the changes going on both at home and in the world abroad; he was a man of the present with a gift for seeing ahead to the future. What he did not understand was the past—or the reasons why Americans so long ago had originally put so much potential power in the office he held. When at last he was to be disgraced, it was because he had broken with the faith that had glued Americans to each other in the beginning to make a republic.

That misunderstanding, of course, was not incomprehensible. Nixon had grown up in California politics and it was in California that the party system had first begun to crumble; in California that the new style of politics was born which was ultimately to corrupt the White House; in California that the postwar restlessness of Americans had first made them prey to the new breed of professional manipulators who were to take over, without ever understanding it, the delicate meeting ground of politics and government.

The early professionals of California politics, whose descendants were to govern from the White House, were quite unlike the "pros" of Eastern politics—the hacks, the ward-heelers, the finance men, the conniving contractors, the ambitious young lawyers who, all together, under the traditional bosses, had nominated candidates and run campaigns since the days of Ulysses S. Grant.

They were different because California was different, and California forecast the shape of the future.

Long before suburbia became the great battleground of American politics in the fifties and sixties, California was projecting suburbia's politics. Its sun-washed valleys by the Pacific were the last stop in the westering urge of American history. For generations Americans had drifted there—they had come first for gold to Northern California, and then been lured south by real-estate promoters who told of fortunes to be made in orange land. Those who came first were old-stock Americans—Protestant Civil War veterans, fortune seekers from Maine, Vermont, Massachusetts, to be quickly outnumbered after the turn of the century by families from Michigan, Illinois, Indiana and Iowa.

California was thus Republican by inheritance. Until 1930 the Democrats of California were little more than a sect, sending to Washington only one Congressman out of the state's eleven, sending to the state capitol at Sacramento only thirteen of the 120 state legislators. From 1898 to 1938, California elected not a single Democratic Governor. And then, in the late 1930's, the political landscape buckled as strangers arrived. They came in hordes—first the Okies, Arkies and Texans, the refugees of the Grapes of Wrath. Then came the war tide—workers, soldiers, Negroes, Jews, who first saw the Pacific Coast on their way to war in the Pacific and were smitten with the California virus; then Mexicans; then all sorts of strivers, land-developers, university people and technicians absorbed by California's new industries of aviation, missiles, electronics.

California politics ever since the thirties had had a peculiar zesty flavor—Dr. Francis Townsend had swayed the state with his Townsend Plan; Upton Sinclair, robed as a prophet, had come near winning the state with his EPIC ("End Poverty in California") slogan. The Republicans had mastered such prewar Democratic insurrectionaries easily. In the postwar forties, however, the growing numerical Democratic majority was not to be wished away. To control the state, the Republicans had to develop a new system of political techniques if they were not to be doomed forever as a hopeless minority.

Republican politicians in suburbia all across the country were struggling with incoming Democratic migrants from the city. In a state of traditional politics like New York, as newcomers poured into counties such as Suffolk and Nassau (now making up the ninth largest metropolitan region in the nation), a Republican Boss Sprague was there to receive them—his party functionaries would man the welcome wagons he sent to greet the newcomers as they poured into the Levittowns; his political machine would make sure the sewer system worked, or offer to help with the hook-up of telephone or electricity if it was snarled. An old-fashioned organization like the Sprague machine could deliver solid, necessary favors in return for the enrollment of solid Republican votes.

But in California no such machine solution was practicable—for reasons that ran deep in the state's history. Party machines had been wiped out thirty-five years before by a waspish, stocky and belligerent Progressive Republican Governor named Hiram Johnson—California's La Follette. Hiram Johnson was a "conscience" Republican, and early in the century his conscience had been violated by the sordid control of his party and state by the Southern Pacific Railroad. That railroad bought and sold legislators and officials in Sacramento as if the state government were its property. In this legislature, said one of its members, "you wouldn't even pass the Lord's Prayer . . . without money." Leading a revolt of moralistic, church-going, Midwestern transplants to California, Hiram Johnson purged the state of the railway's control: his revolt wiped out political patronage more completely than anywhere else in the Union, forbade party nominating conventions, fumigated every cranny of conventional party politics. In the process, he bequeathed to California one of the finest state governments in the Union; a governor with powerful executive control; and a disorganized party system.

It was Hiram Johnson's political legacy that bedeviled California Republicans all through the forties and fifties. Johnson had never envisioned the wave upon wave of the uprooted, wanderers and horizon seekers that would engulf his state.

How could the Republicans reach such people? How could they penetrate the minds of the newcomers who hived in endless suburbs from end to end of the Golden State? How could they, deprived of the apparatus of Republicans in other states, frustrate or lure to their own candidates the overwhelming Democratic majority among these newcomers?

The answer that came in California in the thirties, forties and fifties has now become so standard all across the country that there seems nothing novel about it. You reach suburban America, which by now means most America, not face to face but through manipulative techniques—by sophisticated public-relations planning, by the deliberate management of images, phrases, symbols, by careful orchestration of emotions, by *ad hoc*, specialized, issue-oriented citizen or volunteer committees. Forty years later, such professional campaign management was to be common practice in every major state of the Union. But in the thirties, when Americans still voted on party lines, it had already begun —in California.

Again one must go back to Hiram Johnson. Among his legacies, he had left California the practices of "initiative" and "referendum," a concept of "do-it-yourself" legislation, a turn-of-the-century Progressive's version of what is now called "participatory democracy." "Initiative" lets California citizens petition to put programs on the ballot which, if passed, become part of the state's constitution; "referenda" let citizens request a review of a law the legislature has made and, if enough signatures and votes are collected, repeal that law.

Hiram Johnson had thought of his great reforms as "arming the people to protect themselves." But what it did over the years was to arm specific-interest groups to short-circuit parties, legislatures, established leadership, and twitch an uninformed electorate by its nerve ends. To get an initiative or referendum on the ballot required a certain number of signatures—5 percent of the vote in the preceding election; in Hiram Johnson's day that meant 30,000 signatures, today it means over 300,000 signatures. Public-relations firms collected such signatures at 25 cents per name; moreover, they would provide for a complete political valet service of literature, radio, billboards and, later, television to excite the public to do what the specific-interest group required.

The technique for running a campaign divorced from a political party would probably have been invented by *someone* in the past forty years. Its apotheosis was to be reached in 1972 in Richard Nixon's CREEP—Committee for the Re-Election of the President. But almost certainly it *had* to be invented first in California, where Hiram Johnson's reforms invited shrewd candidates to make of every election a referendum. And thus one comes to the parents of the new professionals of politics, Clem Whitaker and Leone Baxter, truly creative originals.

Clem Whitaker, a tall, asthmatic man who might have been mistaken for a pioneer church deacon except for his penchant for colored sports shirts and flamboyant neckties, was the son of a Baptist minister. Coming back from World War I to report politics in Sacramento, he organized the Capitol News Bureau, which specialized in covering the California legislature.[1] His acid observation of the quality of the California Assemblymen led him to think that, on the whole, it would be cheaper to influence politics by mobilization of pressure at the grass roots than by buying votes retail, one by one, as was then the practice of California state lobbyists. As he expanded his operations, he met and then married his second wife, Leone Baxter, the man-

[1] See "Government by Whitaker and Baxter" by Carey McWilliams in the April 14, April 21 and May 5, 1951, issues of *The Nation*. Also see *Southern California Country: An Island on the Land* by Carey McWilliams (New York: Duell, Sloan & Pearce, 1946), still after almost thrity years one of the finest studies ever published on the subject. The best modern work on California politics is *Dancing Bear: An Inside Look at California Politics* by Gladwin Hill (Cleveland and New York: The World Publishing Company, 1968).

ager of the Redding (California) Chamber of Commerce, a petite, green-eyed, red-haired woman, as bright as he and as fascinated by the manipulation of public opinion. Together they made political history.

From 1933 to 1959 (when California abolished cross-filing in an attempt to give some coherence to party politics) Whitaker and Baxter were to California politics what Tammany had once been to New York politics. Managing sixty campaigns and referenda, in the fifteen years prior to 1951 they had won fifty-five of them. Their clients were men of such eminence as Earl Warren, William Knowland, Thomas Kuchel, Richard Nixon, Goodwin Knight. Their fee for rounding up enough signatures to put a referendum on the ballot was at least $120,000; but for candidates who had money, or could raise money, such professional services were cheap; such services create laws and elect Governors and Senators and Assemblymen.

Not until 1949 were Whitaker and Baxter recognized nationally as new political prototypes—when they offered their services to the American Medical Association to block Harry Truman's health-insurance program and Washington politicians, normally so savvy, recognized the quality of their performance in thwarting the President of the United States. Imitators since then have created the recognized art of political manipulation; refinement of their techniques has followed with the refinement of polling, broadcasting, image-making, telephone banks, direct-mail cross-sectioning. Their principles are now embedded in American political practice, and no American political leader approaches any major issue of right-or-wrong without, in the phrase of the Nixonian White House, weighing "the PR dimension of the problem."

The Whitaker-and-Baxter principles of political technology are perhaps worth recalling, for their principles underlay the campaign of 1972—although the stupidity and criminality of their imitators at the Committee for the Re-Election of the President would have upset and offended them. The first of these principles was unspoken: "Politics is too important to be left to politicians." The second is simpler: "More Americans like corn than caviar." The third is still operational: either party, or any legislature, can be taken over for a specific purpose if enough muscle, enough volunteers, enough grass-roots strength can be coaxed out of the ballot boxes. And there were corollaries to these basic principles: the best kind of campaign is an attack campaign; in any campaign, an enemy has to be invented against whom the voters can be warned; issues are to be few, but must be clear—and must confront the voter with an emotional decision; the independent vote is critical in a close election, and once the party is captured by a nomination, the independent must be the target of all suasion and PR. Lastly, Whitaker and Baxter believed that a campaign must have an inner rhythm, a pace, a timing that would capture the attention of the news system, both print and electronic.

Whitaker and Baxter were themselves sublimely uninterested in any substantive issues. Their ethics were those of a skilled lawyer who does his best to win a case. They could, for their fee, deliver a tailor-made campaign for anybody or any cause; and they usually won.

Whitaker and Baxter provoked, of course, many California imitators, Baus & Ross, Spencer-Roberts and Associates, and others. But all the imitators had learned the same lesson: to attack, to rouse the passions, to disdain party organizations. And thus California politics baffled, and sometimes horrified, Eastern politicians by the violent emotions they roused. Nelson Rockefeller, in his California primary campaign against Goldwater in 1964, hired the Spencer-Roberts firm and restrained it. But even a decade later in 1974, by then a scar-crusted veteran of national politics, Rockefeller could not forget the quality of opposition he had encountered in California and recalled that campaign thus: ". . . rough stuff I mean, this—you know, I mean, everything: from having acid put in the punch at a reception, to having bomb threats almost every night, phone calls, workers, women workers in the party, driven off the road in their cars at night, and so forth. This is a rough business, see?"

PR—public relations—was the name of the game in California. To master PR required ever larger sums of money, and eventually a statewide campaign in California became, by far, the most expensive state race in the Union, except for the Rockefeller campaigns in New York. The cost of politics was going up to its 1972 peak. And perhaps it should be noted that the fund-raising scandals of the national election of 1972, organized by Californians, may eventually bring an end to the PR era that began there—by the restrictive new campaign laws the 1972 scandals have provoked.

Politics in California had not yet reached its peak of expense and of passion in January, 1946, when Navy veteran Richard Nixon returned home from the war. But it was on the way.

The power of Whitaker and Baxter was at its height in 1946, and their practices, rooted in Hiram Johnson's concept of direct democracy, had already become common in elections. California, as one has noted, was a state about to explode with newcomers. From 8,000,000 people when Nixon returned after the war, it was to go to 10,500,000 in 1950, to 16,000,000 in 1960, to 20,000,000 in 1970. Its government, propelled by Hiram Johnson's old reforms and Earl Warren's character, was superb. And its party system anarchic.

The Democratic Party was a shambles, a shuffling non-organization, some of its pockets dominated by dust-bowl Southern Democrats; others, in key metropolitan areas, financed by liberal Hollywood luminaries; or, in the north, penetrated by Communists (political reporters felt that the Democratic organizations in six of the nine counties in the Bay Area were actually dominated by the Communist Party apparatus). Republican Governor Earl Warren's chief political opposition came from lobbyists for special interests in the California legislature, not from Democrats. Warren was the chief star of California politics—but only one among a number of diverse politicans who called themselves Republican, yet operated in the same star system, where volunteer groups or fan clubs were more important than party stucture, and big-moneyed backers substituted for old-fashioned Eastern bosses. Money bought PR. To reach the people Republicans used Whitaker and Baxter, or one of the rival professional firms—and relied on California's three great newspapers, all of Republican proprietorship, to spread the message as if they were house organs.

This was the stage on which Richard Nixon would make his entry into politics in 1946, choosing as his passageway his home-town district, the California 12th Congressional,

south of Los Angeles. Many other young veterans were en-
listing in politics for the first time that year, each coming
home from a good war, determined to make America better. Among them were elected such youngsters as Carl Albert, who would later be Speaker of the House that forced
Nixon to resignation. Among the class of '46 were Jacob
Javits, Otto Passman, Thurston Morton, George Smathers.
Among them also was another Navy veteran, John F. Kennedy, preparing to run for Congress in the Massachusetts
11th, one of his family fiefs in Boston. A failure that year
was a young Armored Corps veteran, Peter Wallace Rodino, who tried his first run in the 10th New Jersey District,
which was then Newark and an overwhelmingly Italian-
American enclave. Rodino lost narrowly on this 1946 try;
but he would run again in 1948, win, and go on to define the
issues of power and its abuse in the proceedings against
Richard Nixon.

All of these young veterans, tempered by war, were of a
passionate patriotism, a patriotism which now, thirty years
later, seems anachronistic. Each would project this patriotism into the future and into politics in his own way—from
his recent experience, from family background, from boyhood memory, from yearnings, wounds, dreams of his own
past.

But, by all measures, Richard Nixon's past was the one
most steeped in striving, scored by ambition and colored by
sadness.

3

POOR RICHARD:
HOW THINGS WORK

The Nixon who held his first political rally in Ontario, California, in November of 1945, aged thirty-two, not yet mustered out of service, was a man already half shaped—totally unknown to his countrymen, and probably unknown even to himself.

Perhaps historians of the future, insulated from passion by the perspective of time, will see him more clearly than his contemporaries. They are the ones who award the badges of merit or infamy to dead heroes and past villains. Good Queen Bess and Saint Louis, Honest Abe and Henry the Navigator glisten as figures carved by historians to instruct the young. Bad King John, Louis the Fat, Ivan the Terrible, Adolf Hitler teach what decent men should not be or do. But Nixon will mystify even the historians; more is known of his inner thinking, and yet more will become known, than of any previous President of the Republic. They will have to balance his known crimes against the achievement of peace and the release of America from thirty years of war. They, perhaps, will be able to weigh his hypocrisies against his convictions. Perhaps they will even be able to explain the essential duality of his nature, the evil and the good, the flights of panic and the resolution of spirit, the good mind and the mean trickery.

But for a reporter of the time, the task is more difficult. A reporter cannot report unless he tries to understand the man and get to know him. For this reporter, who passed successively from loathing for Richard Nixon to respect for him, then to inescapable recognition of his criminal guilt, the task has been particularly difficult. For no one could understand what he was or would become unless he tried to understand both the onrushing forces Richard Nixon faced when he entered politics—and how he had been already shaped and would be shaped further.

The story has elements of an American tragedy.

I had begun as a political reporter to trace the past of Richard Nixon in 1955 when already, as Vice-President, he was a man of controversy. A first run-through of California politics made stark reading. He was loathed by my friends there; disliked by Earl Warren; disdained by Senator William Knowland; and hated by then Governor Goodwin J. Knight, a colorful and vivid-spoken man whose anger seemed to me, then, oddly misfocused on detail. Knight had been physically shoved around at the airport when he, as Lieutenant Governor, had come to meet young Nixon, California's Vice-Presidential nominee, at his homecoming from the Chicago Republican convention in 1952. Nixon's advance men had roughly pushed Knight out of the line-up for photographers, as advance men do, depriving him of that front-page picture which to politicians is bread and butter. Knight was not bitter at Nixon so much as at the men he had gathered around him: it was a quality of criticism I would encounter over and over again for twenty years, provoked by the bristling arrogance of the Nixon guards.

I pursued the Nixon trail in California; he had won three elections by then, each time by a smashing majority, so that one had to acknowledge that the people at least had found something in him. But the man behind his campaigns was nowhere real, except as a silhouette of partisan bitterness. Moreover, the man was not truly a California politician in the sense that Earl Warren or Bill Knowland was. "Dick," said Pat Hillings, then one of Nixon's associates, "is the first lateral entry into California politics. The first time Dick ever visited the legislature at Sacramento was when he came back from knocking off Alger Hiss in Washington."

But if he was not a typical local politician, he *was* quintessentially a Californian, of that endless stream of seekers who suffer as they strive, who learn to smile when hurt, and bring remembered bitterness even to their feasts of joy. He came of Californians who reflect uncounted millions of Americans everywhere who share the same insecurity of not feeling at home in the world.

I drove to Whittier, whose chamber of commerce describes it as "a first-name-basis kind of town. It's a place where people traditionally honor their obligations and pay their bills on time." Already, even then, thriving little businesses were beginning to wipe out the orange groves that had brought its Quaker settlers there, but it was a neighborly place and I visited the only local contact I could make with his boyhood past.

The white-haired lady I met, as gentle as she could be, was reluctant to talk; she had been the debating coach at Whittier High School. She offered the same perplexity I have heard expressed so often since. She remembered and respected his quality—she simply did not like him.

The boy she remembered was smart; he worked hard. He was a poor boy—he could not stay for football practice after school because he had to catch the school bus as soon as classes were over and go to work in his father's general store. Which probably was why he joined the debating team, she said, instead of the high-school football team, whose squad had to practice late in the afternoon. And he had won the Kiwanis Club of Whittier prize for the best oration by a high-school student on the Constitution.[1]

But—there was something mean in him, she went on, mean in the way he put his questions, argued his points. Dick's father, she remembered, was mean, too. She used to live near the Nixon house, and when Mr. Nixon yelled at the boys, everyone for blocks around could hear. His temper frightened people. But, on the other hand, she said, his mother was an angel. Everyone I have ever spoken to over

---

[1] The oration read in part, as reprinted in the high school's yearbook, "The chief desire of man is that his life and personal liberty may be well protected. While our forefathers were struggling for freedom, one of their grievances was that a man accused of a crime was not always given a fair chance to prove himself innocent, and was thus often unjustly punished. Therefore the framers of the Constitution provided for the highest type of justice. No citizen of the United States can be tried for a capital crime without first being indicted by a grand jury. If he is indicted, he is given a public trial by an impartial jury. He may obtain counsel and witnesses. He is not compelled to testify against himself as in times past, nor is any evidence obtained by compulsion." This excerpt, by any means of testing, is excellent thinking for a teenager, but was written long before the days of electronic tape recording.

the years has reported Richard Nixon's mother as if she radiated goodness. Carl Greenberg, the Log Angeles *Times* reporter, calls her "a sweetheart," and remembers her *insisting* on fixing breakfast for him in the kitchen one early morning when he was waiting to interview her son running for the U.S. Senate. Nelson Rockefeller recalls her as "saintly." And when Richard Nixon talks of her, his face softens into a smiling reminiscent glow.

Only those who came of age in the Depression know what insecurity is—and what poverty can do to family life. And few learned more sadly than Richard Nixon.

The most disastrous of all the Nixon forms of political rhetoric is his recollections of his childhood. They were matters of privacy one winced to hear exposed, and made the listener embarrassed to hear the lamentation from the stump.

The Nixon were bone poor, yet proud. Frank Nixon had been a streetcar motorman in Columbus, Ohio; frostbitten in the open cab of his trolley one winter, he left for Southern California, where he sought sun and warmth to ease the pain in his feet which continued for years thereafter. In California he worked as a farmhand, an oil roustabout, a carpenter; and met at a church social and married a Quaker girl, Hannah Milhous, from Indiana. He tried to set up a lemon ranch in Yorba Linda thirty miles outside Los Angeles; as a carpenter, he built with his own hands the house in which they lived; and on January 9th, 1913, arranged the stoves and the fire flues so that there would be some warmth in the cold room of the cottage when his second son, Richard Nixon, was born. Then the lemon ranch failed; and the family moved to Whittier, a Quaker community in the growing orange-ranch development of Southern California. But Mr. Nixon was not destined to make it there either—his general store and gas station provided only the scratchiest of livings. At ten, Richard Nixon hired out as a part-time farm laborer. At fourteen, he hired out as a barker for a fortune wheel for an outfit called Slippery Gulch Rodeo, which was a front for a poker-and-dice room in the back. He would tell later of his mother getting up at four in the morning to bake pies for sale in the store; of the Fourth of July with no fireworks, when other boys had them; of his mother going off to work as a scrubwoman and cook in Arizona because the sanatorium there would, in recompense, take care of his brother Harold, who was stricken with tuberculosis.

One has the picture of the embittered father remaining in Whittier with his other little boys, irascible, drained constantly by medical expenses (another of the boys died in childhood), cooking and caring for them, cuffing them cruelly, until the mother came home again. In Frank Nixon's family there had been only one success—his brother, a Ph.D., "Uncle Ernest," known as "Doc Nixon, the potato man"; and Frank Nixon was driven to see his sons succeed where he had not himself. Nixon remembers his father as "strict," as believing that "spare the rod and spoil the child" was not the way to bring up children. But of his mother, whom he adored, he said once, "We dreaded far more than my father's hand, her tongue."

The Nixons were poor in a way that only the other poor could understand. Ice cream was a rare treat. The boys wore hand-me-down clothes ("I wore my brother's shoes, and my younger brothers were handed down mine"). Given a twist of home atmosphere, Richard Nixon might have become a tribune of the poor, as was Hubert Humphrey, whose outgoing, opera-loving father knew equally hard times. But out of such experience come different perspectives. One either becomes a spokesman of the poor or one is determined to escape and, like Scarlett O'Hara, sleeps all one's life with the dream of never being poor again. Poverty curdles character as well as strengthening it. It crumples some men. It makes others hard. Poverty soiled Nixon; he grew up to be hard—and vulnerable. And as in all those who grow up so vulnerable, the instinct for control, control of one's circumstances and perimeters of dignity, would grow.

Escape from poverty was not easy in the thirties. Graduating from high school, Richard Nixon won a Harvard Club of California prize—a book, the biography of Harvard's Dean Briggs. But the family could not afford to send him off to Harvard. Instead, living at home, he worked his way through the local Quaker college, Whittier, where in his senior year he was elected student-body president. Then off to Duke Law School, on a scholarship. Scholarship boys had, in those days, little time for fun. You made your marks or you lost your scholarship. Nixon spent little time in bull sessions; he studied, to graduate third in his law-school class—and to be turned down by the great-name New York law firms where he sought a job. All his life, from his days at Whittier College, where he had campaigned and won against the campus snobs, it was Nixon against the Establishment.

The early life is graven with the scratch marks of poverty. Nixon himself described it best, years later, in an outburst of reminiscence in New Orleans on the campaign trail in 1968: "When Pat and I first got married—when was that, Pat?—oh yes, 1940, we went to Mexico. That was just after I graduated from Duke and I went from Duke up to Lansing. I still remember that bus ride, and I bought a car with her money—she had the money—a 1939 Oldsmobile, and I drove it back all the way across the country, and then we split the cost of our honeymoon, and went to Mexico for two weeks. Sometimes we drove all night to save the cost of a hotel, and I think we saw every temple, every church in old Mexico and it all cost us only $178. Well . . . a year later we decided to take a vacation, because I think you should take a vacation when you're young, even if you have to borrow for it, we saw too many old folks tottering around in Mexico and decided not to wait that long. Well, we took a United Fruit boat—no, I should say ship, I'm a Navy man—for a two-week trip from California through the Canal to New Orleans. We had the worst cabin in the boat, it was the *Ulua*—our cabin was right down there in the hold with the sound of engines and the smells. So when we came to New Orleans, we decided to eat one meal in a good restaurant. We came to Antoine's and we ordered one Oysters Rockefeller for the two of us, and one pompano-in-a-bag."

It was a money-pinched life: a junior's job in a local law office, an admonition from a local judge about the bungled handling of one of his client's cases. A gamble in an orange-juice-bottling venture that failed. Then the war; separation; and brief residence in New York, where he and Pat shopped at Macy's, and when cheap seats were available, they splurged on two in the uppermost tiers of the old Metropolitan Opera House. Then a few months in Middle Riv-

er, Maryland, working as a contract-liquidation officer for
the Navy on the Martin Mars flying-boat project.

It was the fall of 1945 when the call came, as Nixon remembers it—a telegram from "an old friend, a banker in
my home town of Whittier, who went to college with my
mother in Whittier," spokesman for a committee of local
businessmen. They wanted to find a young Republican war
veteran to run for Congress against liberal Democrat Jerry
Voorhis in the old 12th California Congressional District.
They interviewed a number of prospects and, after a ten-
minute speech by Nixon, decided he was their man.

Politics, for those who choose it as a way of life, is an
exercise in ego—attractive most to those who have a sense
of self, who enjoy the rub of their personality against others
and the camaraderie of the campaign. Of this quality, Nixon had little. What he did share with other politicians was
the desire to write his name on other men's lives, to find
identity in the action. But poverty's wounding is harshest on
those who have talent, drive and ambition but are denied
the entree that comes so naturally to those who are better
born. "If he'd grown up in Boston," said a Bostonian who
came to know him later, "he would have been one of those
people singing Christmas carols outside the old homes in
Louisburg Square or Beacon Street, peering through the
windows, wondering what those kind of people talked about
inside." Invited to become a candidate, he was now for the
first time invited in—not quite to the parlor, but to a career
that was beckoning to thousands of young officers coming
home from the war with their first command behind them
and their futures obscure. It was not a glittering invitation,
for Voorhis was already a national figure and Nixon's
chances were faint. But politics would be his life from then
on. In politics, and politics alone, he would find his identity.

The full-scale biography of Richard Nixon as an individual remains to be written. In the hero-or-villain style of artful biography or polemic reporting, it is easiest to write of
the leader figure as if all his policies, impulses and decisions
flow from inner character. If one hates Richard Nixon
enough, it is easy to describe the implacable vindictiveness
and tenacity of the man as more important than the enormous courage; the recurrent gusts of panic or fury as more

important than the long thoughtfulness; his coarseness of discourse and lying as more important than his exceptional sensitivity to others' emotional needs; the cheapness and nastiness of his tactics as more important than the long-range planning of his exceptional mind. But it is for other writers to delve the psyche of the deeply textured former President and sort out the personal *character* qualities of the man. Yet there are genuine *political* qualities that must be traced from his first campaign on, developing in his later campaigns, to explain the abscessing of his Presidency to disaster.

A generalization first: underlying all Nixon's political qualities, good and bad, is curiosity—a fascination with How Things Work. In any private conversation with Nixon, this characteristic surfaces almost immediately: how do things get done? Those who have perceived this quality only at its most vile in the famous transcripts should be reminded that these were conversations held in the worst season and the worst crisis of the man's life. The same qualities of curiosity, probing, suspicion, reflection as I have heard them over the years, in and out of the Oval Office, can make him also one of the most absorbing and impressive of conversationalists.

Fragments recur to me from years of talk, from the most trivial to the most vital. Casual fragments of conversation on airplanes—on how the airlines manage to take an untrained girl and mold her into a polished stewardess in a six-week course; on how plane-to-ground communication works. On the sociology of politics—how the blue-collars vote, how Italians vote, how Catholics vote, how suburbia votes, how the vote breaks in Peoria. Fragments of conversation on techniques of campaigning—on the relative costs and merits of daytime radio for issue speeches as against evening television for emotional appeal, on Rockefeller's style of campaigning, on Goldwater's style of campaigning, on precisely what mistakes McGovern was making in 1972. I have only twice in some dozen hour-or-more conversations over the past seven years tried to draw Richard Nixon out about foreign affairs. But, inevitably, any conversation with him circles down to foreign affairs, and there again, from the trivial to the supreme: from the problems of

Prime Minister Lee Kuan Yew in Singapore to the grating between Russia and China, to the need of offering friendship to Red China (because they had the bomb, too, and we could not afford to remain on confrontation course). Conversations on how the Presidency works ("I must build a wall around me," or "From now on, no more than two drinks a day, I have to be alert for any midnight call"); on how Congress works; on the functions of a Vice-President; on the need of giving the South its hearing on the Supreme Court and in its decisions. The conversations have run from the brilliant to the humdrum—but always as a theme, the same theme: How Things Work. If you knew how to get to the proper buttons, you could press them.

In 1946 when Nixon began in politics, "how things work" was simple; the lessons came from the school of Whitaker and Baxter. You won by attack—you picked a nameless foe and frightened the voters; or you picked a well-known name and dissected it and pinned a catch-tag on it.

Jerry Voorhis was the first victim of the attack style. For vicious irresponsibility there were few campaigns like Nixon's first attack on Voorhis. Voorhis, a moderate liberal, an opponent of the booming Communist Party, was attacked, denounced and smeared by Nixon as a tool of the Reds— and destroyed. Re-election in 1948 brought Nixon to eminence as the man who pursued Alger Hiss—another dogged, relentless, unremitting attack. The fame of this triumph positioned him to run for the Senate against Helen Gahagan Douglas in 1950 in another mode of attack, surpassing even his slander of Voorhis; and, having won that campaign, he was positioned for choice by Dwight D. Eisenhower as running mate; and when he won, his vehemence of attack escalated.

Already by the late fifties his stump ferocity had made him an object of hatred to millions of liberals. "A ruthless partisan," wrote Walter Lippmann in 1958, "[who] does not have within his conscience those scruples which the country has a right to expect in the President of the United States." "Nixonland," said Adlai Stevenson, "a land of slander and scare, of sly innuendo, of a poison pen, the anonymous phone call, and hustling, pushing, shoving—the land of smash and grab and anything to win." No one could heat the blood of Democrats more quickly than Richard Nixon, who could denounce Secretary of State Acheson's "Kollege of Kommunism, Kowardice and Korruption," or label the Truman administration as "K1-C3"—Korea, Communism, Corruption, Controls," or "Acheson's color blindness—a form of pink eye toward the Communist threat to the United States." "What we need in Washington," he thundered in 1952 against the Truman administration, "is a President who, instead of covering up, cleans up."

Another political quality was also clear in the early Nixon campaigns—clear from the first campaign poster, a red-white-blue placard showing the Navy veteran in uniform, neglecting to label him Republican, saying simply: "ELECT RICHARD M. NIXON—WORLD W. R II VETERAN."

For this political quality, some Americans use the word "patriotism." In France, Germany, Italy, Japan the political type would be simply labeled as a "nationalist" politician, and thus be seen clearly. In America, however, "patriotism" is one of the old-culture words like "motherhood," "honor," "family," "flag," and embarrassing to intellectuals. The patriotism of most Democrats is as deep and genuine as that of most Republicans; but Democrats hesitate to campaign on the theme, for it exposes them to the mockery of the thinking and university classes to whom they normally appeal for guidance and support. Yet patriotism, or nationalism, is a bedrock issue in all national political campaigns, mined most intensively by Republicans, who began to wave the bloody flag shortly after the Civil War.

The bellicose rhetoric of Republicans has always extolled the martial virtues; but the Republicans have led Americans to no wars in this century; they have let the Democrats do that. In Nixon the Republican contradiction between Republican rhetoric and practice runs strong. His political purpose internationally has always been peace; but he liked to have war veterans around him. "Has he seen service?" was a question he frequently asked about prospective appointees. His rallies used the American flag as bunting; and his advance men knew that he liked a motorcade best when children lined the sidewalks in rows, fluttering peppermint-striped handkerchief-sized flags on both sides. Kennedy would go no further in campaigning than having the bands play "Anchors Aweigh" with a Navy lilt. Nixon preferred "America the Beautiful."

Patriotism, in every country, is invoked both by the devout and by the charlatans in politics. In the case of Richard Nixon, patriotism is devout, sincere, unqualified; and sometimes as hysterically emotional as it is among folklore American Legionnaires. Whatever excesses it may mask in others, and did indeed mask among his administration teammates; however much it was twisted into the hypocritical formula of national security and thus became a pretext for true crime—in Nixon, the emotion of patriotism was real.

Service in Washington, first as Congressman and next as Senator, hardened this genuine nationalism in Nixon, both into high policy and into mean politics. Whether Jerry Voorhis was or was not a Communist (which he was not), whether Helen Gahagan Douglas, the "Pink Lady" of his attack, was or was not a Communist dupe (which she was not), there were indeed hard Communist conspirators abroad in the land, in California and in Washington. Alger Hiss was the chief Nixon trophy—Nixon had actually pinned down and brought to trial a State Department official linked, in some way or other, with a Communist penetration of American diplomacy. And from then on, the real or fancied menace of conspiracy always interlocked, as a paranoia, with his genuine sense of patriotism.

Yet there was more to the Nixon service in Washington and the nationalist cause than negative intolerance or the simple unmasking of conspirators, both real and imaginary. He was of the anti-Taft wing of the party; the only Californian to join such liberals as Javits, Keating and twenty-three others to endorse the progressive "Republican Advance Group" of 1950; and voted consistently for liberal foreign-aid measures. His votes on domestic affairs were conservative; but his votes on foreign affairs always, under Truman, were enlightened and supportive. He might denounce Dean Acheson personally, but he would vote generally for Achesonian measures of foreign policy. And later in life, after election in 1968, he was to entertain a warm, almost affectionate correspondence with the man he had called the Red Dean, soliciting his advice.

Nixon's service as Vice-President was, in many ways, a humiliation. Vice-Presidents in those days, if not outcasts, were little more than political decoration. (Not until John F. Kennedy later gave Lyndon Johnson an office in the Executive Office Building was one admitted to real participation in White House affairs.) In Eisenhower's time, his Vice-President, Richard Nixon, operated from two separate offices in the Capitol. As a Senator from a big state, California, Nixon had had an effective staff of fifteen. Now he was reduced to a staff of seven, plus two military aides—and his function, whether chosen by himself or assigned by Eisenhower, was to be the public, outdoor "knife man" of the Republican Party and its political jack-of-all-trades. Chosen by Eisenhower to perform the cauterization of Senator Joe McCarthy, the reluctant Nixon moved to attack the Senator from Wisconsin and thereby estranged himself from the loyalties of right-wing Republicans. Taking to the road in mid-term campaigns to savage the Democrats, he became for them the most venomous figure in the Eisenhower administration. But in eight years as Eisenhower's roughneck partner, he was never once invited upstairs to the parlor floor where Presidents entertain their friends. That galled. And once when Eisenhower was hosting a political rally at his Gettysburg farm, he closed the rally by inviting a handful of friends into the house and left Richard Nixon, in the words of a friend then present, "standing outside there like someone had shoved a finger up his ass, he was so upset."

Excluded from most major decisions, he was permitted to participate in only one matter of substance: foreign policy. His symbolic role as second man in the Republic required constant trips abroad—to Korea, to Asia, to Europe, to Russia, to South America. As Vice-President, he would be intensely briefed by the State Department before each such trip, and his mind learned the way the world worked. Thus to his firm nationalism he added a powerful body of learning, knowledge and acquaintance with foreign chiefs of state. In foreign policy, he could bring himself to clash with theologian John Foster Dulles, then Secretary of State, who saw the Cold War as the conflict of Gog and Magog; and in one such clash over foreign aid he earned from Nelson Rockefeller a note which read, "You were superb. You have no idea what your understanding, integrity, courage and leadership mean to so many of us."

To his patriotism was thus added a detailed, realistic knowledge of what the true, as against the rhetorical, interests of the United States were abroad. Of these, the first was power, the second peace. If, ultimately, his disaster was to come because of his confusion of the interest of national security with the interest of Richard Nixon personally, nonetheless the credentials he acquired as lonesome and solitary Vice-President were to serve the Republic well abroad when he went on to become President.

No man except Franklin D. Roosevelt campaigned more often for national office across the country than Richard Nixon, who made the trip five times. But the campaigns of 1952 and 1960 were so crucial in the development of his political personality that they demand a sifting of their stress points from the chronicle.

It was from the campaign of 1952 that one can mark the freezing of Nixon's attitude to the national news system into one of hatred.

Until 1952, Richard Nixon had made his way in politics sheltered from the cutting edge of hostile reporting by the friendly borders of the Los Angeles *Times* circulation area. The endorsements of the Los Angeles *Times* in those days carried the same crushing power and support for its candidates as, in other days, did the endorsements of Colonel Robert McCormick's Chicago *Tribune* in "Chicagoland," or the support of the Boston *Globe* in eastern Massachusetts today. Such local endorsements were franchises of victory for unknown Republicans, and they were issued to aspirant politicians by Kyle Palmer, chief political correspondent of the *Times*, a grave and somber conservative who accepted his own importance with a quasi-public sense of responsibility. No Eastern political reporter, not even the memorable Jim Hagerty of the *New York Times*, rivaled Palmer in local clout. Once, fresh from Eastern reporting, I checked in at Kyle Palmer's office at the *Times* to consult the dean of Southern California political reporters; after a candid, outgoing "fill" on the story I had come to seek, Palmer apologized for having to cut the talk short. The Governor, he said, was waiting to see him. And it was indeed

Governor Goodwin Knight, hat in hand, waiting to visit the great Palmer in his austere reporter's cubicle.

Palmer could commit the full power of the Chandler family, which owned the paper, to candidates he designated. He had so designated Richard Nixon in 1946; and Nixon had come to accept this fatherly and friendly treatment by the publishing family as normal. Palmer liked young Nixon and offered a stirrup up. So, too, did Palmer's successor, Carl Greenberg, a man more modest than Palmer, an honest craftsman, absolutely meticulous in his reporting, but fond of Nixon personally with no apologies to make for the affection. Later, when a shift in family relations at the Chandler court put the paper in the hands of Otis Chandler, and its management in the hands of a new breed of editors, the reporting of the paper would clinically examine and help destroy Richard Nixon. But in the beginning, the Los Angeles *Times* was Nixon's patron, the publishing family his guardians, and he expected that other publishing enterprises would treat him with similarly unbalanced kindness.

His first years in Washington did little to disillusion Nixon with the press. As always, he was interested in how things work—and the way the press worked seemed simple. He developed, during the pursuit of Alger Hiss, into one of the most useful committee "leaks" that friendly correspondents could seek out. With the nation then at hysteria pitch in the great Red hunt of the fifties, there were many friendly correspondents, and their stories of the young California patriot on the trail of conspiracy made Nixon a national figure.

It was a total shock, then, when in 1952, running for Vice-President, Nixon found himself, for the first time, the object of national press onslaught. He had, as Senator, been the beneficiary of $18,235 in funds from Southern California businessmen, spent on his behalf for political expenses. He considered such a fund commonplace, as indeed it was at the time, nor was it secret. When first questioned, he casually told his Southern California fund-raisers to make the details available; but within days the news system, led by the New York *Post*, had made the story of the "secret fund" a national scandal. The Nixon fund story was followed only a few weeks later by the story of the Stevenson fund—a private kitty of another kind raised by the friends of Adlai Stevenson for Stevenson's use in adding to salaries for his appointees in the Illinois state government. But it was Nixon who in the national press was vilified, while Adlai Stevenson was but gently chided.

The episode rankled; it deserved and received a full chapter in his book, *Six Crises;* it festered further during the years of his Vice-Presidency when to his natural hit-slash-and-smear quality of attack was added the role of political knife man for the Eisenhower administration against the Democrats.

There was, of course, little to do about the news system's hostility. The Nixon stump rhetoric came off the rancid side of the folksy culture that Sinclair Lewis first mocked and that television later scorched; and the cultural tonality of the press was changing.

The Washington press corps had been for generations a brotherhood of underpaid men, posted to the capital by publishers who not only owned but controlled their newspapers and preferred to recruit their Washington reporters from the police beat or the sports shack. As late as the middle thirties, with a handful of exceptions like Walter Lippmann, Raymond Clapper, Arthur Krock and Marquis Childs, the Washington press corps boasted no exceptional names or men of culture. Underpaid—their median salary being $5,400 a year—some got as little as $1,500 a year.[2] Lacking the real dignity or the self-importance of Washington correspondents today, they wheedled information from a contemptuous White House, asked their publishers' questions at press conferences, fawned on press secretaries and Senators for scoops, and existed largely on press handouts. "Investigative reporting" was a phrase yet to be coined.

By the forties the Washington press corps had become the instrument of Franklin D. Roosevelt, who treated its members with lordly, yet friendly paternalism, as if they, like him, were victims of their Republican publishers; and the correspondents, all of them patriots in the war, helped the President get his message to the people. The press ob-

[2] See the classic on the capital's press corps, *The Washington Correspondents* by Leo Rosten (New York: Harcourt, Brace & Co., 1937).

served a certain restraint in those days—no pictures were published of the crippled Roosevelt in his wheelchair.

By the 1950's, however, there had begun that elevation of the press corps into an independent institution of a quality, an education and a self-importance that had transformed it into a national opposition to any President, any Congress, any power system of whatever partisan colors.[a] It members were educated men now, and slowly slipping out of publishers' control.

Nixon, with his homely style of speech, his ferocity of attack, made the nerve ends and aural sensitivities of the new sophisticated press corps wince. When Nixon talks unguardedly on the stump, he talks the hard language of the underprivileged; he can get down to bedrock communication so directly and coarsely as to mystify not only his adversaries but his friends. Once, shortly after the 1960 campaign, I visited President Kennedy in the Oval Office, and he was indulging himself by reading verbatim transcripts of Nixon's stump speeches in the campaign. Kennedy was puzzled. He said, "You know, Nixon is really smart—how can he talk such shit?" To the press corps following Nixon through his Vice-Presidency, and later through his campaigns of 1960 and 1962, whatever Nixon said was just that. His thematic and usually thoughtful radio addresses of 1972, his prepared state messages as President would be ignored—he had cut an outline on the news system which nothing could erase. To man as sensitive and private as Nixon, with his understanding of the importance of symbols, the transmission mechanism of the news system from 1952 on was the enemy. He had overborne that news system once in 1952, conscripting television for his famous Checkers appearance. Television would remain his favorite instrument of communication—but only when he could control or manipulate it. The news system as a whole, however, would become, in his mind, his prime enemy from the campaign of 1952 until the time when his bitterness moved his administration from morbid hatred of that system to crime in pursuit of its practitioners.

[a] See Chapter Ten, "Power Struggle: President Versus Press," in Theodore H. White's *The Making of the President—1972* (New York: Atheneum, 1973).

The 1960 campaign was no less a pivot point in the man's political development than the campaign of 1952.

There was, for one thing, the fact that Richard Nixon not only liked John F. Kennedy, but admired him. Kennedy was naturally elegant; Nixon strove at most for dignity. Kennedy peeled off his best phrases, not from speechwriters' material, but from a spool of poetry in his own mind. Kennedy had a reputation as a womanizer, a reputation to which Nixon could not aspire. Kennedy was rich, Harvard-bred, his father a companion of Presidents, bankers, ambassadors. Richard Nixon was the son of an unsuccessful grocer. And Kennedy's much quoted private judgment on Nixon could not have failed to reach Nixon's ears—"no class" was the way John Kennedy summed up his adversary of the 1960 campaign.

Nixon ran a respectable campaign that year, nonetheless; against Kennedy's eloquence Nixon pitched a major effective slogan, "How to Keep the Peace Without Surrender"; and then washed his live-flesh audiences in the pathos of recollection of his underprivileged boyhood, contrasting it with that of the millionaire Kennedys. He felt, even years later, that he would have had the Catholic working people of the country with him that year against the Democrats, and thus won victory, except for the fact that Kennedy was himself a Catholic. There were few dirty tricks in 1960 on the part of the Nixon campaign—and those little beyond the level of high-school mischief; as were the dirty tricks on the Kennedy side.

Two significant episodes in Nixon's political development mark the campaign of 1960.

The first was technical—a matter of foreign policy. The menace of Fidel Castro, the Communist dictator of Cuba, was being enlarged daily in the American mind by the press, and it was John F. Kennedy who then took the popular hard line against Castro, a campaign commitment later to result in the disaster of the Bay of Pigs. Nixon responded, opposing any intervention in Cuba: "We would lose all of our friends in Latin America; we would probably be condemned in the United Nations, and we would not accomplish our objective. . . . It would be an open invitation for Mr. Khrushchev to come in . . . and to engage us in what would be a civil war and possibly even worse than that." On foreign policy, therefore, Mr. Nixon would not play campaign politics.

Even more important in that campaign was the night of the gnomes—the vote-counting of November 8th, 1960. No one will ever know precisely who carried the majority of 1960, for on that night political thieves and vote-stealers were counterfeiting results all across the nation. The three-o'clock-in-the-morning contest rested on whether the Democratic crooks or the Republican crooks were more skillful.

Historically, John F. Kennedy won by 112,000 or 118,000 votes out of 68,000,000; the final figures were never accurately established; but the margin was less than two-tenths of one percent. And thereafter followed two Nixon decisions, one quick, one slow.

The first was Richard Nixon at his best—he would not challenge the results. From midnight on, reports of vote-stealing and vote-faking had been pouring into the Nixon suite in the Ambassador Hotel in Los Angeles. By the time, the next day, he flew back over the country to Washington to liquidate his office as Vice-President, the Republican leadership had been at work. Fraud in vote-counting was nationwide—both their own fraud and Democratic fraud. Robert Finch was put to work assembling the data. William Rogers, Fred Seaton, Thruston Morton each took a piece of the research puzzle. Democratic vote-stealing had definitely taken place on a massive scale in Illinois and Texas (where 100,000 big-city votes were simply disqualified); and on a lesser scale elsewhere. What to do? Then, as now, there was no Federal election law to guide action. To challenge and demand a vote recount is a matter of individual state law, all the laws differing. In Cook County, Illinois, for example, a vote recount could not be completed for months, and in Missouri, not before spring. Thruston Morton was of the opinion that a challenge to the vote *must* be made. Not that there was any hope of denying the Presidency to John Kennedy; but because a long-drawn-out national inquiry might ultimately purify the vote-count system and make future elections thief-proof. Nixon briefly entertained conflicting advice. To Rogers he said, simply: no, he would not do it. To Finch, the final adviser at the time, he said: the country could not stand another Tilden-Hayes dispute. Besides, he continued, John Kennedy was entering a perilous period of foreign policy; Kennedy had to move with authority; he, Nixon, would do nothing to weaken the authority of the President in the next few months. Drop it.

Thus Nixon at his best. But the residue lingered. A switch of 32,500 votes out of 68,000,000 might have made the difference—if only 4,500 votes in Illinois and 28,000 in Texas had switched, the combined fifty-one electoral votes of those two states would have made him President. Every vote counted. Any future campaign Nixon would run would be bottomed on the conviction that votes, one by one, were decisive; any future campaign he would run would be run to squeeze the maximum vote out of the ballots. However far ahead or behind he might be in the public-opinion polls, the zeal for overreach in gathering the actual votes would be cardinal. And the zeal would be transmitted down to every level of his operations, down from those closest to him to those who worked for the men closest to him, down to the men of third and fourth and fifth levels—that nothing fair or foul could be overlooked which could squeeze that last possible vote. There must never again be the kind of slippage that took place on the night of November 8th, 1960.

Years later, the after-emotions would still be there: Operation Integrity in 1968; Operation Sandwedge, suggested by Jack Caulfield in 1971; and the operations of Messrs. Mitchell, Magruder, Dean, Segretti and all the rest of the crew who broke the law reaching for the last unnecessary additional vote in the 1972 landslide, the largest margin of votes in American history.

There was more to come in the education of Richard Nixon after his 1960 defeat and his ill-advised run in the gubernatorial race in California in 1962. That race had been a disaster. He had risked his national reputation against the amiable "Pat" Brown, and California voters torpedoed him. His frayed nerves snapped on the night of his defeat, and his bitterness toward the press surfaced the next morning in one of the more memorable of his utterances when, without informing his staff, he burst in on a valedictory press conference of Herbert Klein and launched into the tirade that closed with the famous words, "You won't have Nixon to kick around any more because, gentlemen, this is my last press conference." Five days later, taking him at his word, the ABC television network aired a half-hour show, "The Political Obituary of Richard Nixon," graced with the presence of one of his earliest adversaries, Alger Hiss.

With that, Richard Nixon was apparently dismissed from history, and was off to New York, where, he hoped, he could begin a new career in the private practice of law. There, soon after his arrival, in an interview with Roscoe Drummond, he made it clear: "I say, categorically, that I have no contemplation at all of being the candidate for anything in 1964, 1966, 1968 or 1972. . . . I have no political base. Anybody who thinks I could be a candidate for anything in any year is off his rocker."

But New York City was to enlarge his experience further.

New York is so many cities and communities wrapped into one that no single definition contains it. It is the largest industrial center in the world; it is a workingmen's town; it is a homeowner's town; it is the ethnic center of American politics, whose mayors once boasted that New York held more Jews than Israel, more Italians than Rome, more Irishmen than Dublin, more blacks than any African city. It is the intellectual, artistic, cultural center of the Western world.

But it is also the money town. Along the East Side of Manhattan, reaching from Wall Street up through the East Eighties, dwells a community where more wealth, American and foreign, is gathered than anywhere else on the globe. Money in all its mysteries, privileges and tantalizing sophistications is the stuff of conversation and the essence of culture in this unique community.

It was this community of money that Nixon, a relatively poor man, entered in 1963 as senior partner of a respected law firm, Mudge, Stern, Baldwin and Todd. But Nixon, Mudge, Rose, Guthrie and Alexander—as it was renamed—like any other major New York law firm, was one of those temples whose priests' purpose is to guard, cherish and tax-shelter the monies and financial interests of its clients. Such firms arrange estates, bequests, bond issues and taxes, making money dart and dodge like underground streams through the crevices of the tax laws, always legally, but always as if money were a game. And Nixon began to learn "how it works" with money, too.

Richard Nixon had been a frugal father-of-family; he had been a punctiliously parsimonious Congressman and Senator. His secretary, Rose Mary Woods, had first been attracted to the young Congressman when in 1947, as secretary to the Herter Committee, she found young Nixon's expense accounts so tidy (and tiny) among those of other junketeering Congressmen who traveled the world examining American foreign policy. A junket abroad is, for Congressmen, usually an occasion for wine, good hotels, sightseeing and expensive gourmandizing. Congressman Nixon detailed his expenses down to the last penny—for breakfast, for taxis, for lunch. Rose Mary Woods liked that. He had entered the Vice-Presidency in 1952 with net assets of probably $40,000. As Vice-President he was equally frugal, and when he left the Vice-President he left with, perhaps, less than $100,000 in net assets. On 's single book, *Six Crises,* published in 1962, he was to earn almost as much money as he had earned in Washington as Congressman, Senator and Vice-President in all the previous fourteen years.

By 1968, about to undertake another run for the Presidency, Richard Nixon had fattened. He was now worth, net, $515,000. He listed his assets as $858,190 (holdings in Key Biscayne, Florida; a New York apartment; cash of $39,385; personal property of $60,000 including Mrs. Nixon's jewelry; plus civil-service retirement benefits) as against liabilities, mostly mortgages, of $342,360. He had learned a great deal about money and tax laws in the culture of New York finance, and was no longer poor.

In his law firm, now renamed again as Nixon, Mudge, Rose, Guthrie, Alexander and Mitchell, he could rely on experts to guide his income and outgo through the regulations of the Internal Revenue Service. Like most New Yorkers at the six-figure level of income, he left the details of his payments to be worked out by accountants who dealt with secretaries. His tax accounts were made out by the reliable firm of Vincent Andrews; Rose Mary Woods simply sent them the bills and the records. When later, as President, he shifted tax counsel and personal supervision of his affairs to John Ehrlichman and John Dean, or to Herbert Kalmbach and

Frank DeMarco, he was in the hands of far less expert advisers.

There seems little doubt, in retrospect, that Richard Nixon, if he ever reached national office again. would not settle for leaving office as poor as he had left the Vice-Presidency. He had learned too much in New York.

Herbert Hoover and Franklin Roosevelt had been millionaires when they entered office and money was unimportant to them. Money was unimportant to Harry Truman also, who enjoyed Bess Truman's home cooking and found nothing uncomfortable after his return to Independence, Missouri, where Bess had a come-in helper by day and did the dishes at night. Eisenhower, however, enjoyed money —and left rich, under a special ruling of the Internal Revenue Service allowing the hero of World War II to keep his book royalties not as income but as capital gains. And Lyndon Johnson was a greedy man. Starting with nothing, almost as poor as Richard Nixon in boyhood, he had accumulated a fortune. Having earned no larger salary in the government service than $22,500 a year until 1960, Lyndon Johnson died leaving an estate reported at more than $20 million. He was lord of a manor of 3,700 acres—the LBJ Ranch— irrigated until it was a garden place; a helicopter pad had been installed for him by the government; special telephone lines had been strung for his convenience; and his political influence had pried a radio and, later, a television franchise in Austin, Texas, from the FCC. The television station would eventually be sold for a reported $9 million.

One must jump ahead to see how far the money game carried Richard Nixon—and the aides who served him. Early in his second term, in January of 1973, one of the trustees of the Nixon Foundation in California was called by John Ehrlichman and told that the President, after retirement from office, did not plan to be a lawyer or work for a corporation or a university or earn money by writings bound by publishing deadlines. Therefore, suggested Ehrlichman, the President would rent his papers and memorabilia to the Nixon Library and Foundation for an annual fee of $200,000. This sum, added to the pensions, perquisites, privileges of ex-Presidents, would have let him live, if not in the style of Rockefeller, at least in a style so similar as to be indistinguishable to ordinary Americans.

Such schemes, of course, and even the idea of another try for the Presidency were far in the future when Nixon came to New York in 1963. "He was completely shattered," recalled his friend and law partner John Mitchell in a conversation late in 1968. "He'd been a comparatively young man when he shoved off from Whittier, California, to Washington. And all his life until he came to New York he was looking back over his shoulder at the jungle of California politics. In New York, he felt his public life was all behind him and for the first time in his life he let down his guard and began to look at other people, other events. . . . In California, he'd always looked up at the chairmen of the board of the Eastern Establishment; and now he was dealing with them. . . ."

Nixon in New York was a more attractive personality than he had ever been. A stranger in a town of strangers, he would stroll the streets; in late autumn when the cold began to bite, he would pace Fifth Avenue in a light suit jacket, the wind tugging at it. He would go to parties with old and new friends. At a party at Gabriel Hauge's house, having spilled a drink of Christmas glög over his palms, he shook hands with a tart-tongued young lady and when she wiped her syrupy hand and said, "They ought to call you Sticky Dick," he could laugh. He liked reading, too. He was a member of the Book-of-the-Month Club—or so it seemed from the books on the shelves of his apartment at 62nd Street, where the best-read, most conspicuously thumbed volume was John Hersey's *The Wall*, that unforgettable evocation of the holocaust of the Jews. The book moved Richard Nixon.

New York then for Richard Nixon was money, and comfort, and relaxation. But little satisfaction of the identity-craving he had felt since boyhood. Identity was something beyond the security of money.

Nelson Rockefeller, for example, had identity beyond money. Whether or not he was Governor of New York, Rockefeller had identity, and the relationship between Nixon and Rockefeller over the years was as fascinating as the relation between Nixon and Kennedy. Kennedy was the grandson of an East Boston saloonkeeper, Rockefeller the great-grandson of a cancer-cure quack; but two or three generations had intervened and they were to the manor born. They knew how everything worked—ladies, art, politics, institutions, entrees. Try as he could, Nixon could not match their inherited know-how, and his style irritated both of them. When in 1960, as the Republican convention was gathering, Nixon had flown secretly to New York to persuade Rockefeller to run as Vice-President on his ticket, his approach had been awkward. He had told Rockefeller that, according to his surveys, Rockefeller could add two points more to the ticket than any other running mate tested. In Nixon's mind it was probably a compliment; but it had annoyed Rockefeller, who believes that he is worth more than two marginal points in any circumstances. Rockefeller had rebuffed the offer by saying he was not built to be standby equipment and then went on to humiliate Nixon.

When Nixon moved permanently to New York, he bought an apartment in the same building as Rockefeller's, at 62nd Street and Fifth Avenue. But Rockefeller reserved his Fifth Avenue apartment for entertaining close friends; the apartment was his "home" and Rockefeller never invited Nixon upstairs, as Eisenhower had never invited him upstairs. When entertaining candidates and eminences, Rockefeller does so at the imperial Rockefeller estate in Westchester's Pocantico Hills on the bank of the Hudson, and there, on several occasions, as candidate for high office, Nixon *was* invited—to be impressed, as who would not be, by the view of the majestic Hudson flowing far below at the foot of the soft-shouldered green hills and distant palisades. Nixon emulated Rockefeller when he could. It was not only the apartment he had bought in the same building as Nelson Rockefeller's; he would later acquire as adviser Rockefeller's personal foreign-affairs adviser, Henry Kissinger; he would also acquire Rockefeller's personal osteopath, Dr. Kenneth Riland, one of the best back specialists in the business. Only later, after the election to the Presidency, would he attempt to match the splendor of Rockefeller's Pocantico Hills—overstretching his means to acquire the estate at San Clemente, and overstretching a government budget to make it a place of beauty to rival in charm, if not in scale, the Rockefeller crest above the Hudson.

If there was no way of matching Rockefeller in money or personal identity, Nixon could, however, rival him in another way—as a political force. Nixon had lost his base in California politics; in New York Republican politics he was treated as a "non-person"—if invited to a Republican fundraiser, it was only as a paying guest who had to buy a ticket. But the Nixon of Fifth Avenue was nonetheless a man who retained an invisible nationwide base. There were millions who admired him for his tenacity, pluck and conservative politics, as well as for the stigmata of poverty and bitterness they shared with him. Moreover, the Republican Party was moving to the Goldwater rupture of 1964, dismaying regulars and liberals alike, the former by Rockefeller's all-out attack on Goldwater, the latter by the unvarnished candor with which Goldwater put out his ideas. Alone among major Republican figures, Nixon stumped the country, coast to coast, for Barry Goldwater in 1964, earning the grudging admiration of the hard-core right which had distrusted him since he helped undo Senator Joe McCarthy in 1954. In New York, Nixon was small; in the nation, big. Nixon campaigned again in 1966, this time as a one-man mobile rescue unit for marginal Republican candidates in the Congressional elections, carrying by his support at least a dozen seats the party might otherwise have lost—and also, simultaneously, developing his own personal staff, and newer campaign techniques, financed by money raised apart from Republican Party sources. He was always learning. And by the spring of 1967, to the surprise of all amateurs who had dismissed him from importance, he was a leading candidate for the Presidency of 1968.

The Nixon of the 1968 campaign was quite a different man from the Nixon of 1960 or the Nixon of 1952. He had learned. for example, the value of trips abroad in political profile; his connection as special writer for the *Reader's Digest* made him, whenever he wanted to be so, a foreign correspondent—but a correspondent with a news value and silhouette that resulted in predictable jumps in the Gallup ratings with each trip abroad. He was, by far, a better-read man—he had learned something of the disaster of American city life in New York and now approved of open housing; he had, most important of all, deepened and changed his thinking on foreign affairs and begun, as early as 1967, to advocate the ending of the cold war by the first direct approach to Red China. And he had, finally, and ultimately disastrously, learned to commit himself and discipline himself to a staff of people entirely loyal to him personally.

In the development of Richard Nixon, the campaign of 1968, which brought him the Presidency, was to deposit yet another set of political residues in his multi-tiered personality.

There was the war first. The 1968 campaign was fought on many levels—erratic, symbolic, romantic. But underneath all lay the agony of a people trapped in a war they had not sought and could not understand. Nixon was scrupulous in the support he gave Lyndon Johnson's efforts at peacemaking. Frustrated by his inability to lash out on the hard side, as he had been frustrated by his inability to take the cold-war side on Cuba against Kennedy in 1960, he was learning, nonetheless, that the people wanted peace and the next President must give it to them. It startled many to discover that Nixon, within the party, was privately on the dove side. Henry Kissinger, for example, arrived at the Miami convention of 1968 as Rockefeller's guide on foreign policy. Both Rockefeller and Kissinger were prepared to do battle against the platform advanced by the primitives of the Republican Party who wished to call the nation to total victory by a march on Hanoi. Rockefeller was prepared to tear the party apart once more, as he had against Goldwater, if Nixon shared _ ir position of extreme escalation. But in the midst of the pre-convention struggle, Kissinger found himself in contact by telephone with Richard Nixon, then at Montauk, Long Island—and found Nixon to be *with* him and Rockefeller *against* escalation. It was the first of many Kissinger-Nixon understandings in foreign policy, and their alliance underwrote the keynote phrase in Nixon's acceptance speech— "after an era of confrontations, the time has come for an era of negotiation"—which made possible later their state diplomacy.

George Wallace was another influence, at least equally important. If Nixon were to win, he could win only as a center conservative. But on his right he was outflanked by George Wallace, whose appeal rested on simple, homespun racism. To compete with Wallace for Southern votes would make Nixon, too, a racist; to attack Wallace might lose him the South. There was a hard decision which Nixon made—

to win, if possible, in a way that would make him a conservative President who could nonetheless govern without
having mobilized majority white prejudice against minority
black Americans. The narrow victory of this policy left
Nixon at the end with a popular margin only slightly more
visible than Kennedy's in 1960. And to eliminate the threat
of Wallace in the future, he was to use, in 1970, trickeries
against the Alabama Governor only slightly less dirty than
those he used against Democratic candidates in 1972.

Yet a third layer of sediment hardened in Nixon during
the campaign of 1968. Though the street violence of 1968
was directed not against him but against his Democratic rival, Hubert Humphrey, it frightened Nixon—as well it
might have. Nothing makes for more vivid political writing
than riot in the street, but nothing is more frightening in outdoor politics than those moments of campaign frenzy when
the mobs, or the provocateurs, begin to hurl rocks and
brandish placard staves, when blood begins to flow and police respond with reflex brutality to momentary violence.
Nixon's mind, which seeks control and order above all, had
long been scarred by mobs—he had met them first in 1952,
when the stories of his "secret fund" had strung a gauntlet
of provocations at his rallies across the country. He had
been physically endangered by mobs jeering, spitting and
rock-throwing on his trip to Venezuela which he reports in
his *Six Crises*. He had a visceral hatred of street wildness.
And though the street wildness of 1968 was directed against
Hubert Humphrey, it aroused in Nixon's mind a responding, clinical anger that long outlasted the campaign; and a
willingness, as President, occasionally to permit his aides,
with his knowledge, to provoke similar street violence.

There is, finally, the fact that when victory came in
November, it came narrowly. Nixon was a minority President, elected by the smallest percentage of the national vote
(43.6 percent) since Woodrow Wilson's election in 1912
with 41.9 percent. There would be a hostile Congress to
face; and the press, he knew, would be against him, too,
though for the moment it offered him the honeymoon truce
it offers all incoming Presidents.

Thus, on November 6th, the day after election, he was
off to Key Biscayne.

The power was his now, narrowly won, but won beyond

any reasonable doubt. There was no constituent majority to which he could point as the base for his mandate to govern. Missing, too, was one of the unspoken imperatives of good politics—that feeling of men in power that they were put there for clear purposes which the people sought; the internal discipline of a staff that rises from the combat memory of having carried off a common cause.

Nixon's victory had come in a country torn by war and split by race hatreds, and had been skillfully organized by the men who had shaped the campaign, who must now shape a government—by men like H. R. Haldeman and John Mitchell. Robert Finch and Herbert Klein, John Ehrlichman and Leonard Garment, Richard Kleindienst and Maurice Stans, Peter Flanigan and Frederick LaRue and all the others who had moved in and out of the fluid years in which they had become the quarreling and faction-ridden Nixon Team.

Nixon was dependent, thus, not on a majority or a mandate, but on a team.

They would have to figure out with him, in the next few weeks, not how you made a campaign work, but how you made the government of the United States work. Those closest to him in the campaign shared the same fascination with how you made things work; they would move on with him to the White House and create and destroy the Nixon administration.

It is time, now, to look at that team and how it came to

4

THE TEAM:
FROM POLITICS TO POWER

The Nixon team had been shaping for a long time.

But it is important to examine what its members brought from their past as, in 1968, they approached that critical crossroads of American democracy—that point of the process where politics changes into government.

The team had been in the making over a period of twenty-two years, first in the basin of Los Angeles and Orange counties, under the milk-blue skies of the California Southland; expanding by recruitment in Washington; and then, finally, admitting its last recruits to the inner circle in downtown New York.

The Nixon team was, to be sure, as political a team and as power-hungry as John F. Kennedy's had been in 1960. Kennedy's team, however, with the exception of Sorensen, had been much more narrowly New England in origin, dominated by Boston Irish and Harvard men—and cemented together by Kennedy's commitment to causes and style. No such unity of ideas or origins bound the Nixon team together. What bound it, through all its gradations and layers, was a professional fascination with the game of politics. No common political cause embraced all its members except what each of them, in his different way, considered "patriotism." Among them were both the visionary and the hardknuckled, the mean and the gentle, the sweet and the bitter; yet leadership among them had fallen by the end of 1968 to a handful of men almost uneducated in American history, with little background in government or the American tradition of power. In a decade of political war, embittered by defeat and thrilled by victory, they had developed into a crew, managerial and able—but very, very tough.

Murray Chotiner, twenty-two years earlier, had been the first of the Nixon team. He had by 1968 been thrust far, far out from the center of leadership, but it is still important to recall him. A minor-league imitator of the major Whitaker-and-Baxter group, Chotiner was an attorney with offices in the Fox Theatre Building on Wilshire Boulevard, Los Angeles. Short-statured, dark, bright, Chotiner was a police-court lawyer; but, apart from this dingy professional practice, Chotiner dabbled in politics, for which he had a decided flair. Most lawyers in politics speak with marbles in the mouth; Chotiner spoke clearly. He was an attack man in the classic tradition of California politics, a knife man who could write a snappy press release, define an issue sharply, and who loved playing the game of voter emotions. Chotiner was a gut fighter and mean—Nixon's first mentor and campaign manager in 1946.

Second in seniority on the original Nixon team was Herbert Klein, a man quite different in character and style. Klein, a recently returned Navy veteran in 1946, as was Nixon himself, held the title of news editor of the Alhambra *Post-Advocate,* circulation then 8,382. He had reported the first Nixon Congressional race; found Nixon attractive; and, like so many newsmen, been tugged across the line between hard reporting and the warm affection newsmen feel when they meet the candidate of their hearts. Later an elder of the Presbyterian church in San Diego, and editor of the San Diego *Union,* Klein was a man incapable of making enemies. Very slow and grave of speech, he was a person of such soft-spoken gentleness that he would ultimately be considered "weak" by those who came later to the growing team. By the time of the 1950 race against Helen Gahagan Douglas, however, Klein was in Nixon's inner circle as unofficial press adviser to the candidate; and would so continue for twenty years.

Third in seniority was Robert Finch. Robert Finch had yet another quality. Handsome as a statue, he was a Marine Corps veteran (second lieutenant), having volunteered for the war just out of high school at the age of eighteen. Finch's love affair with the American process came to him naturally—his father had been a World War I hero, an Arizona state legislator and cotton farmer who had been driven from his farm to Los Angeles in the Depression. Finch had studied political sicience and history at Occidental College after the war; been elected student-body president there; been chosen by Los Angeles Congressman Norris Poulson as his executive secretary in Washington—and found himself just down the hall from the office of young Congressman Richard Nixon. Their relation became that of older brother-younger brother. Nixon would talk foreign affairs to young Bob Finch—of the political vulnerability Nixon recognized, as a Republican, in his support of the Marshall Plan; or the dangers of unsubstantiated testimony at the hearings of the House Un-American Activities Committee. Finch was always on the sun side of Richard Nixon's character, and later, when the men on the dark side cut Robert Finch's throat, Nixon defended him as "a poet of politics." Finch was a superior type—intent on using politics to make government, and thus American life, better. In a ruminant mood, Finch could indeed talk of the problems of governing American society with an eloquence close to poetry. Despite that, he was a skilled politician (onetime chairman of the Los Angeles County Republican Committee) and a man familiar with the rhythms, the peaks, the organization and the timing of emotions that must go into any well-organized campaign.

The originals were, thus, prototypes of the ultimate team that twenty years later moved into the White House. Chotiner, hard and mean; Klein, amiable and intelligent; Finch, visionary and purposive. Nixon was always aware of the differences between the mean and the gentle men about him. Twenty-five years later, in spring of 1973, when crisis was breaking around him, Nixon asked Leonard Garment to replace John Dean as legal counsel to the President and clean up Watergate. The President was as fond of Garment by then as he had been of Finch in the beginning, but he accompanied this offer to Garment by wondering whether perhaps Garment was too gentle, not mean enough for this tough job. Garment, a very civilized person who had made his reputation in New York as an outstandingly effective litigative lawyer, made the point that Nixon had seen only one side of him—if occasion required, Garment promised, he could be mean enough, too. Several weeks later, at the White House reception for Brezhnev, Garment passed along the receiving line for the customary half-moment of

conversation with Nixon, who, smiling, asked, "Well, Len
—have you been mean to anyone today?"

The original California Southland team expanded when
Nixon first came to Washington. It added from Southern
California James Bassett, then political editor of the Los
Angeles *Mirror,* a liberal Republican who helped steer
Vice-President Nixon through the ultimately successful and
harrowing war with Senator Joe McCarthy in 1954. But it
added non-Californians, too—foremost among them, William Rogers, who had worked with Nixon on Congressional
committees, agreed with the young Congressman on matters of foreign policy, and then became a working ally of
Nixon when Rogers served as Attorney General for Eisenhower and Nixon was Vice-President. Nixon respected
Rogers, trusted his advice, and they had been partners on
the day Eisenhower sent them both to Sherman Adams' office to tell Adams he was fired. Nixon had added Rose
Mary Woods in 1951 as secretary; her political savvy and
absolute loyalty bound them together for eighteen years,
until, in 1969, Bob Haldeman came between. And by 1960
he had added two others of note—Leonard Hall, of New
York politics, and James Shepley, a hard, corrosively intelligent journalist, later to become president of Time Inc.
The roots of the growing Nixon team were still, however,
in the Southland. In 1956, Finch had been chairman of the
Citizens for Eisenhower-Nixon in Southern California; a
friend, Loie Gaunt, in Nixon's office mentioned to him that
one of the brightest men she had known at UCLA was Bob
Haldeman, a young advertising man. Finch enlisted Haldeman as "frogman," and Haldeman turned out to be superla-
tively effective at advance work in the Los Angeles area. By
1960 Finch had become national campaign director for
Nixon's first try for the Presidency. And with Finch's appointment came the first elevation to the national level of
H. R. Haldeman—Haldeman would be the chief of all national advance teams in the campaign.
With Haldeman, other names entered the team.
Haldeman was an effective organizer and, as he justifia-
bly said of himself, he "advanced the state of the art" for
all advance men thereafter. He wanted orderly rallies, insisted on them; he was conscious of television, and all ad-

vance men were instructed to pack the crowd into the television camera; already in 1960 the evening news shows were, for him, the prime target of any political gathering, the "visual" or "photo opportunity," worth more than a thousand words. At the lowest level were young "rally men" who handled midday stops and argued over such matters as whether the bands should play "Buckle Down, Winsocki" (which Nixon personally liked) or "Merrily We Roll Along" (which stirred Nixon crowds better). Above them was a tier of sixteen or eighteen (memories differ) senior advance men, all responsible directly to Haldeman. Some of the advance men went on to become distinguished public servants, such as John Whitaker, Under Secretary of the Interior. Others became important functionaries, like John Warner, later Secretary of the Navy. Others ran for office themselves, or became, with their experience, important industrial executives. But by far the most important was John Ehrlichman, a college classmate of Haldeman's at UCLA. Ehrlichman's first political assignment in 1960 was surveillance. He was to go to North Dakota, pose as a Rockefeller volunteer, infiltrate to judge how serious a threat Rockefeller might be to Nixon in the 1960 pre-convention maneuvering. He wound up driving a car in the Rockefeller motorcade on that first expedition, explaining later, "The Rockefeller people thought I was from North Dakota and the North Dakota people thought I was from Rockefeller."

The campaign of 1960 was a steppingstone in the development of the team. The campaign was centralized on one person—Nixon—and all decisions, whether he wished or not, came to him. "He saw people when he was in Washington every half-hour," recalled Finch shortly after the 1960 campaign. "He went over his own speeches, rewrote them, nit-picked the schedule, scrutinized everything down to the ethnic appeals." Others criticized Finch for letting Nixon be open to so much pressure and so many people. There were always rivals for Nixon's ear, channels of access for old politicians via Len Hall, who was called Campaign Chairman, and other channels via Finch, who was called Campaign Director. And of later fame, but then inconspicuous, was Finch's executive assistant and office manager of the Washington headquarters—L. Patrick Gray, an Annapolis graduate so dedicated to Nixon that he had retired from a promising Navy career to volunteer for the 1960 campaign. Nixon would reward Gray twelve years later by naming him Acting Director of the FBI.

Veterans of the 1960 campaign have variant memories of it. Some recall Nixon as still a jovial drinking companion on the plane flights, ready to laugh and joke. One evening, dining with Barry Goldwater, Nixon asked, "Tell me, Barry —what the hell are you anyway?" And Goldwater, half Jewish, replied, "I'll tell you, Dick, I can stand either as a Jew or a Protestant, whichever will do you the most good"; and the early weeks were enjoyable.

More recall Nixon, as the campaign wore on, developing a strange reclusiveness. He would sit in the back seat of the campaign plane while Governors and eminent politicians sat forward; he did not want to talk to them. Nixon wanted their views and advice brought to him through intermediaries. He felt that the prince should not be open to a tug-of-war between his advisers, that an important man was too often apt to be swayed by the last advocate who caught his ear. He wanted information filtered as it came to him—and he wanted his filterers to filter his will back to those whom he must direct. He was annoyed, for example, by the habit of his running mate, Henry Cabot Lodge, who would break each campaign day for a mid-afternoon nap while he, the Presidential candidate, was barnstorming from dawn to late dark. He asked Shepley to get on the phone and "chew that bastard out"; Shepley refused—he was a staff man, and it was not his job to tongue-lash the New England Brahmin who might soon be Vice-President. Later, Nixon as President would habitually use others for the cruel work of head-cutting—he shrank from the direct confrontation always, even to the very end when he asked Secretary of State William Rogers, during the Watergate crisis in the spring of 1973, to go to John Mitchell and ask him to "step forward" and take the blame.

Haldeman was not then, in 1960, a member of the first team, and did not occupy a regular seat on the campaign plane until the very end. He would come aboard at occasional stops, confer with candidate Nixon and then—you could almost hear his heels click, said one veteran of that campaign—be off to do the candidate's bidding. "Nixon," said James Shepley, who was constantly urging Nixon to

make the important calls and see more people, "was by nature an excluder. Haldeman liked to exclude people. When
Nixon's need met Haldeman's abilities, you had an almost
perfect formula for disaster."

By late October, Haldeman was second man to Nixon on
the plane whenever he was aboard; and on the final fantasy
flight of the campaign, which left Los Angeles on the Sunday afternoon before election for the 7,170-mile flight to
Alaska and back via the Midwest, Haldeman was in charge.
That flight was blamed by others at headquarters on Haldeman's unquestioning obedience to Nixon's will—a waste of
a critical weekend when their candidate might have been
fighting for the decisive swing electoral votes of Illinois
(27) and Texas (24) instead of Alaska's 3. But probably in
Haldeman's mind it was the best that could be done to end
an untidy campaign, poorly planned from the beginning.

That weekend of 1960, from Sunday afternoon to Election Day, Nixon had no more than three hours of unbroken
sleep. Everyone tugged at the candidate, and Nixon had
bound himself to the absurd promise of campaigning in all
fifty states of the Union. It had been the kind of campaign
where visits to states were checked off on a chart like score
points on a baseball card. Speaking in Memphis, Tennessee,
one night, for example, the candidate could be persuaded
that simply by crossing the Mississippi for a late-night rally
on the other side of the river he could check Arkansas off
his score sheet. In all, one of Haldeman's advance men estimated, with all the travel, torment and exhaustion to which
the candidate was subjected in 1960, he spoke during the
course of that campaign to less than 250,000 uncommitted
voters. If ever he had a hand in running a major campaign,
Haldeman knew he could run it more effectively.

By 1962, in Nixon's race for the California governorship,
the team had narrowed back to Californians. Easterners
like Rogers, Hall and Shepley had long since left to rebuild
their careers. Finch had argued vehemently against the local California race that would pit Nixon, a national figure,
against the affable "Pat" Brown for the governorship.
Haldeman, however, insisted that the race would be an easy
victory; and thus, since Finch was *against* and Haldeman
for the contest, Haldeman now emerged as Nixon's campaign manager. Bob Finch, still fond of both Haldeman

and Nixon, but this time technically on the outside, suggested that Haldeman might be able to use as his deputy an inside-office manager, a classmate of Finch's at the University of Southern California Law School, temporarily out of a job—Herbert Kalmbach. Kalmbach enjoyed the campaign, but found himself most useful in the service of another man who was making his first mark as a team member: Maurice Stans, finance chairman of the California 1962 campaign. Under Stans's direction, Kalmbach learned the craft of political money-raising, a subform of the art of politics that impassions many Democrats and Republicans as much as big-game hunting impassions safari aficionados like Maurice Stans. Under Haldeman, in 1962, worked some of the old familiars—like Herb Klein, as press secretary, and John Ehrlichman, who took leave from his Seattle law practice to work in the California campaign. But there were also young newcomers later to become famous—like Ronald Ziegler, who had worked under Haldeman at the J. Walter Thompson agency in Los Angeles, on the Disney World account; and a college friend of young Ziegler, Dwight Chapin, who was also a junior J. Walter Thompson man.

The backfield of the team, the central control, thus, in 1962 reverted to Southern Californians. Yet it would enlarge once more by a quantum jump when Richard Nixon, defeated in the California race, picked up and removed himself to New York, as senior partner of the firm about to become Nixon, Mudge, Rose, Guthrie and Alexander. In New York, Nixon was to meet new people—like Henry Kissinger, who was first introduced to him at a cocktail party at the home of Clare Boothe Luce. Here one of his 1960 volunteers, William Safire, would volunteer as part-time public-relations officer in 1965 and become full-time unpaid public-relations officer for the campaign of 1968. Here he would employ two new speechwriters, Patrick Buchanan and Ray Price. And at his law firm, most important, he met new associates. Nixon, Mudge was not then a political law firm in the sense that New York's insiders recognize Rogers and Wells or Paul, Weiss, Rifkind, Wharton and Garrison as a political law firm. It was a stodgy, meat-and-potatoes firm, lacking glamour but full of bright young men—such as Leonard Garment, Thomas Evans and John Sears, who were fascinated by having a major political personality in their midst and were swept up in the political excitement Nixon brought to their office.

Most of all, Nixon was impressed by a new senior partner who joined the law firm on January 1, 1967, to occupy the office adjacent to his—John Newton Mitchell. Only eight months younger than Nixon, Mitchell, like Nixon, had served in the South Pacific; had, indeed, commanded the PT squadron in which young John F. Kennedy had served. Mitchell was an outstanding bond lawyer. His skill and prestige in his craft were such that if he were interested in a particular bond issue and it received, say, a BAA rating before issuance, then he could lift the phone—and Nixon could see him do it—and get that rating lifted to an A with a single call. Nixon was lonely in New York—he enjoyed visits to Mitchell's country house in suburban Rye, where he could pound the piano and Len Garment, a junior partner, would play the clarinet. Tart-tongued, bald-headed, Mitchell had an almost roguish charm—and an air of tough, unruffled calm. Smoking his pipe, he would sit at a conference table, almost always speak last, then speak with apparent good sense. Moreover, like Nixon, Mitchell had made it on his own, and possessed the compass-true conservative instincts of a self-made man. When, in early 1968, several Southern outriders of the growing campaign team of that year insisted that Nixon appoint a firm-handed campaign manager in New York, Nixon's choice was Mitchell—Nixon would supply the politics, Mitchell the management.

All of these New Yorkers became part of the new Nixon team of 1968, and thus of the later Presidential team. And all of these new men, like the Southern Californians before them, like the Kennedy men and the Roosevelt men, knew that politics is the antechamber to power in America. If the voters can be wooed, swayed, twinged, manipulated, then out of those voting booths which record their choices comes real power—to build, heal, kill, design, confer or withhold favors. There is no way, in the system by which Americans choose their leaders, that one can divorce the raw emotional appeals of politics from the power of the American state to change the nature of history.

And there is no way, thus, of avoiding at this point a brief glance at the infantryman's level of politics, at the code, practice and tradition of American advance men, which was eventually to destroy the Nixon administration.

No internal laws govern a candidate and his campaign, except that the candidate chooses his staff. Thereafter he is at once tyrant and prisoner, and the men about him at once courtiers and manipulators. A candidate's staff is divided by functions, under whatever names they are popularly given. "Strategists" of a campaign are the half-dozen idea men who happen to get the candidate's ear; "finance chairmen" are the shakers of the money tree; "media men" are the barkers and portrait painters, the film producers and time-buyers. But "advance men" are the king's lancers, his companions of battle; for them, politics is the bloodless equivalent of war.

Every political system has advance men—perhaps every animal system has advance men, for both animals and men are clusterers. Those who can cluster together in groups survive, while the scattered solitaries die out; and in any human group, the leader, the politician, needs advance men to call people into clusters. In Communist countries, advance men are organized in what they call "agit-prop" brigades. In England's parliamentary system, the parties have "constituency agents" who call voters to cluster to hear the parties' candidates. Peter the Hermit, who preached at the fairs of medieval France, was the advance man of the Crusades—the recruiting sergeant of an idea. But whatever advance men are called, whether they practice their craft as hobbyists, dedicated advocates or professionals, their function is the same: to race the blood, heat up the consciousness, mobilize emotions so that crowds eventually gather—in some countries to storm the palace, in democracies to pour votes into the polls. And all advance men are wired together into the central purpose of politics—which is the pursuit of power, the control of events.[1]

Much has changed in the professionalization of politics in the past twenty years—specialists can organize telephone banks more efficiently than the old party regulars; direct-

---

[1] See *The Politician Primeval* by Edgar Berman (New York: Macmillan Publishing Company, Inc., 1975) for an amusing anthropological study of American politicians as Dr. Berman observed them.

mail technicians can deliver a message scientifically to precisely sensitive cross-sections better than the old leaflet men; television producers can mold or carve the image of a candidate in thirty- or sixty-second spots better than the old-fashioned two-hour speech. But the advance man remains an anthropologically distinct species, the generator of the direct excitement of an American campaign.

To be an advance man is great fun. Campaign headquarters sometimes attract young businessmen who get three to six months' leave from their corporations; Democrats sometimes enlist young labor leaders who know the proper factory gates and the union halls where workingmen cluster; both parties like young lawyers. For all of these types, politics is the adventure of a season. "It's a once-in-a-lifetime deal," said John Whitaker, the most respected of the Nixon advance men. "They burn out. Advance men have to be over twenty-five and under thirty-eight."

A Presidential campaign is a soul-scorching adventure. There at the point, silhouetted by beacons and lights on the platform, is the candidate—exhausted, sleep-starved, punch-drunk, out of touch with rear headquarters, swept from city to city across the country, pushed, hauled, beaten with advice, moving to a ballet for which he may once have written the theme, but which is now choreographed by others. Back at headquarters, his campaign manager, chief scheduler, PR specialists, the rest, have doled out his time by days, by hours, by minutes, themselves wincing at all the pressure put on them by the party, by special blocs, by citizen groups, or by the Senators, Congressmen, Governors also running for election—all of whom want a share of the attention the national candidate brings with him when he travels. And as he travels, the candidate is increasingly dependent on those closest to him, those who wake and sleep with him, whose advice is the last word in his ear before he rises to speak, or the first word he gets as he rises heavy-lidded in the morning for the day's rounds. He must personally trust those who envelop him as a combat commander in battle gives trust to his battle staff. He will either come to love and trust them (if he wins) or despise them (if he loses).

The immediate advance man on the road is always held responsible for success or failure at each campaign stop.

Not the old party nor the local machinery in any city or county will have to face the candidate if things go wrong. The advance man will. His vision is a five-day vision, no matter how lofty and far-reaching is the candidate's theme. The advance man gets to town four days before the candidate and must organize the rally or meeting; he must find or hire a band; he must contact the local chief of police and struggle with the regulations and wheedle a motorcycle escort from the police; he must tell the local party people just how many and which of the local politicians the candidate wants on the platform with him, or in the pictures for the morning paper, or on evening television. He is responsible for the feel of local politics, for the local message, for housekeeping details, for hotel rooms for the press, for handling baggage, for the stop-off at the local fund-raiser (if the money promises to be large enough)—and then he must see to it that the candidate is flipped off on schedule to the next advance man at the next stop, where there will be a similar rally or event, in Dallas, in Boston, in Milwaukee, in Portland, in San Diego, whatever place the schedule has set.

There is one thing an advance man learns fast: he gets things done right or he gets out. And to get things done right, he must throw away the niceties. He learns quickly, whether he is a Democrat or a Republican, that all local groups have their special interest and their special feuds. These must be ignored; his loyalty is personal—to the man who is running for President. If the local machinery belongs to his party, then it must be conscripted. The mayor. The chief of police. The school superintendent. They must be used as instruments by the advance man, who executes the game plan laid out at campaign headquarters. If the game plan requires that there be on the platform one black, two women and one professor, and if some local politician protests, then that local politician must be overborne. In the transcontinental turmoil of an American campaign there is never time enough to do it all, but the advance man must try. Like a hit-and-run driver, the advance man will not be there to pick up the pieces after the cavalcade moves on.

A camaraderie of battle develops in every campaign, from which the latecomers to victory and power are excluded forever. These advance men of the road are veterans of triumphs and disasters, of forlorn and sullen rallies in the rain and of roaring crowds in the noonday sun when the sound of the cheering is the foretaste of destiny. Whenever the advance men get back to headquarters, they tell one another their battle stories. How, for example, the local school board had a rule that no high-school band could play at a political rally because the schools in that town were supposed to be non-partisan. Well, screw that! We went in and got two local high-school bands anyway, and the fife-and-drum corps of St. Theresa's parochial school, and a football band, and the girls were kicking it up with their pom-poms and it made great pictures and he loved it. . . . Or: Jeezus! There we were rolling down Western Avenue and the press bus broke down and what was I going to do? So I stopped the local bus on the route, and I slipped him fifty and we packed the press on that. . . . Or: The local fire department had a regulation on numbers—no standees in the aisles, and we had a thousand people outside, so we opened the side doors, screw the regulations! Or: That dumb son-of-a-bitch of a mayor had a luncheon all laid on, and when I told him it wasn't on the schedule, you should have seen his face, but we just rolled out and left him. . . .

Advance men, more and more in the age of television, live in a world where manipulation is everything, and they know the opposition's manipulators are out there, too. Advance men do their post-battle briefings in terms of the opposition: They drowned him out. Or: Those college kids stole the TV picture. Or: That AFL/CIO crowd packed the airport against us. Or: Listen, we can't ever put him into Queens, they threw eggs at him last time. Or: You can't put him into an outdoor rally in Boston, that corner of Summer Street and Washington Street is dangerous, they murdered Humphrey's rally there. And always the question, one to the other: How do you know? And the answer: I know, we got information.

Information is vital in a campaign. You must find out whether there will be a riot or a demonstration; at street level this is as important as finding out at top level what the opposition is going to say about Cuba, prices, inflation, busing or world peace. The phrase that Bob Haldeman was later to use before the Ervin Committee, that he tried to run a "zero-defect system," was a phrase taken from the folk talk of modern advance men. Given the transcontinental tour of a candidate, given five appearances in a day, if there is one rally broken up by ugly hecklers or distracted by pretty college girls demonstrating—that is the one that press and television will focus on. Television and press, like people, need instant symbols to make issues clear. So if the message is to come across clear, if the theme is to be burned into the mind of the voter, and through his mind to his gut, then there must be no defects. At whatever cost. The news system must be used; it must be outwitted; it must be made to carry *your* message, not your adversary's. Thus, the candidate needs intelligence; he needs, whether he is informed of it or not, espionage; this is a game for power. So get it done. Don't tell us, damn it, how or why it can't be done. Get it done!

And at this game, in the 1960's, H. R. Haldeman proved himself the modern master.

It would be wrong to paint Haldeman's politics or practices, in campaign or in government, as if they were unique to H. R. Haldeman. The role of chief of advance men, as well as the manic enthusiasms of the deputies whom they select to cluster the American people in campaign blocs, runs back to the beginning of American history. As American democracy developed, as the party system replaced the Colonial system of deference to natural leaders, men who sought power learned to use trusted lieutenants to organize their appeal to common people. James Madison was, in effect, advance man for Thomas Jefferson in 1800. Martin Van Buren organized the campaign of Andrew Jackson— for by the 1830's, when more and more people began to vote, it was clear that the people were sovereign and they could be gathered in the streets by torchlight parades, caused to rock and oscillate to emotion and hope and resentment and favors. Both Madison and Van Buren went on to be President, but we have meager and scanty records of other advance men, famous or forgotten, until the late nineteenth century.

One can draw a direct line from past American Presidential practice to the recent present only with the campaign of the twenty-first President of the United States, Chester A.

Arthur. A large man with glossy chestnut hair, muttonchop sideburns, drooping mustaches, fond of sable-lined overcoats with broad mink cuffs, Chester A. Arthur reflected a portrait of dignified decency. But Chester A. Arthur was one of the more corrupt of the New York State Republican politicians when he was chosen in 1880 to run for the Vice-Presidency with James Garfield. Arthur's responsibility in the campaign, as scholars have recently discovered from his letters and documents,[2] was futuristically modern. Though he was Garfield's running mate, he was responsible for advance and for scheduling. Meticulously, he ran former President Ulysses S. Grant, the chief "name" among the supporting "surrogate" speakers, through Ohio and Indiana. Carefully, he scheduled the speaking tours of other stand-ins through upstate New York. The chief media star of the day was Mark Twain, and Arthur sought to conscript the reluctant writer to kick off a New York rally. "If I were a political speaker I should be glad enough to assist," replied the plaintive author of *Tom Sawyer* and *Huckleberry Finn*, ". . . but I have no strength in that direction." Nonetheless, Twain consented to make "just one little bit of a 15-minute speech."

Arthur was advance man, scheduler, money-raiser all rolled into one. In charge of the shakedown, Arthur demanded (and got) "contributions" from New York's Federal, state and city employees; all postmasters across the state were forced to pay in, some as much as 3 percent of their annual salaries; judgeships were sold for $500; and when Arthur found deficient zeal, he personally signed a circular exhorting his deputies to "push things."[3]

---

[2] See "Chester A. Arthur and the Campaign of 1880," by Thomas C. Reeves, of the University of Colorado, *Political Science Quarterly*, Vol. LXXXIV, No. 4 (December, 1969).

[3] Arthur's leader, James Garfield, was himself no paragon of virtue, tainted and smeared as he was with the graft and scandal of the Crédit Mobilier affair. But when Garfield was assassinated, and the news was brought to the utterly corrupt Senator of New York Republicans, Roscoe Conkling, he boggled. "Chet Arthur—President of the United States?—My God!" legend reports Conkling as saying. It should be noted that, once installed as President, Arthur moved to push through the first Civil Service Act, to purge the system of corruption from which he had so greatly benefited himself. It should also be noted that he was named by President Ford as one of his five favorite Presidents.

From Chester A. Arthur in 1880 to H. R. Haldeman in 1968 stretch three generations and many other advance men who made their mark in American history. But Haldeman was probably the ablest of them—and different. So was American life. So was the art of campaigning. So, too, was the professional touch campaigning required. Finch and Hall and Klein and Bassett had failed in the great try of 1960; Haldeman, too, had failed in the gubernatorial campaign in California in 1962. This campaign of 1968 must not fail—this was to be a score-through. Like Chester A. Arthur, Haldeman had learned that in campaigning you "Push Things."

In a campaign there is no conflict between ends and means. The end is to win victory, and, as in war, the means do not matter—deception, lying, intelligence operations are common in all campaigns; a campaign is no place for squeamish men. But what happens, said one of Richard Nixon's advance men of 1960 long afterward in 1974, what happens when the advance men become government? "What happens when they all sit in the same room in Washington and the President trusts them and nobody is squeamish, nobody is there to say, Wait a minute, is it right or wrong?"

A man of great charm when friendly and of complete ruthlessness when frustrated, Bob Haldeman is impressive in either mood. Lithe, graceful, his body moving with an athlete's suppleness, soft of voice, far more handsome now with his light brown hair cut long than when, crew-cut and flat-topped, he terrified the White House, his entire career can be read as that of a man who swam too far out, beyond his natural depth.

The Haldemans were people of established family—unlike other rootless California newcomers such as the Nixons, the Finches, the Chotiners, the Kleins, the Kalmbachs. The Haldemans were third-generation Californians; they lived in the Hancock Park section of Los Angeles. Like the Chandlers, they were Republicans and patriots. Bob Haldeman's father was an original Nixon man—indeed, had contributed to the so-called Nixon secret fund of $18,000 which enlivened the campaign of 1952.

But Bob Haldeman, as he is remembered by other Southland Republicans, was not particularly active in local politics—not generally known by the precinct workers and bony structure of the Republican Party fighting its losing battle against the growing Democratic tide of migrants to Los Angeles. Haldeman might appear from campaign to campaign, but only in campaigns that involved Richard Nixon. He gave no money to campaigns; indeed, he informed his old friend Bob Finch, in Finch's campaign for the Lieutenant Governorship in 1966, that it was against his principles to contribute money to candidates; he would give him a cocktail party instead. If there were any Haldeman affiliations in Los Angeles local politics, they were to a group that the regular Republicans called "the bully boys." If there were any institutional commitments in Haldeman's life, they were to his school—to the University of California at Los Angeles, of whose alumni association he was president. And beyond that, primordially, to the country, to the flag, to the strange sense of patriotism which causes men to excuse themselves sin. To this day, H. R. Haldeman thinks of himself as a good and decent man doing what he considered best for his country and Richard Nixon.

Professionally, Haldeman was an advertising man, an account executive with J. Walter Thompson, a firm he had joined in 1949, a year after graduation from UCLA. From 1956 on, he took leave from advertising to campaign for Richard Nixon every time he ran, until in 1968, when he finally took leave, even though he was then office manager and vice-president in Los Angeles, he was told that if he went on leave this time he needn't bother coming back.

It was not a hard decision for either side to make. In the J. Walter Thompson headquarters on Lexington Avenue in New York, H. R. Haldeman was seen as a man who simply had not performed. "He was a very buttoned-up guy," said one of his New York superiors, "he was on top of every detail; he wrote famous memoranda." But the Los Angeles office simply was not progressing. Operating in the second largest metropolitan area in the U.S.A., the office ranked twenty-fifth among the fifty-eight worldwide branches of the organization. Its billings never rose beyond $6.5 million in a period when the parent company's billings went up from $315 million to $390 million—and its profit contribution was stagnant. Haldeman could administer; he could not

build. He could analyze a market, not develop it. When the
parent agency transferred the account of Continental Airlines
from the Chicago to the Los Angeles office, Haldeman soon
lost the account; his austere personality and that of swing-
ing, ebullient Bob Six, president of Continental, did not
mesh. "Our records," said his New York chief, "show he
shouldn't be in charge of anything. There was this huge
growth period and our Los Angeles office was stagnant; he
knew we were discontented with him."

Nor did the job make Haldeman personally happy.
Haldeman was a first-class marketing expert; neither a writer nor a creative designer, he was nonetheless an executive
whose interest lay in administration and leadership. The
purpose of advertising is to cultivate desire, to stimulate ap-
petites that research has identified for harvest at supermarket checkout counters or filling stations. It is a game that
young men find intellectually intriguing in the beginning.
But though rewards are large in money terms, few advertising men are happy, and their frustrations as they age are a
shade more intense even than those of schoolteachers and
journalists. After years of administering accounts as Bob
Haldeman did for Blue Chip Stamps, Walt Disney Produc-
tions, Seven-Up, Blue Cross, Carte Blanche, Western Gear,
Garrett Corporation, Douglas Aircraft—what profit was
there to a man's soul?

And Haldeman had a soul; still has. He bared it but rarely—sometimes to his young aide Larry Higby, whom he
had recruited from UCLA. Haldeman was a regent of the
University of California, and as advertising grew boring, he
gave the university half his time. After hearing Larry Higby
speak at a dinner that Haldeman hosted for the top twenty
seniors of the UCLA class of 1967, he invited Higby to join
J. Walter Thompson—and then acknowledged to Higby
how dispiriting advertising was as a game. In late '67,
Haldeman guessed to Higby that Nixon's chance of becoming President was only 16 percent; but he was devoted to
Nixon and wanted to do nobler things than advertising. As
soon as the campaign of 1968 shaped up, Haldeman was in
it; flew East to take up permanent residence in April of
1968 and asked young Higby to join him. Both went on together through the campaign to the White House, the twen-
ty-three-year-old Higby becoming Haldeman's Haldeman—

and thus a very substantial power in the Nixon administration.

There were many qualities in the Haldeman personality that were intriguing to the outside observer. There was the capacity for endless work; the good mind; the professional marketeer's approach that caused one observer to say after a single visit with him, "He knows what America is, all right, but does he know what it's all about?"

Three qualities were, however, especially relevant to what came later.

Loyalty was the first of these qualities. Loyalty to the country, of course—to his vision of an efficient, well-ordered society in America. Then came loyalty to his alma mater, the University of California at Los Angeles. In the struggle between its chancellor, Franklin Murphy, and the highly centralized regime of the University of California, headquartered in Berkeley, Haldeman fought the battle of UCLA with a devotion and a straightforward commitment of energy, skill and political outreach that cause Murphy (now chairman of the board of the Los Angeles *Times Mirror*) to remember him with a personal fondness and admiration that make almost schizophrenic his abhorrence of what Haldeman later became. For Haldeman's ultimate loyalty ran to Richard Nixon, above all other loyalties. "It was a total commitment," says Murphy, "a clear-cut case of hero worship, almost a wedding. The basic loyalty was to the man, not to the Republican Party, perhaps not even to the traditional processes of government. You have to understand that—the tragedy was his loyalty. Covering up for Richard Nixon was not a sin to him—the only sin was anything that might have impeded the reelection. . . . Nixon was an institution for him . . . he felt Nixon was absolutely indispensable to the future of the country. I shake a little and am somewhat frightened . . . [of] what might have happened had the cover-up been successful. Perhaps then arrogance would have known no bounds and we might well have had some dark days."

To this quality of loyalty must be added a second quality —an almost blinding puritanical morality that governed his personal life and his view of other people. He was absolutely incorruptible about money, and he neither smoked nor drank—and frowned on people who did. His rigidity froze all those about him. Once on a campaign tour, when the President, Mrs. Nixon, Haldeman and several aides visited the estate of an eminent Eastern Governor, Mrs. Nixon asked the Governor's wife if they could withdraw from the men. As the two ladies sat alone at the end of the hard campaign day, Mrs. Nixon asked for a dry martini; she sipped contentedly, then asked for another and said, "You know—I don't dare take a drink when Bob Haldeman's around." Well after both he and John Dean had left the White House, Haldeman, acknowledging that the appointment of John Dean had been part of the breakdown of the Presidential "fail-safe" machinery, was still upset by what he had later learned about Dean's free-swinging romantic life as a Washington bachelor.

In addition to his loyalty and self-righteousness was a third quality: his intellectual preoccupation with the techniques of modern management. The rigid self-righteousness coupled with the cold, mechanical, business-school techniques of management were later to make him a man of terror in the White House—unforgiving, cruel, inflexible. But in 1968 Haldeman's techniques of management, applied to campaign politics and contrasted with those in the rival Humphrey campaign, glistened. Haldeman had first applied them on a broad scale in the Nixon California campaign of 1962—his memorandum on the management of a candidate elevated to doctrine the old political maxim that a candidate cannot be at once the horse and the jockey in his own race. A candidate, the 1962 memorandum held, must be insulated; must not be personally involved in money-raising or dealing with the money-brokers; must be kept on course at all times; must never be disturbed emotionally by news of events that he can do nothing about. By 1968 Haldeman in another memo had further refined the technique of campaign management: the news system must be understood as hostile; the dawn-to-dusk style of campaigning was over; rallies were important only to give a candidate a feel of the people and to provide items or visuals for television and newspapers. Votes are to be harvested not retail by personal appearances but wholesale by marketing approaches, one television snatch of ninety seconds on the evening news being worth, in exposure, several thousand times any given personal exertion of the candidate in the flesh at a rally. And, always, the candidate must be protected, his energies husbanded. One of the traveling members of the campaign entourage of 1968 remembers Haldeman on the plane, in the closing weeks, carefully reading the recently published book of Peter Drucker, *The Effective Executive,* and slowly marking various passages with different-colored pencils as he studied, presumably, the immensely complicated job of the Presidency which his effective candidate would soon take over.

Long before those closing weeks of the 1968 campaign, the final Nixon team that was to manage the United States had begun to jell. If one had had foresight, one might have been able to discern in the erratic development of the campaign toward its uncertain climax the outline and mechanics of a future Nixon administration.

This 1968 team had developed almost as if it were a carry-over from the specialized Nixon "Congress-66" task force, a group of young New York lawyers and businessmen that met regularly either at the Metropolitan Club or the Links Club on the fashionable East Side. Occasionally, Haldeman would fly in from California to join its sessions; and Finch, who had been elected Lieut...ant-Governor of California in 1966, would make his input by telephone.

It was a rather friendly group that thus began the 1968 campaign, certainly more relaxed than those of previous Nixon campaigns, more open to the press than any before. Nixon was of course still wary of the press in 1967; at one of his first planning sessions it was laid down that he wanted to keep his rival George Romney in the headlines as long as possible; the news system, he felt, would massacre Romney, and Nixon's personal dictum was "Keep him out on the point." But as for himself—under Klein's persuasion, Nixon opened himself to off-the-record interviews, entertained correspondents both friendly and hostile and could, at the beginning, even joke with them. On the night of his official campaign kick-off in February, 1968, standing teeter-totter on a wobbly chair in one of the cocktail rooms of the New Hampshire Highway Hotel in Concord, he mocked the necessary charades of any Presidential campaign; apologized for what would be his necessary name-dropping; apologized again for how many times they'd have to listen to his "B" speech ("I know some of you will be able to deliver it better than I before I'm through"); and when, finally, a reporter asked him why he wanted to be President, he laughed and answered, "All I can say is anybody who wants to be a reporter . . . well, I think covering a Presidential campaign is worse than running in one."

A warm, easy-going team set out on the early primary road in 1968. Richard Kleindienst of Arizona was already operational across the country in backroom politics, dividing the nation into delegate-scouting regions, planning the convention roll call. Len Garment in New York was in charge of television. Maurice Stans collected money. William Safire free-wheeled as philosopher. Herb Klein, tiring now from so many road campaigns, planned public relations, and Nixon traveled with Pat Buchanan as "press contact," Ray Price as speechwriter, Dwight Chapin as personal orderly and Rose Woods as secretary. The team rolled on from primary victory to primary victory—New Hampshire, Wisconsin, Pennsylvania, Indiana, Nebraska, Oregon. "It was all warm and friendly and cozy," recalled Rose Mary Woods later, "until suddenly, in May, Bob Haldeman arrived."

A winning campaign always acquires an inner dynamic of its own. It starts with the candidate, a handful of men, a theme and a plan. By November of election year it has enlisted hundreds of thousands of volunteers, politicians, state staffs, national staffs, media specialists and has become an enterprise; it must be managed differently. By the end of April the Nixon campaign of 1968 had already outgrown the reach of the nuclear team of the spring primaries. Mitchell was overburdened managing the New York office with its ever growing cross-country connections. The candidate needed a personal manager, too—that man who in every campaign is "custodian of the body," as Kenneth O'Donnell was for Kennedy, as Louis Howe was for Franklin Roosevelt. And the best and most trusted custodian of the body, the most devoted personal manager Nixon had ever known, was Bob Haldeman.

"It was a lot of fun," recalled Kleindienst later, "for those first three months of 1968—Len Garment, Peter Flanigan, Charlie McWhorter, a real happy political experience. And then at the end of April, Mitchell called us into the Park Avenue office and gave us the change of concept. Haldeman was going to be the personal chief of staff, to give Nixon time for the big issues, and if we had a problem, don't bother Nixon, take it to Haldeman. From then on, except for occasional telephone calls on the convention delegate count, I never talked to him again." It was the beginning of isolation. At the end of the year, Nelson Rockefeller, familiar with Nixon from other contests, asked John Mitchell how they had handled Nixon and the problems of this campaign. "Simple," replied Mitchell, "if we had a problem, we never let it get to him, we solved it on our own."

It was only a few weeks later that John Ehrlichman arrived, invited by Haldeman to handle convention logistics. They had been together in UCLA politics; in the campaign of 1960; again in 1962; and now in 1968 would go on to a common end. An Eagle Scout in boyhood, a decorated (DFC) lead navigator on twenty-six high-risk bombing missions over Germany, Ehrlichman had settled down as a Seattle lawyer, an amateur environmentalist, a devoted father of five children. Like Haldeman a Christian Scientist, deeply religious, Ehrlichman, too, neither smoked nor drank. Affable, intelligent, a thoughtful conversationalist, he was also an amateur artist—and a stranger on a plane with him one stormy day remembers the kindliness with which Ehrlichman soothed a frightened mother and terrified child by drawing sketches of child and mother to entertain them until the plane stopped bucking.

Ehrlichman was, however, anything but kindly or friendly when he arrived in New York in 1968. He was Haldeman's man. Bustling with derivative managerial efficiency, Ehrlichman demanded planning budgets for all convention expenditures, budgets that were not to be exceeded; arranged the hierarchy of rooms and different-colored passes and badges that set every man's access and rank at the Hilton-Plaza Hotel, which was to be Nixon's Miami headquarters. And only a few weeks passed before the earlier members of the 1968 team felt the bristle of his personality.

As the convention gathered, with the outcome by no means certain, the Ohio delegation held a critical fifty-eight votes, at stake between Rockefeller and Nixon. One of the two key men of the Ohio delegation was the National Chairman, Ray Bliss, and Bliss arrived at the Hilton-Plaza with a professional politician's curiosity as to how Kleindienst's delegate command shop was operating—to be stopped at the downstairs lobby and told he was not cleared. "Politics," says Kleindienst, "is the art of making friends, and I get this call saying that John Ehrlichman has barred Bliss from coming up. I tell John he just can't do that, and he says yes he can—no clearance, no entry, no matter who it is." It was the first of the Ehrlichman-Kleindienst clashes that were to grow in the next five years. Momentarily, Kleindienst, as floor manager of delegates, won: his personal visitors would, for the duration of the convention, be cleared directly through to him. But when the convention was over, Kleindienst was out of it—shipped off to Washington to run the Nixon liaison office with the Republican National Committee there while the main headquarters directed events from New York.

Nixon headquarters in New York after the 1968 convention was anything but cozy. Perhaps it is foolish to expect coziness in the headquarters of a major-party nominee within reach of the highest office in the land. But one could notice certain things about this headquarters that cast shadows ahead to 1972.

For one thing, it was managing a California-model campaign. It ignored the structure of party regulars and the Republican National Committee. The Republican National Committee was, to be sure (apart from a first-class research department), a retirement roost for old party faithful, the despair of the succession of National Chairmen who passed through its leadership, a resting place, in Nixon's words, of "hacks." Yet its symbolism was large; it was the party. Now, once a week it was invited to send a representative to New York, where Nixon's personal campaign was conducted from three offices, all near each other, on midtown Park Avenue. The party was expected to take its orders from New York, do what New York wanted, mobilize the faithful and execute the wishes of the advance men and PR men.

In New York was housed the growing research-and-speechwriting team; in New York also, Maurice Stans captained the money-raising drive; in New York was PR control; and in New York were John Mitchell and Bob Haldeman. These two men had met first in early spring, stalked each other warily and then, as Tom Evans of Mitchell's law firm said, reached their *"détente"*—Mitchell would administer the campaign of 1968 (as he was supposed to again in 1972), and Haldeman would be in charge of the body, time and person of Richard Nixon. It was a compact among equals, but the balance tilted to Haldeman as the post-convention weeks wore on, for it was Haldeman, not Mitchell, who controlled access to the candidate. It was Haldeman's man John Ehrlichman who was to be tour director for the traveling candidate, closest to him at morning and at evening, managing the transcontinental adventure. And it was Haldeman's young protégé Ronald Ziegler who would be in charge of press relations on the plane. The traveling tour directed by Ehrlichman moved with almost unprecedented efficiency—press well cared for, time left for writing dispatches; the proper politicians aboard; arrivals and departures punctual. Ehrlichman merited "first-class" in all departments of management. To which was added the personality of the then-young Ronald Ziegler—eager, helpful, warm, energetic. When, early in 1969, Ziegler was elevated to press secretary of the White House, the appointment was greeted by the press with pleasure. Mary McGrory, one of the climate-makers of Washington, wrote, "he has such an early-morning face and such a palpable desire to please that to bait him would be like kicking a puppy." She was to change her mind shortly thereafter, well before she wound up as number twenty on the White House's prime enemy list.

There was yet another characteristic of the Nixon campaign which would assume much greater importance later: suspicion.

Suspicion was bred into the Nixon campaign of 1968, and it ran from topmost level down to street floor. Regularly, once a month, electronics experts swept the headquarters for bugs, wire-taps and listening devices. They remembered how Lyndon Johnson's Democratic administration had spied on and harassed Barry Goldwater in the campaign of 1964, and they knew they were running against the same administration. Back there in 1964, the "Five-

O'Clock Club"—the Johnson attack group—had first directed the practice of dirty tricks from the White House. Sometimes the White House would have the advance text of a Goldwater speech, even in Spanish, before he could read it off the teleprompter himself. The White House would acquire Goldwater advance schedules in time to precede and follow him with speechmakers on local press and radio, to outflank the Republicans with headlines of their own stimulation. Goldwater recalls to this day, more with rue than with bitterness, his shock when two correspondents arrived to question him on a proposal he had not yet made—that he was about to promise to send Eisenhower to South Vietnam. To his certain knowledge, he had discussed this thought with only two members of his personal staff. Yet the two correspondents had heard the story at the Johnson White House.

The Nixon campaign of 1968 was directed formally against Hubert Humphrey. But in the background was still the same White House apparatus of Lyndon Johnson and other enemies. At the Miami convention of that year, for example, one of the Nixon walkie-talkies with its secret wavelength was filched and delivered to the Reagan headquarters so that the Reagan team could monitor the command messages to Nixon captains on the convention floor. By some imaginative mischief or accident, the local AFL/CIO campaigners in New York made the sidewalk below the Nixon headquarters at Park Avenue and 57th Street a rendezvous point where their bicyclists, after work, could volunteer to come and pick up anti-Nixon literature for distribution in their neighborhoods. Suspicious of New York, the Nixon headquarters had had assigned to it a special liaison with the New York Police to guard security—a man called Jack Caulfield, later to become famous, too. And the campaign wound up with an authentic, certified instance of cable- or wire-tapping—the surveillance of Mrs. Claire Chennault, co-chairman of Nixon's national women's committee, by Federal authorities who suspected her of disturbing the Johnson diplomacy by direct communication with South Vietnam. That wire-tapping and presumably others were, of course, scandalous and might have become prime explosive political material—except for the refusal of Hubert Humphrey, that good person, to use wire-tap material in the closing weeks of the campaign for his personal political advantage.

The suspicion was not only external but internal. There was, for example, the experience of Dr. Glenn Olds, a scholar of philosophy who had been brought into the campaign by the joint intercession of Donald Kendall, president of Pepsi-Cola, and Leonard Garment—an unlikely pair of sponsors, but both close to Nixon. Olds's assignment was exciting: that he settle down with a staff of four and examine the whole structure of American government. Which people in the bureaucracy truly moved the levers? What talents must a new President recruit to govern? Olds began to analyze the government by function, then to accumulate files of possible appointive names. His mesh was wide—fellowship winners of universities and foundations, Chamber of Commerce lists, Junior Presidents of America lists, Civil Service lists, Future Farmers of America lists. In all, by his October 28th deadline, Olds felt he had found over 1,000 promising names, "50 absolutely top people, 150 excellent ones, 250 first-rate people," to which a Nixon administration might turn for appointees.

But Olds *was* an academic; his long explanatory conversations, the windiness and ruminations of his thoughtful mind annoyed the curt managerial men at the top. Moreover, the names and backgrounds he was accumulating were uncontrolled by the top members of the team—and such names, such options might actually get to Nixon. In September, Olds's personal journal was stolen from his desk at the Park Avenue headquarters. It upset Olds, for his work was supposed to be secret. In October, Olds interviewed Adam Yarmolinsky, a Kennedy-Johnson liberal who had been active in Johnson's War against Poverty; Olds had been seeking guidance on how the new administration might come to grips with the welfare problem, and Yarmolinsky had had enough experience to offer thoughts. Olds wrote a thank-you note to Yarmolinsky. A few days later he was summoned to John Mitchell's office, where Mitchell brandished a Xeroxed copy of the thank-you note. "He was agitated, pacing his office," said Olds later. Olds had been caught dealing with Yarmolinsky, a known "radical," and this, for Mitchell, was sin. Olds checked the Xeroxed copy of his private letter to Yarmolinsky and, by the markings, discovered it could only have been purloined from his personal files.

Few trusted each other; the campaign ran in compartments; to break out of a compartment meant danger. Haldeman's managerial sense had changed the pattern of a Nixon campaign from the radial model of 1960, with all men reporting to the President, to a concentric model. Each man had his own orbit, each must stay there unless permitted an open discussion in the presence of the candidate. All the feuds that were later to rowel the White House began to sputter in the campaign of 1968—Mitchell against Finch; Mitchell against Colson; Kleindienst against Ehrlichman. Younger men, like John Sears or Richard Whelan or Kevin Phillips, who tried to break through their compartments to the candidate found themselves frustrated, and quit, either during the campaign or shortly thereafter.

There were great issues in the campaign of 1968 and Richard Nixon handled them as best he could. But the most important issue was the war in Vietnam and Nixon was never in any doubt that peace must be made shortly or the country would come apart. In the final weekend of the campaign, when Lyndon Johnson announced his bombing halt and implied that peace was at hand, the Nixon campaign all but collapsed. By Saturday of the last weekend of the campaign it was Haldeman's opinion that a vote that day might give the victory to Humphrey. But the Haldeman team was now effectively organized. And since their private polls showed that it was the woman's vote that was slipping to Humphrey, the Nixon team drenched television's soap-opera time of day in every key region of his appeal with a Nixon special on the "mother and boyhood theme"; and added two full hours of telethon time, a question-and-answer show, on Election Eve, broadcast out of Los Angeles. And the next morning the group took off.

By that morning, Tuesday, November 5th, the final Nixon team had all but jelled. It was an apprehensive group that boarded the campaign plane, the *Tricia,* festooned with balloons, in Los Angeles. By then the master and chief of staff, second in command to the candidate-about-to-be-President, was Bob Haldeman, busy finally with a thick folder on the problems of transition. He spent the flight pondering the White House staff structure—how does one choose the men, place them properly, install them in the right places to give a President the control of the things that the United States government must do?

What thoughts or conclusions Haldeman reached are unknown. But when the plane reached Newark and limousines sped its passengers to the Waldorf-Astoria, where the next President would await the voters' verdict, the pattern of the campaign distributed the staff almost naturally into the centers where they would remain for the long night and all the next four years.

Richard Nixon sat alone in his suite's bedroom. In his antechamber sat the cluster that controlled access—Haldeman, Ehrlichman, Dwight Chapin and Haldeman's Higby. In another chamber down the corridor sat old-timers Finch, Klein, Chotiner and, oddly, John Mitchell. In a third chamber sat the President's issue men: Garment, Price, Safire, Buchanan.

The issue men—Safire in particular—gave the President-designate his theme when he came downstairs at 12:30 the next day to speak to the nation: a snatch of reminiscence of the campaign, an evening in Deshler, Ohio, on the road, a depressed evening for Nixon, when a young girl had held up a placard with the yearning message: BRING US TOGETHER.

BRING US TOGETHER would, thus, become the first public theme of the first Nixon administration. But it would have to be translated into practice, into government, into program, into administration before it meant anything—and thus, that afternoon, the party was off to Key Biscayne to translate theme into policy, to translate politics into government, to translate purpose into control.

Control.

Control is what politics is all about. Theoretically, in a democracy ultimate control is exercised by the people who vote on the alternate directions that candidates offer them. But at the executive level, for a President, control is much more complicated. There are 2,000,000 men and women in the armed forces. There are 2,700,000 in Federal government employ. There are 30,000,000 clients of the government drawing Social Security benefits. There are almost 200 Federal agencies, bureaus and commissions with power over airlines, water, environment, investment, television and radio, credit and banking, crops and prices, railways, trucking. And a new President, with the right to choose some 1,200 men and women in the eleven-week period between his election and his inauguration, must move the entire mass forward by choice of names.

Names. Every President of modern times, supervising a change of regime, is confronted with the same problem: what are the names, who are the men through whom he can exercise the control he must place on events?

The problem worried Richard Nixon in the weeks after his election. The Olds research and lists had never reached him—blocked off going up the line. He had flown restlessly around the country for five weeks, from November 5th to December 11th—from New York to Key Biscayne, to Washington, to New York, to Key Biscayne again, back to New York, to Washington, to California, back to New York —pondering names. He had earlier had a concept of how he would manage his government—a Big Team and a young, hard team. The Big Team would be in his Cabinet, famous names, men of stature, outstanding Republican Governors, like Romney, like Scranton, like Rockefeller; or even eminent Democrats like Hubert Humphrey or Henry Jackson, to give his Cabinet a bi-partisan, bring-us-together flavor. But beneath them would be an operational team of young men, men who could work all night, men who would bubble up with ideas.

Names, though, were hard to come by, as all Presidents discover. When finally placed in authority, they find that the authority even of a President goes so far and no farther —it cannot conscript. Nixon sought Democrat Hubert Humphrey to be his spokesman at the United Nations— and after a few days of thinking it over, Humphrey declined. Nixon sought Democratic Senator Henry Jackson as his Secretary of Defense—but Jackson declined. So much for bi-partisanship.

Among Republicans, Nixon sought David Rockefeller as his Secretary of Treasury. But Rockefeller, just named chairman of the board of Chase Manhattan Bank, did not want the post. Nixon sought William Scranton of Pennsylvania as Secretary of State. Scranton, too, declined. Nixon sought to make Franklin Murphy Secretary of State. But

Murphy did not want it either. Nixon next sought Nelson Rockefeller as Secretary of State. At a breakfast meeting in the apartment block they both lived in, Nixon felt out Rockefeller for the post—but Rockefeller, either knowingly or unconsciously, would not receive the signal. "He kind of floated the idea across the breakfast table," said Rockefeller, later recalling, "but it wasn't a hard offer." The President-elect had been reading the writings of Harvard Professor Daniel P. Moynihan. He proposed Moynihan as Secretary of Labor; but George Meany of the AFL/CIO vetoed that idea because, said Meany to Nixon, Moynihan had no administrative experience. There was no adequate Secretary of Agriculture he could find. Neither was there a Southern Republican of quality he could find for the Cabinet.

Choosing the Big Team, his Cabinet-government team, became an obsession with Nixon during the first few weeks of the passage into the Presidency. He expected total personal loyalty from all who worked for him. But as President he had hoped to command extended loyalties from many other men, larger men; and, like so many Presidents before him, discovered that such loyalties are not to be compelled. He would be dependent, thus, for control of his government on the political loyalists of his inner circle, who had captained the team to victory—and that control, the real control, had already been established, almost casually, within days of the election.

Nixon had flown to Key Biscayne from New York the day after the election for a five-day rest at a villa he rented from Senator Smathers (which he was to buy for himself along with an adjacent villa a few weeks later). The leaders of the campaign, Haldeman, Ehrlichman, Finch, Mitchell, had accompanied him, and in a series of rolling sessions they had begun the task of putting a government together. One night they gathered in hard talk. The President had wanted Finch to be his Attorney General. Finch was adamant with his no. Except for Nixon, he was the only man in the room who had ever been elected to public office. Two years before, running for Lieutenant Governor of California, he had won by the largest margin in California history (almost 1,300,000), outrunning Ronald Reagan's margin by 300,000 votes. His had been an issue-oriented campaign, based on civil liberties and environmental controls. Finch

insisted he did not want to be chief cop of the new administration; he wanted to be its social-issues man, its Secretary
of HEW, which might be molded someday, with appropriate legislation, into a Department of Human Resources.
The group then turned to John Mitchell. Mitchell had for
weeks been insisting he wanted no part of government,
wanted simply to go back to his law practice in New York.
Under intense pressure now, Mitchell grudgingly said all
right, he'd take the goddamned job. Thus, the Attorney
General.

John Ehrlichman was difficult, too. He maintained that
he was on his way back to Seattle to practice law. The President had to put pressure on Ehrlichman privately. On their
drive to the Opaloca airport to meet Hubert Humphrey
(and get *his* turndown for the U.N. post), the President
pleaded that Ehrlichman come aboard for just one year, to
be his personal counsel—adding that it would do Ehrlichman a lot of good as a lawyer later to say he'd been counsel
for the President. On that basis Ehrlichman accepted for a
year only. Thus, the President's personal counsel.

The President admonished the group that he wanted no
Sherman Adams in his office; he was very strong about
that, and went on at great length about Eisenhower's gift-
taking Chief of Staff. Obviously, his choice for personal
Chief of Staff had to be Haldeman the incorruptible. The
President felt Haldeman would understand him, whereas
Sherman Adams had not understood Eisenhower.

With that the governing trio had already been installed
—Mitchell, Haldeman, Ehrlichman—two advance men and
a bond lawyer, none with any experience in government;
and the three flew back to New York with the President-
elect to fill in Cabinet posts in the next three weeks. If
Scranton, Murphy and Rockefeller did not want the State
Department, they agreed that someone else Nixon trusted
would do—William Rogers, an old friend from Eisenhower's time, a key team member in 1960. And if Jackson
would not take the Defense post, they could fall back on a
party man, old stalwart Melvin Laird. And all other Cabinet appointments were padding, announced to the nation on
TV on December 11th.

The organization of his government always seems more
important to an incoming President than the organization

of his White House. Government expresses national policy —the people have voted you in or out on what they sense to be your policy. But the White House is administration— how, personally, you get things done to make policy effective. While Nixon concentrated on Cabinet, ideas, policy, he was quite sure that the staffing of the White House would take care of itself. For that task he would have Bob Haldeman.

During the campaign Haldeman had declared, "I've never concerned myself with the issues, I'm a political mechanic. I work programs, not issues, not speeches, not phrases. Dick says there has to be a few sons of bitches in any organization and I'm his. I'm putting it all together." The statement was one of Haldeman's characteristic self-put-downs; issues *did* matter to Haldeman because they mattered in politics, and mattered to Nixon—fiscal responsibility, order in the government, in society, on the campus. But of all the issues in the transition period, the most important was the war in Vietnam. "There's this task of making the Republican Party a majority party," Haldeman said one day in the transition period. "We can do it, but it all depends on what happens in this damned war. If we can end it, we can do it."

Since foreign policy was Nixon's first concern, and Haldeman was observant of every nuance of Nixon's mind, Nixon's first grasp at foreign policy must have been instructive as they prepared for operating the White House. The President had appointed his old friend William Rogers to State. But he had also appointed Henry Kissinger as his personal foreign-policy adviser on the White House staff. Which would be on top? Even before inauguration, Kissinger's impending authority over the National Security Council had met resistance from the State Department; and Rogers, reflecting the view of the State Department, had questioned the large circumference being drawn for Kissinger's authority and activities. This objection, in the President's mind, and thus in Haldeman's mind, seemed to be inspired by the State Department bureaucracy, which objected to an enlarged National Security staff in the White House giving the President the last choice of options in foreign affairs. Three times before the inauguration, the State Department offered its remonstrances against a personalized foreign policy. Three times the President had to turn Rogers away, and finally, tartly, himself sent the word: "No further objections will be entertained." The White House would direct policy through the President's own men, men like Kissinger—or Haldeman; the Cabinet was to be an administrative or executive body, subordinate to the President's authority. The President's authority was personal, to be exercised by his personal man—Bob Haldeman.

Haldeman was to be way out there—with little reading in history to guide him, with no legal background to instruct him on the reach and stretch of the law. Whatever training he had brought with him from management and marketing had been deepened only by the philosophy of campaign advance work—that all structures must be compelled or conscripted to do what his personal hero wanted done. Now, however, he would be up against institutional adversaries of a new kind—against a resistant bureaucracy that he would come to hate; against a Congress of the United States that he disdained; against a national press that he despised. He had told a friend early in the campaign of 1968, "Frankly, I'm never going to permit to happen again what happened at the end of the Kennedy campaign or the 1962 campaign —this man can't take pressure, he must be protected to think his way through the problems of the country." Haldeman's loyalty lay only to Richard Nixon; and no man served him worse.

There is an old Latin phrase, used by friends of Nixon in the early days of the Watergate scandal, to excuse the excesses of the administration. *"Licet Jovi, non licet bovi,"* runs the old phrase—"What is permitted to Jupiter is not permitted to an ox." It is a good and sound phrase, for those who govern other men always enjoy privileges which are not permitted to ordinary citizens. A President may have a freedom of action and decision which no other man may enjoy—there is no other way for a President to do his job.

Yet the reverse of the old Latin phrase is equally compelling: *"Licet bovi, non licet Jovi"*—"What is permitted to an ox is not permitted to Jupiter." Jupiter, or the President, must have higher standards than an animal of the fields. What deviltries, malice or dirty tricks are permissible to advance men in the coarse struggle of an American election campaign are not permissible in the office of a President. The President is sworn to uphold the law; all of us breach the law, whether by speeding beyond the limit on a highway or fouling a pure stream with our litter. All politicians in every campaign I have reported for over twenty years have, in one way or another, broken the laws of election practice. But a President, once elected, is the man who must *not* breach the laws. Such is his sworn oath.

Yet now, step by step, over the next five years, in the beginning perhaps unknowingly, later knowingly and with full malice, the President's team, and then the President himself, would cross that line, set by law, which separates the use of power from its abuse.

5

THE WHITE HOUSE OF RICHARD NIXON: FROM STYLE TO HERESY

The inner style of the White House was set within six months of the first inauguration of Richard Nixon. It took several years for the style to develop its full swing publicly, but what was to go wrong began there. For the style was Richard Nixon's, and the man he chose as first minister was H. R. Haldeman.

From their long adventure in politics they had developed an unspoken code—the concept of control, the belief that events can be, *must* be, managed. What they had not learned is the essential difference between the roughhouse code of political management and the majestic responsibilities that must attend the management of a government.

For Bob Haldeman, the White House was the great challenge—an opportunity to test on the supreme level the management techniques that had so long fascinated him. Shortly before the President took office, Haldeman had consulted Dwight D. Eisenhower—and Eisenhower had stressed that the chief service Haldeman could give the incoming President was to keep him away from "day-to-day trivia" and guard him to concentrate on just a few "overwhelmingly important issues." Lyndon Johnson repeated exactly the same advice. And the advice suited both Haldeman's style and his knowledge of his leader.

Organizing the White House was no simple task. You have a situation here, Haldeman told his apprentice Higby as they moved into Washington, where we have to put together the biggest corporation in the world in forty-five days. Haldeman drove himself; for his first three months in Washington he lived as a hermit, without wife or family, working normally eighteen hours a day, sometimes twenty. Haldeman insisted that policy and substance were for others to decide. He was simply an instrument of the President, responsible for structure and personnel placement. But inevitably, thus, Haldeman was instant arbiter of the order and rank of all those newcomers and veterans who, at the beginning of each new administration, pour into Washington and circle one another at the summit of power.

The weaving of a new administration is a craft for which no handbooks are written. Personalities, colors, symbolisms —of politicians, of learned men, of campaign veterans, old cronies and interior loyalists—must all be threaded into the tapestry. Governors, accustomed to being number one in their own states; eminent academics and famous thinkers; businessmen of powerful corporate achievement; Congressmen with baronial influence in key committees on the Hill —all arrive and shuffle about in the first weeks of a new administration until, sooner or later, they learn the first rule: power depends on access to the President's ear; reward and favor depend on compliance with the President's will. Their own authority extends downward. But influence upward over high policy, victory or failure in the vicious clash of bureaucracies and interests, depends on access to the President's thinking.

Secretaries of the Cabinet disperse to their huge offices and bureaucratic cocoons full of high hopes and stern purpose, convinced after their wooing by the President in the engagement conversations that they are wired into his central purpose. But then, once enclosed in their own empires, most find themselves trapped—snared by their permanent bureaucracies who know much more than they, besieged by Congressmen who find a Cabinet department the easiest place to exercise leverage, plagued by a press and columnists whose specialists frequently have far more perspective and better judgment over particular matters than the new Cabinet members. Trapped by all these, they still must confront the real America, whose future their departments must guide. And the only way out of the interlocking traps is by triggering the President's authority. This authority can be reached only through White House staff members. Their defense of the President's time must be penetrated in order to invoke his will. But any President's time, vitality, attention span are limited—so that the interpretation of his concern, outreach or availability is, in fact, controlled not by him but by his staff. Just as, in a campaign, the sheltering of the candidate's energies is decided on by his chief of advance men.

There was, as the Nixon White House began to shake down, a neat pattern in its thinking. There would be three chief areas of concern in the White House: foreign affairs, first; then domestic affairs; then, as it was called in the White House, "operations and administration"—the process of Presidential leadership. And it was on the process that Nixon was to be hanged.

The first area, foreign affairs, was the business of war and peace. Of all the responsibilities of his office, foreign affairs had interested Nixon most in the past and was to engage his best thinking. Here his deputy was a newcomer— Henry Kissinger. Kissinger's mind and the President's mind meshed. Both loved to deal in the fixed quanta of power that come packaged in states and sovereignties. No matter how bizarre the game of international diplomacy, it deals fundamentally in measurable matters—armies, terrain, national interests, the statistics of trade. It is an immensely complicated game, more intricate than chess (Kissinger was so fond of chess that he read books on the game for relaxation). If Nixon was an aficionado of game strategies from football field to convention floor to baseball diamond, Kissinger was a connoisseur of the cultures, histories, fears, faiths and personalities of the world's great diplomats, past and present. The minds and priorities of the two men fitted perfectly, the man who had grown up in Whittier, California, and the man who had come as a refugee boy from Fuerth, Germany. In the White House, the advance men who had graduated to power from domestic politics were bewildered, yet dazzled, by Kissinger. "You watch him get ready for a press conference," said John Ehrlichman once, in wonder, "and he's tripping over his shoelaces, his fly is unzipped, he's shuffling his papers around, trying to find a document—you think he can never bring it off, then he goes out to face them and he's absolutely superb, he does it." In foreign affairs, Kissinger proved he could get things done as well as any advance man. Within a year Henry Kissinger had become a model for all other White House personnel.

But the second area of responsibility—domestic affairs

—was an area of blur. Arthur Burns, for one, had a piece of the action. As senior Counselor to the President, his first assignment was to translate Nixon's campaign promises into a program of domestic legislation. But Daniel P. Moynihan, as nominal chief of the "Urban Council," had another piece of the action. A scholar of eloquence and charm, a Democrat who had served both John F. Kennedy and Lyndon B. Johnson, Moynihan had learned in previous administrations how resistant were the cross-currents of American life at home to solution by simple power strokes. Both men were academics—Moynihan from Harvard, Burns from Columbia. Both shared the intellectual habit of self-questioning, both were aware of arguments against as well as for any course of action they proposed. But they clashed; and fond as Nixon was of both, their rivalry annoyed his sense of order.

Last came H. R. Haldeman's area—"operations and administration"—and Haldeman, from the very beginning, never felt any self-doubt or indecision. His responsibility, the process of translating Presidential will, policy, impulse or instinct into action, never troubled him. Nor did he or anyone else recognize what "operations and administration" had really come to mean in the long years since World War II. Over those decades, the once powerful Cabinet departments had become further and further removed from national policy; policy had become too complicated to be settled by single departments. Their conflicts had to be meshed and made into national policy somewhere else. That somewhere else could only be in the White House, in the office of the President; and, starting with Eisenhower, then intensifying under Kennedy and Johnson, the White House staff had become an unrecognized fourth branch of government, the policy branch, easily as important as the traditional executive, judicial and legislative branches of the Constitution. In presiding over the President's instruments, Haldeman was presiding, without recognizing it, over this new policy branch of national government—with little sense of history, or any experience, or any understanding of what national government is.

Each of the three large areas of Presidential operations developed its own philosophy—a reflection of Richard Nixon's thinking.

In Kissinger's office, which dealt with absolute national interest in foreign affairs, the philosophy ran clear: that America, though it must abandon its role as the world's dominant power, must remain the world's first power. Its purpose was to make peace. This philosophy turned out to be revolutionary, correct and triumphant.

In domestic affairs, the philosophy was more difficult to define; the urges that rip and tease American life at home are maddeningly contradictory, and harden beyond any simple solution in public opinion, Congressional blocs, community pressures. Moreover, the secrecy and stealth necessary in foreign affairs simply do not work in domestic affairs, where persuasion rather than force is premium. Not until Ehrlichman had become Director of the Domestic Council in 1970 could one perceive a coherent movement toward a point of view: a conservative impulse, which distrusted government centralization, abhorred Washington's increasing intrusion into the private lives of ordinary people, and moved to lessen that power.

Ironically, in Haldeman's operations-and-administration shop, practice ran directly contrary to this philosophy. The President wanted control of events, control of his bureaucracy, control of his administration, even if his purpose was to decentralize government control. And Haldeman, thus, centralized controls. Unspoken, his philosophy ran, "Let the President's will be done." And among the young men that Haldeman favored, the ladder of ambition, the way to his attention and thus to the President's attention, was performance—fast, quick, hard.

By spring of 1969 the Nixon administration had roughly sorted itself out. The Governors—George Romney, John Volpe and Walter Hickel; the political stars—William Rogers and Melvin Laird; the important businessmen—men like Maurice Stans, David Kennedy, a leading Chicago banker, and David Packard of the Hewlett-Packard Company—had all been dispersed to their imposing Cabinet offices and bureaucratic satrapies. One old-time Nixon man, Robert Finch, had opted out of the White House to become Secretary of HEW—his idea of control was social: how many new hospitals would the country need? how many new medical schools to staff them? what kinds of programs could his arthritic huge bureaucracy launch to make life in America more human? Another Nixon intimate had also opted out of the White House: John Mitchell, who sat in the Attorney General's office, and whose idea of control was at once stern and flexible—stern to enemies, flexible to friends.

Then came the young men of the White House, Haldeman's men, those who manned the new fourth branch of government. These inexperienced young men, unaware of the responsibilities of power, were quickly intoxicated by its privileges. And Bob Haldeman was the chief dispenser of both powers and privileges.

The greatest of all privileges for one who works at the White House is simply to work there. The laminated color-photo identification card that the Secret Service registers for all people with access to the White House is a pocket-sized badge of status. To flash the card, to be of the White House, to be able to use the blue-and-white White House stationery reserved for White House staff members and surpassed in prestige only by the stiff apple-green stationery reserved for at least forty years for the President's signature alone, is to have status.

There are also, to be sure, more tangible privileges—White House cars, access to the car pool to speed one's parting guest, plane flights and instant reservations, mess facilities in the prestige-filled Executive Dining Room. But perhaps the most important privilege of all is symbolic—the telephone. When one lifts the phone, one knows that some other man's secretary will announce, "The White House calling." It is amusing to sit in the President's private lobby in the White House and see important visitors lift the white princess telephone from its cradle (EXT 880) and furtively sneak a call home just to thrill someone with that phrase, "White House calling." The words "White House calling" wire men into power, make them part of the mechanism of control of life and of government. It is difficult to resist such intoxication, especially for young people or provincials new to power; and the men Bob Haldeman packed into "operations and administration" were very young and very new.

There is a political topography within any President's White House, changing with every new administration; and the arrangement of his men in their chambers maps the orbits of power about the central presence in the Oval Office.

A quick tour of the downstairs inner corridors about the Oval Office in the first months of the new administration explained matters graphically. To the left, as one entered the lobby, through the antechamber of the West Wing, encrusted by newsmen as it had been for so long that memory runneth not to the contrary, was the office of the new Press Secretary, Ronald Ziegler, a graduate of the campaign of 1962, an advertising man who had risen with Haldeman. As one circled the inner corridor, past the Cabinet Room one came to Dwight Chapin's office; he, too, was an advertising man, younger than Ziegler, handsome, bright, but of equally little government experience. Chapin was nominally the Appointments Secretary; but appointments with the President were all cleared through Haldeman, and Chapin's chief formal duty was to watch the buzzer system in the President's office to his left—one buzz meant that the President was free, two buzzes meant that the President was ready to entertain the waiting visitors. On the other side of the Oval Office, a partition away, sat Haldeman himself, and in other offices just above sat his two personal aides, Alexander Butterfield and Higby. Downstairs in the basement, with a basement-eye view of the legs of passers-by on West Executive Avenue, sat Henry Kissinger, as Walt Rostow and Mac Bundy had sat before him, subject to the President's buzzer too. (Once the old press quarters had been cleared out, Kissinger would move upstairs to the first floor where the President sat.) In the room just above the Oval Office sat John Ehrlichman, where Larry O'Brien, John F. Kennedy's chief political aide, had sat before him; and on all three floors, all secretaries (except Rose Mary Woods), all aides (except Kissinger and Moynihan), assistants and liaison men were subject to Haldeman's personal orders. And Haldeman ran a tight shop. The eight young ladies in his secretarial pool ate their lunches normally at their desks and were expected to stay until eleven or midnight—until the day's paperwork was cleaned up. The civilian guards who sit as they watch the passages in the inner White House were instructed to rise to attention when any member of the senior staff passed. Haldeman wanted the windows kept closed in the car that drove him to and from the White House; a chauffeur who forgot and left one window open was promptly fired.

This West Wing is the soul of the President's operation in the White House, and, normally, the importance of men in a Presidential court can be judged by where they sit. To be quartered in the East Wing, which is an honor, too, is to be one ring removed from power; the East Wing is largely ceremonial and those who sit there see the President but rarely. If one inhabits the President's West Wing, however, one is close—the President, restless or tired or elated, may walk around the inner rim of the corridor and shuffle (as Lyndon Johnson did) or probe (as John F. Kennedy did) and out of curiosity or boredom poke his head in on underlings to gossip, chat, inquire, find out what is on their desks and get the feel of things for the moment. Such moments are precious to those who serve the President. And even if they do not see the President, there are other values in being in the West Wing. In his rivalry with Arthur Burns in the first year of the administration, Moynihan opted for a tiny office in the basement of the White House West Wing, next to Kissinger's, while Burns opted for a large suite of offices for himself and staff across the street in the Executive Office Building. Moynihan, whose wisdom is at once profound and practical, had made the better choice—"Why, it meant I could piss standing next to Haldeman in the same toilet," he said one day, explaining the strategic geography of the White House.

Until the time of Richard Nixon, the outermost ring of the court was always in the Executive Office Building; and that handsome dove-gray building reflected the bloat that had come to the Presidency over the years. Once it had housed the entire State, War and Navy departments of the United States; some of the brass doorhandles in its basement marked *"Semper Fidelis"* still reflect its occupation by the U.S. Marine command. But the military services had long since departed, and in the post-war years the State Department had left for a home of its own, too. Gradually, the building had filled with all the expressions of the new and growing power of the Presidency—the President's Science Advisory Council, the President's Council of Economic Advisers, assistants to assistants at the White House, Secret Service personnel, logistic personnel and countless pockets, bureaus and administrative expressions of Presidential purpose.

Now, under Nixon, the Executive Office Building, or at least its first floor, became part of the White House itself, in spirit if not in physical fact; and the corridors of that floor might aptly be called King's Row. It was King's Row not only because the restless President chose to conduct a very large part of his political business from his hideaway on the east corridor, but because the first floor was Haldeman's domain, too.

The writers who draft Presidential speeches and messages are considered a personal facility of the President, and Haldeman quartered the 1968 campaign writers—Buchanan, Price, Safire, reading from right to left—on the west corridor of King's Row. To these he added two more: Jim Keogh, a tough-minded graduate of the *Time* magazine staff, and a pale, gangly youth called Tom Huston. When Charles Colson rose to eminence, he was given the EOB office next to the President's. When Egil Krogh rose to direct the Plumbers' operation, he was moved to a room up the hall from the President's office. Herbert Klein, an old friend of the President, merited the old conference room of Cordell Hull, and his Office of Communications occupied several ornate rooms down the hall, filled with such Haldeman nominees as Jeb Magruder, Gordon Strachan, Herbert Porter. John Dean, when he joined the White House, earned an office on King's Row, Room 106. (When he was replaced by Leonard Garment, Garment moved into 106, to be followed there shortly by Fred Buzhardt, while, from January of 1974, James St. Clair, the President's impeachment counsel, sat nearby.) And downstairs in the basement under King's Row would be installed in Room 16 the Plumbers' office of Messrs. Howard Hunt, Gordon Liddy and David Young.

The first-floor offices, with their handsome fireplaces, carved woodwork, high ceilings, are no more opulent than those on the second floor, where Spiro T. Agnew was sent, or on the third floor, where so many functional agencies went about their statutory tasks. But to be on King's Row carried almost as much prestige as to be in the West Wing itself. King's Row had a life of its own; and on King's Row developed that underground of irregulars whose reckless *esprit de corps* did so much to bring down the administration.

When the gears of this apparatus engaged, the machinery worked something like this. Those closest to the President would rise at 6:30 or 7:00 in the morning. At 8:00, various sub-groups would meet to review the day's schedule—the Domestic Council would meet in a group of its own, the Congressional liaison team would meet in another group, the foreign-policy group would meet in a third. By the time, usually 8:30, the President's counselors met in the Roosevelt Room, a fairly accurate picture of what was bubbling up in the nation, short range or long range, would emerge, as if in some political developing fluid. To this picture Ziegler, always in attendance, would add a survey of opinion, anticipated questions and pressures from the news system; and with this composite picture, Haldeman would usually enter into direct conference with the President at about nine o'clock for what was normally a half-hour session. There, the day's calendar would be sorted out, the appointments listed or corrected, the requests from Cabinet members for audience handled, the Congressional wars reviewed, the trip schedules planned.

To this Haldeman profile of pressures and decisions pending, the President would add his own input. Nixon's mind, ever racing, kept turning through the night; as soon as he entered office he had had installed in his bedroom on the second floor a special bed light and pad system to jot down his thoughts; later he added two Dictaphones to catch these night thoughts; and to these were frequently added his scribbled comments on the daily in-house news survey prepared overnight and topped off at 7:00 in the morning by Patrick Buchanan. The news report was important to the President; if it was not there by 8:00, he would call. The news often upset him—sometimes his comments expressed pure curiosity, but just as often they expressed annoyance, irritation and concern at leakage. Haldeman would leave the President after their morning conference to go to his own office and translate his jottings of Presidential will— sometimes, he said once, in an exaggerating mood, as many as a hundred of them—into dictated, crisp, one-paragraph memos. The top copy of the news report, with the President's jottings, would go eventually to the National Archives; but from Haldeman's out basket the memos went to young Lawrence Higby, who was to see to it that things got done. Haldeman spoke for the President on the highest level; Higby spoke for Haldeman on an operational level; and whether it was an affair of state or a spurt of annoyance with the press, the machinery moved to respond.

It was difficult all too often to tell who was speaking as the memos and directives worked their way in and out of the White House to get things done. When messages came to Cabinet secretaries, they came at the high level—from either Ehrlichman or Haldeman. A Finch or a Romney, later a Kleindienst might bridle at the relayed message. But unless they wanted to make an issue of the matter and appeal over the machinery to the President himself, they submitted. Mel Laird at Defense was the most difficult—he would visit the White House only to talk with the President; would accept no instructions he disagreed with unless he could first see the President himself. A very savvy operating politician, Laird laid down the rule that no one in the entire Defense establishment could entertain *any* request from the White House unless it was cleared with one of two special deputies. If, for example, the office of his Secretary of the Air Force received a message (as it did) that the White House wanted an animal to be flown by an Air Force plane from St. Louis's zoo to San Diego's zoo, the request had to be channeled through one of Laird's two deputies, who would find out whether Mrs. Nixon herself actually wanted an Air Force plane used for such a purpose or whether someone in the White House was using her name. Laird had been around Washington for a long time and was used to the phrase "White House calling"; he always insisted on knowing who specifically at the White House.

There is a disease that affects all men who serve a President—it is the disease of abnormality of obedience, of inability to differentiate between a wish and a command. So much can be done by a twitch of the President's finger, so specialized are the facilities at his disposal, that his slightest expression, his muttered exasperation, unless properly interpreted, may set vast or tiny matters under way. White House personnel still tell a parable about Ike and the squirrels. Eisenhower was putting one day on his special green on the White House South Lawn when a squirrel ran across his putt. "Get that goddamned squirrel out of here," the good-natured President is reported to have snapped. And the next day, strolling on the lawn, he saw a corps of Parks Department men chasing and trapping squirrels all over the twenty-acre South Lawn. "Who the hell ordered that?" asked the President angrily—and was told that he had himself. Someone had interpreted his desire.[1]

Even within the West Wing of the White House it was impossible to be sure what Richard Nixon personally wanted, or who was speaking in his name. "How many times," said Diane Sawyer, the most effective member of the White House press office, "have I seen those memos from Bob's office, 'Get this done' or 'Do it.' You always assumed that Haldeman was talking for the President, but we were always one man away from the President himself. One man away is too far."

There is no doubt that the new President sensed his vulnerability from the very beginning.

The antagonism of the Democrats he took for granted; and at the beginning of his administration, no particular viciousness either private or public marked his approach to the old struggle between the parties. He took for granted, too, control of the Congress by the Democrats, courting some, attacking others, accept the fact that every major committee of both houses would be led by a Democratic chairman; with some he compromised; with others, like Mansfield, he achieved friendship; others he set out to destroy.

Much more bothersome to him was the bureaucracy; all Presidents are appalled by the sluggishness of the millions of men and women who turn the wheels of government— or who slow those wheels when the President attempts to

---

[1] The validity of this worthy tale has of late been contradicted. Former Chief Usher of the White House, J. B. West, tells in detail in his memoirs of Eisenhower's insistence on elimination of the squirrels, and how the Secret Service prevailed on him not to shoot them, but to have them trapped and taken off to be set loose in Rock Creek Park. West's account is almost certainly true. But the way the story is still told in the White House carries a historic truth too large to dismiss.

speed them up, or who cling to the familiar out of inertia when a President wants a change. To this permanent affliction of all Presidents was added the real condition that the Federal bureaucracy for forty years, with the single interruption of the benign administration of Dwight D. Eisenhower, had been staffed by Democrats, and its leaders promoted by Democrats. The bureaucracy, too, had a philosophy of its own and that could be changed only very slowly, if at all.

Most bothersome of all, however, were the press and the news system. Nixon's anger at the press had been building ever since 1952 (see Chapter Three), but now that he was President, it intensified. The news system was the carrier of ideas, the manager of the stage, the molder of images; and it was, simply, an element completely out of his control. No other leader in any country lives with such a press as America's, for it is the only absolutely free and uncontrolled press in the world, cramped only by loose libel laws and the dictates of making a profit. No President can tamper with it, except at his peril.

To Nixon, the news system was the "PR problem"—a wording which underscores the elastic line in his mind between politics and government. By the autumn of his first year in office he had taken the time to express his attitude toward the press in writing, to the executor of his wishes, Bob Haldeman. His memorandum to Haldeman of September 22nd, 1969, is far too long to quote in full; it must have taken a full day to prepare:

"In memoranda in the future," he wrote to Haldeman, "I shall use the letters PR whenever I am referring generally to a project I want carried out on the PR front. Until we get a full-time man I think we need in this field, you will have responsibility for seeing that these decisions are implemented. What is particularly important is that I be informed as to what action has been taken and, if action is not taken, why the decision has been made not to take it. . . ."

There follow then particular matters of the day and season that bothered the President, then an operational paragraph.

"PR. Every Monday, I want a week's projection as to what we anticipate will be the major opposition attacks so that we can plan our own statements with those in mind. I realize that we sometimes may not have such information, but, on the other hand, a careful checking with the offices of Kennedy and McGovern et al will yield us some pretty good information as to what their plans are. . . .

"I have reached the conclusion that we simply have to have that full-time PR Director, who will have no other assignments except to bulldog these three or four major issues we may select each week or each month. . . .

"I know this is a subject that troubles all of us, but I do not want to continue to slide along with what I fear is an inadequate response, and an amateurish response to what will be an enormous challenge in the next two or three months. This could be a subject for discussion and decision next weekend at Camp David, among other subjects." [2]

[2] Nixon's September basic directive on PR was not long in producing its flow of responses.

A good example of early reaction was that of Jeb Stuart Magruder, in a memorandum to Haldeman, dated October 17, 1969.

Magruder was at that point just beginning to make his mark and he had scanned 21 requests from the President in the thirty days just previous, all seeking some counter-action to news reports made by a list of reporters or commentators running from Dan Rather and Ted Lewis to John Chancellor, Walter Cronkite, Jack Anderson, Howard K. Smith as well as *Time* and *Newsweek*.

Magruder felt that calls to specific editors, from Pat Buchanan or Herb Klein, protesting unfairness had been "unfruitful and wasteful of our time." In his memo entitled "The Shot-Gun versus the Rifle," Magruder preferred the shotgun.

"The real problem," he wrote, ". . . is to get to this unfair coverage in such a way that we make major impact on a basis which the networks-newspapers and Congress will react to and begin to look at things somewhat differently. . . . The following is my suggestion as to how we can achieve this goal.

1. Begin an official monitoring system through the FCC as soon as Dean Burch is officially on board as Chairman. . . .

2. Utilize the anti-trust division to investigate various media relating to anti-trust violations. Even the possible threat of anti-trust action I think would be effective in changing their views in the above matter.

3. Utilizing the Internal Revenue Service as a method to look into the various organizations that we are most concerned about. Just a threat of an IRS investigation will probably turn their approach.

4. Begin to show favorites within the media. Since they are basically not on our side let us pick the favorable ones as Kennedy did. . . ."

Magruder concluded in his final paragraph, ". . . we seem to march on tiptoe into the political situation and are unwilling to use the

Much later, I asked one of Nixon's personal staff the same question I asked so many of the group: "What went wrong?" His answer was, as in every case, short of the reality, but it was nonetheless interesting. "We were operating in a totally hostile environment. Press. Congress. Bureaucracy. And our people were young and inexperienced. If we made any mistakes at all, they would get us, even the same mistakes previous administrations had gotten away with. They were out to get us. And we made a lot of mistakes."

What was happening in that first year of the Nixon administration was, however, far worse than "mistakes"; and it had begun months before the Nixon PR memo of September. It had already begun, as a matter of fact, on February 17th, 1969, just four weeks after the inauguration, when Bob Haldeman reported to John Ehrlichman in a private memorandum, "Bebe Rebozo has been asked by the President to contact J. Paul Getty in London regarding major contributions. . . . The funds should go to some operating entity other than the National Committee so that we retain full control of their use. Bebe would appreciate your calling him with this advice [on how to handle the funds legally] as soon as possible since the President has asked him to move quickly." That first step had been neither illegal nor unprecedented. Lyndon Johnson had set up a President's Club of contributors of $1,000 or more to his politics; but that was an open operation, members getting color photographs of Johnson, invitations to White House dinners or seats at national conventions. The Nixon-Haldeman-Rebozo private fund was to be entirely secret, a personal resource to help the President's men get done what they thought the President wanted or needed.

What came next was genuinely frightening. In retrospect,

---

power at hand to achieve our long term goal which is eight years of a Republican Administration. I clearly remember Kennedy sending out the FBI men to wake-up the Steel Executives in the middle of the night. It caused an uproar in certain cases but he achieved his goal and the vast majority of the American public was with him. If we convince the President this is the correct approach, we will find that various support groups will be much more productive and much more cooperative. . . ."

the easiest way of explaining what happened—and the generally accepted explanation—is that of a planned and purposeful conspiracy developing within the White House to subvert the law. Except that that was not the way it was at all; and the subtleties of the disaster make it the more difficult to retell.

What happened began invisibly in those first months, with uncoordinated little steps, with tiny roots, with the impulses of inordinately self-righteous men who realized only much too late that they were breaking the laws of the United States. It began with style and ended in crime.

There was, to start, one rootlet that ran from the office on the second floor of the West Wing, just above the Oval Office, where sat John Ehrlichman, Counsel to the President and tour director of the victorious campaign of 1968. As tour director, Ehrlichman had met and come to like Jack Caulfield, a very trivial character with whom to start a major story.

Jack Caulfield, detective second grade of the New York Police Department, was assigned originally as police liaison in 1968 to Nixon's campaign headquarters on Park Avenue, and was then sucked up into the roving campaign, on leave from the police force, to keep his eye on "candidate security," as he exaggerated it; the Secret Service contemptuously referred to him as the baggage handler, the room-assignment man when the campaign tour moved through various towns.

An ambitious man, Caulfield had won a place in the Police Department's Bureau of Special Services, to the resentment of his colleagues there who considered themselves an elite unit—most of them college graduates, all competent in a second language, assigned to surveillance of subversives, exiles and the violent conspiratorial groups that abound in New York and plague the United Nations. His friends on the force remember Caulfield as a man on the make. "A real paranoid" but, at the same time, "a fun guy" was the description of one of those who wanted to get Caulfield out of the Bureau of Special Services.

There were to be many others of similar writhing upward ambition later in the Nixon administration, but Caulfield is a minor prototype. During his assignment to the liaison detail with Nixon headquarters in 1968, he had struck up an acquaintance with John Ehrlichman. The Nixon victory and his acquaintanceships heated Caulfield's ambition to the point where he felt he might ask for the post of Chief Marshal of the United States. Turned down for that, he received an offer from John Ehrlichman in March of 1969, two months after the inauguration. Ehrlichman was trying to develop a political "intelligence capability" for the President, something more personal than what the FBI and the CIA could offer. He suggested that he would like to have Caulfield set up a private security agency to provide "investigative support" for the White House. Caulfield said no—he wanted to join the White House Staff. And on April 8th, 1969, there was Caulfield, installed in the Executive Office Building as a White House employee setting up a private intelligence system for Ehrlichman and, thus, for the President.

A one-man private intelligence system is, however, not much of an intelligence system. Caulfield had a friend at the Bureau of Special Services, Tony Ulasewicz. In May, John Ehrlichman flew to New York to meet Ulasewicz, secretly, at the VIP lounge of La Guardia Airport and interview him. But Ulasewicz would not be, as Caulfield already had been for a month, a government agent. He would indeed be an agent of the Presidency, but a secret political agent, paid for not by the government but by private funds. In June, Ulasewicz flew down to Washington to meet Herbert Kalmbach, dispenser of the President's private political funds, and the matter was explained: he would be paid $22,000 a year directly from Kalmbach's office (later raised to $24,000 a year) plus $1,000 a month in expenses and would receive his orders from Caulfield. His assignment was simple—political espionage for the White House. Ulasewicz was never to see Ehrlichman again; his orders would come through Caulfield. Ulasewicz, a disciplined policeman, would not question his orders or where his reports went. But Ulasewicz was a step into the blur of law. Whether or not a White House counselor is entitled to command intelligence operations by agents on the official White House payroll is questionable, but probably legal. Whether a White House intelligence operation can, however, command intelligence, search and espionage paid for by private political funds is something else again. Thus, Ulasewicz was now installed in Washington, not in breach of established law, but not legally either. His assignments, as he recalls—and he might get thirty or thirty-five assignments a year—concerned the sex, drinking and family problems of political opponents of the President, or of contributors to the President's rivals. All reports were verbal—to Caulfield. Where they went, up from there, he did not know. And his first major assignment was to find out exactly what Ted Kennedy had been doing that night when Mary Jo Kopechne was drowned at Chappaquiddick in July, 1969, in no way a matter of national security.

Whether it is within the law for a President in the White House to command, as his party's leader, such a private intelligence capability is unclear; but the style is dirty. What followed next, however, as we trace this early root system of what happened, was quite clearly not only dirty but definitely illegal. It concerned Joseph Kraft, a maverick among Washington journalists.

Inexhaustible, a stunningly lucid reporter, Kraft, unlike most of his colleagues, is unpredictable in his political reactions. And to Richard Nixon, who had pegged Kraft as an early Kennedy loyalist in the campaign of 1960, Kraft's reporting of the 1968 campaign was a pleasant surprise. Kraft coined the term "Middle America," defining Nixon's constituency; he reported with consternation and eloquence the riots of the Democratic convention of 1968. Kraft's thinking and writing, like those of Moynihan, another realistic Kennedy Democrat, appealed to Richard Nixon. They spoke several times during the campaign of 1968. After Kraft broke the story of LBJ's plans for a summit journey to Moscow in 1968, Nixon was impressed enough so that later he approached Kraft about a job in the new administration.

Thus, Kraft's adverse reporting of the first months of the new administration came as a second surprise to the new President. Nixon had groped for several months for a new approach to the Vietnamese negotiations in Paris; but in early May of 1969, Kraft reported that Nixon's new proposals were futile, they would not work, the war could not be ended the way the President proposed. Here, a man the President had thought of as a friend had turned out to be a newsman.

Who was influencing Kraft? The Democratic bureaucracy? Could it be Kissinger himself? (The President had telephoned Kissinger once and located him in Kraft's home, a guest at a dinner party.) Or could it be one of the lesser White House staff—someone like John Sears or Bob Ellsworth, campaign aides who had been friendly with Kraft in the campaign? The President wanted to know; he passed the word to Ehrlichman; and from Ehrlichman it went to Caulfield, who commissioned another private agent, John Ragan, to place a legally unauthorized wire-tap on the phone of a private citizen, without sanction of court order. And thus, one June evening, a wire-tap was installed at Kraft's Georgetown home while Kraft was off for the weekend. The tap brought little information—chiefly the conversations of Kraft's Spanish-speaking maid—and was removed after one week. But a law had been broken, whether by the President's personal direct order or by Ehrlichman's interpretation of his exasperation is obscure.

If the wire-tapping of Joe Kraft had been the first definite illegality, the month of May, 1969, saw the beginning of another system—one that was to culminate in further and widespread breaching of law as the imperatives of national security and the rights of private Americans blurred in the new administration's practice.

All that spring Nixon had been incubating his new diplomacy. The stakes were high—peace in Vietnam, stability in the Middle East, agreements on nuclear-arms limitation, *détente* with the great Communist powers. All these initiatives were ultra-secret and, as the Pesident saw them, "closely interrelated." Success or failure depended on this secrecy, insisted Nixon later, explaining that "Leaks of secret information about any one could endanger all."

In April, Nixon discovered, as all Presidents had before him, that for the press, national security was always a legitimate story to probe. On April 6th, 1969, the *New York Times* reported a secret proposal to end the Vietnam War by withdrawing American troops. On May 1st, the *Times* reported five secret strategic options for the arms-limitation talks—before the National Security Council had considered them. And then, on May 9th, 1969, the *New York Times* front-paged a story by correspondent William Beecher

("CAMBODIA RAIDS GO UNPROTESTED") reporting that American B-52's were raiding North Vietnamese supply and troops concentrations in Cambodia with the tacit approval of Cambodia's chief, Prince Sihanouk.

This was not seen as betrayal of a presumed friendship, as Kraft's columns had been. This seemed to be an outright leak from within the bureaucracy, damaging Sihanouk's ability to co-operate, threatening every delicate link in the chain of Nixon's secret diplomacy.

Kissinger, weekending with the President on Key Biscayne, was on the telephone to J. Edgar Hoover, chief of the FBI, as soon as he had read the *Times* of May 9th. According to Hoover's memorandum of the day, Kissinger said that Beecher's story was "extraordinarily damaging and uses secret information." Hoover was told to find out immediately who had leaked to Beecher, using whatever resources were necessary but "discreetly, of course." By five that afternoon Hoover reported back that "it is the conclusion of the contacts we have made that it could have come and probably did from a staff member of the National Security Council"—Kissinger's own office—and from someone else in a Pentagon bureau whose staff members, said Hoover, were "largely Kennedy people and anti-Nixon." Indeed, the two suspected men were described as "so-called arrogant Harvard-type Kennedy men." Hoover's memo concludes, "Dr. Kissinger said he appreciated this very much and he hoped I would follow it up as far as we can take it and they will destroy whoever did this if we can find him, no matter where he is." It must have seemed quite clear to the President: the hostile bureaucracy, the hostile press, Kennedy men, all out to get him—and on a matter of national security where he felt firmly, morally right as world peacemaker.

Thus, on May 12th, in the name of national security, the process was authorized: four taps on government officials, three in the National Security Council, one in the Department of Defense; the next week, two more in the National Security Council; the next week, two on newsmen. Over the next few months the list expanded to a total of seventeen with two more newsmen and seven more government employees, the taps on all of whom were described later by

Attorney General Mitchell to the Ervin Committee as "routine."

Yet they were anything but routine. Though wire-taps for national security were legal at that time (and until the Supreme Court decision in June, 1972), these new wire-taps were a sharp departure from years of FBI practice, years in which J. Edgar Hoover had been brought under ever tighter control by successive Presidents. Wire-taps on racketeers, organized crime, embassies in national-security cases had indeed been common practice. But wire-tapping of government officials had been rare, and of newsmen almost non-existent.

The rights and wrongs of the practice ran directly to J. Edgar Hoover, whose role for decades in American politics had been obscure. Hoover, autocrat of the FBI, sovereign over his bureau, thought of himself as an institution, and he had seen eight Presidents come and go. Dean Rusk said once, "You know, my impression, though I was the senior member of the Cabinet, talking with J. Edgar Hoover was about like talking to President Charles de Gaulle." But Hoover was abnormally sensitive about his public image. Before his Congressional appearances he would cut off many wire-taps so that if questioned he could report a minimum number in effect. About wire-tapping American newsmen he was particularly careful, except for the Communist *Daily Worker*, which Hoover considered fair game; when it came to tapping foreign newsmen, the Army intelligence agencies were given the job. When columnist Joseph Alsop complained to Lyndon Johnson that he thought *his* phone was being tapped, Johnson directed his Attorney General, Nicholas Katzenbach, to ask Hoover—who shot back that he wouldn't be so stupid as to tap a newspaperman. Eventually a tap on a newsman's phone would become public, said Hoover, and "the press would murder us."

Hoover could not decide, on his own authority, who was to be wire-tapped. Authorization for all wire-taps, in either criminal or national-security cases, had to be signed by the Attorney General; and such papers were hand-carried upstairs to the AG's office by an FBI courier, who waited for their approval. Katzenbach came to recognize, however, that Hoover considered a single authorization as perpetual.

"If Calvin Coolidge had authorized a wire-tap," said Katzenbach, "Hoover would think it still operative." Thus, Lyndon Johnson—who at times spoke like a stalwart of the American Civil Liberties Union and at other times listened gleefully to Hoover's bits of gossip or relished secret transcripts—tightened control over Hoover. Henceforth, he ordered, all wire-taps of any kind must be renewed every ninety days by signature of the Attorney General.

Even before that time, Attorney Generals had become very cautious about wire-taps. William Rogers, Attorney General from 1957 to 1961, recalls authorizing none on American government officials, none on newsmen. Robert Kennedy, his successor, used wire-tapping and bugging, both extensively, particularly in his war on labor racketeers and the Mafia; and forwarded to his brother, the President, some of the more romantic passages of a tap put on a Martin Luther King conversation with a lady, which had been installed as a security matter. But Katzenbach, Kennedy's successor, tightened controls considerably. In Katzenbach's time, only two taps were put on government employees—one on an Air Force sergeant suspected of being a Russian spy; the other on a State Department official fingered as being a Russian contact man, whose friends in the department felt he would be cleared of suspicion if his phone were tapped at a particular moment when those who had informed against him said the Russians would be in touch with him. The official was cleared by this tap; the anticipated call never came through. And Ramsey Clark, Katzenbach's successor, continued the scrupulous patrol over government wire-tapping until 1969. Thus then, for years before Nixon took office, so far as is known, only two government officials had been wire-tapped by the FBI—and no American newsmen except, perhaps, those on the *Daily Worker*.

What is interesting about the wire-tap and surveillance system set up in May, 1969, is the quality of inevitability of the historic "glide"—the glide that Nixon's men took, unconsciously in the beginning and then very consciously and maliciously, across the line of law. The President himself, on his second day in office, told this reporter that he had instructed Mitchell to govern wire-tapping "with an iron hand." He wanted no "climate of fear" in this country.

Four months later, he had himself authorized the widespread wire-tapping of newsmen and government officials in a matter of national security; and his authority helped all those below him to glide across the laws, too.

One can fasten on a man who, in his way as minor victim, is almost as unimportant as Jack Caulfield in terms of power—Morton Halperin of Henry Kissinger's staff. Halperin is a marking point in the glide from legitimate national security to political espionage. Halperin was one of the original four wire-tapped; a scholarly type, he did not hold a very important job on Kissinger's staff, and was given no access to sensitive material after Beecher's story of May 9th. In August, he asked to resign; in September, he left. He retained title as consultant to Kissinger for another six months, but worked only one day in that capacity. Yet his phone was tapped for another year and a half, until February 10th, 1971, by which time he had been a private citizen for a full year—and a consultant to Edmund Muskie, whose Presidential campaign was then crescent. Other taps, too, were applied, or continued, on individuals not even remotely connected with national security—on John Sears, for example, Mitchell's former junior law partner, who had clashed with his boss in the 1968 campaign.

The beginning of the glide across the law had begun with high purpose—to protect the President's diplomacy, and thus the national security, from leaks or news plants that could cripple it. But leak-plugging became an all-embracing purpose. By mid-1971 Nixon raised the matter to Cabinet level, each Cabinet officer to be responsible for checking leaks in his department; and in Haldeman's presence, told them that Haldeman was to be "Lord High Executioner" of the program. The rationale for continuing wire-taps was explained by John Ehrlichman in his testimony before the Ervin Committee—that "not everyone in the Executive Branch" shared Nixon's purposes, that "holdovers" from the Kennedy and Johnson administrations "actively opposed the President's policies, especially his foreign policy, but also in the area of domestic affairs," and "These people conducted a kind of internal guerrilla warfare against the President," they were "trying to frustrate his goals by unauthorized leaks of part of the facts of a story, or of military and other secrets, or by just plain falsehood" to discredit the President with Congress, the press and abroad.

Little information of any use came from the wire-taps, and Nixon himself summarized their value quite accurately when, according to a later-published transcript, he told John Dean on February 28th, 1973, that the taps "never helped us. Just gobs and gobs of material: gossip and bullshitting. . . . The tapping was a very, very unproductive thing. I've always known that. At least, I've never, it's never been useful in any operation I've ever conducted." Useless as the taps were for national security, Nixon himself had set the climate for their use—and roots of other systems of abuse were growing in that climate, too.

Of these other abuses, perhaps the most important was the pressure on the instruments of civil government, and of these, the pressure on the Internal Revenue Service was the most alarming. That pressure traces back to July 1st of 1969, and to a character who ranks in unimportance with Caulfield and Halperin as a man of power, but one of far more symbolic significance—Tom Charles Huston.

A skillful writer, something of an intellectual, a young man of the right, Huston had been national chairman of Young Americans for Freedom, and had also served in Army Intelligence for several years before joining the White House staff early in the administration. There, as an aide to Patrick Buchanan's news-monitoring team in the Executive Office Building, he was listed as a Presidential speechwriter. Tall, sallow, gangling, only twenty-eight when he arrived, Huston shared with many of the later culprits the thrust of violent ambition, to which he added a quality rare in the other managerially ambitious types—the fervent and fanatic conviction of a true believer. A picture of John C. Calhoun hung in Huston's office; his service with Army Intelligence had convinced him that the country was worm-eaten with domestic enemies and subversives; his ferocity frightened other men on Writers' Row.

Most of his colleagues were glad when Huston shortly made his way up on the ladder of ambition to Bob Haldeman's attention and, though still occupying the same office, became the central White House clearing agent for all information on subversives, demonstrators, insurrectionaries from other Federal intelligence agencies. To this assignment Huston swiftly added his own initiative—he had been around Washington long enough to measure what impact a White House memorandum has in the bureaucracy, or the phrase "White House calling." He understood the instrumentation of pressures within the government, and was convinced that it must be used against the peril of what he fancied was real subversion.

Of record then, in the name of young Tom Charles Huston, is the first twitching of government's most frightening agency of confiscation—the Internal Revenue Service. On July 1st, 1969, Huston demanded that the IRS begin to check on the financing, funds and tax exemptions of "Ideological Organizations." Three weeks later (on July 24th), the income-tax people convened thirteen revenue agents to discuss "an extremely important and sensitive matter in which the highest levels of government are interested." Under discussion were some seventy-seven organizations seen as a possible "threat to the security of the United States," and, the agents were enjoined, "one of our principal functions will be to determine the sources of their funds, the names of their contributors, whether the contributions given to the organizations have been deducted as charitable contributions, what we can find out generally about the funds of these organizations. . . . we do not want news media to be alerted to what we are attempting to do or how we are operating because the disclosure of such information might embarrass the Administration."

This initial step, taken at Tom Huston's initiative, was, again, probably legal. Insurrectionary groups, violent groups, demonstration groups have, ever since 1968, been occasionally funded by good-willed cause-people, old ladies and young scions of great fortune, as philanthropic contributions, free of the strictures of reporting that cover formal political contributions. But the threatened use of the Revenue Service as the punitive political agent of the administration would, over the next few years, be stretched into what foreshadowed the most dangerous abuse of power of all.

Thus by midsummer of 1969, if anyone had then had the wit, knowledge or information, one could have perceived in the Nixon administration the beginning of three separate efforts at control of the political process—not yet linked in a conspiracy, but all of them pressing against the thin membrane of the law. There was a political intelligence arm operating out of John Ehrlichman's office, stockpiling political rumor, gossip and filth for the partisan wars; an official, legal surveillance system, directed by Attorney General John Mitchell and FBI director J. Edgar Hoover, designed legitimately to protect the President's diplomacy, but slopping over to include press and individual officials in no way connected with national security; and a first attempt to distort the instruments of the Revenue Service for use against political enemies, a method up to then used chiefly against gangsters.

It was sometime in early spring of 1970 that the hunger for control of events, which ran all through the Nixon White House, was challenged from the streets by a madness which alarmed not only the management of the White House, but millions of ordinary Americans as well.

1970 opened as a year of violence, the skein of traditional American politics torn by the spasms of a true terrorist movement. On March 6th, a quiet brownstone house on New York's sedate West 11th Street exploded—and its neighbors learned that a crude but effective bomb-making factory in its cellar had been working in their midst. Two young women fled, and three dead bodies were found in the ruins. The week after that, March 12th and 13th, bomb threats caused 15,000 people to be driven from their place of work in Manhattan. Two weeks later, two more people were blown to bits at another bomb factory in Manhattan. And all through the year, violence would continue—a judge and three others killed in a courtroom fracas in San Rafael, California, an innocent mathematician blown to death in a research center at the University of Wisconsin, a university building burned at Harvard. In all, by December, 3,000 bombings and 50,000 bombing threats causing search or evacuation of buildings had been reported during the year.

The violence was clearly political and came from the left —and as unprecedented as it was resistant to analysis. Encapsulated in dogma and wild rhetoric, the members of this revolutionary movement may have numbered a few hundred or a few thousand. No one knew for sure. Nor could anyone define clearly the sectarian fissures in this wild-left underground. One tightly organized element was the Black Panthers; the other, more violent element was made up of white youths, organized in underground communities called by various names, of whom the most paranoid were the Weathermen. No coherent doctrine bound these terrorists together; the Weathermen spurned black revolutionaries and white working-class masses alike, believing that simple chaos would usher in their opportunity for making a perfect new brotherhood of the American people. American history has enjoyed its full share of political lunatics, dream-seekers, wild men—but what was startling about the new revolutionaries was their willingness to kill. Never before had American politics known groups so ready, in their fanatic cruelty, to maim and injure innocents, to perpetrate wanton murder, arson and brutalities, all absolved by the programless morality of bleak nihilism.

Facing the terrorists, the Nixon administration also faced a real responsibility to the American people to protect them from such enemies. For the self-righteous in the Nixon administration—men like the puritanical Haldeman and Ehrlichman—the violence that spread across the country must have been the visible signature of the creeping "moral decay" they had been elected to purify. The language, the faces, the beards, the rhetoric, the sex lives, the habits of the people they despised seemed to culminate naturally in just such violence. And they were disturbed by the inability of the FBI or any of the other official agencies of the American government to cope with this present and rising menace.

Since so many elements were entering the crescendo of decision on terrorism in the spring of 1970, one must pause to consider a slow and growing default in the obsolete thinking of the FBI.

For years the Domestic Intelligence Division of the FBI had become an increasingly barren place to visit—even when its officers would consent to talk with visiting reporters, their conversation was sterile. Their thinking had been shaped by the comforting concept that all evil lay in the Communist Party, the instrument of Russian Bolshevism. This thought had guided their covert activities for years, as the FBI penetrated cell after cell of the Communist Party to root out conspiracy. But the Communists, at some point in the late 1940's or early 1950's, had ceased to be the nursery of American radicalism. Communist influence had simply withered; Communist control, whether over unions or the liberal mind, had vanished. The radicalism that began in the late 1960's and persists today in such groups as the Symbionese Liberation Army, however dangerous, was an expression of native American nuttiness; the enemy was no longer likely to be a Russian or an Algerian agent, but a native American crank who could kill and maim with the frenzied self-righteousness of a John Brown. And the new "Cointelpro" groups of the FBI had little success in fathoming their minds.

For the White House people, it was disconcerting to find that the government's chief official agency of control was devoid of ideas and incompetent to deal with mobs in the street.

All this was of great moment as events in the spring of 1970 came out of control and boiled into the streets and campuses in what became known as the Cambodia-Kent crisis. On the domestic front, all spring, had come the tattoo of random bombings, violence, terrorism, the sputtering of the drug epidemic. On April 30th, Nixon ordered the most successful American offensive of the entire Vietnam War—a strike by American forces across the unmarked border of South Vietnam and Cambodia into the sanctuaries which the North Vietnamese had made their major war bases—and with that act the college campuses of the country ignited. The outrage was inflamed in a day when Richard Nixon was heard on air denouncing "these bums . . . blowing up campuses . . . burning books."

Looking back now, the firestorm of emotion that burst in the first two weeks of May, 1970, may be seen as the last massive nationwide protest of the insurgency of the 1960's. But those who had to meet it could not know it was the last crest of a receding tide. It was a frightening moment. The trial of Bobby Seale, Black Panther leader, was approaching, and the president of Yale, Kingman Brewster, had proclaimed that he doubted "whether any black revolutionary could get a fair trial anywhere in the United States." From all over New England, students were marching on New Haven to see Bobby Seale freed. The Pentagon was on alert; Federal marshals and National Guards with bayonets were mobilized; the 82nd Airborne Division of the U.S. Army was put on standby. In Washington, in the underground war room of the Pentagon, civilian officials of the Nixon administration gravely studied blow-up maps of the streets of West Haven, North Haven, New Haven; intelligence pinpointed the whereabouts of Bobby Seale and Brewster as it had pinpointed the whereabouts of Fidel Castro in the missile crisis.

Bayonets and tear gas dispersed the students later on the New Haven Town Green; Bobby Seale did get his trial and charges against him were dismissed. But there was worse to come than the New Haven riots. On Monday, May 4th, 1970, on the campus of Kent State University in Ohio, after a weekend of trashings and burnings, a unit of abominably commanded National Guardsmen fired point-blank into a knot of students, killing four and wounding nine. At once and for weeks learning was suspended from coast to coast. A score of colleges had previously protested the Cambodian invasion; the day after the Kent State killing, schools were closing nationwide from Yale to Stanford—80 colleges on strike two days after the Kent killings, 200 by week's end, 400 by the beginning of the following week. Examinations were canceled, classes suspended, within days students and parents alike were pouring into Washington to lobby Senators and Congressmen for their cause.

The inflammation spread. Politicians thundered, editorialists denounced, intellectuals mourned. Two hundred fifty members of the State Department signed a manifesto to denounce the policy they were supposed to shape. Businessmen joined in the panic; the stock market had been sinking since March. In May, in its worst week in forty years, it broke wide open, plunging toward an eight-year low (631.16) on the Dow-Jones average in a 17,000,000-share trading day on May 26th. "Whirl is King," wrote Richard Rovere in *The New Yorker,* "and Richard Nixon is First Minister."

It had been a bad spring for Richard Nixon. He had already been humiliated twice by the Senate when it rejected two of his nominees to the Supreme Court. ("Even the Republicans he relied on," said one White House aide, "people he trusted, turned against him in the Senate. It was a question of whether anybody could govern the country with the

machinery he had.") Inflation was moving up, unemploy-
ment was growing, the press was savaging him. Of the two
major achievements of his new administration—environmental policy and the successful invasion of Cambodia—
the former had been ignored, the latter denounced. And
now from all over the country, mobilizing in the presence
of television, students, demonstrators, welfare clients were
marching on Washington. Events seemed thoroughly out of
control. People had been killed already; more killings
seemed inevitable.

At the White House, counsel was divided. There was, on
the one hand, the moderate counsel of Robert Finch. In the
riots of the late sixties, certain tactical practices of moderation had been worked out by university administrators, and
in some cities by mayors like John Lindsay of New York.
This moderate doctrine held that it was wisest (and worked
best) to *talk* with demonstrators, to cool their passion by
parley rather than by fire. Finch proposed to set up (and
did) a conference central in the basement of his HEW,
where assistant secretaries or under-secretaries, including
Pentagon staff men, would be available to talk with any
demonstrator in person or answer questions by telephone. It
was another one of those Finch proposals that tagged him
to his old teammates as soft. But at the White House, the
inhabitants saw themselves as under siege—not rhetorical
or fancied siege, but real siege. Terry Lenzner, later to be
Assistant Chief Counsel to the Ervin Committee, lunching
at the White House mess one day in May, heard a group at
the next table discussing the advisability of setting up machine guns on the lawn to mow down the first demonstrator
who attempted to storm the gates.

To the stay-at-home American who sees only snippets on
the television news, riot and demonstration may be very
disturbing, yet are unconsciously accepted as one way of
delivering a political message. But those who followed the
outdoor politics of the 1960's in America remember riot
and demonstration in street, in ghetto, on campus as fearful
and savage. The sound, the jeering, the foulness of language, the rocks hurled, the people injured, the blood
streaming, the provocations of young people or black people intoxicated with self-righteousness, the counter-cruelty
of indiscriminate police were the ugliest face of American

politics, bowel-tightening. And to none more so than Richard Nixon, for whom riots have always been offensive,
emotionally disturbing, infuriating to his neat way of thinking.

"They'd driven one President from office, they'd broken
Johnson's will," said Henry Kissinger later of the events of
1970. "Were they going to break another President? They
had him on the edge of nervous breakdown."

Whether or not Richard Nixon came close to nervous
breakdown in the events of May, 1970, is debated seriously
by his aides. There is a log recently made available, however, of the President's behavior on the night of May 8th-9th,
1970, when demonstrating students had encamped all over
Washington, had occupied its public places and were holding vigil at the Lincoln Memorial. Nixon had spoken that
evening on television, then tried to fall asleep; but sleep
eluded him. At 10:35 that evening, he began to reach out
by telephone: to Rose Mary Woods, his secretary; to his
daughter Tricia; to Secretary of State William Rogers; two
minutes later to Henry Kissinger (10:37); to Bob Haldeman a minute later (10:38); to Mrs. Nixon a minute thereafter (10:39); to Dr. Norman Vincent Peale (10:50)—
and then, racking up thirty-eight more calls in three hours,
he ran on: Transportation Secretary Volpe, Congressman
Fountain, Hobart Lewis, William Safire, Secretary Shultz,
Secretary Laird, Henry Kissinger again, Billy Graham,
John Ehrlichman, Bob Haldeman (a second time), Secretary Hickel, Rose Mary Woods (second), Bebe Rebozo,
Pat Moynihan, Congressman Monaghan, Haldeman
(third), Cliff Miller, Rose Woods (third). It was now past
midnight and the calls went on: Haldeman again at 12:18,
Haldeman again at 12:20, Kissinger again at 12:24, and
Alexis Johnson, Kissinger, Haldeman, Ziegler, Buchanan,
Kissinger, Nelson Rockefeller (at two minutes of one in the
morning), Herb Klein, newscaster Nancy Dickerson, Zieg-
ler, newswoman Helen Thomas, Bebe Rebozo again, John
Mitchell, Governor Thomas Dewey, Bob Haldeman again,
Rose Woods again, Kissinger again at five minutes of two
in the morning. Then came a pause. At 3:24 he began tele-
phoning again—to Paul Keyes, to Kissinger (3:38 A.M.), to
Ron Ziegler, to Helen Thomas.

Another pause and then at 4:22 in the morning he called his valet, Manolo Sanchez, and without word to Secret Service or aides, set out. At 4:35 Sanchez had the limousine at the South Lawn and Nixon was off—first to the Lincoln Memorial for a warm and pleading conversation on peace, foreign affairs and environment with the students encamped there. Then, still wound up, he drove to the Capitol, giving Sanchez a tour of the empty chambers of the Senate and of the House where he had once sat (he fitted himself into his old seat). By this time the Secret Service had joined him, and Bob Haldeman, Ron Ziegler and Dwight Chapin, having been awakened from sleep, caught up with Nixon and Sanchez outside the Capitol. All five then went to the Mayflower Hotel for a breakfast of corned-beef hash, returning to the White House at 7:30 A.M.[3]

There was no doubt that the events of May had disturbed the President—as well they should have. Commanding a successful military offensive, unable to reap its diplomatic harvest abroad because of near-insurrection at home, perplexed by a street madness which seemed beyond the control of either his staff, his own efforts or the FBI, he groped for solutions.

There are always in Washington many solutions being offered for any given problem; solutions become policy, however, only when the President chooses one or another. In Dean Acheson's great phrase about life in the Washington bureaucracy, "Policy bubbles up from the bottom, decisions are made at the top." The President was now approaching one of the critical policy decisions of his career without knowing it.

Violence had plagued the country for five years now. Not only his campaign pledge ("law and order") but his Constitutional obligation ("to insure domestic tranquility") burdened Richard Nixon. No one had a clue, much less a working analysis, of how to cope with this ferment of the

[3] For a vivid account of this incident see *Before the Fall*, by William Safire (Doubleday and Company, 1975), which is the best-balanced and most thoughtful story from an insider at the Nixon White House published yet.

season and the time, not even his intelligence agencies. But he felt they should, they must.

On June 5th, the President summoned to the White House the chiefs of the American intelligence community —Richard Helms of the CIA, J. Edgar Hoover of the FBI, General V. Bennett of the Defense Intelligence Agency, Admiral Noel Gayler of the National Security Agency, and gave them, in the memory of one who was present, a blistering rubdown. He was dissatisfied with them all, the President is remembered as saying; they were overstaffed, they weren't getting the story, they were spending too much money, there was no production, they had to get together. In sum, he wanted a thorough coordination of all American intelligence agencies; he wanted to know what the links were between foreign groups—al-Fatah; the Arab terrorists; the Algerian subsidy center—and domestic street turbulence. They would form a committee, J. Edgar Hoover would be the chairman, Tom Huston of the White House would be the staff man.

Tom Huston had by now become a large man in the King's Row hierarchy. His views, on the memo circuit between the EOB and the White House, had engaged the attention of Haldeman. Huston had left the humdrum servitude of Writers' Row and become, in effect, the White House expert on internal intelligence. And his ambition had grown with his authority. His conviction was that the country was infiltrated by foreign agents; that the CIA and the FBI were locked in a fools' rivalry of spies; that the intelligence agencies were wasteful and duplicative; and that only the White House could knock their heads together.

There are few more memorable figures in the story of derivative power in the White House than young Tom Charles Huston. Because he was a man of the White House, because he was a favorite of Bob Haldeman, because his ideas had reached the President, he could sit with the masters of American intelligence, commanding billions of dollars and thousands of agents, and dominate all but one of them, J. Edgar Hoover. It is an axiom of any working group, public or private, that the staff man who writes the report can, if he is skillful enough, manipulate the rationale and conclusion of the group's decision. Young Tom Huston was the staff man; it was his responsibility to write the report which, through Haldeman, would reach the President for decision; his only antagonist on his way to dominance of American intelligence was seventy-five-year-old J. Edgar Hoover, a wily and experienced bureaucrat.

By June 25th, Huston could report to Haldeman on the progress of the intelligence planning meetings. The recommendations of the group, drafted by Huston, spelled out a structure of super-police and super-espionage such as had never before been known in America. Only Hoover had resisted. Reported Huston: "The only stumbling block was Mr. Hoover. . . . When the working group completed its report, Mr. Hoover refused to go along with a single conclusion drawn or support a single recommendation made. . . . his objections are generally inconsistent and frivolous—most express concern about possible embarrassment to the intelligence community . . . from public disclosure of clandestine operations." In the eyes of Tom Huston, J. Edgar Hoover, the indiscriminate nemesis of American liberals and Communists, was almost a civil-libertarian. "At some point," wrote Huston later, "Hoover has to be told who is President. He has become totally unreasonable and his conduct is detrimental to our domestic intelligence operations," or "Hoover can be expected to raise the following points. . . . (a) 'Our present efforts are adequate.' The answer is bullshit! This is particularly true with regard to FBI campus coverage." Earlier he had written, "Mr. Hoover should be called in privately for a stroking session at which the President explains the decision he has made, thanks Mr. Hoover for his candid advice and past cooperation, and indicates he is counting on Edgar's cooperation."

By mid-July, Huston's report on the new intelligence plan had met the President's approval. On July 14th, Haldeman memoed Huston: "The recommendations you have proposed as a result of the review have been approved by the President. He does not, however, want to follow the procedure you outlined. . . . He would prefer that the thing simply be put into motion on the basis of this approval. The formal official memorandum should be . . . the device by which to carry it out. . . ."

On July 23rd, Huston's memo was secretly issued to all American intelligence agencies in the President's name. Policy had bubbled from the bottom up into a decision at the top that tore apart the fabric of both law and Constitution. The law, so ran Huston's rationale, had been ripped up by the bloody people of the streets and the hiding terrorists. Thus, then, the law-enforcers themselves might dispense with law. National security, and its imperative privileges, now ran to confront domestic dissent and domestic protest.

"The President," said the memo, "has carefully studied the special report of the Interagency Committee on Intelligence . . . and made the following decisions." The "following decisions" were mind-boggling. The National Security Agency—the code-cracking and cryptographic worldwide surveillance arm of the U.S.A.—would be allowed to intercept the cables or correspondence of any American citizen communicating overseas. All intelligence agencies were now empowered to penetrate or spy on "individuals and groups who pose a major threat to the internal security." Restrictions on legal "coverage" of domestic mail, between Americans, were to be removed—which meant the government could read anyone's private mail. Government would be empowered to burglarize and enter private homes, by a doctrine of justified surreptitious entry. Colleges and students were special targets. In the aftermath of the Cambodia-Kent State outburst, coverage of violence-prone campus and student-related activities was to be increased: "All restraints which limit this coverage are to be removed." All these measures were to go into effect by August 1st, and by September 1st, before the new campus season began at schools, the President expected all agencies involved to report.

The memorandum, invoking the authority of the Presidency, was signed by Tom Charles Huston. And, to make matters clear, a supporting document on Organization and Operations instructed: "The President has assigned to Tom Charles Huston staff responsibility for domestic intelligence and internal security affairs. He will participate in all activities of the group as the personal representative of the President. . . The group shall meet at the call of the chairman, a member agency, or the White House representative." Tom Charles Huston, now twenty-nine, was in charge of the super-police.

The coup, of course, could not last, did not last more than five days. Hoover could recognize what was happening. He went immediately to his superior, John Mitchell, Attorney General. Mitchell swiftly interceded with the President. Such a memo, of total, flagrant illegality, must not, could not be the policy of the United States government, expostulated Mitchell. Five days later, down through channels—from Nixon to Haldeman, to Huston, to all the spy-masters—went the word that the Huston memo had been revoked. And, attempting to erase from history what had happened, each recipient was instructed to return his copy. It would be as if it had not existed; except that in an age of photo-copying, copies would be available three years later for the Ervin Committee to show to America.

The downfall of Tom Huston came swiftly thereafter. A few more months of rear-guard action followed, Huston still firing memos against J. Edgar Hoover like a tail gunner in hopeless flight. Slowly, he found his memos went unanswered, and his access to Bob Haldeman, who guarded access to the President's thinking, was blocked. He toyed again with prodding the IRS to action against subversive plotters and then, discouraged by such liberal measures as Nixon's welfare plan and new federalism, he quit in the spring of 1971, convinced that Richard Nixon, whom he still admired, had been seduced by liberals. Of Tom Huston it can be said that he was true and loyal to what he felt was right, and a menace to the Republic.

However casual a decision the President made in approving the memo of July 23rd, however correct he was in revoking that decision only five days later, its residue lingered. Momentarily he had revealed one side of his mind, the side that believed the term "national security" could be stretched all the way—all the way to every mailbox, every college campus, every telephone, every home. The passions and the killings of spring, 1970, would be forgotten, but not the President's reaction to them; and however tightly the decision had been held, the atmospherics at the White House had now changed. Up until that point, the President's will had been interpreted chiefly by the self-righteous and puritanical Haldeman and Ehrlichman. This new decision was to be interpreted by many. Not only did Haldeman, Ehrlichman, Mitchell, Hoover, Gayler, Helms, Bennett, Huston know of it. So did their assistants, staff men, secretaries. So did many anonymous others. "There were quite a few spare characters at the meeting from the White House staff," recalled John Ehrlichman later of the meeting with the President to approve the Huston plan. And those who did not know of the meeting directly, or of the President's fleeting approval, were not slow to catch the rhythm to which their ambitions might dance. The President had approved, for five days, a breach in the guarantees that America's Constitution holds for its citizens. The Constitution is not an easy document to interpret; it is full of contradictions; Nixon had been caught in one of those contradictions, as had many Presidents before him; and the nature of his later crime could be understood only by quickly glancing back at that Constitution. Long before anyone dreamed of Watergate, that Constitutional contradiction was on Richard Nixon's desk.

The contradiction in the United States Constitution has frozen into basic law forever the romantic politics of the young revolutionaries who in 1783 forged the first republic since Rome.

These young men had taken to arms and fought for seven years against the tyrant George III and the tyranny of all monarchs. After their victory, they had experimented for six years with government by a confederation of states, without any president or any national leader; all strong executives were feared as embryo "monarchs" or "tyrants." Under this leaderless confederation of states, however, national currency became worthless, commerce and industry stuttered, Indians raided frontier settlements, dreams faded. Such a confederation would not work. As the young men matured, they sought a new strong leadership that would yet not be a tyranny—and thus they wrote their Constitution, a masterpiece of political craft, installing a dominant and powerful elected executive called President, in whom was vested all executive power, but a power balanced and checked by legislative and judicial powers.

The strong executive Presidency resulted, thus, from a compact between the states which could not live prosperously unless a strong President brought them together for one national purpose. But how could the citizens of these states be brought together, and how were their liberties to be protected from executive power? In what would today be called a "deal," it was agreed that to the original Constitution there would be immediately tacked on ten amendments which we call, today, the Bill of Rights. Without the Bill of Rights, the Constitution is a working bargain of states agreeing on a common executive. With the Bill of Rights, the people become part of the bargain, too—their loyalties, their privileges, their inalienable rights are directly guaranteed by the Federal government, by the President. They are citizens owing loyalty and life both to their states and to the nation.

Despite the Bill of Rights, the contradiction between executive power and the civil rights of citizens is inherent in the Constitution; but Richard Nixon, for all his devout patriotism, never quite grasped the complexity of the contradiction. The President is elected to see to it that the laws are faithfully executed. So he swears, right arm uplifted, on Inauguration Day. But the purpose of the Constitution makes that pledge more difficult to fulfill than would appear. That purpose is, as the preamble says, "to form a more perfect union, establish justice, insure domestic tranquility, provide for the common defense, promote the general welfare, and secure the blessings of liberty." But then come the first ten amendments, the Bill of Rights. And there is the rub: freedom of religion, of speech, of press, of peaceful assembly guaranteed; freedom from unreasonable searches of person, houses, papers and effects and the further guarantee that no person shall "be deprived of life, liberty or property without due process of law."

The contradiction between these amendments and the preamble to the Constitution has plagued all Presidents ever since—how to provide for the common defense and insure domestic tranquility without trampling on one of the guaranteed civil rights. Many Presidents have grappled with this contradiction. Lincoln, suspending the writ of *habeas corpus* in the Civil War, was violating the Sixth Amendment in order to provide for the common defense and insure domestic tranquility vital to save the Union. Franklin D. Roosevelt, violating the First and Fourth Amendments to put Japanese-Americans in concentration camps, was doing what he felt he must under the injunction to provide for the common defense. The thought of common defense ran just as strongly in the Constitution as the thought of liberty. The founders tried to insure both. Long before Richard Nixon, the simple phrase "common defense" had been translated into the phrase "national security"; and in the name of national security many Presidents have committed breaches of the law.

The phrase "national security" was to be the governing phrase of the Nixon defense all through 1973 and 1974. Which laws should a President choose to execute when there is a contradiction between national security and personal liberty? How far can his clerks, aides, assistants, counselors and deputies go in balancing one against the other?

In approving the super-police and Huston memo of 1970, Richard Nixon thought he had come down on the one side—common defense and domestic tranquility—as against the other—the Bill of Rights. But his assistants would carry that decision further. Neither he nor they recognized that the thoughts they entertained breached not simply the law and the Constitution, but more than that. The United States, with its polyglot constituent stocks, is a nation only by faith—that all are bound together in their pursuit of happiness by common belief in their personal liberties and equality before the law. What had happened in 1970, under the provocation of street violence, was that Richard Nixon had breached that faith. Although he revoked the Huston plan and did not act on it, he had been guilty, in religious terms, of an Act of Heresy, or truly dangerous thought.

What crimes and and abuses had occurred up to that point were no worse than those committed by previous Presidents. But from 1970 on, the heresy of the President was to sanction his lieutenants on their road to unpardonable crime.

6

THE UNDERGROUND:
FROM CRIME TO CONSPIRACY.

By the summer of 1970, after the spring violence, after the Huston heresy, an observant insider might have been able to detect a change not only in style but in quality of the Nixon administration.

Large matters, where large and good men ran affairs, were shaking down—or at least shaping into reasonable, sometimes exciting plans. Though the Paris negotiations with the Communists of Hanoi seemed paralyzed, American troops were coming home—115,500 had already come back by April 15th, with another 150,000 due home in the next twelve months. A masterful three-part plan for environmental reorganization had been designed—it had a research branch, NOAA, the National Oceanic and Atmospheric Administration, which patrolled oceans, seas, sun, air, coastal zones scientifically; a three-man Council on Environmental Quality to guide the President personally; and a new, tough policing branch, the Environmental Protection Agency. The scheme was already in operation and would shortly make America the world's leader in environmental management. Integration was moving in the South, and would move there faster and farther and more peacefully than under any of Nixon's predecessors, until by the beginning of 1974 the eleven states of the old Confederacy had the highest degree of racial integration in the nation—only 29.9 percent of their black students were attending public schools still 80 percent or more black. Housing, though in a momentary slump in 1970, was on its way to the boom of 1972; more Federal housing assistance would be granted by the Nixon administration than in the previous thirty-four years. Never had Federal funding for the arts and humanities done better than under the Nixon administration, rising steadily from an annual budget of $12 million a year to $81 million a year. The Post Office was about to be reorganized; so, too, was rail passenger traffic; a welfare plan was before Congress (which would fail) and a revenue-sharing plan (which would succeed) was on the drawing boards.

Many good men were working at hard problems and groping for real solutions—interpreting in their way the President's will at its best.

And yet, simultaneously, at the nerve center, all along King's Row were others interpreting the President's will at its worst—the irregulars.

There are irregulars everywhere, in every large corporation, in every large municipality, in every large enterprise —the men who cannot wait to get ahead and must cut corners. Ambition is a healthy, useful quality. It surges naturally in every White House; but, usually, for those who work in the White House, this ambition is guided, or restrained, by the causes and convictions that brought them to the service of the President or the country in the first place. Not so, however, on King's Row.

On King's Row it was impossible to define any purpose that brought the irregulars together except the common hustle to move fast. Pushing, squirming, elbowing each other to the sun at the top, they strove for the attention from Haldeman or Ehrlichman that might bring them forward to the President's notice as those who served him personally, above all causes, all restraints. To let loose such people at the delicate interconnection of politics, policy and government, at the center of power controls at the White House, would have been perilous even if planned. Unplanned as it was, it was even more perilous—for their only common bond was their competition to reach the evil impulses of revenge and bitterness that, they sensed, lay as surely in Richard Nixon's personality as the good. "These guys," said Mel Laird, "behaved the way they did not because they didn't understand politics; they didn't understand the difference between right and wrong."

In the White House, ambitions are compressed; time is short, the span of a four-year term; one must move fast to win attention, to earn that burst of ego gratification conferred by notice in the press or on television as a national figure. After such notice, later, come great jobs—offers to head worldwide corporations, mighty foundations or universities, great lobbies, law partnerships, even nominations for high office. But the hustle on Nixon's King's Row was sharper by several degrees than in previous administrations. Nixon's world was peopled by enemies; the irregulars considered themselves at war; and among them, by late 1970, one could single out several men who were paradigms of limitless ambition—three outstanding white-collar roughnecks, each of whom, in his own way, would interpret the President's will to the President's undoing, as the siege summer of 1970 provided the sanction of heresy for what their ambitions devised.

They were John Dean, Charles Colson and Jeb Magruder.

John Dean had not seemed like a pivotal personality when he arrived at the White House in the summer of 1970. A reshuffle had just taken place as, once more, Richard Nixon sought to get control of the cumbersome machinery of government and make it work as he thought it should: Ehrlichman to be Chief of the Domestic Council, George Shultz to be Director of Management and Budget, Finch to leave HEW (and be replaced by Elliot Richardson) and come aboard as first Counsellor to the President. Thus, a gap—who would replace Ehrlichman as Counsel to the President, personal attorney for the President, to guide him through the laws? It is unclear who first recommended Dean to Bob Haldeman, but it was of no little moment that John Mitchell, for whom Dean then worked at Justice, *objected* to Dean's transfer to the White House. Dean was too able a talent, said Mitchell to Haldeman, to be wasted on a job as low-level as Counsel to the President.

Dean's record, viewed by Haldeman, was indeed glittering. Dean was young, only thirty-one. Wooster College, Ohio. Georgetown Law School. Good experience on the Criminal Law Reform Commission. Good contacts on the Hill. Quick mind. "A bright, able, handsome, super-ambitious young guy," Haldeman later recalled of his first meeting with Dean, whom he had summoned out to San Clemente for a half-day's conversation before approval.

Haldeman had made a hobby of speaking to managerial groups on personnel choice. What one looked for in young men, he would say, were the three "I's"—Initiative, Intelligence, Integrity; their superiors could supply wisdom, experience and guidance. Initiative and intelligence were relatively easy to identify; integrity, admitted Haldeman later, was the hardest thing to measure, you couldn't get a fix on it. And on this matter of integrity, Haldeman's administrative fail-safe mechanisms had stuttered; he later claimed that he did not call for clearance on Dean from the FBI, resting his approval on the recommendation of John Mitchell and previous Justice Department clearance. His story was that he had no way, then, of knowing that Dean had left his first law office under a cloud. Dean had earned $7,500 a year then in 1965; in 1970, as Counsel to the President, he was to get $42,500.

John Dean arrived at the White House in July as the siege panic of 1970 was fading. He was not to carry the rank of "Assistant to the President," as Ehrlichman had, but to be simply "Counsel to the President," seated in Room 106 on King's Row, responsible to Haldeman as a slot-holder in "Operations and Administration." Haldeman made clear the job description—Dean would be responsible for no less than twenty traditional areas of Presidential legal work, in a supervisory fashion. In addition, he would track the new laws on campaign funding and be responsible for keeping an eye on campaign intelligence.

In the summer of 1970, when Dean came aboard, when the President's nerves were still raw from the Cambodia upheaval, the atmosphere of the White House itself gave direction to his initiative. His new replacement, said John Ehrlichman later, was required most importantly to "be a self-starter." From his experience at Justice, the new counsel was already aware of the flexible use of the government's suveillance facilities; and in his new post, Dean found that John Ehrlichman had bequeathed to him Jack Caulfield (and Tony Ulasewicz), described by the outgoing chief as "a kind of facility of the counsel's office . . . he sort of went with the job." The law, as seen from the White House by the new counsel, must have seemed elastic; and he was its interpreter.

If John Dean was the white-collar striver as conniver, then Charles Colson, another of the emerging class of 1970, was the white-collar hustler as bully.

Colson's was without a doubt the shrewdest political mind, after Richard Nixon's, in the White House. A Bostonian of thirty-eight years, he could be, though a rogue, a man of refreshing candor and humor. His round face with its underslung jaw, his spectacles through which the eyes stabbed, his stocky body—all made him the kind of figure whose portrait, if dressed in eighteenth-century garb, might have hung as a Yankee founder in the Boston Museum of Fine Arts. But back home, Colson fitted into the category known as "Swamp Yankee"—one of those vanishing aboriginal Protestants left behind by the successful families of the old stock as they withdrew to their stockades on Beacon Hill and Commonwealth Avenue while Irishmen, Jews, Italiano, French Canadians, Slavs, Blacks and newer breeds swarmed through the wards of the old Hub.

Colson's politics may have been shaped by this experience; his father had been left behind (a functionary in the local Securities Exchange Commission office) by the more successful Yankees of the Hill; Colson's bitterness at the Establishment was personal. He found more in common with the newcomers who, like himself, had to strive in the hard-knuckled contest for a living. His politics thus could be described as almost Southern Californian in strategy, though not in origin. Republicans in Massachusetts have been a more outnumbered minority for far longer than Republicans in California, and the search by traditional Republican Protestants for allies among Massachusetts ethnic blocs is thus crucial. This searche is of different style from the search in California, but the thrust is the same—to win, lure, trigger, divide the majority of Democrats by issues or symbols until there is a big enough breakaway to give Republicans electoral victory.

Colson had first practiced his concept of ethnic-bloc politics for Leverett Saltonstall when that Republican Senator, in 1960, won an astounding upset victory on the same day that John F. Kennedy was sweeping Massachusetts for the Presidency as a Democrat. Colson had thereafter practiced law in Boston, earning a comfortable six-figure income a year; dabbled in politics from time to time; served with the Nixon campaign of 1968 as an "issues man"; had his first feud with John Mitchell in that campaign; and then come to the White House in 1969 to practice "bloc politics" as a Presidential political strategist. He was to reach out and court the AFL/CIO, to reach out and woo and win the

Teamsters Union, to reach out and urge positions against birth control that would sway the Catholic hierarchy, to reach out for any organized, traditionally Democratic ethnic group that could be shaken loose from the Democratic Party, then in full course to the convulsion that resulted in George McGovern.

Colson was slow in making his presence felt, and not until the election of 1970 was he truly of the inner circle. He had successfully masterminded a public-relations smear of Democratic Senator Joseph Tydings that summer, had been invited to the President's personal campaign post-mortem in Key Biscayne, and by early 1971 had risen to be a major force. Colson's operating philosophy seems to have come from his service in the Marine Corps where he had learned their formula for partisan warfare: "YOU CAN'T WIN OVER THE HEARTS AND MINDS UNTIL YOU HAVE THEM BY THE BALLS."

The first set of testicles for which Colson reached in the White House struggle for power was that of the man who sat in Cordell Hull's old suite on King's Row—Herbert Klein, director of the Office of Communications. The Office of Communications reflected the Nixon White House's emphasis on the PR dimension of politics. A simple Press Secretary could no longer deal with public relations; the news system was television, talk shows, radio spots, promotion, a maze of transmission mechanisms which required professional manipulation. But Klein was an old-fashioned newsman by origin, and had come to regard the changing press with a low-key melancholy, and the news system as a whole with sadness. It was not that the news system was necessarily, or even frequently, inaccurate in its reporting of the Nixon administration. It was simply that it behaved as a chromatic screen—it screened out the good on Nixon, and headlined the bad. If Nixon went to New Orleans, as he did in the summer of 1970, to meet with Southern community leaders and enlist them in finally getting on with the job of desegregation, Klein would see the President front-paged with a picture of two scowling white policemen as background and a story that implied Nixon had flown South to stiffen resistance to desegregation. For Klien, this skew of the news system was simply a cultural barrier that separated him, Nixon and Middle America from the news masters. He had to live with it and do the best he could.

For Colson, however, the news system *was* the enemy— or, if not the enemy, the mechanism that must be intimidated, or misled, if his kind of symbolic politics was to get through to the people with any success. To gain his ends, Colson had absolutely no scruple—leaks, plants, forgeries, lies were all part of the game as he played it. Klein was made of softer stuff; and in the contest between them to serve the President best in his PR interest, there could be absolutely no doubt of the outcome. Klein was "soft," Colson was "tough." Moreover, by early 1970 Bob Haldeman had already installed a personal agent in Klein's office, Jeb Magruder, to make sure that PR was managed as it seemed to Haldeman and the President that PR must be managed.

Of Jeb Magruder it may be said that he was the white-collar hustler as weakling. Moderately smart, handsome, attractive, he was described by an older advance man at the White House as "one of those salute-and-go-over-the-hill type of guy." There was no detectable philosophy in any conversation with Magruder except that of managerial slick. At once friendly, weak and ambitious, he had, successively and unhappily, betrayed on his way up or was to betray further, first, Bob Finch, one of his original sponsors for an administration post, then Herbert Klein, then John Mitchell, then everyone with whom he dealt, up to the President of the United States. He would do whatever seemed appropriate to him at the moment, under the pressure of people whom he feared.

Magruder was another instance of the Haldeman "fail-safe apparatus" gone wrong. Even the President felt that Magruder was a Haldeman mistake. But the early checks made on his career showed little of Magruder's weakness, except that his was a rather sad, probably emblematic story of the endless upward striving of the junior white-collar executive. It ran: public high school on Staten Island, New York, where he was a minority WASP; then on to a good college (Williams), where he majored in political science and studied ethics under the Reverend William Sloane Coffin, later chief moralist of Yale. Then: good service in Korea; night classes and a degree from business school; sales; supermarket advertising; job-shifting; merchandise managing. And the notches rose from $7,000 a year (at Crown Zellerbach) to $10,000 a year, then to $22,000 (at Jewel Tea Company), then to $30,000 as cosmetics buyer (at the Broadway-Hale chain in California), as he tried to bend and weave to the needs of his various bosses and various organizations. And always—pliable and adaptable, comfortable to have around.

There was also a Magruder dabbling in politics on the side to please the inner man. He was a Republican by heritage. In 1960, while working in Kansas City, he joined in the Nixon campaign as ward chairman. Action came again in the 1962 and 1964 campaigns; action for Nixon as an organizer in Southern California in 1968; and then, in Haldeman's search for bright young men of initiative, intelligence and integrity, his name came to Haldeman's attention as one of those interchangeable white-collar managerial parts that might pull Herb Klein's loose-structured office together.

For the President, and thus for Haldeman, Herb Klein's office was not doing the job. The paperwork coming back from Klein's office to the White House seemed sloppy. Moreover, Klein was *not*, simply *not*, getting the control of press response that he should.

Magruder, a management man, as deputy, was supposed to put that to rights without disturbing Klein.

"He was," reflected Klein later, "not forced on me. I was looking for a deputy. What they wanted at the White House was a game plan for public relations—something like a six-day game plan for the PR on welfare, with items to fill TV programs or talk shows, which people on which newspapers to be contacted, with the contact for *Meet the Press* listed. They had a system of paperwork—like: 'Action Memo No. 746, Why haven't you reported back?' Jeb was very skillful, he wrote beautiful memoranda, and he was so skillful running things over your desk at a given moment, with a 'by-the-way.' . . . There was this feeling of Bob Haldeman that they could do anything better than anyone else, so you got a highly competitive, a secret group of inexperienced people with this high degree of competition. There were these young people who'd drop the name of the President as if they ate, drank and golfed with him, and I'd get memos from Jeb saying, 'The President wants this' or 'The President wants that.' "

In the White House, Magruder's reputation grew on the basis of the apparent clarity of the memoranda that moved across from his desk on King's Row to Haldeman's office. On paper, Magruder, who had never before dealt with the press, sounded, nonetheless, like a man who knew what it was supposed to do. As vice-president for public relations of Ford, Mobil or IBM, he might have been a conspicuous success—but there the nature of the product would have been clearly defined by responsible engineers.

By 1971, Magruder had learned the polarity of powers up and down King's Row. He had, early that year, been caught in the squeeze between Klein and Colson; and, moved by a managerial territorial imperative, Magruder had urged Klein to protest Colson's intrusion into their field of news management. All three had gone to lunch together at Washington's most fashionable downtown restaurant, the Sans Souci, to resolve their differences. At lunch, Colson had brutalized Klein and refused coordination, with such roughness that Magruder came away in near physical fear of Colson and with a sense of Colson's growing power.

By spring Magruder was in direct contact with Colson; one can trace a new web, Magruder-Colson-Dean, as early as April 14th, 1971. Magruder had learned from the Department of Commerce of the collapse of an airy scheme called the Main Sugar Industry, one of the bubbles of the hot-stock boom of 1969; somehow Maine Sugar had arranged government funding for a sugar-beet mill in a scheme that would persuade Aroostook County's potato growers to raise sugar beets instead. The scheme had failed. Could Senator Muskie of Maine, the leading Democratic contender, be involved? The family of memos traces a clear action connection. From Magruder to Colson: could Muskie be implicated in the press? Next day, from Colson to Dean: could Jack Caulfield be put on the detail to "dig out the facts"? Colson needed facts for the smear to be slapped on Muskie: "I have ways of getting this out but I do need the facts which apparently, as you will see from the enclosed, are available from Fagan of the Commerce Department. He is a political loyalist and can be dealt with confidently."

There was thus, in the spring and early summer of 1971, a movement to and fro along the offices of King's Row that wired together an undefined but real underground. In Magruder's office, he controlled his own deputies—Robert Odle, Herbert Porter, Gordon Strachan. Out of Dean's office, Caulfield and Ulasewicz still operated as Presidential agents for political intelligence. And in Colson's office, a staffing up for supermanipulation of the press that would result shortly in the hiring of E. Howard Hunt.

A larger system of events should frame the story of the development of the underground and the handful of ambitious young men who helped destroy a Presidency. History was moving on a much more important level than their knowledge or comprehension, for at this point the Nixon administration was feeling its way toward its great *détente* with Russia and China. This approach to the hostile power centers of the Cold War, the hope of peace, rested on the secrecy with which Nixon and Kissinger could execute this maneuver.

And at this point an event took place which, to Richard Nixon, seemed to demonstrate once more the unholy alliance between the enemy press and the treacherous Democratic-inclined under-bureaucracy, neither of which he could control. That event—the publication of the Pentagon Papers—was to rouse the ultimate fury of the White House, and stimulate the underground to escalate its sporadic little illegalities into major continuing lawlessness.

On June 13th, 1971, the *New York Times* began to publish what have since become known as the Pentagon Papers—a secret Pentagon study of the whys, wherefores, motives and thinking that led to the disaster of the Vietnam War.

The contents of these papers are prime material for some later history of the Vietnam War—but they revealed little of relevant action secrets. Turgid, endless, harrowing in their picture of bureaucratic confusion, they might have been deplored by Mr. Nixon and then accepted publicly as a portrait of how stupidly the Democrats under Lyndon Johnson had led the nation to its sorrow.

And indeed just this thought, to reveal how blunderingly the Democrats had led the nation to war, was the initial reaction of the White House and became one of the roots of the famous Plumbers' project. Haldeman was on the telephone the Sunday of their publication, June 13th, to Dr. Richard Allen, a distinguished scholar of international affairs. Allen, a decided conservative, had been campaign consultant on foreign affairs to Richard Nixon in 1968 and had hoped for the National Security post that was eventually to go to Henry Kissinger.

What did he think about the Pentagon Papers? asked Haldeman now. Allen advised that the White House do nothing. A few days later, Haldeman called again—the President thought it might be a good idea to declassify everything; what was Allen's opinion? Allen was this time enthusiastic—declassify all the inner stories, he said, Kennedy's Bay of Pigs papers, Roosevelt's Yalta papers, the Berlin papers. But he cautioned that it must not be done simply as a history of Democratic blunders—Eisenhower's Lebanon papers should be declassified, too. Asked to write a memorandum, Allen began, "The proposal to declassify certain documents from previous administrations dating back to the Roosevelt administration is, in my view, a sound idea. Properly and skillfully implemented . . . the President would . . . be known as the man who 'leveled' with the American people"; and Allen went on to outline a program.

The memo provoked another long telephone call from Haldeman to Allen. Would he, Allen, do the job? Allen said no; he knew himself to be tagged in academic circles as a "right-wing scholar," and the whole project would become vulnerable in the eyes of liberal historians because of his leadership. But the project would go forward anyway, he was assured; and Egil Krogh would lead it, he later learned.

But events were quickly to twist the President's mind from his original purpose of demonstrating that the Vietnam War had been Lyndon Johnson's war. First, there was no doubt that the Pentagon Papers had been stolen from government files. They had been stolen by one Daniel Ellsberg, a former Pentagon bureaucrat, in violation of both civil laws and laws of national security. Secondly, the *New York Times* (and the Washington *Post* later)—as the Supreme Court ruled on June 30th—broke no law by publishing them. Thirdly, the effort of the Nixon administration to stop publication made the *New York Times,* the *Washington Post* and other organs of the leadership press defend their right to publish and, in substance, to become public confederates of Daniel Ellsberg.

Here, finally, the administration saw its nightmare proven: the Eastern Liberal Press publicly joining an ex-bureaucrat in what Nixon considered a clear and undoubted breach of the law. The President was furious. If the Supreme Court refused to bar these newspapers from publishing what they would, the government must tighten internal discipline so as to stop those leaks at their source; and what had begun in his mind as a declassification project took on a new character.

Already, in early June, David Young, of Henry Kissinger's National Security staff, had been detached for an assignment described to Kissinger as "declassification." But if declassification had once been the pretext for setting up a special unit, the concept was already changing. It was merging with the assignment the President had given John Ehrlichman a few days earlier—to find as much information about Daniel Ellsberg as possible. Ehrlichman now handed on this assignment to one of his favorite young men, Egil Krogh. But to the rising alarm of both Kissinger and the President, now engaged in the most delicate negotiations of twenty years with both China and Russia, the leaks continued in early July. At a dinner in mid-July in Los Angeles (at Perino's, a somber but excellent restaurant on Wilshire Boulevard) the President dined with his closest—Kissinger, Haldeman, Ehrlichman—discussing, with bitterness and concern, the leak problem. There, the President decided to see Egil Krogh himself as soon as he returned to Washington. But the day that Nixon saw Krogh was Saturday, July 24th—one day after the *New York Times* had broken a story (by William Beecher) detailing the secret American fallback position in the strategic arms-limitations (SALT) talks with the Russians. "The President was livid," said John Ehrlichman of that talk. "He gave Krogh an overcharge." The President's later public recall of that talk was more restrained: "I told Mr. Krogh that as a matter of first priority the unit should find out all it could about Mr. Ellsberg's associates and his motives. Because of the extreme gravity of the situation, and not then knowing what additional national secrets Mr. Ellsberg might disclose, I did impress upon Mr. Krogh the vital importance to the national security of his assignment. I did not authorize and had no knowledge of any illegal means to be used to achieve this goal."

Egil Krogh's is a name much more significant than those of most of the others lifted from anonymity by the great scandals. The names of Caulfield, Ulasewicz, Magruder, Dean, Chapin and the soon-to-come names of Hunt, Liddy, Segretti, Barker *et alii* might well have been called Sockready, Muckseller, Slurtz, Sly, Hungerman or Jones. There were no essential personalities among them. But the name of Egil Krogh is the link between the high puritanical moralities of Ehrlichman and Haldeman and the tools they were bunglingly trying to employ. This was not their business and they made the worst of it.

Egil Krogh, who had been in the Ehrlichman law firm in Seattle, his sister the best friend of John Ehrlichman's wife, was a man of immaculate personality, behavior and character. Originally assigned to help in the ceremonial and security responsibilities of the first Nixon inauguration in Washington in January of 1969, he had afterward been named political liaison man with the FBI. After this first contact with agents of official surveillance, he was then assigned as White House liaison man with the narcotics people. There was a moral imperative on the narcotics front: the drug epidemic then raging in America was as perilous as plague. (In New York City alone, in the decade 1960–1970, heroin deaths had risen annually from 199 to 1,100 to become the leading cause of death among teenagers, rising from 29 a year to 225 a year in the five years up to 1969.) If the drug peril required clandestine social and police detection, few would legitimately question or be squeamish about the combat and intelligence tactics involved; American lives were at stake. Krogh, thus, had learned something about covert operations before he was summoned to higher things; but he remained an innocent at heart. "This was the kind of guy," a friend remarked, "who, if you had put him in charge of a big wedding back in Seattle, wouldn't have known how to call the police station and get a couple of cops to help with the traffic."

To put Egil Krogh in charge of a secret police operation was equivalent to naming Frank Merriwell chief executioner of a KGB squad. He would do his best, but it was not his turf. In America, tradition had trained few, if any, major talents in political espionage, deviltry or harassment. No trained corps of domestic partisan spies exists like the agents of the CIA, the G-men of the FBI, the accountants of the IRS. In operations of domestic malice, as in the operation of campaign intelligence, one recruits what one can get—usually remainder men from old campaigns, drifters, amateurs of such awkwardness, ineptness and silliness as must inevitably carry matters awry. To risk so much with such poor instruments was probably the height of managerial incompetence. But Ehrlichman and Haldeman both pressed for speed; the President had inflated the adventure to a matter of highest national security; and to Eagle Scout Egil Krogh, zeal was of the essence.

Krogh, on the managerial table, was responsible to Ehrlichman. But Ehrlichman, like Tom Huston before him, had lost confidence in the FBI; on some occasions he called it "a sieve," which it was indeed becoming as the aging Hoover's discipline faltered and his lieutenants struggled for the succession. Ehrlichman was suspicious of an alleged acquaintanceship between J. Edgar Hoover and the father-in-law of Daniel Ellsberg, toymaker Louis Marx. Ehrlichman wanted a White House investigative staff entirely independent of the FBI and official surveillance agencies; and Krogh was empowered to recruit the new staff members. David Young had already been seconded from Henry Kissinger's staff as a leak plumber. Colson had recruited just a few days before his fellow Brown alumnus E. Howard Hunt, a failed functionary of the CIA, to help him in his various caprices for manipulating the press and planning the public shame of Dan Ellsberg; Hunt was now also transferred to Krogh's unit. Krogh himself had earlier come to know G. Gordon Liddy, a remainder man of county politics in New York State, who had been one of his contacts at Treasury when he supervised the drug patrol. Liddy was aboard by July 19th. And all three of the famous Plumbers' unit were soon at work in the basement of the Executive Office Building. There, one day in late July, Dr. Allen, the original drafter of the declassification project, was emerging from the basement gym in the building and, turning the corner to mount a staircase to the first floor, noticed on Room 16 a blue shield. The sign said, simply, "PLUMBERS." He opened the door, for the sign was new; and there, behind a desk, was sitting David Young, who supposedly was working on declassification. What did the sign mean? asked Allen. "I'm a plumber," replied Young, laughing at his joke, "I fix leaks. Like it?" Beyond that, the suite was barren—a shelf full of the quarterly *Foreign Affairs,* a few books and no more. And out of the corner of his eye, Allen noticed an agitated man watching him suspiciously—a civilian guard, thought Allen, assigned to protect the security of classified documents. The man was introduced to him as Gordon Liddy and then Allen left, asking himself, "Oh my God, what are they doing?" But by August few strangers entered Room 16. There, with an alarm system, three private phone lines, three-way combination safes and war-room charts for ongoing projects, Young, Hunt and Liddy could play spy at their will, supervised only by Egil Krogh, whose guidance was taken from Section One, the Hiss chapter, of the President's book, *Six Crises*—the obligatory reference manual for all those to whom the President entrusted security work.

The Plumbers' unit had a broad range of activities, for it was a facility that could be used by Colson as well as Ehrlichman; but none, by Presidential directive, was more important than the undoing of Daniel Ellsberg. A psychiatric profile of Ellsberg, composed by Hunt's former colleagues at the CIA, proved valueless. They needed more on Ellsberg—not only evidence for his approaching trial, but slander material which Colson could feed the press. By late August, Liddy and Hunt had flown to Los Angeles to survey the office of Ellsberg's psychiatrist, hoping to purloin, find or wheedle defamatory material from it. By Labor Day, Liddy and Hunt had recruited three Cuban hirelings to assist them and were ready (they had a penchant for break-ins on holiday weekends, as was evident in their first break-in at the Democratic headquarters Memorial Day weekend 1972). The Cubans jimmied open the locks; found nothing; bungled everything. If not insane, the mission was wildly extravagant and useless. If any evidence had turned up, it would have been, as any Justice Department lawyer might have told them, tainted evidence invalid in court. They had conscripted agents with ties to the CIA, thus implicating that agency without its knowledge. They had broken half a dozen laws at once by the entry—and gained nothing. When, finally, the results and methods were made known to John Ehrlichman, who had authorized "a covert operation," stipulating that it be "done under your assurance that it is not traceable," he was dismayed. And shortly thereafter the White House special unit was, at least in name, disbanded. But the personnel were still there, for use as the underground wished.

The atmospherics of the fall of 1971 are probably more important than the way events followed one another, for by the fall of 1971 it becomes impossible to describe events in sequence. They were happening over a broad spectrum of underground activity, with many competitive players vying in their ambitions, all suspicious of one another, each more royalist than the king and infinitely nasty. Haldeman, Higby, Ehrlichman were all taping their own phone conversations with unsuspecting callers, and Colson had plugged an IBM recorder to his phone. Some at the White House, like Finch, suspected that they, too, were being tapped for leaks that might be pinned on them. At one point, briefly, the White House experimented with a video-telephone system so that people might watch each other's faces as they talked on the phone—but that was shortly canceled. And the President, too, unknown to any but Haldeman's personal staff and the Secret Service, had begun that winter of 1971 to tape-record all his own conversations.

There were too many circuses going on all at once in the same darkened hall to be patterned.

In one ring, John Dean and Jack Caulfield directed a tax-crackdown operation against political enemies, far more sinister and extensive than anything the departed Tom Huston had envisaged. It ran from an attempt to put a tax bite on off-beat producers Emile De Antonio and Daniel Talbot, who had made a satirical anti-Nixon film in New York, all the way to a tax probe of the august Brookings Institution, whose staff not only hated Nixon, but infuriated the administration because of the massive intellectual resources it could train on him as target. The tax operation embraced an effort to help the Reverend Billy Graham and John Wayne (both outstanding public friends of the President) with their income-tax problems, and also an effort to get the once-friendly but now hostile Los Angeles *Times*. The

Long Island *Newsday,* a subsidiary of the Times Mirror company which also publishes the Los Angeles *Times,* had printed an investigation of the finances of the President's closest friend, Bebe Rebozo. Thus, in the fall of 1971, after an investigation by Jack Caulfield, Dean sought to find out whether the anti-trust division of the Justice Department might crack down on the Los Angeles *Times.* The Justice Department reported there were no grounds for suit. The *Times* had supported Richard Nixon in every election from 1946 to 1968, and was to call for his re-election in 1972; but Dean had been a child when the Los Angeles *Times* launched Nixon's career, and Nixon had now turned against the Chandler family. If the Justice Department could not, or would not, crack down on the Los Angeles *Times,* Dean could at least try to get the reporter who had written the story—*Newsday*'s Robert W. Greene; and Caulfield was authorized to send an anonymous letter to the tax authorities suggesting a check of Greene's tax returns and triggering an audit of the reporter.

Use of the tax threat was not simply an initiative of the daring young men of the underground showing off their *machismo* to each other. It was policy that came from the top. Later, John Ehrlichman decided that getting Lawrence O'Brien, Democratic National Chairman, in whose former White House office Ehrlichman now sat, was a political priority and the income-tax people were the ones to get him. When they failed to do so, Ehrlichman told then Commissioner of Internal Revenue Johnnie M. Walters, according to Walters' recollection, "I'm goddam tired of your foot-dragging tactics." Ehrlichman himself, in executive testimony before the Ervin Committee, recalled the incident more clearly: "I wanted them to turn up something and send him to jail before the election and unfortunately it didn't materialize."

There was yet another circuit that collected enemies' names. Every President, from George Washington to Lyndon Johnson, has had his list of personal peeves. Lyndon Johnson's peeves were collected vaguely in an "anathema list," limited to cultural and intellectual figures who were opposed to the Vietnam War. The managerial men of the Nixon administration made the procedure much more efficient and, in its sweep, terrifying. The circuit of contributions to the enemies list had started in Charles Colson's office, next door to the President's in the EOB, in May or June of 1971, probably out of his preoccupation with bloc politics. In Colson's effort to make sure that "our" labor leaders, not "their" labor leaders, that "our" blacks, not "their" blacks, were invited to symbolic social functions at the White House, Colson had been compiling an adversary list. By August, 1971, the list had been institutionalized by John Dean. "This memorandum," he wrote in an early broadside, "addresses the matter of how we can maximize the fact of our incumbency in dealing with persons known to be active in their opposition to our Administration. Stated a bit more bluntly—how we can use the available federal machinery to screw our political enemies." Dean circulated an original Colson list; other members of the underground checked off the prime enemies; and all began to contribute new names as if each name earned them a Brownie point. The total list came to over 300, the prime list to 20, in no recognizable order except that beginning with Picker, Arnold and Barkan, Alexander and ending with McGrory, Mary, it was largely a list of hostile journalists and contributors to Democratic candidates. Nor was it an idle list to be frustrated by the bureaucracy; it had the force of a Nixon-administration "action-memo."

For example, number seventeen on the list was CBS correspondent Daniel Schorr. Dean had circulated his "screw our enemies" memorandum on August 16th. On August 17th, the next day, the President made a speech to a Catholic gathering in New York promising that aid to parochial schools was on the way. The day following, August 18th, Schorr reported that no such program of aid to Catholic schools was in the works and commented on air, "We can only assume the President's statement was for political or rhetorical effect." The day following that, the 19th, the President, while flying over Wyoming en route to California, learned of and was infuriated by Schorr's remarks. Haldeman communicated the President's wrath to his aide, Lawrence Higby, and Higby, from the plane, telephoned J. Edgar Hoover demanding a complete background check on Schorr. By the next morning, an FBI agent was at Schorr's office at CBS, another was calling CBS News President Richard Salant at his home in Connecticut, and other agents, ranging from the American Embassy in Bonn to agents in Baltimore, St. Louis and Virginia, were off the mark, interviewing twenty-five of Schorr's friends, relatives and employers in seven hours. The public pretext of the investigation was that the government was considering Schorr for a job. There was no such job. It was simply the underground pressing buttons on the apparatus to get the man whom the President, in one of his transcribed conversations, described as "that son-of-a-bitch Schorr."

As the election of 1972 approached over the horizon of 1971, one can sense from the documentation the gathering of all the elements of the King's Row underground for that effort—and the addition of more. Jeb Magruder had now moved catercorner across the street, to 1701 Pennsylvania Avenue—to CREEP, the Committee for the Re-Election of the President. He had arrived there at the beginning of May, 1971, as Deputy Director to hold unsteady and uncertain leadership until John Mitchell would replace him in 1972. Magruder, on his way up as usual, with a pay raise of several thousand dollars to $38,500 and a large blue chauffeured limousine at his command, was the joint choice of Bob Haldeman and John Mitchell. Magruder had been around the White House underground long enough to know the rules by which they played the game, and was familiar with most of the circuits. He had also sat around Herb Klein's office while that veteran of many campaigns talked of the past—and of the dirty tricks the Democrats had played on the Nixon campaign in 1960, the organized jeering, the public-address systems cut when Nixon rose to speak in Michigan, the rotten eggs thrown at Nixon in Ohio. What message of experience Magruder took away from his easy-going mentor is impossible to weigh. But the administration, as Magruder knew well, would expect him to interpret imaginatively the budget item marked "campaign intelligence" in his new office.

Every political campaign that this writer has ever covered has had a budget item, under whatever rubric used for decency, which was devoted to campaign intelligence. Never, however, has campaign intelligence reached as far as Jeb Magruder was willing to take it in his direction of CREEP. In the secret war room of CREEP, across the street from headquarters at 1701 Pennsylvania Avenue, hung a sign with the legend: "WINNING IN POLITICS ISN'T EVERYTHING, IT'S THE ONLY THING." Magruder had hired a director of youth operations, Kenneth Rietz, three months after his own appointment—Rietz was to operate youth spies on campuses. Magruder had brought with him from Herbert Klein's office a deputy, Bart Porter. Porter would be the recipient and coordinator of campaign intelligence from Rietz. The White House was constantly demanding more information on Democratic plans. A spy in Muskie's headquarters was needed, and Ken Rietz reported back that for $1,000 a month a chauffeur could be planted as a volunteer driver there; the "volunteer" was a retired taxi driver who also purloined Muskie campaign documents. The operation—code-named Sedan Chair—amounted to little, was paid for out of petty cash by Bart Porter, and was liquidated in three months. Espionage on Hubert Humphrey's campaign was needed. Thus, another spy operation—Sedan Chair II, costing $6,000, for a young Kentucky detective who volunteered at Humphrey's Philadelphia headquarters and quickly rose to be second in command there. In the Far West, George Wallace was threatening to split the right-wing vote in California. Thus, a $10,000 grant to a dissident Wallacite for a clandestine keep-Wallace-off-the-ballot effort. And more, and more. The White House was always informed via Gordon Strachan, once Magruder's deputy in Herb Klein's office but now promoted to minor responsibility in Haldeman's office. Strachan's function was to know what was going on at the Committee, where those who saw him taking notes in meetings referred to him as "Haldeman's spy."

In the underground, it is impossible even now, and probably will be forever, to catalogue the shifting actions of all the platoon lieutenants pursuing their dark and sometimes clashing ends. Caulfield, for example, seeing the action building, sensing the swelling of the campaign purse across the street at 1701, wanted to set up a spin-off, an independent detective agency which he himself would head, contracting for espionage and dirty work. "Project Sandwedge," as he outlined it, would cost $511,000 in order to set up offices in Chicago, New York and Washington. Caulfield, as so often before in his striving, was to be disappointed. Offered instead a post as aide with John Mitchell—which he hoped might make him Mitchell's personal deputy—Caulfield discovered, sadly, that he was expected to be a pistol-packing bodyguard, not the confidant and intelligence master for the about-to-become-chairman of the campaign.

There were yet other operations, both sinister and vulgar, of which perhaps the most frivolous was the Chapin-Segretti "dirty tricks" operation, authorized directly by Haldeman from the White House. Dirty tricks are as old as American campaigning, as old, indeed, as electoral politics, dating back to republican Rome. But they had been elevated to a minor dark art by another graduate of a Southern California university, the celebrated Democratic prankster Dick Tuck, a political wit who had specialized for twelve years in plaguing and pin-pricking Richard Nixon's campaigns. But the art was now degraded to buffoonery by its freshly recruited leader, Donald Segretti (hired by his USC classmate Dwight Chapin), who had no experience in politics, a thirty-year-old man of outstanding naïveté and stupidity. Segretti was the kind of man who, coming into a strange city (like Tampa, Florida), would simply telephone local Republican headquarters and ask the anonymous answering voice on the phone (as he did) to recommend a trustworthy individual to do "part-time work" in his secret enterprise.

So much was going on, so confusingly and in such erratically inter-linked compartments, that any superior management man would have been outraged. But the suspicious White House ran by compartments. Bob Haldeman had passed the responsibility for overall campaign intelligence to John Dean. John Dean knew nothing of politics to begin with, had never before been active in a campaign; and by now the distinction in his mind between the illegalities of national security and the practice of American politics had been lost. Thus, wholly ignorant of what might happen, John Dean in December of 1971 inserted the name of G. Gordon Liddy into the political campaign—and what happened thereafter was like the burning of a slow fuse that would eventually explode everything.

John Dean had met Gordon Liddy when Liddy worked as a political appointee at Treasury and Dean himself at the

Department of Justice; he had become more familiar with Liddy as a member of the Plumbers' unit in the White House; and when that unit was disbanded at the end of 1971, Dean had suggested Liddy as intelligence chief to Jeb Magruder. Magruder, complaisant as always, accepted this new chief secret agent aboard his team at CREEP with the title of General Counsel. Once aboard, Liddy was soon joined, at Colson's suggestion, by his imaginative partner in the Plumbers' group, E. Howard Hunt. And together the two went about putting together the most ambitious espionage apparatus ever fielded by any American political party except the Communists.

By the end of December, all intelligence units financed by CREEP—Sedan Chair I, Sedan Chair II, the Rietz operation—were taken out of the hands of young Bart Porter and assigned to Liddy. By January the clumsiness of the Segretti dirty-tricks team in the field was causing backfire from Republican leaders gearing up for primaries in states like New Hampshire and Wisconsin. What was going on? they asked Magruder. On inquiry, Magruder learned from the White House that his old friend Chapin was directing Donald Segretti in a dirty operation in the field that rivaled his own; Magruder insisted that the Segretti operation be assigned to Liddy and Hunt for coordination.

Whatever had gone on before Januray was a mixture of illegality, absurdity, national security, malice and stupidity. But what followed at the end of January, 1972, was an outrage: the open suggestion to the Attorney General of the United States to violate the laws and the Constitution—and his tolerance of that suggestion.

Ultimately, the Judiciary Committee of the House of Representatives was to charge that the President "had violated his constitutional oath 'to take care that the laws be faithfully executed.'" But the man on whom, in first instance, this burden falls is the President's Attorney General; he is required by duty not only to execute those laws, but to be aware, to investigate if he believes others conspire to break the law—and to convict them. Not so John Mitchell. Both good and mean men in the Nixon administration later examined their consciences as to what they might have done to search out and frustrate the crime net that had been building for so long in their midst. But the most precise and clear responsibility came first to John Mitchell on January 27th, 1972, while his President was preparing to fly to Peking to make peace with China. Whether the matter of that day seemed serious or not, John Mitchell chose to ignore it—he had learned in the campaign of 1968 not to bother Richard Nixon with detail. Mitchell was about to become campaign chief again for 1972. But he was still Attorney General, bound by oath as was the President, when he received his visitors that morning in the highest office of the law.

The office of the Attorney General, with its imperial waiting room, is one of the grander offices of Cabinet members, more so than that of Secretary of State or Secretary of Defense, as grand as the ornate office where once sat the Postmasters General of the U.S.A. And on the frieze of the building that houses it runs the legend, "NO FREE GOVERNMENT CAN SURVIVE THAT IS NOT BASED ON THE SUPREMACY OF LAW."

There, at 4:00 on the afternoon of January 27th, 1972, arrived Jeb Magruder, John Dean and G. Gordon Liddy. Mr. Liddy can be described in no other terms except as a gun-loving psychotic; an ex-FBI agent, a former local prosecutor in Dutchess County, New York, a member of New York's Conservative Party, he was a man of violence, a hater, a frightener of children, a histrionic who once fired a gun in a courtroom to stress his point, a toughie who had once demonstrated his strange self-control by holding his hand over flame and burning it to show his ability to withstand pain. His warped sense of patriotism caused him to see enemies everywhere—Communists, subversives, liberals, students, rioters, Democrats alike. By now he had pulled together the espionage activities of both the Chapin-Segretti and Magruder teams, and had designed a million-dollar plan for clandestine campaign activities.

Spreading his charts on an easel before the Attorney General, Gordon Liddy outlined his fancies—kidnapping suspected radical demonstrators at the Republican convention, then scheduled for San Diego, and hijacking them to Mexico; wire-tapping Democrats at their headquarters in Washington and at their convention in Miami; compromising Democratic delegates to that convention by luring them aboard yachts where they might be seduced by "high-class call girls." The Attorney General averred that that was not what he had in mind, and furthermore the price was too high; Liddy should redraw his plans more modestly.

The trio was back again a week later, on February 4th, and Liddy had reduced his plans to more modest proportions. But again the Attorney General demurred—too expensive, too risky.

There followed a third session almost two months later, on March 30th, 1972, at a villa which Bebe Rebozo had rented for Mitchell at Key Biscayne. Absent now were John Dean and Gordon Liddy, present were Jeb Magruder and his office *alter ego*, Fred LaRue, a wealthy Mississippi oil man and a Republican pioneer in Southern politics.

There are various views of John Mitchell at this twilight moment of his career. He had resigned as Attorney General on February 15th and wanted rest before he took up fulltime direction of CREEP on April 13th. He had been, in his vigor in New York, a severe and effective lawyer with the hard-bitten quality that impresses Richard Nixon. But his marriage had been going sour; his second wife, Martha, who saw herself as a Southern belle of the old school, had been making his personal life an agony for years, and she grew worse in Washington. There, as Mrs. Attorney General and one of the *grandes dames* who practice Cabinetry, her ego had grown, as had her eccentricities. John Mitchell was drinking more, too. For a full month he had suffered through Senate committee hearings on the International Telephone and Telegraph affair. That rogue corporation had recently offered $400,000 to subsidize the Republican convention in San Diego; but the summer before, ITT had eagerly accepted a proposal of John Mitchell's Department of Justice offering to settle out of court three anti-trust cases against them. Senators wanted to know whether the ITT money was a flat-out payoff to the Republican Party for favors delivered. John Mitchell's honor was in question and the headlines stabbed him each day. His hands quivered; his friends were saying he was strung out, over the hill. He had gone to Key Biscayne to rest and relax and bleach out the nerve strain in the sun. But all winter, decisions had been piling up in Jeb Magruder's office in the planning of the campaign, decisions at every level which he, as deputy, had to clear with Mitchell.

Magruder and LaRue arrived in Key Biscayne with some thirty action memos or decision papers, and all morning on March 30th the three shuffled papers, initialing decisions for Magruder to take back to Washington.

The last paper was the third revised Liddy proposal for campaign intelligence. They paused before that one for roast-beef sandwiches and beer, and then examined it. None was enthusiastic, but the proposal had been before them now for two months; the White House was pressing for a massive intelligence screening of Democratic rivals; Liddy was frustrated and growing angry.

"We discussed the proposal for ten minutes or so," writes Magruder, "and all of us expressed doubts about it. We feared that it might be a waste of money, and also that it might be dangerous. 'How do we know that these guys know what they're doing?' Mitchell asked once. . . . Mitchell, as we talked, scribbled on the paper Liddy had prepared, which listed the amount of money he wanted, and the number of men and types of equipment he'd need. Finally, Mitchell told me that he approved the plan, but that Liddy should receive only $250,000. We discussed the targets of the wiretapping program, and it was agreed that Liddy should go ahead with the wiretapping of Larry O'Brien's office at the Watergate, then we'd see about other possible targets."

Mitchell had approved many wire-taps in the previous four years in the name of national security and in his role of Attorney General. He had learned about political espionage in the campaign of 1968. And, thus, a next step, though larger than any before, seemed small and easy to take. Now the once-chief of law of the United States, its former Attorney General, was authorizing breach of the law by G. Gordon Liddy and E. Howard Hunt and those they might recruit. If they succeeded, the laws of the United States would become pliable as putty for as long as the Nixon administration held any authority over the country.

What followed happened swiftly. Within a week, Liddy had received $83,000 in cash from the Finance Committee to Re-Elect the President. He had begun the purchase of equipment for his clandestine platoon; he had targeted the McGovern headquarters for penetration; tried, failed, shot out the streetlight in front of the headquarters the night of that adventure in a moment of frustration. The Sedan Chair penetrations of Muskie and Humphrey continued; so, too, did the amateur operation of Donald Segretti; and Liddy himself from a safe distance captained the first wire-tapping of Democratic headquarters on Memorial Day weekend 1972.

The first wire-tapping was, as so much else in the bungling operations of the underground, a fiasco. The tap on O'Brien's phone failed to work; the second tap had been misplaced on the phone of another headquarters functionary, from which the tappers could gather information on the social life of his secretary, but nothing of any political importance. Mitchell was exasperated by the nonsense yielded by so risky an operation. Liddy must do better. And thus, on the night of June 16–17th, the second break-in—and disaster.

The elements of stupidity that went into this second break-in defy any rational standards even of purposeful malice. The equipment used was cheap; the techniques employed would have appalled the CIA, the Mafia, the New York Police Department or the KGB. Spring locks were taped horizontally across tongue latches, not vertically so as to be inconspicuous. Having been stripped once by a routine guard inspection in the night, the latch-tapes were reinstalled in exactly the same conspicuous horizontal way, thus causing the guard to summon police. Not even the most primitive kind of disintermediation, the use *only* of outside personnel, was employed—the chief wire man being James McCord, the security chief of CREEP, who was himself present at the break-in. No cut-off between McCord and Hunt/Liddy was set up. Identification of the participants, if caught, was assured by their papers and notes. The cash they carried, in $100 bills, had come through the Committee to Re-Elect out of a batch of $114,000 from a Miami bank which, by law, had to record the serial numbers, and so the bills were easily traceable back to the Committee. And the political thinking was appalling—no secret of any value could be found in the Democratic National Committee except the size of its debts; whatever O'Brien, the National Chairman, had to say he had said over and over again in print, and a good clipping service would have provided it all at thirty cents a clipping. Finally, the perspective of real politics outside made the risk frivolous. Nixon had just returned from Moscow and a peace-making triumph; the Democrats had just torn their party apart in California; George Wallace had been eliminated from the campaign; peace, prosperity, domestic tranquillity all were there to bring Americans to vote for Richard Nixon. Yet those involved were still, in their ambitions, pressing on.

The disaster had been building since the spring of 1969, working its way up from the dark places, where the underground was poisoning politics, to the desk of the former Attorney General himself. And the initiating detonation happened in fifteen minutes.

The law-and-order thrust of the Nixon administration had made Washington its target city for cleaning the streets of muggers and terror. A strengthened Washington police force was reducing the incidents of assault, violence, thuggery, month by month with extended patrolling, faster response to cries for help. With the cry for help from Frank Wills, the black custodian of Watergate, at 2:00 in the morning, the new, effective patrol system rushed a car to the scene; and on the sixth floor of the Watergate building found the bunglers in Larry O'Brien's office. "Don't shoot, we give up," is the way legend has the manner of their surrendering.

There was probably little doubt in the minds of any of the culprits that their superiors, stretching up through the Committee to Re-Elect to the former Attorney General, who was now about to become executive director of the sprawling underground, could surely arrange for their release and, after appropriate explanation, cover up the episode.

No shred of evidence nor any serious allegation made by anyone indicates that Richard Nixon was party to, or instigator of, the grand stupidity of the break-in. He had been too long in politics to run so great a risk for stakes so small; and besides he was too busy for such trivia. He had, of course, sanctioned the climate of lawlessness two years before with the Huston memo; but it is doubtful whether anyone except John Dean knew the full extent of what had happened since, in all its incriminating detail. But the President was now consciously about to sanction the cover-up. Yet it would be several days before he got to that point—days of utter, complete and farcical confusion.

When the Saturday-morning break-in came to light, first at the Washington Police Department, then at the White House, the masters of the underground were spread loose and unready across the country and around the world—John Dean in the Philippines, Mitchell and Magruder in California, Haldeman and the President in Key Biscayne, Ehrlichman in Washington.

It was the Los Angeles branch of the traveling underground that was alerted first—by a telephone call from Gordon Liddy to Jeb Magruder, then eating breakfast in the fashionable Polo Lounge of the Beverly Hills Hotel. A quick consultation between Mitchell, Magruder and Robert Mardian, former Assistant Attorney General, decided that the easiest first course was the quick fix; and Liddy was instructed to seek out Attorney General Richard Kleindienst (he found him at the Burning Tree golf club) and ask that the Department of Justice get CREEP's man, McCord, out of jail.

The affair was bad, they knew, but not quite bad enough to call off the great party to which they had been invited that night. Taft Schreiber, a vice-president of MCA, the entertainment conglomerate, and a rare Republican among the Hollywood overlords, was playing host to them in his mansion on the hills overlooking the basin of twinkling lights in the city below. Schreiber was doing his best for the Republican cause that evening and had invited some of Hollywood's most dazzling stars, promising Henry Kissinger as guest of honor. But Kissinger, on learning that Martha Mitchell had been invited too, had canceled out. He could not stand the lady. Instead of Kissinger, then, the White House had rushed out Mrs. Nixon herself and the party was a success. The stars—Charlton Heston, John Wayne, Jack Benny, Zsa Zsa Gabor—eyed the political celebrities, and the celebrities eyed the stars; the food was first-class, the entertainment superb. Except that, as Schreiber kept noticing, Magruder was preoccupied, darting in and out to the telephone, calling Washington. Hours before, in Washington, Kleindienst had driven Liddy out of the golf club locker room in anger for suggesting a police-court fix; and Step One of the prelude to cover-up had died at birth.

In Washington that Saturday afternoon, Secret Service agent Patrick Boggs telephoned John Ehrlichman to say that the police had found a notebook belonging to one of the burglars listing the name of White House employee E. Howard Hunt. Shortly thereafter Jack Caulfield checked in with the same news. "My God," Caulfield remembers Ehrlichman as saying, "you know, I can't believe it." Then said Erlichman, "Well, I guess I had better place a call to John Mitchell," and Caulfield agreed that would be appropriate. But almost immediately Erlichman realized this was a problem that had to go to the very top, and telephoned Ron Ziegler, who would pass the news to Haldeman and the President at Key Biscayne.

Sunday, as the news of the break-in first surfaced in the Washington *Post*, was a day of confusion, with long-distance calls crisscrossing the country—Haldeman calling Magruder and Mitchell in California; John Ehrlichman telephoning Colson and Haldeman; the party in California hastily arranging flights back to the capital; John Dean arriving sleep-starved from Manila in San Francisco, telephoning his office in Washington and learning what had happened, then being instructed to get back to Washington as fast as possible. And finally the President in Key Biscayne calling Colson. "He was so furious," said Colson later, "that he had thrown an ashtray across the room at Key Biscayne and thought it was the dumbest thing he had ever heard of and was just outraged over the fact that anybody even remotely connected with the campaign organization would have . . . anything to do with something like Watergate."

By Monday the high command of the underground was gathered in Washington (except for the President and Haldeman, who would return that evening). Confusion worsened. In the Monday circus, some of the grotesqueries began to clarify. The job at Watergate had been a Hunt-Liddy job; thus now, early in the morning, John Ehrlichman assigned John Dean to find out the nature and structure of the story. Recalling the buzz and confusion on King's Row, almost none of the participants have been able to keep their recollections straight: there was a frantic effort to locate Howard Hunt's files and prove that he had been dismissed from the White House on March 30th; calls from Howard Hunt to get his safe cleaned out; conferences buzzing through Ehrlichman's office, Colson's office, Dean's office; Dean's meeting in the street with Liddy and Liddy's paranoid remorse, expressed to Dean ("He told me that he was a soldier and would never talk. He said if anyone wished to shoot him on the street, he was ready"); Dean's effort to reach Kleindienst, who had line authority over the FBI, and Kleindienst's exasperated reply to Dean that "his superiors at the White House never understood that once an investigation begins, it runs its full course." Then in late afternoon the rifling of Hunt's safe in the Executive Office Building with its documents, its forgeries and slanders of John F. Kennedy, its pistol, its electronic equipment and its cash. And, after that, the evening gathering at John Mitchell's apartment in the Watergate—Mitchell, Magruder, Dean, LaRue, Mardian—all five aware, either instinctively or specifically, of just how deeply they were personally involved. And wondering how the matter might be covered up—for, as three out of the five of them knew as lawyers, they must go to jail if they concealed their knowledge. Yet —if they told the truth, might they be striking a body blow at their campaign to re-elect Richard Nixon?

It was not until Thursday that the managers of the underground had evolved a plan as Step Two in the prelude to the cover-up. Their problem was the FBI, and the FBI was moving fast. It was one of those engines of government, like the Army or the IRS, that had been wound up by law years ago to do its duty; it was doing the duty it had been trained to do; and had traced the burglars' banknotes directly to CREEP, which had converted checks at a Miami bank into cash that had been forwarded to Washington. No one could call off the FBI, even with friendly Pat Gray in charge, except the CIA. And no one could direct the CIA to do that except the President.

One must pause here to look at the President as he received news of the crisis—and examine again that strange duality of his personality, the evil and the good, the discipline and the instability, the planned purpose and the vengeful impulse.

Again and again, as one probed the men closest to the President at the end of his administration, when their own loyalties began to run thin, there would come this reference to that duality. One poked at Pat Buchanan, dedicated, loyal, honest—and after the best long answer he could give, one poked again with the same old question, "What went wrong?" And, in exasperation, he would burst out, "It runs to the President himself. There's a mean side to his nature you've never seen—I can't talk about it." Or even Ehrlichman, long after it was over, who loved the President, "There was another side to him, like the flat, dark side of the moon." Or, again, from another, "There was a chemistry between him and Haldeman, when they were alone together something happened that brought out the worst in both of them." Or from someone who had listened to the tapes, "You ought to hear his conversations with Chuck Colson—it was dirty-boy talk, like two little boys pulling wings off flies." Or from his former law partner Tom Evans, trying to reconstruct from the outside what had happened in Washington, "I can almost see and hear it—all of those people in one room, none of them wanting to play chicken, everyone trying to outdo the other in toughness." Or, finally, as Leonard Garment summed it up in the best analogy, "There were people around him who brought out in him and each other what I can only call a negative synergism—a set of negative qualities which, instead of canceling each other out, multiplied each other."

It is essential thus to recapture the sequence of events and the mood of Richard Nixon as he learned of the break-in and its impending uncovery. That sequence of events had massaged to afflatus what Henry Kissinger was later to tell friends was "the Walter Mitty streak" in Richard Nixon's character, that captivating iridescence he saw in any invitation to toughness.

For six weeks prior to the break-in, Nixon had been accepting such invitations to toughness and performing as the tough guy, gunslinger, riverboat gambler of global politics. On May 8th, 1972, he had faced an enemy offensive in Hanoi and had toughed that one out with a brilliant decision —mine Haiphong, if necessary challenge both China and

Russia at once in the gamble of war and peace. He had won that gamble. He had gone on, two weeks later, to Moscow—and toughed it out with Brezhnev and Kosygin. Though, as it turned out later, the Russians outbargained him on the giant wheat deal, he had wrung out of them a limited balance of missiles, bringing peace conspicuously closer.

And thus now, in the third week of June, after such immense and successful gambles on the world scene, there came to him this apparently trivial thing—this break-in at the Democratic headquarters. Whether he learned the full details on the 20th, in a first conversation with Bob Haldeman, of which eighteen and a half minutes were deliberately erased from the tape, or whether he learned only on June 23rd of his danger from an FBI investigation is immaterial. His mood was of that inner grandeur which caused him to keep in his private cubicle off the Oval Office the only photograph hung there—of himself and Churchill, the great world statesmen. And the episode that Haldeman was relating to him shortly after 10:00 that morning of June 23rd ran back to the kindergarten of his political life in California, to the old roughhouse style of cut-and-slash—stupid, certainly; embarrassing, definitely. But important?

In the presence of Haldeman, and by the transcript of the conversation, it was apparent that the President had no sense of lawlessness or law about this matter. The chemistry between them was tough, managerial, ruthless. "It was Haldeman and him in the room together," said Kissinger later. "If it had been Al Haig there, or myself, or someone else who might have asked a question about it, it would all have been different. He would have played to us."

The President now played to Haldeman. Haldeman had been told by Dean that Dean and John Mitchell had conferred and recommended that the CIA be called in to obstruct the FBI. A short interchange and then,

Haldeman: "And you seem to think the thing to do is get them [the FBI] to stop?"

The President: "Right, fine."

Haldeman: "They say the only way to do that is from White House instructions. And it's got to be Helms [CIA chief] and to ah . . . Walters. . . . And the proposal would be that Ehrlichman and I call them in, and say, ah—."

The President: "All right, fine. . . . well, we protected Helms from one hell of a lot of things."

After the big gambles of war and peace, this decision was not even a dice throw; it was button-pushing, and with his streak of *machismo* surfacing against the Democrats, negligible adversaries compared to those he had been facing, he went on:

"Play it tough. That's the way they play it and that's the way we are going to play it."

With that to a second matter—John Mitchell.

The President: ". . . Well, what the hell—did Mitchell know about this?"

Haldeman: "I think so. I don't think he knew the details, but I think he knew."

Mitchell was a good friend. Mitchell was involved. But Mitchell was also manager of the campaign. Mitchell had to be protected, out of both loyalty and political need. The critical exchange could not have taken more than five minutes, with no pause for that distinction between trick and crime, mistake and sin, between politics and government.

And with that quick exchange the President was impeachable.

Within those five minutes he had crossed the line of the law, like so many of his lieutenants, without quite realizing what he was doing, and would be forever unable to retrace his steps. It was all there in those five minutes. Not purposeful crime, but worse—the thoughtless abuse of power. The habit, the atmosphere, the chemistry of his White House had all been urging him on to this casual moment of intoxication with power.

This was not a wayward thought, nor even a heresy as the Huston memorandum had been. It was a directive, an act —precise, tiny, easy. He had struggled so hard to establish control over the government and its resistant bureaucracy, and all the pieces were in place. He had replaced the late autonomous J. Edgar Hoover with a personal loyalist—L. Patrick Gray, his campaign office-manager in the campaign of 1960. The present Attorney General was Richard Kleindienst, his convention delegate manager in 1968. His old friend Lieutenant General Vernon Walters had been installed as deputy director of the CIA, to watch and control its chief, Richard Helms. The President controlled it all, as he had sought so long to do—what could go wrong?

And within five days the scheme had come to naught.

Within hours, on the afternoon of June 23rd, Haldeman had put the Dean-Mitchell plan into execution. By half past two the eager-to-please Walters was in the office of L. Patrick Gray, urging suspension of the investigation until he could find out whether it would lay bare national-security secrets if pressed further. And for the next three days Walters, Helms and the CIA struggled with the facts and their consciences.

Walters' memos to himself, written for his files on June 29th, trace the course of the CIA thinking. Walters had tried on June 23rd to cooperate on the investigation with Gray, who described it to him as "a most awkward matter to come up during an election year." By June 26th, when young John Dean, thirty-three, summoned veteran Vernon Walters (Lieutenant General, fifty-five) to his office on King's Row, Walters could report that he "was quite sure that the Agency was not in any way involved [in the break-in] and I knew that the Director [Helms] wished to distance himself and the Agency from the matter. . . . I said that I was sure that none of the suspects had been on the Agency payroll for the last two years." On June 27th, Dean summoned Walters again to his office and Walters, repeating the agency's refusal to help a cover-up, said the risks were simply too great. "Involving the Agency," he said, "would transform what was now a medium-sized conventional explosive into a multi-megaton explosion and simply was not worth the risk for all concerned." Dean was now trying to get money from the CIA's unchecked funds to protect and hush the defendants, and on June 28th, the next morning, he again summoned Walters to his office. This time Walters laid it on the line. "I repeated that as Deputy Director I had no independent authority. . . . The idea that I could act independently was a delusion. . . . I said that I realized he had a tough problem, but if there were Agency involvement, it could be only at Presidential directive and the political risks that were concomitant appeared to me to be unacceptable."

And so the underground was on its own—no help from the CIA.

By Wednesday, June 28th, this much was clear: John Mitchell, John Dean and Jeb Magruder were all involved in crime. Bob Haldeman, John Ehrlichman and at least half a dozen others were tainted by knowledge of the crime, and thus conspirators after the fact. And, so, too, was the President of the United States, who wanted the purging of the matter postponed until after the election. Further, they would have no help from the CIA, no help from the FBI, no help from the Department of Justice, no help from any organ of the bureaucracy. All of whom they must now scheme to outwit.

The scheme that evolved on this Wednesday, June 28th, was both mad and amateurish. To begin with, John Mitchell would leave the chairmanship of the Committee to Re-Elect (that had been decreed over the weekend at the White House). But Magruder would stay—he was too weak, or too vulnerable, or too hot to dump. But whether in office or not, Dean, Mitchell, Magruder and LaRue would become, in effect, the general staff of the grand cover-up for the next six months. And the new cover-up would proceed on two levels at once—first, bribery; and, second, perjury.

The payoff may not have seemed like bribery when it began, the next morning; and certainly the Mafia or one of the great multi-national corporations that deal in international bribery would have handled the matter better. On the afternoon of the 28th, after a meeting at Mitchell's office, and with the approval of Haldeman and Ehrlichman, Dean had urgently telephoned Herbert Kalmbach in Los Angeles to fly to Washington. Kalmbach, catching the Los Angeles Red Eye express flight, arrived in the capital for breakfast, met Dean in Lafayette Park and received his assignment to raise cash to pay legal and support costs of the defendants. By midday Kalmbach had passed the message to Maurice Stans, who arrived in the Statler Hilton Hotel with a briefcase filled with $75,100 in $100 bills. By the following day, Tom Ulasewicz, general handyman of dirty work, had arrived in Washington to pick up the greenbacks, pack them in a laundry bag and begin a misadventure of nine days, of false rendezvous, of missed telephone calls, of bungled signals trying to deliver cash to the defendants and their law-yers.

It was to go on that way for nearly three months—Kalm-bach raising cash either from CREEP or from corporate contacts ($75,000 from the chairman of the Northrop Cor-poration alone), delivering to Ulasewicz, Ulasewicz deliver-ing to designated recipients. Cover-up was costly and re-quired exertion: $40,000 delivered by Kalmbach, after a flight to New York, to Ulasewicz at the fashionable Regen-cy Hotel on Park Avenue. Another $28,900 for delivery at the Statler Hilton in Washington. The Northrop chairman's $75,000 delivered at the Airporter Inn near the Orange County, California, airport. A last delivery on September 18th or 19th—and a final reconciliation of accounts in John Dean's office on the 21st. By this time, with some $220,000 of cash moved, both Ulasewicz and Kalmbach had had enough of it.

They had traveled, with a bit more consciousness of their course than the others, on the same glide path across the boundaries of the law: from an impulse of compassion and comradeship to a situation where, clearly, they were break-ing laws. Kalmbach, a lawyer, and Ulasewicz, a veteran cop, could recognize blackmail when it was rubbed into them—payments not only for defense lawyers, but pay-ments requested for Mrs. Liddy's psychiatrist, payments for Mrs. Hunt, payments to meet extravagant and extortionate demands. But by September 19th, when they made their last delivery and quit, the first hazard, at least, had been capped—the culprits caught at Watergate had all been in-dicted and the indictments were safely contained: the four hired agents, plus Messrs. Hunt, Liddy and James McCord. Kalmbach and Ulasewicz were, for the moment, safely out of it; what further cash was needed must come out of Bob Haldeman's secret fund of $350,000, which was delivered to Fred LaRue.

So, too, for the moment were Jeb Magruder and John Mitchell out of it. Perjury was their route. Their cover sto-ry had begun in the same week in June that the payoffs had begun, and was a more elaborate operation. The object was simple: to cut off the link of criminality at Hunt and Liddy, before it got to Magruder, whence it would inevitably move to Mitchell. The fiction was that of course there was a budget in CREEP's campaign for intelligence operations; large sums of money had indeed been used. But the intelligence operation had been designed for checking out the safety of all the "surrogates" who would be traveling on troubled campuses and in troubled cities; and Gordon Liddy's chief assignment had been to check out the safety and security of San Diego as a convention site, on which site the President himself had insisted because it was a short and convenient helicopter ride from his ocean-front estate of San Clemente only sixty miles away. According to this story, what more Gordon Liddy and Howard Hunt might have done, including the break-in at Democratic national headquarters, had been deplorable, an excess of zeal, unauthorized, illegal, regrettable. This story—to be told to the grand jury of the District of Columbia—was rehearsed again and again. First in John Mitchell's private law offices at 1701 Pennsylvania Avenue; then, again, in John Dean's office in the Executive Office Building, with Dean firing questions at Magruder, playing the role of tough prosecutor while Magruder played the role of clean-cut, innocent young manager betrayed by underlings' zeal. The President's chief legal counsel, Dean, and the government's former Attorney General directed, and Magruder rehearsed, a *danse macabre* to make meaningless the law.

There is an unreality to the summer cover-up—as if a handful of men with nominal authority could outwit the vast outside reality of the American system: the offices of the prosecutors, the hidden loyal underground of civil servants, the remorseless grinding responsibility of courts, the curiosity and appetite of the press. It was as if, intoxicated by the power of the White House, they truly believed that they could circumvent what it had taken 200 years of American civilization to build. They had been, after all, responsible only for a small crime. Nixon's election victory could not have been jeopardized by their confession or prosecution. They could not imagine that to use the powers of office to erase the crime would wipe out all that Nixon had really accomplished, and would bring the country to its first real Constitutional crisis since the Civil War.

August and September passed smoothly for the conspirators. John Dean, even while he rehearsed and manipulated Jeb Magruder, was reporting upward to Ehrlichman and thus, via Ehrlichman, to the President, that the scandal had not touched the White House. The President was pleased. On September 15th, after both Mitchell and Magruder had already perjured themselves to the grand jury, John Dean met the President face to face and was congratulated on his handling of the matter. Dean lied to the President as he told the story, blandly, outrageously, unconscionably. But the indictments had come down from the grand jury that day precisely as planned: the small fry were summoned for trial, and Mitchell and Magruder were home free; and the trial would not take place until January, after the election was safely over.

After thanking Dean for his performance, the President reviewed the prospects. "They should just . . . behave," he said of his troops at CREEP, "and recognize this . . . is war. . . . I wouldn't want to be in Edward Bennet Williams' position after this election. . . . Because afterwards . . . that is a guy we've got to ruin. . . . You want to remember, too, he's an attorney for the Washington *Post.* . . . We are going to fix the son of a bitch." He continued with his preview of the future after victory, "I want the most comprehensive notes on all of those that have tried to do us in. . . . They are asking for it and they are going to get it. . . . We have not used the power in this first four years, as you know. We have never used it. We haven't used the Bureau and we haven't used the Justice Department, but things are going to change now."

All seemed clear for the President and his men to consider what they would do with their country when the victory that was visibly approaching would give them the power of complete control.

7

VICTORY 1972:
DESIGN FOR CONTROL

All election landslides have had an intoxicating effect on Presidents. The word "mandate" is immediately slapped on the tally, and the President, a man whose ego is normally larger than other human beings', can, momentarily, be swept to a perception of himself as an instrument of destiny.

Few Presidents have been able to cope with the psychological after-effect of a landslide—the delusion of omnipotence. Roosevelt in 1936 (victory by a 60.8 percent, 11,000,000-vote landslide) went on nearly to wreck his second administration by his proposal to pack the Supreme Court. Lyndon Johnson (61 percent, 16,000,000-vote landslide) went on in 1964 to plunge the nation simultaneously into a social revolution, an unauthorized foreign war and an inflation that still, in 1975, rages uncontained. Richard Nixon (60.7 percent, or 18,000,000-vote margin) was suffering from similar intoxication the morning after his 1972 re-election—but an intoxication oddly sullen, quite different from the exuberance with which his predecessors had greeted their mandates.

The logic of his mind had been reaching for control of events for all four years of his first term; and had been frustrated except in foreign affairs. Now he had carried every state in the Union but one; his sweep almost defied analysis. Only the Roosevelt landslide of 1936 matched Nixon's in the stupefying geographic response to his call. His majorities ranged from the merely huge in the industrial North and East (in the high fifties or low sixties) to the enormous in the South (over 70 percent), peaking at 80 percent in Mississippi. Catholics had given him their majority as well as Protestants; blue-collars, farmers, businessmen all had voted for him. Congress, the press, even his own party bore him little good will—but the people, in every single region, had spoken for him and overwhelmed his adversaries. He was the nation's President. Thus, alone yet triumphant, he could envision control in his second term on a scale grander, and yet more personal, than any President had ever conceived before. He could envision a turning in domestic affairs—in housing, in race relations, in agriculture, in welfare, in tax structure, in house-cleaning of the obsolete—almost as far-reaching as the turning he had already achieved in foreign affairs. But it would be, nonetheless, a difficult task.

I had traveled with him the previous day, the day the people were voting, shaping the invisible landslide in the beautiful land that unrolled below his plane. I had spent half an hour talking with him and had been struck by the somber, almost emotionless mood in which he had discussed this violent shifting of political loyalties down below;[1] I felt I had caught him in a moment of weariness after a long week of final campaigning and a will-testing diplomatic confrontation in Vietnam. It turned out, however, not to have been a passing mood—for the next day, many others, much closer, would catch the same grim mood of the President who had won the largest vote of confidence ever given by the American people.

Nixon had spent most of election evening alone, in the Lincoln Room on the second floor of the White House, before the fireplace. The palace guard had separated into its parts—the first echelon of Haldeman and Ehrlichman upstairs in the long and gloomy corridor that runs through the second-floor living quarters. Downstairs in the White House lobby were the television sets and a vote-analysis center for those next closest; and two miles away at the Shoreham Hotel gathered the lesser staff, speechwriters, and public dignitaries of the Republican Party in the traditional jubilee reception of anticipated victory. Nixon had visited the jubilee, spoken on television to the nation, then come back to his Executive Office hideaway, where he ordered a snack from the White House mess and from one o'clock to three

[1] See Chapter One, "The Solitary Man," in Theodore H. White's *The Making of the President—1972* (New York: Atheneum, 1973).

o'clock in the morning talked with Charles Colson and Bob Haldeman about the meaning of his victory and what came next.

The next day, Nixon was up late and, after a visit from a dentist who replaced a crown which had broken as he ate dinner the previous night, met with the White House staff at 11:15 in the morning in the Roosevelt Room. He spoke briefly, referred to an account of Disraeli in a book he had been reading and insisted that the new term was not going to be just more of the same—that he was not an "exhausted volcano." He urged that they immediately report to Haldeman about their own plans—what their interests were, what jobs or projects they wanted to work on in the second term. The second administration would be an entirely new administration. When he left, Haldeman rose and required that everyone hand in immediately a *pro forma* resignation, along with a one-line suggestion of what each wanted to do next ("not a flowery one," said Haldeman; "if we need it, you can send a flowery one later"). Most listened disturbed. What was happening?

The President then walked to the Cabinet Room, where, as he entered, his Cabinet rose and burst into applause. Then he began to talk. Said one Cabinet member present, "There was this joyless, brooding quality as he talked, you almost had the impression he had lost. This was the biggest landslide ever, it was an occasion of joy or uplift. He thanked us for what we had done, and he began to brood. He'd been reading, he said, about Presidents in their second term, how they all go downhill. He wasn't about to go downhill. He'd studied American history, and he was looking ahead. There was this foreboding in the way he spoke. There was a vague reference about our submitting resignations, but it was so indirect. Then he went back to how he didn't want to go downhill. Then he left us and went out through the corner door to the Oval Office, and Haldeman chased after him. In about two minutes, Haldeman came back and stood in the corner and he said, 'I'm not entirely sure you people understood what the President said—when he said he wanted your resignations, *he meant he wanted your resignations.*' I was watching Volpe's expression and I could see Volpe was stunned. Volpe had knocked himself out in the campaign, talking two or three times a day for Nixon. He couldn't understand it. I couldn't."

What was happening?

What was happening had begun to happen vaguely in various minds at the White House from at least as far back as 1970, and with planned precision since September before the 1972 election.

What was planned was surgery on the government of the United States, the extension of the concept of executive control of government by the elected President from that of tradition to an entirely new political theory—an attempted change in the nature of the Presidency, almost, but not quite, amounting to a Constitutional change.

The President was about to streamline by fiat the entire Executive Branch of government, install within every department a personal agent of the White House staff to supervise it, create about himself a super-cabinet lodged in the Executive Office Building, officially remove traditional Cabinet members from access to him, and purge the bureaucracy until it became the unquestioning subordinate instrument of the White House policy center which he alone would direct.

So serious were the changes involved, and some of them so sound, that the episode might become forever after a benchmark in American political history. The American government as Richard Nixon had found it had, without a doubt, grown too cumbersome to cope with the tangles of the post-war world at home and abroad. Reorganization was necessary. Good thinking went into the new plan—and bad men. The ideas were fascinating—but the men involved, all too many of them, were dangerous to liberty.

Only a handful of people close to the President had worked on the ideas. I had caught only veiled references to the master plan before the election. Such a reference might come, say, in a conversation with Bob Finch when I would ask him what he'd been working on that day. There's the Richardson problem today, Finch would say. What's the Richardson problem? Well, that's the problem of what we do with Elliot. He's so good. He's got to move up. Where do we put him? State or Defense? And then Finch, so much more interested in government than in politics, would begin to talk about why the government had to be reorganized. It had to be structured by *function*, not by department, not by constituency, he said; there were eleven Cabinet-level departments and almost 200 bureaus, councils, commissions and agencies; you couldn't get government to work simply by bureaucratic reshuffling or reorganization. Each department, each agency had its own Congressional base, its committee with its chairman and his privileges, its supportive pressure group with its compulsions; and Congress was fixed in concrete. The national government had to function differently—to grasp and pull together the problems of today's America, fragmented and uncoordinated in the old bureaucracy.

I caught echoes from other conversations, but could not at first identify whether or how these ideas were reaching the President. Yet it became quite clear as October passed into November that the President himself was reaching for a new way to direct government. By the end of October his election was no longer in doubt—the issues had set the election and George McGovern (like Landon and Goldwater before) had joined debate on the issues so sharply, and so much on the wrong side of American emotion, that McGovern would lose. By the weekend before the election, at San Clemente, the President could all but ignore the campaign that was coming to an end; and on Sunday and Monday, he was preoccupied there with two major matters. One was the war in Vietnam, where the Hanoi regime was frustrating his design for peace. The second was the reorganization of the American government. All that weekend he talked of reorganization with Haldeman and Ehrlichman. On the flight back East on Election Day, he spent several hours in his private compartment talking reorganization with Finch, Ehrlichman, Haldeman; and by the weekend after his election, the outline of the Nixon plan was common conversation all through Washington's upper tier of journalists and civil servants.

The concept of how a President can govern America has increasingly perplexed all serious observers. There had been a first Hoover Commission on reorganization of government which reported in 1949. There had been a second Hoover Commission on reorganization, set up under Eisenhower, which reported in 1955; there had been an Ash

Commission in the early years of the Nixon administration for the same purpose. Many men and scholarly institutions had pondered the awkwardness of American government. But John Ehrlichman now, in December of '72, made more sense than anyone else: he had had a task force working for several months before the election, cross-clearing with the Department of Justice and the Office of Management and Budget on what had to be done, and what could be done without going to Congress to ask for new laws.

Four Cabinet officers, according to Ehrlichman's scheme, would be elevated above all others and named Assistants to the President, forming a super-cabinet, with offices in the Executive Office Building. These four master supervisors —in Economic Affairs, in Human Resources, in Natural Resources, in Community Development—would control all lines of access to the President, not only from Cabinet-rank departments, but also from all other agencies whose functions fell, by the nature of things, within their supervision. In addition, Henry Kissinger would preside over National Security, coordinating Defense and State. And then, finally, he, Ehrlichman, would give up the Domestic Council (no longer necessary under this scheme) and take over from Vice-President Agnew the hitherto meaningless Office of Intergovernmental Relations, which would now deal with governors and mayors of the country, giving them an entirely new direct channel through him to the President to express their needs.

"These people," said Ehrlichman of the name points in what he called a six-pointed Presidency, "will not be named by statute, but by designation, and will only keep the President informed." His own bent toward governmental decentralization ran with the President's phrasing of it at his second inaugural, "We have lived too long with the consequences of attempting to gather all power and responsibility in Washington"; and his own new office could bring about "a revolution in local government; we would give them the resources to decide on their own local priorities." Present government, thought Ehrlichman, had clogged the channels. You had problems today, he said, that no one was dealing with, like energy, because it cut across too many departmental and agency lines. Energy was a Presidential matter and top priority. Another problem was housing. A third was civil rights. A fourth was the budget. Too many people were involved in all these problems for the President to make clear decisions. "You can't have fifteen people coming together to give the President advice in a Cabinet session," said Ehrlichman. "They're all arguing with each other for their own interests and he gets confused. What he decides has to come to him in an orderly way."

A reporter could go from an Ehrlichman to a Pat Buchanan, and Buchanan, a much-learned person for one so young, with passions that have ripened into conviction, would speak of the grand plan on another level.

"Our fault in the first four years was that we never came to grips with government. There's been an absence of this relentless effort to penetrate the bureaucracy, to make it move. We've been a thin film of dust on a hardwood table; if we left now, we'd blow away. R.N. left it to the Cabinet officers to clean out the bureaucracy, and they didn't have the energy or the determination to do it when we got here. We've got to do more than just clean out the two thousand Schedule C's; you've got to move them out of Washington, you've got to shift them out of D.C. We have to get control before we reorganize them. We can't even trust our own phones, you never know when one of our phone calls is going to pop up in the Washington *Post*. It goes all the way back to the New Deal. Ike didn't even shake the bureaucracy when he ran the government. We've been getting this recalcitrance from the bureaucracy ever since we got here four years ago. The immediate thrust is to get control over the bureaucracy, and we've got to use the President's mandate in the next six months to get things going—we can't waste our mandate just reshuffling bureaus."

Control was still the word, all the way from top to bottom, as it had been in the beginning. Ronald Ziegler—whose function in government was transmitting authentically, or else stonewalling from the press, the thinking of the President—ran the reorganization plan through conversation this way:

"No government can be responsive to what the people want with all this bureaucratic crap in between. We're asking what was the original purpose of all this legislation, what structure did it set up to do what it wanted to do— and how did the original structure and purpose disintegrate in the bureaucracy? The President is going to clean out the bureaucracy, not by massive firings, but just enough to make it responsive. In two years, this President is going to have the government operating and responding. He's been approaching it for a long time and he feels that in the next term, 'There's no question that I'm going to put into effect exactly the way the government should operate. I'm going to structure this government in a way that will work.' These guys like George McGovern and Frank Mankiewicz read it wrong, because they let themselves be dominated by this town, not by the nation. So what if this town did think the President was a bigot? You can't call a man a bigot because he wants to talk to Catholics or invites hard-hats to the White House. We're the nation."

But the master plan had other features besides those of rational efficiency. None of those who put together the plan had a deep acquaintance with the simple controls of the Soviet Union, but their plan reflected similar thinking. The Council of Ministers which is the government of the Soviet Union does indeed govern. But the men who control that government are agents of the party Politburo. Politburo agents observe, check, report on personnel in every department; they recommend promotion and demotion on the basis of competence plus loyalty.

Now, as one put the names of the new master plan for Washington together, it began to appear somewhat akin to Politburo control. Constitutionally, legally, nothing would be changed; there would still be the Executive Branch, run by the President, with the statutory executive officers, Cabinet secretaries and agency heads required to testify before Congress; these would direct executive action in the bureaucracy. But in all of these executive agencies and independent bureaus there would eventually be installed a loyal White House personality, someone connected by direct pipeline to the White House central staff. Some of the names were first-class, men of social consciousness, sensitive, honest—like geologist John Whitaker, scheduled to move from John Ehrlichman's White House Domestic Council to the new branch of Natural Resources, where he would hold the titular slot of Under Secretary of the Interior; and Alexander Butterfield, who would go to the Federal Aviation Administration. But then came other names: Egil

Krogh would be White House man at the Department of Transportation; Jeb Magruder at the Department of Commerce; Ehrlichman's assistant Edward L. Morgan (who later pleaded guilty to back-dating documents connected with Nixon's tax returns) at the Treasury. And others.

Theoretically, much of the idea *did* make sense; government in Washington is smothered in paper and embalmed in regulations ("Washington today," said one official, "is a place where three hundred thousand people come to work every morning and, after they finish their coffee, they write a memo back to someone who wrote a memo to them yesterday"). Somewhere, somehow, new men are needed to slice through layers of fat to get at the problems. But all too many of the names in the new central surveillance net were from the White House underground, with the underground's code of ethics. Said one senior civil servant as he reflected on the scheme later, "Our system of government is really, truly, at the point of breakdown. The trouble is that Richard Nixon thought he could solve it by putting sons-of-bitches in command."

Eventually, the bureaucracy was to survive the new plan —both the best of the bureaucracy, resting on the sworn integrity of men in the Justice Department who eventually destroyed both administration and underground, and the fossilized worst, which would require some future President to make better use of his mandate than Richard Nixon had.

Yet, even as they survived through the months of November, December and January, the servants of the government winced as the palace guard surveyed them, one by one, putting each man's career to hazard as his merits were weighed.

The planned reorganization moved both swiftly and ruthlessly. Nixon was off for Key Biscayne with the privy staff on Wednesday after election and then off to Camp David, where he awaited the helicopter to bring his ministers, by what the press called "the Mount Sinai shuttle," to hear their fate on the mountain.

Some of the Cabinet secretaries had decided to get out as soon as they heard their resignations called for, some even earlier. Finch, theoretically senior White House Counsellor, had already decided to give up that post and return to California to resume his political career. Laird, Romney, Rogers of the Cabinet were all leaving of their own volition. But others were thrust out brutally—Volpe was given half an hour's notice to decide whether he would accept the ambassadorship to Italy or leave entirely. He accepted the embassy and, on inquiry later, learned that the Cabinet was being purged of people who "had a base of their own." But others waited for the helicopter to bring them to the architects of the new plan who, from Camp David, were designing the new structure.

Friday, November 17th, for example, the helicopter brought to Camp David the following: Weinberger, Shultz, Peterson. Caspar Weinberger, director of the Office of Management and Budget, learned he was to be moved, in a complex lateral shift, to Health-Education-Welfare, a good place for this thoughtful and genial man, where he would replace Elliot Richardson, now moving up to be Secretary of Defense. He, Weinberger, would in turn be replaced at Management and Budget by businessman Roy Ash. For George Shultz there was a promotion. He would now be not only Secretary of the Treasury, but also one of the four new special Assistants to the President, the economic czar who would gather together the threads of economic affairs for the President's decision.

For Peter G. Peterson, Secretary of Commerce, it was the knife. Peterson, as Assistant to the President for foreign economic policy in 1970 and 1971, had been given a corner office on King's Row. Having performed admirably, he had been promoted in 1972 to be Secretary of Commerce, whereafter he, like almost all Cabinet members, had found his access to the President cut off. His White House link to policy, after this nominal promotion, had become Henry Kissinger, and together they had worked out the interlocked economic-diplomatic parlay which made the Moscow meetings of 1972 a success. But Kissinger, as protector of personnel at the White House, could scarcely rival either Haldeman or Ehrlichman. Thus, then, Peterson, seated with the President at Camp David and expecting acknowledgment of service performed, heard the President begin in an extravagant burst of enthusiasm—about how much he, Peterson, had contributed to the success of the Soviet negotiations; how, in fact, he was a superb Secretary of

Commerce. And therefore—since this was to be the year of Europe, since Peterson understood both economics and foreign policy, Peterson would be leaving the Cabinet and would go to Brussels, Belgium, with the title of Super-Ambassador, to advise on how economic and foreign policy might be pulled together in Europe.

It took Peterson several days to realize his throat had been cut. He was no longer to be a Cabinet member—but what was the new job? He suggested in a memorandum that, since his job was to mesh economic and diplomatic planning, he ought to spend at least several months in the United States working out the strategy before being sent to implement it. Besides, he had five children and it was difficult to leave at once. His memorandum went to John Ehrlichman with the support of both Kissinger and Shultz; but within twenty-four hours Ehrlichman had turned it down; Peterson was to get out of Washington—now.

Peterson, in no sense naïve, was willing to leave, but wanted to know why, after superior service, his dismissal was so peremptory. Colson gave him the answers, as if reading them from a dossier the underground had compiled. Without any unfriendliness, quite candidly, Colson explained: first, Peterson had been going to parties at the home of Katharine Graham, the publisher of the Washington *Post;* not only that, he had even spent a weekend at her country home. Next—he had entertained a feeler from CBS, an approach made by the broadcasting system to learn whether he would like to be a candidate to succeed Dr. Frank Stanton as president of the network. Even though Peterson had turned away the approach, said Colson, it was unbelievable that a member of Nixon's Cabinet could be "cavorting" with unfriendly CBS. Third—the Petersons had been friendly with and seen too often consorting with liberal columnist Tom Braden and his wife, Joan. Thus the dossier. Peterson could only observe stubbornly that he did not feel it appropriate for him and Sally, his wife, to change their way of life or give up their friends. With that, Peterson was out, telling friends that, obviously, he was too fat at the calves, he couldn't click his heels sharply enough. No occasion was given Peterson to say farewell to the President—the last time they had met, the

President had told him he was the greatest Secretary of Commerce since Herbert Hoover.

"Peterson's fault," a member of the underground (who was to be in jail two years later) explained to me that December, "was that he tried his own PR bypass, which you can't do in this administration. There's only one star, Richard Nixon, the current President. All those first team players we named four years ago didn't understand— Hickel, Laird, Romney. There's no first team. If you try to act like a first-team player and publicize yourself, then you aren't going to make it. If you get your head out too far, what happened to Peterson is going to happen to you."

Others besides Peterson were getting the same message in the interim between Term One and Term Two. They would be the instruments of the President's policy or they would be nothing. Ten days after Peterson's visit to Camp David came the visit, on Monday, November 27th, of Richard Kleindienst, Attorney General. Kleindienst had been no inconsiderable quantity in the Nixon team of 1968; he had been known at that year's Republican convention as Richard Nixon's Genghis Khan. But Kleindienst had been feuding with Ehrlichman since those days, and now he sensed he was on the way out. Kleindienst had tired to frustrate the President on the ITT matter; more important, he had frustrated the effort of the underground to control the Justice Department's investigation of Watergate. An archconservative, but a Goldwater conservative, Kleindienst was not malleable. If he was to go, he wanted nine more months as Attorney General—until September of 1973—to find a new job. He arrived in Camp David to see the President, but found himself sitting instead with Haldeman and Ehrlichman. You want to be Attorney General until September? they asked him. OK. But now we'll tell you what you're going to do—you will fire every political appointee in the Department of Justice and fire everyone in every grade from C-15 up.

Kleindienst said that they must be kidding—there were men working at the Department of Justice for $32,500 a year who could make twice that much in private practice. The tone of the department, he explained, its leadership, depended on the morale of its top civil-service officers. Kleindienst refused to do the firings. It was explained to him that the President insisted that people in Justice be responsive to him personally; the President this time had won by a landslide, he did not need any longer to keep people on in response to pressure groups. Kleindienst retorted he would be responsible for the loyalty of the men in his department. Not yet knowing what the civil servants in the Prosecutor's office would soon find out about Watergate, Kleindienst could make the pledge unaware of what Haldeman and Ehrlichman might or might not fear about the upcoming trial of the Watergate small fry. The other two insisted he must sweep the department clean. Kleindienst responded that he would quit right then rather than do that. With this threat, and by the intercession of Barry Goldwater and John Mitchell, Kleindienst was allowed to keep his job for the next nine months—except that other events were to shorten that period of grace.

Across the board then ran the word: Let the President's will be done. Franklin D. Murphy, an old friend of Bob Haldeman's, disturbed by the public report of the resignations being demanded, asked Haldeman what the housecleaning meant. Haldeman replied: You're goddamned right we're cleaning house, we're going to have loyal people now, who take their marching orders from the White House, no Cabinet officer is going to be able to make his own deal with Congress. Murphy, once chancellor of the University of California at Los Angeles, felt it tragic that the White House should continue in its estrangement from the world of scholars. He sought an appointment with Ehrlichman and Haldeman for Roger Heyns, once chancellor of the University at Berkeley and now, as President of the American Council on Education, spokesman for all higher education. Murphy hoped Heyns could explore some way of rapprochement between government and learned men. Haldeman set up the appointment; and Heyns reported back to Murphy that he had never seen such arrogance; they felt they needed no one now, especially from the academic world.

James Reston of the *New York Times* had visited the White House on a similar mission, calling on Henry Kissinger, pointing out that after so overwhelming a Nixon victory perhaps the time had come for some reconciliation between the administration and the free institutions of the country, including the press. Kissinger had replied, "It will not come from this House until the press acknowledges it was wrong."

It was a confusing period because the front lobes and posterior lobes of the President's mind were at cross-purposes. He wanted men of quality in his new administration; yet he wanted total obedience. For example: the President had always admired, with his characteristic respect for the gentry, the patrician Republicans who had made the party great. He had just chosen George Bush, of the Connecti-cut-Yale Bush family, as chairman of the Republican National Committee. Bush was a personal favorite of his. Bush's father had been a Senator, a symbol of starched yet intelligent decency, a New England Yankee. ("I'm really glad Dad's not alive," said Bush when the impeachment of Nixon seemed inevitable, "it would have killed him to see this happen. He thought we were the party of virtue and all bosses were Democrats.") George Bush had gone off to Texas, become wealthy in oil, and a Houston Congressman, but remained a Yankee at heart. As newly appointed chairman of the National Committee, Bush was telephoned from Colson's office at the White House and told they were sending him a political statement he must sign personally and release immediately. Bush said: What? They repeated: This is a statement *you* are making today. Bush told them never again to call the chairman of the Republican National Committee and talk to him like that.

George Bush, in the Nixon entourage, was as close to being a hereditary member of the old Establishment as one could find—except for Elliot Richardson, pure-bred Boston Yankee. Richardson's experience in the new plan and his reflections on it are very illuminating.

As Secretary of HEW, Richardson's surgical quality of mind had attracted Nixon and earned Richardson some affection, which Richardson reciprocated. Richardson remembered one of his conversations with the President while he held the HEW post in 1972. "You know," said Nixon to Richardson one day, "there's no one I work with more closely than Kissinger, Ehrlichman and Haldeman—but I never have them over to lunch. No, I've had lunch with Haldeman twice—but that's the way I work."

Now, elevated to Secretary of Defense, Richardson felt

he must get to know his President better. He wanted to have some direct grasp of the President's thinking and add his own reflection to that thinking. He suggested to Haldeman that there ought to be a series of regular conversations between the Secretary of Defense and the President, so that the Defense Department would have a clear view of the President's ideas for guidance. Haldeman replied that if he suggested that to Nixon, the President would shy off—but he would try nonetheless to set up one first unstructured meeting. It was arranged; lasted almost an hour. Richardson wanted to talk large matters, the shape of defense; instead, the President, pressed by these concepts, responded with specific "projects, crotchets, prejudices." The meeting was cordial but useless; and there were no more, except for specific and immediate purposes. And later, when Richardson replaced Kleindienst at Justice, the pattern was repeated—never any grappling with the concept of Watergate until too late, in the showdown over the firing of Archibald Cox. The Richardson-Nixon chemistry did not work.

When I asked Richardson later what went wrong, he responded metaphorically. "I thought I could help him, I wanted to help him," said Richardson. "His flaws were always there. But it's like looking at a landscape at the end of the day, with shadows over the canyons and the mesas. There's such a dramatic contrast with how that landscape looks at high noon. I first saw him at high noon, and the contours of the landscape were different then, the map looked different from the way it looked with night coming on, when you see the flaws clearly. He was never able to accept the fact that he was President of the United States. If you're President, there isn't any 'they'; the President has to be first among 'us.' People want the President to succeed even if he thinks of them as the enemy. I told this to Ehrlichman, I told it to Colson. But the President was never able to overcome the psychology that got him where he was and conditioned him. His use of football analogies was so revealing—anything was OK except what the referee sees and blows the whistle on."

There was an underlying development in these transition months which rarely captured either Nixon's full thoughtful attention or the attention of the front pages, but which framed more clearly than any other development the profound underlying contradictions in the Nixon philosophies of government.

This was the condition of the national economy, at that point skidding on its way to the unforeseeable inflationary disaster of 1974 and the depression of 1975.

There were, and always have been, three great issues in American national politics: the first is war and peace; the second is black and white; the third is bread and butter. And in this area of bread and butter, or the condition of the national economy, Nixon was confronted with paradox. He held, as a leadership credo, that the President must control the government personally; but he held, as a political credo, that the Federal government must get rid of most of those controls—social, administrative, economic—which the Democrats had so long concentrated in Washington. In 1971, he had exercised the former by violating the latter credo to impose sweeping wage-price controls over the entire national economy. And, miraculously, that had worked—conditions in 1971 had been ideal, the capacity of industry under-utilized, the sharpness of government action deflating the psychology of inflationary expectation within weeks. But Nixon, from the beginning, had been uncomfortable with the wage-price controls he had imposed. It was a political heresy that he recognized; he hoped to end such controls as soon as he could. And with the boom of 1972, cresting in his triumphant re-election in November, he felt the moment had arrived when his economists could loose free private enterprise again to operate as it previously had in America at peace.

There was much to support his confidence. 1972 had been one of the greatest years of American economic history, a boom larger and more fairly distributed to ordinary people than the boom of 1929. The Gross National Product had risen that year to $1,155 billion; and even in "adjusted dollars," dollars adjusted for inflation, the real growth of American production had been an astonishing 6.5 percent for the year and an unbelievable 8.5 percent for the last quarter! Nixon had set his sights in his 1971 control program for a rate of inflation of something between 2 and 3 percent a year; and he had almost made that, too—various economists estimated the rise in the cost of living in 1972 at either 3.6 percent, 3.4 percent or 3.2 percent. In pride, the President's Council of Economic Advisers let its normally technical prose rise, in its annual report, to the hyperbole of "By the end of 1972, the American anti-inflation policy had become the marvel of the rest of the world." The *New York Times,* scarcely a well-wisher of Richard Nixon, headlined its annual economic report of January, 1973, with: "ECONOMIC UPTURN THROUGH DECADE APPEARS POSSIBLE." And the story began: "The United States is in the midst of a new economic boom that may prove to be unrivaled in scope, power and influence by any previous expansion in history." For the rich, the stock market was moving up to a historic high. All economists, in harmony and chorus, predicted more boom. And for the poor—well, five pounds of sugar still cost 71 cents, hamburger still 78 cents a pound; and the price of the Christmas turkey was still only 39 cents a pound. A year later, that Christmas turkey would cost more than double—90 cents a pound. Gas was still only 41.9 cents a gallon; two years later, it would cost 55 cents.

If there was a moment for Nixon to return to the political philosophy of free enterprise, it was now, at this moment of interpassage between administrations, with the towering authority of his mandate from the people. There were other reasons, too. Labor, which had given a larger share of its votes for President to him than to any other Republican since World War I, was growing restive at wage controls. "There was the question," said one member of the Council of Economic Advisers, "of just how long George Shultz could keep George Meany happy by playing golf with him on weekends." And more than that: industry was now working at full capacity, shortages of supply were developing and price distortions were puckering which only intense economic police action would be able to control. It was time to go back to fundamentals.

From September through to the beginning of the new year, Richard Nixon let his economists analyze and recommend solutions to the problem of getting back to those fundamentals. Economics to him was an annoyance, and they must write the scenario.

On January 11th, 1973, he thus announced that, on the

best advice, he was now indeed de-controlling the American economy—abolition of all wage and price controls, except provisionally for those on food, on medical services, on building construction. The economists had seen the transition measure, called Phase III of the Nixon economics, as a measure of cautious unleashing of the economy, with the government retaining its powers of surveillance and, if necessary, intervention. PR translated it to industry and labor as full freedom to go for broke for as much as they could get. Nixon followed with another measure, on February 12th, which devalued the dollar in foreign trade by 10 percent, a devaluation which, when added to his previous devaluation of the dollar by 8.57 percent in 1971, changed the dollar from one of the world's weakest and most overvalued currencies to one of its most undervalued.

It would be entirely unfair to blame Richard Nixon for the disaster which was now about to happen to the American money system in the next year, or the crisis of confidence in all values which was about to take place in the next two years. If anyone could have given him the right advice, he would have taken it—for bread and butter, as he knew, moved politics. But his economists were reaching the margin of their own understanding of the world, as were all economists. His economists, like their Democratic counterparts, could not be faulted either for scholarship or for dedication. But the discipline of economics can study the expression of people's needs and greeds only from the statistics handed down by the past—and their dismal science rests on the premise that people's past behavior indicates how they will behave in the future. Economists are very much like reporters—and as necessary. The best of them can tell you exactly where you are, the exceptional ones can tell you how you got there—but none can predict how you go from where you are to where you want to get. And it is as unwise for a President to let his economists tell him where to go as for a President to let his generals tell him what the aims and purposes of a war should be. Richard Nixon, in following the best advice he could get in an area of life which interested him only in terms of politics, was no different from any other President, as he let slip the controls he himself had taken to government and opened the national economy to the whirlwinds of chance.

Looking back today, there is still no unanimity among economists as to what happened in those months of inter-passage. They point out the many-rooted causes of inflation and the unpredictability of world events. Who, for example, could guess that the schools of fingerling anchovies that abounded off the Peruvian coast and gave the world millions of tons of high-grade protein feed for its meat-raisers would suddenly disappear—whether from a change in anchovy sex habits or a shift in the cold Humboldt current, no one yet knows. But the reduction in the world's supply of livestock protein was instantly reflected in the pressure on American soybean prices, which were to go from $3.25 to $12.00 a bushel in the next eight months. Or, who could guess the price of wheat, which had risen to $1.73 a bushel in September, 1972, would then soar upward to $2.06 a bushel in 1973 (March) and then up to $4.78 at its peak in that year? And that, in its soaring, wheat would carry the price of a loaf of bread from 27 cents to 60 cents two years later? Or, who could guess that Nixon's brilliant support of the Israelis in 1973, under attack from Egyptians, Russians, Syrians, would provoke the oil exporters of the Middle East to blackmail the United States and the oil consumers of the world with their embargo?

Long before this, however, during the period of interpassage of 1972–73, ordinary greed in America, pent up by the controls of 1971, was beginning to work. Already in October of 1972, when it was apparent that the election was won, the Federal Reserve had begun to tighten credit; and, in response, the prime bank rate for best borrowers had risen from 5½ percent to 5¾ percent. In December, that rate went from 5¾ to 6 percent, and businessmen began to complain. (A year and a half later, the prime rate would be 12 percent, and America would be in the throes of double-digit inflation.)

So many elements were working their way toward the impending catastrophe in the interlocked American and international economies that not even the economists could analyze them all. But two elements, directly linked to Richard Nixon personally, are significant here.

The first, of course, was the economic consequences of his peace.

Nixon had probably never read John Maynard Keynes's

classic *Economic Consequences of the Peace,* written after the Versailles peace treaty of 1919. And no one has yet written the book on the economic consequences of the Nixon peace.

Technically, his economic advisers had urged on him the devaluation of the dollar in February of 1973 as a measure to ensure American control over both the dollar itself and the nagging American deficit in international trade which had been developing for years. The dollar should have been devalued years before, in the 1960's, and long since have been removed as the fixed target for speculation of the gnomes of international banking. To devalue the dollar now, they explained, would at once give America control of the terms of its international trade and, at the same time, have little effect on the cost-of-living index, that political-economic barometer which interests all politicians most. Only 7.5 percent of all America's daily living cost rests on purchases from abroad; thus, a 10 percent devaluation of the dollar would raise the cost of living in America only by approximately three-fourths of one percent. What could not be foreseen was that the devaluation would provoke from an already overstrained American economy such a spurt in exports to foreign countries, a demand from abroad so large, as to trigger at home the price rises that scarcity always provokes.

What ran to Nixon personally was his own concept of peace—that peace is always temporary, only the passage of time without war between rival powers; and his corollary to that thesis—that enlarged and fruitful world trade best expresses the good will that must cement such a period of peace together. In practice, Nixon's four-year-long pressure for peace meant that Communist Chinese, Russians, the exuberant enterprise economies of Germany and Japan, as well as the laggard economies of the underdeveloped world must all have access to the world's resources of copper, oil, energy, bauxite and protein—and to America's commanding resources of food, timber, coal, credit and technology. With his devaluation of the dollar on February 12th, Nixon made this access to America's resources almost unlimited —Americans would have to compete with Frenchmen, Englishmen, Germans, Japanese, Russians, Chinese and supplicant Indians, Africans and Latin-Americans for their own resources of food, of energy, of technology. And thus prices must inevitably go up at home and abroad—spurring on the great inflation of the seventies, creating the crisis of confidence in America which now, at this time, dominates all politics.

The second element that ran to Richard Nixon was the matter of confidence in government leadership. The free-enterprise system is at once a system of production and of psychological attitudes. Attitudes rest on confidence in government. The strength and vitality of the system of which Nixon was so proud came from the freedom this confidence gives people to plan their own futures—to risk their money, plan their savings, gamble their fortunes, prepare for their years of retirement in their own way. What this system does is to divorce the individual—whether a free-wheeling financier or a small bookshop merchant—from any master plan which, under communism, makes his livelihood or future subject to bureaucratic will.

Above all, the American system leans forward, resting on the expectation of the rising tide which will float all boats. There will always be more—more buyers, more consumers, more audience, more everything. Thus, in America, the idea of "more" moves all—an immigrant father to send his son to college, a dabbler in real estate to put his money into new garden apartments, a great corporation to install a new paper mill. But these myriad, overlapping individual plans are all based on confidence in the government, that government will keep the rules of the game roughly as they were when the plans were made, that government will be firm, dependable and effective.

When confidence in any government weakens, men think in terms of a week, a month, a year—not the long-range future. Planning in a period of uncertainty, whether individual or corporate, must focus on the *now*, the short-range gratification, the quick price increase, the quick purchase, the immediate fulfillment of wish. It expresses itself in hysterical grabbing and spending. Eat steak today, because tomorrow hamburger will cost more than steak today; back the union to jump the scale now, to keep ahead of inflation, instead of next year when the chance may be lost. Inflation is the characteristic disease of all societies which live under a government losing its authority—from the days of the

Sung dynasty, which invented paper currency, to the collapse of all its successors in Asia, Europe and America that have experimented or relied on currencies and credit as a medium of exchange.

The great inflation would have been a problem of major dimensions even if Americans had had no political crisis to sap their confidence in government. But their confidence in government was oozing away in the early spring months of 1973—and Richard Nixon was too preoccupied with other matters to realize, until too late, that he, personally, was central to this loss of confidence.

Emmet Hughes, writing about his experience in the Eisenhower administration in his book *The Ordeal of Power*, recalled with amusement how, after having been close to affairs at the center of the White House, he would read the news system's reporting. "The daily press, radio and television," he wrote, "*has* to make an intelligent report on national affairs, even though the matters reported may have been handled in a most unintelligible way. . . . Thus, at the end of a day of administrative disorder . . . there was an almost tonic effect in reading, in the evening's news columns, a most tidily organized account of all that had happened."

In those months of interpassage between the first and second Nixon administrations, no such tonic effect could have been experienced by the men of the Nixon White House. Neither within nor outside that White House was there a coherent overall grasp on affairs. Too many major matters were draining the President's attention span and emotional energies in the months between December and March. His negotiations with the Hanoi regime broke down. Thus, in almost absolute loneliness he had to overcome a recalcitrant Pentagon and a resistant Air Force which felt that the cost of bombing Hanoi to bring it to the table again on American terms was not worth the effort in planes and men lost. The President at the same time had to fire, inspire, dismiss, chasten and elevate the men who did not fit into his new managerial plans for the second administration. He must prepare his speech for the second inaugural. He must consider the budget. He had also to think about Congress, and about the burblings and murmurs in the press about Watergate—but that was, at that moment, the old PR problem again.

By January 9th, sharp bombing and precision technology had persuaded the Hanoi regime to settle. Then the prisoners of war were coming off the planes, kissed and hugged by people who loved them. Thus, sometime in early February, as the television cameras showed the men who had been given up for lost, the esteem of Nixon among his countrymen rose to its peak, surpassing in every public-opinion poll the approval he had won in the official count of his votes in November. In the Gallup poll, he rated 68 percent. Dow Jones had just indexed the stock market at its all-time high (1,051.70), and the Nixon bull market seemed about to run away.

He seemed all-powerful. At the annual AFL/CIO convention, old George Meany, never lavish with praise, looked to the President as the only man who could stop the disturbing rise in food prices. "I think you can do anything you want to do," said Meany, "when you have the machinery of government and you have got a very strong President in the White House who has complete control of his own party, complete control of the administration and, at the present moment, practically dominates the Congress." The smiling President and the gruff old labor leader stood together for their photograph.

Yet the President could not do anything he wanted to do, either abroad or at home.

Abroad, he was facing the undeclared war of the Arab oil states on the Western economies. And he was as unprepared to face that undeclared war as the Western states had been unprepared to face Hilter's undeclared war in 1937 and 1938, when they rested ungirt and defenseless before the menace. Energy even then, at the beginning of 1973, was the first Presidential priority; he perceived, and could explain to visitors, the connection between energy and the growing inflation. But two years would be lost before any President of the United States, or its government, would have the authority to face that energy crisis squarely. And Richard Nixon could not master the energy crisis because his personal energies, from February on, were being drawn away by a crisis of personal authority.

At home, on King's Row, hidden matters were slipping

out of control. The episode of Watergate had been compounded from burglary to felony to conspiracy; conspiracy was being undermined by blackmail. What had been originally dismissed by Richard Nixon to his underground staff as an administrative matter was abscessing.

The President, sooner or later, would have to attend to this Watergate abscess personally. From February to March of 1973 it would grow to be his chief preoccupation as the ordinary living costs of Americans became a bewilderment of rocketing prices and their faith in their government was challenged by the relentless reporting of the press. Only a strong, overbearing President with full authority might have summoned Congress and nation to face up to the realities of peace, energy and inflation. Richard Nixon was engaged in a fight for personal survival and he could not. His mandate had run out within four months of his election victory. But not for another year and a half would people know how desperate and tormenting had been his fight for survival, or how his mind approached it—not until the publication of the transcripts of his inner thoughts, an act unprecedented in all history, anywhere, any time.

8

THE TAPES:
A TOUR INSIDE THE MIND OF
RICHARD NIXON

From the moment that Scott Armstrong and Don Sanders, two young staff members of the Ervin Committee, began privately to grill Alexander Butterfield on Friday afternoon, July 13th, 1973, in the basement of the New Senate Office Building, a Constitutional crisis was inevitable: the government would have to invade a President's mind and privacy.

Alexander Butterfield had been a friend of Bob Haldeman at UCLA; and so had been invited to join the White House staff, where for three years he sat next door to the Oval Office as Haldeman's deputy for personal attendance on the President. Butterfield on this Friday afternoon had been under questioning for hours, and had been answering in such orderly fashion that Armstrong remembers the interview as the most rational they had conducted that far. But there was an awkward gap in Butterfield's explanation of how notes were taken at White House meetings. His inquisitors pressed him further—were there tapes?

"I was hoping you fellows wouldn't ask me that," is the way Butterfield's reply is remembered. And then came the revelation: there were tape recordings. He was told to stay in touch with the committee.

Over the weekend, Butterfield sought guidance from the White House's then-Watergate-counsel, Leonard Garment. But Garment was away that weekend and could not return Butterfield's calls until Monday morning, when he located Butterfield in a barber shop getting a haircut. Butterfield reported what he had told the committee investigators, and added that now, this Monday afternoon, he must talk publicly. Garment instructed Butterfield to tell the truth. And then added, "Get a good haircut—you'll have a national audience today." Garment was a lover of the arts, a habitual drama-goer; he knew the rules of the stage: If a gun is placed on the table in the first act, then it must go off in the third act. This gun would go off to make history with unique irony—for history itself had been the progenitor of the tapes, at once their foster father and their intended legatee.

The idea of preserving, or recording, the way great leaders make decisions is not new. History has invited it since the beginning of time. Learned men build a nation's legends and faith out of the memories, scraps and shards left behind by national leaders who acted in torment, madness or exhilaration to shape the past. And many such leaders have for centuries, even before the invention of magnetic sound tapes, done their best to leave records behind to help the chroniclers who would come after make myths of them. Ego is the disease of great leaders; some leave pyramids, some leave tapes; and Clio, the muse of history, symbolically offers them a choice between a fanfare of trumpets and the dripping clepsydra.

In Richard Nixon's mind, the idea of a tape recording for history had been there for years, off again, on again—as follows:

Item: The day is March 12th, 1954. In his hideaway office of the Senate, Room P55, the then Vice-President Richard Nixon was sitting with his friend James Bassett. Bassett, knowing that the purging of Joe McCarthy, an enterprise in which he and Nixon were partners, was a matter for history, was keeping a diary. His notes that day describe Nixon as lolling on a green baize settee, Bassett with his feet up on the round black dining table Vice-President Nixon used as a workbench. Bassett's diary reads:

"RN said wistfully at one point in our rambling chat that he'd love to slip a secret recording gadget in the President's office, to capture some of those warm, offhand, great-hearted things the Man says, play 'em back, then get them press-released."

The idea of taping was there, then, nearly twenty years before.

Item: The first real knowledge we have of any recording system in the White House dates from Franklin D. Roosevelt's day—when the Army Signal Corps installed an experimental RCA pick-up microphone in a lamp in the

President's Oval Office; how well it worked, we do not know. The same lamp was shown in pictures of Harry Truman's Oval Office, but whether the microphone was still in it or not is uncertain. Eisenhower, so far as is known, made no tape recordings. But John F. Kennedy did. His taping system ran only to the Cabinet Room, but may have recorded other discussions. Neither of his two closest aides, Ted Sorensen or McGeorge Bundy, knew of this taping system. Probably only Robert Kennedy and the Signal Corps knew; and the tapes are now being processed in the Kennedy archives temporarily located at Waltham, Massachusetts.

Lyndon Johnson, of course, taped conversations in both the Cabinet Room and the Oval Office, a fact known to almost everyone doing business with Lyndon Johnson. Those taps, expurgated, rest in the Johnson Library at Austin, Texas. But Johnson's taping system, as so much else in Johnson's style, was offensive to Richard Nixon. On November 12th, 1968, traveling from Key Biscayne to New York, President-elect Nixon stopped off in Washington to discuss the transition of government and learn how the White House works. He and his staff were shown around and Johnson's taping system was explained to them.

En route back to New York, Nixon confided to Bob Finch that the very first thing he planned to do was rip out the Johnson taping system. No one, he felt, should be bugged in the President's office.

Item: So Richard Nixon instructed the Army Signal Corps to rip out the old taping system, which it did on February 15th, 1969.

And Nixon's resolve held for two years. On November 11th, 1969, I visited the President—Washington seethed that week with anti-war protesters, rallying about the Washington Monument, preparing for their "death march" about the White House itself. But the President was undisturbed as he talked of war and peace. We sat facing each other on the two sofas before the fireplace and then, though I had heard nothing, he casually said, "That's a broken fan squeaking—it's not a recording device." He explained that he had been trying to get that fan fixed all day, it just proved that even a President couldn't get things done the way he wanted. And added that he did not have recordings of his conversations as other Presidents had.

Which was true as of that moment—and many other visitors probably heard the same story.

Item: The President was at his best receiving visitors who were ordinary citizens—Jaycees, Four-H winners, widows or mothers of war heroes. Speaking to such Middle Americans, he could reach a degree of eloquence voiced neither in his state documents nor on the stump. A staff deputy would be assigned to take notes—but it was hard to catch the flavor. Persistently, the sycophants of the staff urged that such passages of Nixon inspiration be recorded for posterity.

Item: In September of 1969, the President had taken title to his new San Clemente estate by the Pacific, the Western White House had been built and the trustees of the new Nixon Foundation had been named. Seven were to form an executive committee: Messrs. Mitchell, Haldeman, Kalmbach, Ehrlichman, Garment, Finch and Mrs. Patricia R. Hitt. Nineteen others would also serve as trustees. The President joined a meeting of this group and—according to Richard Moore, who was present—talked in broad brush strokes about "pretty heady stuff."

Other Presidents had left imposing memorial libraries and depositories. The custom ran back to the remarkable Hoover Institution on War, Revolution and Peace, in Stanford, California. But Nixon did not want his library to be a collection of dry records. There should, of course, said Nixon, be a depository of papers for scholarly research. But nowadays there ought to be film as well, video tapes perhaps, ways of making the Presidency come to life. Nixon hoped the trustees would talk to the Disney people, who at Disneyland had a wonderful dramatization of Lincoln talking. Nixon wanted real voices—he could visualize some ordinary guy listening on tape to a Presidential decision in the making.

A committee of five was named to plan the library and records this administration would leave to history: Leonard Firestone of Firestone Tire & Rubber Company, Donald Kendall of Pepsico, Ross Perot of Electronic Data Systems, John Ehrlichman and Taft Schreiber of MCA. The committee visited the Library of Congress, glanced at some

650 files in the National Archives, visited the Smithsonian Institution, talked with the chief archivist of the United States. "One thing came through loud and clear," said Schreiber, "that, starting with Franklin D. Roosevelt, every President had emptied his archives and left the files empty."

A President's papers and thoughts were his personal property.

Three of the committee members, Perot, Firestone, Schreiber, then flew to Texas, to consult with ex-President Lyndon Johnson at the LBJ Ranch about the future Nixon library. LBJ was both cordial and grumpy, as was his style, and began, irritably, about how Congress didn't do enough for ex-Presidents—why, he couldn't even get a $300 paper-shredder for his library. And he explained to Schreiber why he needed it—he had called so many of those Senators and Congressmen sons-of-bitches, said so many things, you couldn't let that stuff be printed. "Ain't that right, Bird?" he asked of his wife, who was present in their living room at the conversation.

On his way back to the Austin airport, Schreiber talked with the chief librarian of the Johnson Library, a Federal institution. The librarian made it clear—historians do not want to work with material that is salted; whatever was to be preserved in the future Nixon Library should be preserved in toto; he was doing that with the Johnson papers.

In making his report to Bob Haldeman, Schreiber made it clear: whatever was recorded or preserved, it should be preserved intact, all of it. Haldeman then told Nixon, as the President recalled later, "They [the tapes] were made, curiously enough, in a very offhand decision. We had no tapes, as you know, up until 1971. I think one day Haldeman walked in and said, 'The library believes it is essential that we have tapes,' and I said, why? He said, well, Johnson had tapes—they're in his library at Austin, and these are invaluable records. Kennedy also had tapes. . . . I said all right. I must say that after the system was put in, as the transcribed conversations clearly indicated, I wasn't talking with knowledge or with the feeling that the tapes were there. Otherwise I might have talked differently. My own view is that taping of conversations for historical purposes was a bad decision on the part of all the Presidents. I don't think Kennedy should have done it. I don't think Johnson should have done it, and I don't think *we* should have done it."[1]

Haldeman's recollection of the tapes' origin is fuzzier, although he does remember that once they decided to do it, the President decided not to be selective, not to cosmetize, but to record all of it, every bit of it. "I think," said Haldeman later, "if he had died and it had been my decision, I would have had them all destroyed." Schreiber took a more technical view, as a professional of the entertainment industry: "It was for the library, it was a private thing, so they put in this inadequate system and equipment. They didn't want to go outside for the money. It was all to be a secret, so the recordings were really lousy."

Thus, then, sometime in February of 1971, the Secret Service installed a more elaborate, if faulty, recording system than any previous President had had. The system in the Oval Office and in the Cabinet Room began operation, according to the logs, on February 16th, 1971. Several techniques were used. In the Oval Office, the system was voice-activated; inconspicuous microphones were hidden in all corners of the room and probably in the mantel over the fireplace; and as the President leaned forward in his customary chair at his desk to talk to a visitor, six tiny microphones picked up the conversation through almost invisible perforations in his desktop. In the Cabinet Room, the system was switch-activated; to the left of the President's customary seat, underneath the Cabinet table, were four buttons, two of which were significant—one marked BUTTER-FIELD, the other HALDEMAN, to conceal their purpose. When the President pressed the Butterfield button, the tape rolled; when he pressed the Haldeman button, the tape stopped. But this on-off switch system missed important conversations, just as the on-off switch system under Lyndon Johnson had. Thus, a few weeks later, the switch system for the Cabinet Room was transferred to Butterfield's office down the way; Butterfield would remain responsible for all on-off switchings as soon as the Cabinet gathered.

The system quickly expanded. On April 16th, 1971, the

[1] The above comes from an outstanding interview with the President on May 14, 1974, by James J. Kilpatrick of the Washington *Star* Syndicate, which should be read in full.

President's hideaway in the Executive Office Building was wired with a voice-activated system, and so were the three White House telephones the President habitually used. The last installation did not come until May 18th, 1972—in the President's cabin at Camp David; and that was also the first to be removed—on March 18th, 1973, before the visit of Communist Party leader Brezhnev of the Soviet Union.[a]

Thus the tapes ran—sporadically stopping and starting, spinning and halting as they wove the web that was ultimately to trap Richard Nixon. Of this web, aside from the few specialists in the Secret Service Technical Division, only four men knew: Nixon, Haldeman, Butterfield and Higby. No others. Not Ehrlichman, not Mitchell, not Kissinger, not Connally, not Finch, not the President's Cabinet members or lawyers.

Only history was to hear the real Richard Nixon—someday far in the future. And as the months wore on, the real Nixon himself almost certainly grew accustomed to the inti-

---

[a] As Fred Buzhardt said later, "The voice-activated tapes were a technical solution to a human problem. They didn't want to lose anything, as previous Presidents had done with switch systems." The voice-activated systems made later listeners frantic with ear strain. As soon as the President entered the hideaway, the reels started spinning with the sound of his footsteps; they would pick up the squeaking of his pen; they would pick up the moving of a chair. An hour or sometimes two hours would run by with no voice or sound except what electronic technicians call background noise, and later listeners would have to wait and wait for voices to surface. When it was decided to have the tapes copied to be transcribed, the secret assignment was given to the National Security Agency, with its superlative listening devices, cryptographic experience and audio technology. It, however, was told to make copies of the tapes without letting any of the engineers listen to adjust for sound. The engineers thus made tape copies by meter level, without any auditory adjustments. Thus the vague, large stretches of incomprehensibility, particularly in the rectangular Executive Office hideaway. A high pitched voice like that of John Dean would come through fairly well; a low, deep tone like that of Ziegler's voice would frequently be lost; and the overlapping microphones would pick up the clearest, loudest voice in a conversation, losing the under-mutters and interjections. Listening to the tapes was a chore few wanted, and James St. Clair, the President's lawyer, was particularly unwilling to suffer the boredom of listening directly. "My God," he said to Buzhardt after one early attempt at listening, "do you mean you can actually hear anything at all on that thing?"

macy of history and spoke without awareness of the tapes
—at his best and at his most base.

One should make a generalization here as the Nixon administration passed from its zenith of control to its breakdown in the spring of 1973.

The breakdown happened in the personality of one man,
and the transcripts tell the story, framing it in those tor-
mented months of March and April when Nixon was confronted with himself. But the fragments that pressure and
law have extracted from the transcribed tapes are fragments of the worst moments in a man's life, of a leader doing
the dirtiest of his business, a President flirting with crime.
There was much else in that mind, too, as much good as
bad. And though the bad was absolutely overriding at the
crucial point where the law must pass judgment, the good
in the mind was enormous, too.

For most people who have known Richard Nixon moderately well, it is as impossible to have imagined the coarseness and insecurity of the personality self-transcribed as it
is ever to forget the robust clarity of that mind in other
conversations. For myself this is particularly so, for the last
opportunity I had to visit with Richard Nixon was during
those two months of torment, on March 17th, 1973, just
before its first climax—and never had I spoken to a President who gave the impression of being more completely
self-possessed or in command of his job.[s]

His feet that Saturday were up on the table in his Executive Office Building hideaway; he was at ease, his mind roving, sorting out problems and priorities of national affairs;
and mostly he talked the shop talk of power—power as
Mao Tse-tung sees it, power as the Pentagon sees it, power
as the President must use it. The President, he felt, must
single out a few problems of the thousands and thousands
of immensely complicated affairs that clamor for his attention, and must concentrate on those. He must wall himself
off from detail. And the tapes of that conversation, as he
explained how he saw a President's role, should if ever published reveal much about that other Nixon, the one he

---

[s] See pp. 353–60 in Theodore H. White's *The Making of the
President—1972* (New York: Atheneum, 1973).

wanted historians to find in his library generations hence.

Occasionally, Nixon would toy with his gold watch and I would make as if to go, for I had long overstayed the usual half-hour or hour allotted to a visitor to the President. But he kept motioning me to stay and talked on—talked with a serenity, an introspection, a sweep of historic happenings that held me fixed for fully two and a half hours. Later, when I read the transcript of his conversation that morning with John Dean, it was this quality of serenity that came back to me most sharply. He had swept the morning dialogue with Dean from his mind; he was out there, far, far out there in history, talking as a President should.

His serenity could not have been feigned.

Yet any man who sat in that chair should have known, long before that morning, that crisis was approaching at a speed and with a deliberateness that not even a President could predict or control. It had been approaching, indeed, for almost a year, and he had not recognized it either at its beginning or even then as it was closing on him.

The transcribed tapes tell the story best.

The initiating personal crime had come technically June 23rd, 1972, when, so casually, Nixon had authorized use of the CIA to halt the FBI in its investigation of the Watergate break-in. Thereafter the matter had become an administrative matter for the underground, which successfully contained the scandal until after election in a manner with whose details, quite evidently, he was unfamiliar but found acceptable. ("John," he said to John Dean later on March 21st, 1973, ". . . you had the right plan, let me say, I have no doubts about the right plan before the election. And you handled it just right. You contained it.")

Then, however, as the Senate moved to set up the Ervin Committee to investigate the Watergate incident and other irregularities of the election of 1972, the tapes show the beginning of a genuine concern. It was apparent that the Ervin Committee would set off a PR clash of first magnitude—the press, the liberals, the Establishment all lined up against him unless he could outsmart them, as he had done so often before, by his own PR counter-offensive.

Through the early transcripts of 1973 runs the thrust of this dominant PR strategy—to overwhelm the Ervin Committee's anticipated revelations by making headlines of his own. If the Ervin Committee was going to hit with stories of Republican dirty tricks or the Republican bugging of Watergate, he would counter with the trickery and surveillance by Democrats against Nixon in the campaign of 1968. He, Nixon, had been personally bugged then—J. Edgar Hoover had told him so. Nixon believed Hoover, and it was up to Dean and Haldeman to get that story of 1968 documented. Since Hoover was now dead, perhaps his one-time deputy William Sullivan could confirm that story. If not Sullivan, then Cartha DeLoach, another old Hoover confidant. DeLoach *had* to talk because he now worked at Pepsi-Cola, whose chief was the President's friend Donald Kendall. Within two days of the authorization of the Ervin Committee on February 7th, Haldeman was firing off, on February 9th, an action memorandum to Dean: ". . . go ahead and have Kleindienst order the FBI project on the 1968 bugging so as to gather the data on that and get the fullest possible information. Also, Mitchell should probably have Kendall call DeLoach in and say that if this project turns up anything that DeLoach hasn't covered with us, he will, of course, have to fire him."

Thus the early concept of the problem—a high-stake game of PR. Yes, the Republicans had bugged the Democrats in 1972, but the President had acknowledged it already as "deplorable." And Lyndon Johnson had bugged Nixon in 1968. That's the way the game was played. So what?

All the inner events of the White House from February, 1973, on, may be taken as a refusal to accept what has been called the Chappaquiddick theorem by that political observer, James Doyle. The Chappaquiddick theorem, derived from Senator Edward Kennedy's experience after the drowning of Mary Jo Kopechne in 1969, is very simple: There is no good time for a political figure to tell bad news except right away. If there is bad news, devoted advisers will tell the principal to wait until tomorrow, or wait until next month when the bad news can be covered with a good headline. But all such well-meaning advice is wrong: the longer a political leader waits to put forth his bad news, the worse will be its effect.

The Nixon advisers were not unaware of the truth behind the Chappaquiddick theorem; in their strange dialect it was called the "hangout" route—an effort to tell the story, or as much of the story as was safe to tell, before the press forced the story into the open, in fragments and distortions.

From the transcribed conversation of March 13th on, one can see the President groping his way to that road, then drawing back from it, then turning futilely again to "hang out," then again drawing away. His initial personal involvement in the cover-up on June 23rd, 1972, was known only to Haldeman for certain, probably also to Dean and Mitchell. But what Dean, Mitchell, Haldeman and Ehrlichman and the lesser men knew of how they had carried out his directives had never been told to the President himself in detail; and the more he was to learn, the more difficult would become the hangout.

On March 13th, the conversation shows the beginning of the problem of revelation.

The President is talking that afternoon to John Dean in the Oval Office, still hoping that with Sullivan's help they can override the story of Watergate by the story of Lyndon Johnson's misdeeds in 1964 and 1968. And the President is brought up short by the almost casual remark of Dean that the transcripts of the Watergate wire-taps actually did come to the White House, to the desk of Gordon Strachan, one of Haldeman's young assistants. What ran to Strachan ran to Haldeman, what ran to Haldeman ran to the President.

"He knew?" asks the President, startled. "He knew about Watergate? Strachan did?"

"Uh huh," Dean answers.

"I'll be damned," says the President. "Well that's the problem in Bob's case, isn't it? It's not Chapin then, but Strachan."

The President ponders the fact, apparently new to him, of Strachan's involvement; and, of course, weighs it against the thought of "hangout," of telling the whole story; the story cannot be told if it implicates Haldeman via Strachan. Yet without telling it all, says Dean, "they would never believe it."

"Who is they?" asks the President, and Dean responds, "The press, the Democrats, the intellectuals."

Which provokes an outburst from the President: "They

got the hell kicked out of them in the election. . . . Basically, it's the media, uh, I mean it's the Establishment. The Establishment is dying, and so they've got to show that . . . 'well it just is wrong [the election] because . . . of this [Watergate].' . . . They are trying to use this to smear the whole thing." He is irritated, annoyed; but seems still to believe that PR can thwart the Establishment.

Four days later, on March 17th, though the President is still on the PR track, the tension escalates by several degrees as he talks that morning with John Dean.

They begin with a discussion of the Ervin Committee again, of the need of some plausible story to give, or to fabricate before the committee begins hearings. They agree they will hang out to the extent that they will say the White House of course had knowledge of a Republican intelligence operation, but no knowledge of any criminal intent. Dean reminds the President he had heard discussions of bugging in John Mitchell's office and the President interjects, "Well, you won't need to say in your statement the bugging," and goes on to edit aloud how the statement must read, explaining how necessary intelligence was to the campaign of 1972. "Not only be legal but that it was totally necessary because of the violence, the, ah, the demonstrations, ah, the heck—the kind of activities that we knew were threatened against us in our convention and in our campaign. . . ."

They go on spinning quite a plausible story until Dean mildly raises the point of his own vulnerability because he did learn of the Watergate buggings later. The President dismisses that easily; for him the after-knowledge is not yet clear as a crime. ". . . you," he tells Dean, "you have no problem. All the others that have participated in the goddamned thing, and therefore are potentially subject to criminal liability. You're not. That's the difference." It is the case of the others, the men who authorized the bugging, that bothers the President; and so he is on to Magruder, toying with the thought of offering Magruder as chief villain in the hangout story. But he is familiar, obviously, with dangers in the Magruder story and rejects it: ". . . Sloan, Sloan starts pissing on Magruder and then Magruder starts pissing on, on, who, even Haldeman. . . . Can't do that."

Who can be sacrificed to make the story work? The President himself now brings up Segretti's dirty-tricks operation. That runs to Chapin and here the President is ready to make a sacrifice for the hangout. ". . . Chapin, all of them have just got to take the heat. Look, you've got to admit the facts, John, and that's our—and that's that. . . . I just think on Segretti, no matter how bad it is—it isn't nearly as bad as people think it was. Espionage, sabotage, shit. . . ."

Dean catches the rhythm of what he is supposed to write, spins it about for a moment and agrees, "I have no problem with the Segretti thing, it's just not that serious."

And then Dean jolts the President abruptly. "The ah, ah, the other potential problem, ah, is Ehrlichman's," he says. Dean is telling his story to the President like Scheherazade to the Caliph and he closes this session with a cliff-hanger —that Ehrlichman was directly involved in the break-in at the office of Daniel Ellsberg's psychiatrist in Los Angeles.

"What in the name of God was Ehrlichman having something (unintelligible) in the Ellsberg [break-in]?" asks the President.

"They wanted to get Ellsberg's psychiatric records for some reason," answers Dean.

"Why?" asked the President.

"I don't know," says Dean.

"This is the first I ever heard of this," says the President, "I, I (unintelligible) care about Ellsberg was not our problem."

Dean: "That's right."

President: "Jesus Christ."

One notes, reading this conversation, that the President has thus learned of an illegality that can undermine the government's case in the ongoing trial of Ellsberg; but he will do nothing about it until April 25th, five weeks later, when Kleindienst, the Attorney General, will officially tell him of the matter and force him to act.

One notes, further, that the hangout route has now acquired a new dimension of hazard. Full hangout means Nixon must reveal Ehrlichman's connection with the Ellsberg break-in; which thread would lead to the Plumbers; which leads back to the Huston memorandum; then to the entire irregular operations of the past two years; which involve Haldeman, Mitchell, Ehrlichman—and Nixon himself.

One notes, finally, the underlying assumption of the President, still unshaken at this point in mid-March, that the interlinked episodes are all matters for his subordinates to manage. He is still confident that no evidence can be brought against him and his inner circle because no one else knows of the tapes, and they will be forever protected by executive privilege. His mind is thus not focused on his real problem—the fact that two separate crimes have been committed. The first was a third-rate break-in and burglary, but the second, more serious, is the continuing action by the President to prevent the law from pursuing and bringing to justice the authors of the first crime. The distinction is probably, in his mind, of the order of those little details which, he was to say that afternoon, a President must wall off from himself. And thus, as I have said, when he met his visitor that Saturday afternoon he was apparently absolutely serene.

That weekend, however, the distinction between these two separate crimes and their importance began to be thrust on the President, for now a third and critical pressure would be added which must involve him personally: blackmail.

That weekend, March 17th-18th, for John Dean was blackmail weekend. E. Howard Hunt, spy, novelist, "patriot," participant in the break-in at Watergate, had decided to make his move. A devoted father of four children whose wife had been killed in an airplane crash the preceding December, Hunt was awaiting sentence for the crime of break-in to which he had pleaded guilty January 11th. And the sentence could run to thirty-five years unless Hunt sang. What price silence? Who would take care of his motherless children? Hunt had already tried to negotiate a promise of clemency from the President, via his old friend Charles Colson. The reply relayed back had not been solid enough. So now he would squeeze.

Ironically, E. Howard Hunt had no real reason to squeeze for money at this point. He had just collected $260,000 in insurance money for the death of his wife. Six days before, his brokers had actually bought for him $109,872 in stocks in the Nixon bull market. But now Hunt wanted an immediate $130,000 more in cash—$60,000 for legal fees and $70,000 for himself. Which message he passed to officials at CREEP, who passed it to John Dean. Hunt was demanding $130,000 in cash now, before sentencing on March 23rd—or else he would talk of the "seamy things" he had done in service of Richard Nixon!

But there was no more money. The irregulars had used up all the cash Maurice Stans could deliver, all the greenbacks that Herb Kalmbach could collect, at least $132,000 of the $350,000 greenbacks that Bob Haldeman had turned over to Fred LaRue. As much as 429,500 "jars of jam," the prosecutors were later to charge, had been spent to buy the silence of the seven caught in the Watergate break-in. CREEP could find no more loose cash; blackmail is endless; John Dean had to bring the problem to the President.

On the afternoon of March 20th, Dean described the situation first to John Ehrlichman, then to Richard Moore, Special Counsel to the President. At 7:30 that evening, having asked for an appointment with the President, he received a call instead. It was a long call of fourteen minutes; the transcription is full of disturbing, continuing unpleasantnesses. Dean wanted to see the President to "just paint the whole picture for you, the soft spots, the potential problem areas." The President agreed, "I want to know where all the bodies are first"; and they set the next day, March 21st, for a thirty-minute audience after Dean had once more assured the President that "there is not one scintilla of evidence" of wrongdoing beyond what had previously been stated.

The next morning, March 21st, would not have been a pleasant one for the President with or without John Dean's visit.

The political euphoria of January and February had steadily been oozing away. The market was dropping in New York, and interest rates were climbing. The cost of living as reported by the Labor Department was going up again and, worst of all, food prices had evidently risen in February by 2.5 percent, the most abrupt jump in nearly twenty years—an annual rate which, if continued, would see food 25 percent more costly by year end. L. Patrick Gray was testifying before the Senate, as its Judiciary Committee considered his fitness to be chief of the FBI—and Gray was trapped. How was it that the famed FBI, under his direction, could trace delivery of transcripts of the Watergate buggings all the way to 1701 Pennsylvania Avenue, where the offices of CREEP received them, but could not trace them further? The press had been picking and chipping away at Nixon for weeks on the Watergate scandal, and now, today, was breaking the story of an ITT offer of $1 million to the CIA to help overthrow Allende. There would be more to that story, and the President knew it.

All this was going on when, at 10:12 that morning, John Dean and the President sat down in the Oval Offce, to be joined after a while by H. R. Haldeman. The taped conversation shows some chatter about the original PR plan to counter the Ervin Committee. But Sullivan has been reluctant to talk; and in any case that plan has now been overtaken by events. John Dean now wants to talk, in his allotted time, "because in, in our conversations, uh, uh, I have, I have the impression that you don't know everything I know. . . . We have a cancer—within—close to the Presidency, that's growing. It's growing daily. It's compounding. . . ." Dean has obviously thought through his briefing carefully.

"How did it all start," asks Dean, "where did it start? It started with an instruction to me from Bob Haldeman to see if we couldn't set up a perfectly legitimate campaign intelligence operation over at the Re-Election Committee." Dean tells a straight narrative of the cover-up; of the hush money; and then, for the first time, tries to make clear to the President that the danger is not really the burglary of Watergate, but what happened afterward. Later, in the transcripts, the word "aftermath" would become a favorite phrase of Nixon's counsellors to wriggle around the stark fact of cover-up. But, this day, the political portent of "the aftermath" is not yet clear.

On one point, Dean is quite clear: they are now being blackmailed by Howard Hunt, whose demand is immediately critical. Dean says Hunt wants at least $120,000. And more to come, perhaps $1 million. Dean suggests that Mitchell should be charged with raising the money, and the President responds, "I would think so, too."

They go on. The President says that Dean has to keep the cap on the bottle. His mind is boxing the problem now at a new level. "Well for Christ's sakes . . . get it," says the President. It is impossible to misinterpret the flow of conversation: the President has ordered Dean to buy time for him; and that night, after telephone calls between Mitchell, Haldeman, Dean, LaRue, $75,000 was apparently passed to Hunt through his lawyer.

What to do with the time bought? Dean, says the President, must prepare a basic position paper, some chronicle of events, which the President can give to the Cabinet to explain what happened. "We just better then try to tough it through," says the President. And, shortly thereafter, Dean goes along with the tough defense: "I can give a show that . . . we can sell . . . just about like we were selling Wheaties."

The overall strategy has now discarded the early PR concept. There are three ways out, only three ways: first, they can let all hang out, tell the whole story. Or, secondly, they can beat the Ervin Committee to the punch by convening a special grand jury, at which White House personnel will waive executive privilege and tell the grand jury what they know. Or, lastly, they can stonewall it, deceiving Cabinet, press and everyone else besides. The President favors the hangout route; he does not like the grand-jury route; but waits for another council of war that afternoon.

That afternoon, the President speaks with Ehrlichman and Haldeman. It is a subtle conversation, for of these three, only two, Haldeman and the President, know at that time that the root of the problem goes to the Presidential directive of June 23rd, 1972, of which Ehrlichman was ignorant. Ehrlichman favors the hangout, tell-all story. They consider the grand-jury route; but that is too dangerous; they drop that. What they must devise is a story of apparent candor, a limited hangout, a story that purports to tell all but does not. That will be Dean's job; he is ordered to prepare it.

Yet the heart of the conversation remains: How could one tell all, yet without telling all? How does one square a circle? Or, in the President's phrase that afternoon on March 21st, at six o'clock: "What the hell is he going to disclose that isn't going to blow something?" There was no way of lifting one corner of the cover without lifting the whole cover, not simply on Watergate but on all the operations of the underground in the years before.

The decision made, the President went upstairs to his living quarters, where, as was his custom, he talked into his own Dictaphone machine in the Lincoln Room, holding dialogue alone with Clio, the muse of history.

The voice of Richard Nixon talking to himself is quite different from the voice of Richard Nixon, tough guy, talking to the other tough guys. It is devoid of profanity, malice, viciousness. Nixon alone that evening is a puzzled man —neither bitter nor vindictive, just puzzled.

"As far as the day was concerned," he tells Clio, "it was relatively uneventful except for the, uh, talk with Dean. Dean, really, in effect, let it all hang out when he said there was a cancerous growth around the President. . . ." He is worried by the Dean talk. "As I examined him it, uh, seems that he feels even he would be guilty of some, uh, criminal pra-, uh, liability, due to the fact that he, uh, participated in the action which, uh, resulted in taking care of the defendants while they were, uh, under trial. . . .

"Uh, the Haldeman selection of Magruder is still a very hard one for me to figure out. He was, he's made very few mistakes, but this is one case where Rose [Rose Mary Woods] was right. He picked a rather weak man who had all the appearance of character but who, really, lacks it when the, uh, chips are down."

The President balances the loyalty of his men against their blunders and his heart tugs him to reciprocal loyalty. All through the transcripts there is this one admirable combat quality in Nixon—he wants to stand by the men who stood by him. He will push loyalty to the furthest until, when he withdraws it, he withdraws it only to save himself. This night, though, as he speaks, "I feel for all the people involved here, because they were all as I pointed out to them in the meeting in the EOB this afternoon, involved for the very best of motives." They had covered for a crime they were not responsible for, in pursuit of that great election mandate which would give Nixon the authority to bestride the world as Supreme Peacemaker of the Twentieth Century. The crime that still bothers him most is the burglary, the break-in. "I don't think that, uh, certainly Haldeman or Ehrlichman had any idea about bugging," he explains to Clio. "I, I—and of course know Dean didn't."

But what course of action to take?

"They are going to meet with Mitchell in the morning," Nixon continues, "and I, uh, hope that Mitchell will really put his mind to this thing and perhaps out of it all can come so—some sort of a course of action we can follow. Uh, it seems to me just to hunker down without making any kind of statement is really, uh, too dangerous as far as the President—(57-second silence)—I got over to the house quite late—"

There the tape ends as far as transcribed and published.

One small crime, a simple burglary, had been committed. But a larger crime loomed ahead—not simply payoffs, but cover-up. Something had to be said to the American people; the President admits to himself this is the wisest course; but how could one tell the truth without telling all?

With that conundrum Richard Nixon wrestled for the next three weeks.

Next morning, Nixon was busy with official duties—the traffic of documents—on international load lines, patent classifications, the Annual International Economic Report, other signatures required. There were the meetings, ceremonial and cosmetic—briefings on foreign and domestic policy, meeting on marijuana and drug abuse, meetings with George Bush, and with the outgoing Latin American chairman of the Inter-American Committee of the Alliance for Progress; meetings with many others including Mrs. Bruce Bedford, Lawrenceville, New Jersey, ninety years of age—Mrs. Bedford had met nine Presidents in her lifetime and wanted to shake hands with a tenth, a wish Nixon graciously accorded her.

At 2:00 in the afternoon in the Executive Office Building, the President met with the high command of his irregulars—Messrs. Mitchell, Haldeman, Ehrlichman and Dean. The meeting lasted nearly two hours.

What they discussed, however, bore no relation to the blackmail crisis of the previous day—that had, apparently, been taken care of overnight. Nor did they talk of the underlying long-range problem. Instead they began by wincing to the crunch of that morning's events. That morning, Pat Gray, before a Senate public hearing, had finally cracked. He had said that John Dean "probably" lied, which meant that the Senate committee would almost certainly summon

Dean before it to explain the accusation. And that would compound the problem. Dean was the President's personal lawyer, bound by office and professional ethics to confidence. Now, however, the PR dimension of the problem would require rethinking of Dean's shelter of executive privilege—and John Mitchell advised that perhaps the smartest thing to do was to yield a bit here.

Executive privilege is a matter of vital importance to the conduct of the American Presidency. Unless the President can talk frankly, and listen to frank advice, he cannot think clearly enough to act effectively. Whoever invades his privacy weakens the Presidency. It was Richard Nixon's misfortune and guilt to invoke executive privilege, not to protect the Presidency, but to protect himself.

So they decided to yield on executive privilege. Then they went on to other matters. The night before, the President, alone, had told his dictabelt he favored bringing the story out via grand jury rather than on the Ervin Committee's television cameras. His team had discussed this course in the morning, objected to it; so now the President reversed himself. No grand-jury route. Then the President reverted to the plan of a basic strategic narrative written by John Dean to cover all—Dean to go to Camp David at once to write the story on which the President would "bottom" his whole defense.

The President then brought up the war for the headlines that the Ervin Committee would set off. But when Dean left the room for a few minutes, the President turned to his friend John Mitchell and said, "I can't let you go, go down." Then came a quick rumination on what had happened to Sherman Adams, Dwight Eisenhower's Haldeman, in whose firing he, Nixon, had been involved. Adams had made a mistake, said the President to Mitchell (who must have felt a chill), "but he shouldn't have been sacked, he shouldn't have been," the President repeated. "And, uh, for that reason, I am perfectly willing to—I don't give a shit what happens. I want you all to stonewall it, let them plead the Fifth Amendment, cover-up or anything else if it'll save it—save the plan. That's the whole point."

After that outburst, the President regained self-control. "On the other hand, uh, uh, I would prefer, as I said to you, that you do it the other way." The other way was to tell all. Because with the number of "jackass people they can call," the Ervin Committee's story would be a "hell of a lot worse" than the story as it really was.

Again the swing back and forth: how to tell without telling? Then the point of honor: he had to protect his men. "It's unfair—Haldeman and Dean. That's what Eisenhower, that's all he cared about—Christ, 'be sure he was clean.' Both in the fund thing and the Adams thing. But I don't look at it that way. And I just— That's the thing I'm really concerned with. We're going to protect our people if we can."

Finally, to Mitchell's interim strategy, from which he had privately hoped so much the night before. Mitchell, too, looked at it as a PR matter—and from that point of view again advised that concession was necessary. They should cooperate with the Ervin Committee, waive executive privilege, skip a special grand jury, make the public see they were cooperating. Mitchell, of course, did not know of tapes, could not foresee the danger of their disclosure. They were thus back exactly where they had started two hours earlier, and the meeting closed with the President escaping from it all: "Bob—what time is the—is my takeoff scheduled [for Florida] for 4:30 today?"

They left for Florida that Thursday afternoon and would not come back from the palms of Key Biscayne until the following Monday; by which time matters had grown unbelievably worse. For on Friday morning, March 23rd, John J. Sirica, the Federal District Court judge, had summoned for sentencing Hunt and the four Watergate culprits who had pleaded guilty two months earlier. A stern jurist, he had earned his nickname of "Maximum John" by throwing the maximum possible sentence at those his courts found guilty. Sirica's intelligence and dignity had been insulted by the testimony before him in January. Now, passing sentence on the guilty, he declared that they were being sentenced provisionally to an astonishing thirty-five years in jail for Hunt, forty years for the four others. But, added the judge, there was another way out. "I don't think the government wants a pound of flesh out of you. That is very little benefit to society . . . there will be a flurry of publicity as a result of your guilty pleas, naturally, but in a week or so it will be forgotten about. But, you see, I don't want it forgotten. So I have told your attorneys that the sentence that I will impose on you—and I am making no promise of leniencies . . . but the sentence I will impose will depend primarily on whether or not you cooperate with the . . . United States Senate. . . . I fully expect you to cooperate absolutely, completely and entirely with whoever from that [Senate] committee, whether it is a Senator or whether it is a staff investigator. Whoever it is who interrogates you, you will openly and honestly testify."

Not only that. The judge also released a letter he had received from James W. McCord who (along with Liddy) had earlier pleaded innocent but nonetheless been convicted. McCord, seeking leniency, acknowledged in his letter that political pressure had been applied to the defendants to remain silent, that perjury had been committed, that others, too, were involved. In short, Mr. McCord was ready to sing even before sentencing.

The news reached Mr. Nixon in Key Biscayne. He telephoned John Dean that afternoon to say "you were right in your prediction"; there could be no "cap on the bottle," and by that weekend the press was off with a new gush of revelations. The Ervin Committee investigators were on the trail. Not only those under Sirica's threat but those up and down the ladder of cover-up were volunteering to talk to them. And Ervin Committee members, as well as their staff members, were leaking to any newsman shrewd enough to find the tap points. By Monday, March 26th, the Los Angeles *Times* had surfaced the first leak: that McCord had told Samuel Dash, the committee's chief investigator, that he felt that John Dean and Jeb Magruder were both involved. The Washington *Post*, the *New York Times*, the weeklies and networks would all follow. In a few days, John Mitchell's name was added; and so much more, the White House knew, could follow. A race was now on. Those who felt themselves suspect raced to get to the United States Attorney's office fast enough to trade their testimony for immunity by plea-bargaining. The White House raced to get its story out before the Ervin Committee went public or leaked more.

One must follow these varied frenzied races on different

tracks: the search for scapegoats; the betrayals; the fogged and confused memories; the negotiations at the U.S. Attorney's office; and Tuesday, March 27th, as Jeb Magruder flew to New York to consult his old boss John Mitchell, the growing crisis was reviewed once again by the inner circle —Nixon, Haldeman, Ehrlichman—at the EOB hideaway from 11:10 to 1:30 P.M.

The problem of the council was simple: the press now had the names of John Dean and Jeb Magruder, with John Mitchell's soon to come. Since their guilt led to the White House, the President must move his version to the public as quickly as possible before the Ervin Committee foreclosed the opportunity. How?

Two new approaches were offered this afternoon. Dean had suggested a super-panel, similar to the Warren Commission on the Kennedy assassination. This would be a three-branch panel made up of leading statesmen of the Executive, Judiciary and Legislative branches of government who would investigate, call witnesses, impose penalties. ("Wonder if the President has the power to set up such a thing," asks Nixon. "Can he do that sort of thing? You know, that's the whole point, I don't think so." But the beauty of it, Haldeman points out, is that "the President maintains the ultimate stroke on it because he always has the option on January 19th to pardon anybody . . . so the potential ultimate penalty anybody would get hit in this process could be about two years.") The panel idea catches on with the President, and the name of William Rogers is suggested to head it ("Get Rogers over here for me," says the President); then another new idea, relayed from Kleindienst—to appoint a special prosecutor. That idea is dropped for the moment; it would come again later.

No other governing new approach is raised at this March 27th session and attention is still focused on the break-in itself, not on the "aftermath." But gliding gently, almost without realizing it, they approach the purge. They will get rid of Gray at once; he is a liability and the President fantasizes the statement of withdrawal Gray should make. Then the President toys with the idea of getting rid of Kleindienst, too, but decides to keep him for a few months more. Of course, Magruder must go. He must be forced to tell his story, and tell it fast, to keep the White House out front. He must be discredited immediately. The President: "Say that he is trying to lie to save his own skin," to which Haldeman responds, "It'll bend—it'll bend him."

But the sacrifice of Magruder may force the sacrifice of Mitchell. There is now no more talk of stonewalling it, of protecting Mitchell to the end. Mitchell has to be forced out. The President muses about what Mitchell can possibly say that will not put him in jail. The two others, however, savor the thought of Mitchell against the wall. Ehrlichman, who had disliked Mitchell since the 1968 campaign, hopes that the sacrifice of Mitchell will satisfy the baying press outside. "He's the big enchilada," says Ehrlichman. "He's the one the magazines zeroed in on this weekend," chimes in Haldeman; and then, later, "The interesting thing would be to watch Mitchell's face at the time I recommend to Magruder that he go in and ask for immunity and confess."

The President, even with his tough guys, cannot be that harsh. He is disturbed because he must see Mitchell tomorrow; "having this long seance with Mitchell tomorrow is going to be very difficult," he says; "well, I will get it done."

One notes: There is now a plan for a special panel—to be limited to the break-in at Watergate, as the "aftermath" still does not seem important. Mitchell is being considered for sacrifice. And the President has resolved to tell all, really all, at no matter what cost. But his resolve extends only to the Watergate break-in, not to the story of the underground or the aftermath. That story, or so he believes, is still reserved to himself by executive privilege.

Meanwhile the business of government cranked on. On this day, the President sent to Congress the Annual Report on the National Endowment for the Humanities. He had raised the budget of the National Foundation on the Arts and the Humanities from $12 million to $81 million (and proposed raising next year's budget to $153 million), more than any other President had ever given to arts, letters, the cultural spirit of America. He vetoed the Vocational Rehabilitation Bill as fiscally irresponsible. He met in the afternoon not only with Secretary of State Rogers in the Oval Office, but with the widow and family of Hale Boggs, the former House Majority Leader, who had been lost on a plane flight in Alaska the previous October. And he declared Alabama and Mississippi major disaster areas as a result of storms and flooding.

Perhaps Martha Mitchell, with a psychic sense of what had been happening in Washington, was the only one with a grip on the inner decision. "I fear for my husband," she telephoned the *New York Times*. "They're not going to pin anything on him. I won't let them."

The day had closed in typical confusion. Neither the President, Haldeman nor Ehrlichman could see the nature of the charge clearly; but outsiders were beginning to see it better. The next day, talking to John Ehrlichman over the telephone, Richard Kleindienst tried to make matters clear: "You have the Watergate inquiry by Senator Ervin, that's the political side of it," said Kleindienst. "And then you have the obligation imposed on us to investigate criminal conduct. Two separate distinct operations. They're getting all fuzzed up."

Fuzzed up they were. Dean had failed to deliver his basic Wheaties story from Camp David, where he had been sent to meditate. Neither Mitchell nor Haldeman had come up with a strategy. The press was now printing the leaks sprung by Sirica's stern sentencing and the Ervin Committee's initial investigations. More was being reported than the President at that point knew himself; and so, to close the week, on Friday, March 30th, he assigned a new responsibility to John Ehrlichman—a full, detailed, in-house investigation of the entire matter from beginning to end. And Ehrlichman would report back to the President as soon as possible. That done, the President was off once more to escape from Washington and the Eastern headlines—this time to San Clemente, where he would stay for nine days, from the evening of March 30th to Sunday, April 8th.

Nixon was beginning to be uncertain about whom he could trust. In San Clemente, he invited one of his earliest loyalists, Bob Finch, to come down from Los Angeles to visit him. Five months earlier, Finch, on the plane flight of election day to Washington, had tried to see Nixon alone, but had told Haldeman that he wanted to talk to the President about cleaning up Watergate; Finch had not been permitted a private conversation. This time, Finch did see the President alone—and when he left, a nervous Haldeman asked him just what it was they had been talking about.

Nixon seems to have enjoyed himself that week in California—President Nguyen Van Thieu of Vietnam arrived to consult, confer, be photographed and be feted. The California Angels were opening the baseball season in a night game with the Kansas City Royals, and the President enjoyed the outing. He was guest of honor at the annual dinner of the American Film Institute, where he awarded the Presidential Medal of Freedom to director John Ford. Routine moved easily across his desk and the nine-day stay was tranquil, except for one episode, one more major blunder: John Ehrlichman offered the directorship of the FBI to Judge Matt Byrne, then presiding over the trial of Daniel Ellsberg in Los Angeles. The offer, if not an actual bribe, was atrociously bad ethics. The President had known since March 17th that Ehrlichman had authorized the break-in at the offices of Ellsberg's psychiatrist; he had withheld that information from both the Department of Justice and the judge's court in Los Angeles. He should have known, if he did not, that the concealed break-in made a mistrial or a dismissal of charges likely; but he had withdrawn Gray's nomination from the Senate that week and wanted to offer quickly a new, impeccable name, a tough man of his own ("a Democrat, Irish, Catholic," he described his new candidate, Byrne, to Secretary Rogers some time later, "bachelor, forty-two years of age. . . . Thank God there's a jurist of that kind . . .").

By the time the President flew back to Washington on Sunday, the palace group had evolved, if not a plan, a new set of tactics resting on what Ehrlichman's interim investigation was discovering. Their concoction ran like this: The aggrieved President was just learning how deeply implicated Mitchell was in the break-in itself; thus, Mitchell as well as Magruder would be thrust forward to tell all; and John Dean, who had coordinated the aftermath, would testify before the grand jury, thus forestalling public testimony before the Ervin Committee.

Yet every trip to escape that the President made seemed to coincide with an escalation of the crisis in Washington; a new phase had begun almost simultaneously with his departure. On the weekend of his flight to California (March 30th), two of the key figures of the conspiracy, John Dean and Jeb Magruder, independently began to break. Mistrusting each other, caught in the same closing trap, each wanted to be first in the race to win grace from the prosecutors. On Thursday, Magruder had telephoned his attorney, James Bierbower, and arranged to fly to Bermuda for a conference with him on Saturday. On the previous day, Dean had met with his lawyers, Thomas Hogan and Charles Shaffer, and told them all.

Dean's lawyers were first off the mark—they were negotiating with the prosecutor's office by Monday, April 2nd, and for the next two weeks, until April 15th, Dean was telling as much as he felt he safely could—first about the events leading to the break-in, then more and more about the cover-up and his own role in it, then to the roles of Ehrlichman, Haldeman and the President. (On April 8th, Dean had telephoned Haldeman in California, the morning of the President's return flight. Without telling Haldeman that he had *already* begun confessing, he reported that he was considering talking to the prosecutors. Haldeman warned against that: "Once the toothpaste is out of the tube, it's going to be very hard to get it back in," he said.)

Magruder's lawyers were slower in persuading him to talk; but by Thursday, the 12th, they too were negotiating with the U.S. prosecutors, and on Friday, the 13th, and all morning Saturday, the 14th, in Bierbower's office at 1625 K Street N.W., Magruder was confessing, telling all, bargaining, settling finally for a one-count felony which, with judicial mercy, could be reduced to twenty months in jail.

When the President returned to his White House on Sunday, April 8th, he was in more trouble than he knew. And in the next ten days, Richard Nixon passed his point of no return.

The transcripts, read them how one will, make all coherence impossible, for they reflect the chaos inside the mind of Richard Nixon. The taped conversations slither about, intertwine, shift gear and thought in mid-sentence; they serpentine in and out of the President's conscience, his loyalty to his loyalists, his responsibilities, his vulnerability, their vulnerability, the principle of executive privilege, the political dimensions of the Ervin hearings.

The single thread that runs through them, if any thread

can be found at all, is the thread of non-comprehension and his assumption of his own innocence. He had not, *knew* he had not, been guilty of ordering the Watergate break-in; his men had done that. But it was as if his chauffeur had been caught breaking a speed limit. His June 23rd directive to Haldeman to slow up the FBI investigation, if he remembered it, was of as little moment as if he had tried to fix a police ticket for his chauffeur. And now it had all gotten out of hand; the details of what had happened led back to more details, to the Huston memo, to the entire underground, and his mind apparently could not quite grasp what it all meant.

Strangely for a man trained in the law, Nixon had forgotten one of the most ancient definitions of crime in Anglo-American jurisprudence: misprision of felony. Misprision, deriving from the old French word *mesprendre* ("to make a mistake"), is the guilt of an official who should be able to recognize a crime but either fails to or refuses to bring it to court.

Over the next ten days, that area of his personal vulnerability was finally to be made clear to him—as were many other facts and details in the behavior of his men which he should long since have known.

One should pause in this telling of the critical ten days in April to note a minor but significant event. On the plane back from California, the President, by a tug of his better self, had decided that it would be useful to have new advice, and so had ordered that Leonard Garment be invited in as counsel to prepare his staff's defense before the Ervin Committee. On Monday, April 9th, Ronald Ziegler passed the word to Garment, and the next day Garment saw the President, who told him, simply, to "go ahead and find out all [he] could about the Watergate matter." It would become a vital assignment, but here it is important as a fluctuation in the Nixon character. There was always a cluster of honorable men like Garment who served Richard Nixon —William Rogers, Robert Finch, Elliot Richardson, Daniel Moynihan, speechwriters Price, Buchanan and Safire; and later men like Fred Buzhardt, Melvin Laird and Alexander Haig. Nixon liked these men. But to post such men about one of his selves was to post sentinels against the other self, and set them against the men who protected that other self. When he posted Garment to investigate those who guarded his tough side, he began that sequence of appointments which a year and a half later would climax in the palace insurrection that led to his resignation.

All through this week—while Magruder and Dean were making their way to the prosecutor's office—the President idled, while Ehrlichman and Garment made their separate investigations.

Ehrlichman was finished first. In California, Ehrlichman had interviewed the key officials of CREEP; Kleindienst, the Attorney General, his old enemy; Herb Kalmbach; and others. In Washington, Ehrlichman continued his interviewing, ending on Friday, April 13th, at 5:00 P.M. with a talk with Charles Colson, Mitchell's old enemy; and Ehrlichman's final notes on Mitchell, reproduced in his own neat handwriting by the Ervin Committee, read thus:

> JNM [for John N. Mitchell]: Unbalanced,
> stress,
> didn't want to go to 1701,
> drink
> disorg
> never under control
> wife

With this, the puritan John Ehrlichman was ready to report to the President the next morning, Saturday, April 14th, the first event in a weekend of anguish.

The transcripts of the grotesque weekend of April 14th and 15th, running on to the mini-decision of April 17th, make no sense if one seeks the working of sequential minds. They can be read only as a record of agony as Nixon gradually realizes that it is the cover-up, not the break-in, for which his staff must stand trial.

The clearest of the conversations is that between Nixon, Haldeman and Ehrlichman, which begins in the Executive Office Building hideaway at 8:55 on the critical Saturday morning, April 14th, and runs for two and a half hours.

Ehrlichman has submitted his oral report and he is the protagonist of this conversation. He makes sense to start with. He reports Colson's opinion of the previous day—that this weekend is the last chance to get out front. By next week Hunt, Magruder, Mitchell may all be before the grand jury and, with the leaks, all will come unstuck. The President says, "I want to get all the pieces in my mind if I can," and Ehrlichman runs through the payoff, winding up with his conclusion that Mitchell and Dean have to be put against the wall, and fast. The conversation sticks on Mitchell; Ehrlichman thinks he must go; John Connally has also advised that Mitchell go; then all agree that Mitchell must go, today. He is only two hours away in New York, a plane can be sent for him.

Ehrlichman does an arabesque on how the story will play in the news magazines. It can run, says Ehrlichman, displaying a rewrite man's skill, as "The White House may have its cover-up finally collapse [sic] last week when the grand jury indicted John Mitchell and Jeb Magruder," or it can run, "Events moved swiftly last week, after the President was presented with a report indicating for the first time that suspicion of John Mitchell and Jeb Magruder as ringleaders in the Watergate break-in were facts substantiated by considerable evidence." The latter news story is preferable. But Ehrlichman speaks further from conscience. He had this week been listening to a taped telephone conversation with Jeb Magruder and he says, "I sit over there in Bob's office and listen to that tape of one of the co-actors saying flat out on the tape that he was guilty and that Mitchell (unintelligible) was going to force our fall . . . and I said to myself, 'My God, you know, I'm a United States citizen. I'm standing here listening to this, what is my duty?' "

Their duty, of course, was clear—to act. But now the race has accelerated—it is not a race against the press, it is a race for the record, Ehrlichman points out, so that "sometime two months from now, three months from now, a year" the record will show that the President acted; that he moved the moment he was given the solid information Ehrlichman has now brought him. So they must crack down on Mitchell now, today. The President says Mitchell must be confronted by someone who knows the case ("I can verse myself in it enough to know the thing, but I am not sure that I want to know"); then goes on, for it is all becoming clear to him. "The cover-up . . . well, basically, it's a second crime. . . . Isn't that right, John? . . . Do you think they [the Ervin Committee and press] would keep going on the cover-up even if Mitchell went in?"

Ehrlichman tells the President he assumes so; and thus they go on to the public scenario to cover the cover-up, which brings them to John Dean. The President is still obviously unfamiliar with the details of the payoff and hush money and would remain so for months, probably on some of the details to this day. But the new scenario reads that the money paid will be publicly described as compassion money, not hush money, or rather like the contributions left-wingers made to pay for the defense of the Chicago Seven and the Berrigan brothers. This scenario also requires a public culprit and it can only be the administrator of the cover-up, John Dean. All three agree. However the record may ultimately read, this conference has been the official Ehrlichman report on wrongdoing, and Ehrlichman, thinking clearly, says, "You are now possessed of a body of fact . . . you can't just sit here. . . . You've got to act on it . . . you've got to make some decisions and the Dean thing is one of the decisions that you have to make."

But first Mitchell must be confronted that afternoon— and jettisoned. Ehrlichman rehearses his pitch to Mitchell ("Far better that you [Mitchell] should be prosecuted on information from the U.S. Attorney based on your conversation with the U.S. Attorney than on an indictment by a grand jury of 15 blacks and 3 whites"). The President serpentines once more, but finally agrees: "We have to prick the boil and take the heat. Now that's what we're doing here. We're going to prick this boil and take the heat. I— am I overstating?" To which Ehrlichman responds, "I think that's right. The idea is this will prick the boil. . . . The history of this thing has to be . . . that you did not tuck this under the rug yesterday or today, and hope it would go away."

Thus to technical detail. By now all have accepted wire-taps and tapings as common practice. The conversation has woven through the taping of Magruder, of Kleindienst, of others, and now they have to set up Mitchell.

Ehrlichman says: "I would like a record of my conversation with both Magruder and Mitchell. I think personally that maybe I ought to get my office geared up so that I can do that."

"Why don't you just gear it up?" replies the President. "Do you know, do you have a way to gear it up?"

Ehrlichman: "Yeah. I've done it before."

President: "Well go gear it," and then immediately in the same phrase, "No, no. Well, wait a minute. No, I think that's too—" One wonders whether the President is speaking with consciousness of his own taping, running even at the moment; or from decency; or simply from friendship, an inner loyalty that is still deeply felt—but ultimately squelchable.

These decencies of personal relationships tug constantly underneath the operational decisions. Nixon is pained by what he must do to his friend Mitchell. He feels that Dean, too, is truly not guilty, or if he is, only in terms of law: "What Dean did, he did with all conscience in terms that the higher good—" Magruder hurts, too: "I was thinking last night, this poor little kid . . . lovely wife and all the rest. It just breaks your heart. And say this, this is a very painful message for me to bring . . . also I would first put that in, so that he knows I have personal affection." One recalls Lewis Carroll's "The Walrus and the Carpenter" eating the oysters: " 'I weep for you,' the Walrus said, 'I deeply sympathize.' "

So the conversations wore on through the afternoon; with Mitchell arriving; talking to Ehrlichman; refusing to walk the plank; and the President getting that report. Finally, he attended the annual banquet of the White House Correspondents Association—arriving by careful arrangement just after a $1,000 prize was awarded to Messrs. Woodward and Bernstein of the Washington *Post* for their work in unearthing the Watergate scandals.

After the dinner, he returned to the White House; telephoned Haldeman; then telephoned John Ehrlichman at 11:22.

That conversation heightens the movement of tragedy. The day's events, the race for the record have caused the three to cast many friends overboard. Now the President, who is clear, finally, about the nature of the second crime, obstruction of justice, is beginning to weigh its full implications, his full vulnerability. Should he get rid of Haldeman, too? he asks Ehrlichman, as if the question were a way-out fancy. He has obviously already talked about this thought with others: Kissinger, he says, is against jettisoning Haldeman, Ziegler is against jettisoning Haldeman; but Garment is for it. Ehrlichman, however, stands firm with his old college classmate. Then, with another erratic jump across a canyon of association, the President's conversation brings him to the doom side of the trail that may lie ahead. "You know, I was just thinking tonight," he says to Ehrlichman, "as I was making up my notes for this little talk, you know, what the hell, it is a little melodramatic, but it is totally true that what happens in this office in these next four years will probably determine whether there is a chance, and it's never been done before, that you could have some sort of an uneasy peace for the next 25 years. . . . whatever legacy we have, hell, it isn't going to be in getting a cesspool for Winnetka, it is going to be there."

If Saturday night was uneasy for the President, it would have been more so had he known what his Attorney General, Richard Kleindienst, was hearing that night. For it was in the course of that night that the President lost his race for the record. The Saturday conversations had been bottomed on the premise that the President would be the first of record to force the culprits, his lieutenants, to justice. Cruel as the decisions were, they were obligatory if the record was to read that he had acted on his own.

But this same Saturday the culprits had beaten him. For days, the two most vulnerable of the underground net, Dean and Magruder, had been telling all they knew to the prosecutors in the hope of the mercy which justice yields to those who cooperate. And so, from 1:00 to 5:00 on the morning of Sunday, April 15th, while the President slept, the Attorney General had been listening to his department's prosecutors give him the full details of the cover-up as far as they had learned it then; which was in more detail than the President or Ehrlichman knew. The Attorney General knew he must act at once and telephoned the White House at 8:41 A.M.

At 1:12 Sunday afternoon, Kleindienst was in the President's EOB office, spreading out a story which made the previous day's scenario obsolete. The President that morning had finished worship services, lunched with his clerical guests, listened to the Rochester Male Chorus, been photographed with the singers at 1:05. Then Kleindienst. Kleindienst said the Department of Justice now had what he felt was a full story: John Ehrlichman, Bob Haldeman and John Mitchell were all indictable. It probably gave Kleindienst little pain to report on Ehrlichman and Haldeman; they had tried to fire him four and a half months before at Camp David. But the case against Mitchell troubled Kleindienst; the two had been friends; Mitchell had supported Kleindienst as his successor as Attorney General. It would be inappropriate for him, Kleindienst, to prosecute his friend; and so, once again, Kleindienst urged the appointment of a special prosecutor. This time, Kleindienst added force to the plea: he had discussed the matter with the Chief Justice, and the Chief Justice also supported the idea of a special prosecutor. By midnight of Sunday, after four conversations that evening with Henry Petersen, Assistant Attorney General in the Criminal Division, the President had a clear, if disastrous picture of the situation. Petersen had almost enough evidence from Dean now to indict Mitchell; Dean had offered to tell all, but had told Petersen that whatever sentencing package was to be made of his felony in the cover-up, that package must include Haldeman and Ehrlichman, too. And so the Saturday scenario had totally blown.

A few options were still open to Richard Nixon for the next forty-eight hours. There was the option of doing justice, as a President should—of ridding himself of his own guilt by confession, and letting the law take its way with all others. There was the option of hanging John Mitchell and John Dean separately and then, by destroying his tapes, making it their word against his if they tried to implicate him in open court. There was the option of telling all—all about the Plumbers, all about the wire-taps, all about the IRS, all about the underground—and, at the same time, appointing a special prosecutor or investigator who simultaneously would report the same story directly to him and to the American people.

Yet for the next day and a half the President would choose none of these options. All day Monday and into Tuesday, he wandered through conversations, picking his words toward a public statement that could not be long delayed. Once more he is wrestling with the problems he could not solve on March 22nd—how to tell anything without disclosing everything. Early Monday, he confronts Dean with a demand for resignation—but Dean outfaces him, demanding that Haldeman and Ehrlichman go, too. He rambles with Haldeman and Ehrlichman, trying to weave a scenario that tells as much of the underground story as they can; but that does not work. He sees Henry Petersen for almost two hours in the afternoon and explains why speed is urgent in getting out a statement: we have to "keep ahead of the curve," he explains; "The President should be out front," he says later. But Petersen can see no way of getting out front except to put Haldeman and Ehrlichman overboard now.

Thus, in total confusion of purpose, through the morning and midafternoon of April 17th, with Petersen, Ziegler, Haldeman, Ehrlichman all tugging at him, the President approves a public statement on Watergate, his first on a road which would, finally, take fifteen statements or open letters, eight press conferences and four TV appearances to make matters clear before August 9th, 1974.

This first of his long sequence of explanations, his statement of April 17th, set the tone for the rest. He grudgingly yielded what had to be yielded—waiving executive privilege so that White House aides could testify to the Ervin Committee in public. And ambiguously admitted what could now no longer be denied: "That on March 21st, as a result of serious charges which came to my attention," he had begun a whole new investigation, as a result of which he would send before the grand jury anyone in his administration suspect of criminal activity with no promise of immunity from prosecution.

But the President was still behind the curve; the noose was tightening. He had cast overboard to justice Mitchell, Dean, Magruder, LaRue, Strachan, Chapin as well as all the lower-level crawling things of the underground. But he was not yet ready to go that far with Haldeman and Ehrlichman, and in protecting them he was breaking law and ethics as a man with jackboots crunches glass without feeling it beneath his feet. He promised Petersen on April 17th that all that Petersen had told him, including Petersen's desire to move against Haldeman and Ehrlichman, would be private between them, between a President and his law-enforcement officers. Within minutes he had broken his word and explained to Haldeman and Ehrlichman their dilemma and his. They offered to resign, but the President said no— yet assured them if it came to that he could always find places for them in the Nixon Foundation. Indeed, they had joked among themselves as Haldeman had needled Ehrlichman, "You can handle traffic cases," and Ehrlichman had replied, "Well, I'm not too pleased with the traffic cases." The President was loyal to these two as long as he could afford to be, certainly until the next weekend, when, on Friday, the 20th of April, he was off, this time escaping to Key Biscayne.

His return to Washington, as always in these critical weeks, brought more bad news. On Wednesday, the 25th, Kleindienst, just learning the story, told him the details of the break-in at the office of Ellsberg's psychiatrist. The President had known of Ehrlichman's involvement in that caper since March 17th; but Kleindienst now insisted that the information had to be relayed to Judge Byrne, holding court in Los Angeles, which would probably cause the Ellsberg case to result in a dismissal of charges.

The true panic begins to build that same Wednesday, April 25th. It begins that morning, in Nixon's conversation with John Ehrlichman and Bob Haldeman, which runs almost three hours, from just after 11:00 to just before 2:00 in the afternoon. Ehrlichman thrusts the action with considerable bravery and candor. They are facing the threat of John Dean to tell all; and, says Ehrlichman, "I think it's entirely conceivable that if Dean is totally out of control and if matters are not handled adroitly that you could get a resolution of impeachment. . . . I don't know if you've thought of this or not, but I got to thinking about it last night. Uh. On the ground you committed a crime . . . and there is no other legal process available to the United States people other than impeachment." The dread word has been spoken; they must face the Dean threat; they decide that Haldeman will listen to the tape of the March 21st conversation immediately and measure the threat.

Haldeman is back within three hours, at 4:40, to report to the President on what actually had been said in that pivotal conversation. There is almost lunatic lucidity to Nixon's conversation now. As Haldeman reports, the President arrays the evidence of his own words against himself: "I said a million dollars. With a million dollars (unintelligible) clemency. You couldn't do it till after the '74 elections. That's an incriminating thing. . . ."

The thought suddenly occurs to him that Dean may have had a tape recorder in his pocket, but Haldeman is overriding, coaching his President in reconstructing and stagelighting the conversation: "At this point, you're, you're investigating. . . ." Haldeman goes on with his coaching, the President perceivng all the dangers in his own words while Haldeman, still serving the man he loved, tries to weave a protective screen around the President's words. And the President knows, his mind sharp, that this protective PR screen may not work, ". . . you, Ehrlichman and I have got to put the wagons up around the President on this particular conversation. I just wonder if the son-of-a-bitch had a recorder on him. (Tape noise.) I didn't notice any but I wasn't looking."

By the end of the day it is clear that what is at issue is the impeachment of the President, and the vulnerability of Haldeman and Ehrlichman. The centerpiece of the action is the words of March 21st. Can they be kept secret? A quiet hysteria has built in the President, his suspicions having gripped on John Dean's possible tape recorder. And that is the subject of the last recorded conversation of that day, a telephone call from the President to Haldeman in the evening, the President starting abruptly: "Is there any, uh, way that, uh, even surreptitiously or discreetly or otherwise I mean, that, ah, way you could determine whether Dean might have walked in there with a recorder on him? . . ." Haldeman tries to soothe the President's panic, remove the obsessive thought. But the President in his nightmare persists, "but . . . even the smallest ones are bulky enough that you mean, with a fellow like Dean you'd sort of see that wouldn't ya, where do you carry them, in your hip pocket or your breast pocket?" Haldeman: "Oh, under your arm, you know, where you carry a pistol holster or something . . . it's so remote as to be almost beyond the realm of possibility." The President: "In this matter nothing is beyond the realm of possibility."

Haldeman soothes the President, re-assures him that there can be no Dean tape-recording. Haldeman seems to be in a hurry to get back to his tape listenings that evening as the conversation closes. They, the men of the Presidency, control the tapes—so long as the Presidency shelters them from evidence they are possibly safe.

If Wednesday, April 25th, was a bad day, then Friday, April 27th, was dramatically, climactically worse. That afternoon, the President learned that the *New York Times* was about to break a story by its indefatigable investigative reporter, Seymour Hersh—and the story would claim that Dean's testimony implicated the President himself in the web of unraveling crimes.

The President summoned Henry Petersen to the Oval Office at 5:37 that Friday. One must remember that he has now been under mounting pressure for days—from Kleindienst, from Garment, from Rogers, from Petersen—to get rid of Haldeman and Ehrlichman. But now he himself is a target. Is the Hersh story true? he asks of the Assistant Attorney General. Does his chief official prosecutor have charges or information against the President of the United States?

"Now, Henry, this I've got to know. . . . Now, understand, I have told you everything I know about this thing," says the President.

Petersen promises to call U.S. Attorney Titus and Silbert, Glanzer, Campbell, his prosecuting team, to find out whether Dean had in fact implicated the President.

"Do you mind calling them right now?" asks the President.

Petersen leaves to telephone his staff, returns in twenty minutes; and the President, as if reading his face, greets him with an almost Shakespearean phrase: ". . . as like all things, some substance, some falsity?"

Petersen reports that Dean's lawyer, Charles Shaffer, has said, has, uh, threatened, "We will bring the President in—not this case but in other things." The President is almost incoherent for half an hour ("You've got to believe me, I am after the truth even if it hurts me"). He is bitter about John Dean—though he has just called him to wish him Happy Easter. He calls in Ron Ziegler for corroboration:

"since March 21st when I had that conversation with Dean, I have broken my ass to try to get the facts of this case. Right? Tried to get that damn Liddy to talk." Turns again to Petersen after Ziegler has left: "if there's one thing you have got to do, you have got to maintain the Presidency out of this. I have got things to do for this country and I'm not going to have—now this is personal. I sometimes feel like I'd like to resign. Let Agnew be President for a while. He'd love it."

Then the President composes himself. He reviews cleanly, with the old clarity, the options left him—to let the grand jury act at the prosecutors' behest; to put out on leaves of absence those under charge; or force his men to resign. The lines of his authority are, up to this point on Friday, April 27th, still clear. The President is talking to one of his instruments, Henry Petersen, Assistant Attorney General, whom he can reward or punish. He is musing to this civil servant as if Petersen were, indeed, his to control; he is musing whether or not the Department of Justice should grant Dean immunity. The thought here, in the back of the Presidential mind, must have been that by refusing immunity to Dean he might still be able to hush Dean, and so protect Haldeman and Ehrlichman. "Now, in Dean's case, I do not want the impression left . . . that by saying 'Don't grant immunity to a major person,' that in so doing I am trying to block Dean giving evidence against Haldeman or Ehrlichman. . . . Do I make myself clear?"

But he is brought up short. The toneless transcripts read:

Petersen: "Yes. Let me make myself clear."

President: "Yes."

Petersen: "I regard immunity authority under the statutes of the United States to be my responsibility, of which I cannot divest myself."

President: "Right."

Petersen: "And—ah—we take opinions, but I would have to treat this as advisory only."

The transcripts give no sign of breath, pause, alarm. But Henry Petersen, a Level IV Presidential appointee, had told the President, to his face, that he considered himself under command not of the President, but of the law.

And the President had lost control.

If there had been any doubt about the fate of Haldeman and Ehrlichman, there was doubt no longer. If Dean was determined to bring everyone down, and if Petersen refused to hold Dean in pawn by denying immunity—then the whole story must break, and Nixon's two closest would have to be discarded. He cherished both men; needed them; had refused for days to accept the resignations they had offered. But now they must go.

It was Friday evening now, and he must act. On Saturday he took counsel. Garment, who had been for the firing of Haldeman and Ehrlichman for over two weeks, recalled the wisdom of Gladstone—that a great prime minister must sometimes be a butcher. And suggested that the President appoint Elliot Richardson as Attorney General in Kleindienst's place. Nixon called his Secretary of State, Rogers. Rogers supported the nomination of Richardson to replace Kleindienst and undertook to call Richardson that afternoon at his home to explain the need of his accepting the post, to which, after some reluctance, Richardson agreed. The President further asked Rogers whether he would do the firing of Haldeman and Ehrlichman. Rogers replied that since he had not hired them, he could not, would not fire them. The President asked whether Rogers would join him at Camp David the next day and be with him, present in the room, when he fired Haldeman and Ehrlichman. Rogers again said no. The President asked Rogers, finally, whether he would come anyway to Camp David just to be there, to sit around and wait while he was doing the firing. To this, Rogers agreed.

So all journeyed out to Camp David on Sunday, April 29th, for the butchery. The President, Len Garment, Bill Rogers, Ray Price, Rose Mary Woods, Haldeman and Ehrlichman. Kleindienst and Richardson were later to put in separate appearances—Kleindienst to be dismissed and Richardson to be appointed. Richardson was assured in face-to-face conversation with the President that the President was not involved personally in the scandal ("He told me so, convincingly," recalled Richardson later). Garment was appointed acting Counsel to the President for Watergate matters on the specific promise, recalls Garment, that he would have access to all data (which he would not get) and the President's assurance of his own "non-involvement."

At Laurel Lodge, Garment and Price both worked on the statement that was to be issued the next day, which they wanted as short and direct as possible. And the President then went about the work of dismissing Haldeman and Ehrlichman at Aspen Lodge while Rogers sat in an adjacent room. Haldeman keeps his recollection of that day to himself. Ehrlichman remembers being greeted by the President on the terrace of Aspen Lodge and being told it was to be a very painful conversation. They went inside and there the President broke down and wept, and offered to help Ehrlichman with his attorneys' fees from a large sum of money he had available to him—which Ehrlichman refused. The President then asked if there were anything else he could do for Ehrlichman and so Ehrlichman later reported: "I said he could explain to our children why he was asking me to leave. That, basically, was the end of the meeting."

By this time, early in the evening, the deed had been done and Rose Mary Woods was given next day's statement to type, which she remembers reading for the first time in a state of shock. And the President and his Secretary of State, Rogers, had dinner alone together. Rogers remembers the dinner as very gloomy, the President non-talkative, contemplative, fully aware of the consequences that must follow. He broke out in bitterness about Judge Sirica once, and Rogers tried to explain that Sirica was only trying to get the truth out. Nixon referred guardedly to "other things" that might lie ahead, but Rogers did not know what they might be. Mostly they talked of how much good they, two old friends, had done for the country and the cause of peace, and of how in the long run that was what would count. "You accomplish a lot of things," Rogers recalls Nixon as saying, "you're active—and there are hazards to it."

The statement of April 30th was better, but only marginally better, than the statement of April 17th. It had the hardness of new facts in it. The President was accepting the resignations of Haldeman and Ehrlichman ("two of the finest public servants it has been my privilege to know"); and also that of Kleindienst with regret. Also that of John Dean—with no comment. And he was appointing a new Attorney General, Elliot Richardson, to whom he gave authority to name a Special Prosecutor. Leonard Garment would be appointed Counsel to the President in place of John Dean, to study all matters relating to Watergate, and would report directly to him.

Nixon was busy the next two days in Washington—Tuesday and Wednesday—with the state visit and state dinner of West German Chancellor Willy Brandt. He carried off his other public duties with equanimity, but found time, privately, to lose his temper with Garment, who had, immediately on taking over his new office, thrown in twenty-one FBI agents to guard the files in the offices of Haldeman and Ehrlichman around the clock. Garment, like Richardson, like the other new appointees to come, took his assignment seriously, unbelieving that there could be a conflict of national interest with the President's interest. And Garment had been put down and insulted too often by Haldeman and Ehrlichman to believe that they did indeed represent the true interests of the President he was attempting to save.

By Thursday, with Brandt en route back to Germany, Nixon could leave Washington—for Key Biscayne, where the next day, Friday, May 4th, he appointed General Alexander Haig to be his Chief of Staff to replace Haldeman.

Others of the Haig caliber would soon join what, in effect, was a new administration of the Presidency—Laird, Richardson, Garment, Buzhardt. But they were loyal only to the public policies of Richard Nixon, his proclaimed purposes, the record that had won for him the largest popular election margin in American history. He could trust such men to serve such public purposes, but not to protect him personally. He was alone—all alone against what he had told Petersen a few days before was "the system."

And on May 17th, as the Ervin Committee gaveled open its hearings, "the system" took over.

9

THE SYSTEMS RESPOND: SPRING 1973

It was customary to say, during the two years when Richard Nixon was being driven from power, that "the American system worked."

The phrase perplexed me, and as 1973–74 wore on, I had to examine both what was meant by the system and what was meant by power. For if I could not explain them to myself, then the ordeal of the two years was meaningless—a detective hunt for the key to a series of squalid crimes, a bungled burglary authorized by bad men who happened to be in power by an accident of history. No one had been hurt, imprisoned, tortured in those years. None of the criminals had grown rich by extortion or bribery. None had conspired with foreign powers. Almost all their crimes had happened before in American history—but the intensity of the response to them was a watershed.

As I pursued the response, I began to see that there was no such thing as "a system." The central armature of government was the Federal state; and about this state and within it circled many "systems," all of them attempting to sway the state, move it, bend it to their purpose, or wall themselves off from its interference. Though each of the systems acted by its own internal dynamics, its own internal ethos or greed, all together in their action they buttressed the state—they gave it life and vigor, moved it in one direction or another. The state itself, however, had its roots not in this circle of systems but in faith; faith and confidence are the bedrock of all states, free or tyrannical. Without faith, no state can survive.

I had during the Second World War seen a real revolution and I had written glibly about "the system" collapsing in China. In retrospect, now I can see that there was no system in China of any kind, and except for a handful of divisions loyal to Chiang Kai-shek, nothing to buttress the state. Provincial divisions in the same army distrusted each other. Landlords did not trust each other. Peasants trusted no one. Nobody trusted the paper money that served as currency, the banking system least of all. The academies had been destroyed by the Japanese invasion of 1937; they could offer no help to the state. And the state simply dissolved as its supporting systems dissolved because confidence and trust had dissolved first.

Sun Yat-sen had once called his people *"I pan san sha"* —a sheet of sand, particles of human beings with nothing to bind them, and in Honan, in 1943, I learned what he meant. In Honan that year, 2,000,000 peasants died of starvation in the great famine, and through the worst of it the colonels of Chiang Kai-shek were extorting from the peasants even their seed grain. I saw dogs eating dead bodies in open fields. But no Chinese reporter was allowed to publish this story. Yet, the next year when the peasants of Honan finally took their pitchforks, knives and guns and fought alongside the Japanese invaders against their own government, it came as a surprise to Chiang Kai-shek and his ministers of state. Just as it came as a surprise to the world when an entirely new party, the party of Mao Tse-tung, simply shrugged off the old state and made a new Communist state—whose bedrock was faith.

I had also in my youth lived through what we Americans called a "revolution" in my own country—the Depression of the thirties and the response to it of the American government. It was up to government, to the state, to save us— and lo, the state did, with relief, with public welfare, with make work. Roosevelt masterfully co-opted a number of old systems, created one new system (that of the labor unions), then invited another system—academia—to enter government, change the direction of state and thus save it as we knew it. He restored faith in government—and brought to its support all those new systems which persisted for a generation as a Democratic majority called the Roosevelt coalition.

The Republican Party was one of the classic examples of a party mobilizing systems to sway government of the state.

Far back in the last century it had become apparent that neither of the two contemporary parties nor the government could contain the crisis of slavery. And so a system of old moralists, led by the Protestant churches of the North, threw up new institutional leaders who founded the Republican Party, which mastered the slavery crisis by a war, changed the country's culture, but retained its form of state.

That party had been born out of faith in union and freedom; had co-opted the aggressive leaders of a new business and industrial system during the war; and then, though it remained the governing party for half a century, saw its constituent systems divide, the men of civic good against the men of greed. Underlying the stupendous election victory of 1972, more than a century later, was the first major recognition by the Republican Party of its need to co-opt new systems. What the American people voted for in voting for Richard Nixon was, first, peace, which he pledged—and, next, his consent to let the ethnic communities and local governments of the United States lead their own lives with minimal interference by the Federal government. What brought about his downfall was the contradiction between his smothering public pieties and his ruthless private conduct—for as soon as any of the systems in America could expose these, none of the systems that had supported him in the election would stand in his defense, because he had breached the faith on which all rests. Abstract this faith, and Americans would be like Sun Yat-sen's Chinese—a world of sand particles.

What is unique about the crisis of 1973–74 is how very much it was divorced from conventional politics. The Democratic Party did not attack, the Republican Party did not defend; the business system, the banking system and the labor-union system stood apart; so, too, did the clergy.

It was three specific systems acting by themselves and by their own dynamics—the press from outside, the judicial system and Congressional leadership acting from within—that moved first tentatively, then inexorably to bring about the downfall of Richard Nixon. Together they wrote a story which gave the American people the intolerable choice between cynically accepting an aberration in conventional political practice or dramatically repudiating the hereditary faith in their national government. And the American people had to affirm faith or else see their state transformed.

If any of the managerial conservatives in the White House had ever paused to read the writings of John C. Calhoun, or pondered on Calhoun's theory of "concurrent majorities" they might have understood what they provoked in 1973. Calhoun held that no government could long operate without a general concurrence of its systems—if any one of the social or community systems felt its survival threatened, it would resist by all means possible; it would make war to survive. Which theory of Calhoun's explained both the Civil War of 1861 and the movement of the news system in 1973–74. For, though the action of the news system began with routine professionalism, it was to move on to a historic level because the survival of its freedoms turned out to be at stake.

By the beginning of 1973 the news system of the United States had been pushed to the wall. Its practitioners had been spied on, intimidated, tax-harassed—and they feared worse. In defending itself by counter-attack, it was defending far more than the news system. It was defending the rights of all Americans; if individual reporters and newspapers and TV outlets were not safe, then no one was safe from the same search and seizure, harassment, tax menace and reprisal to which the news system felt itself subject. That the news system did vent its prejudices in 1973–74, that some of its leading members perhaps indeed violated law (particularly in seeking or revealing grand jury testimony), that it certainly whipped up passion—all this is undeniable. But whatever their extravagance, the men and women of the news system could take their absolution from Barry Goldwater's campaign keynote of 1964— "Extremism in the defense of liberty is no vice! . . . Moderation in the pursuit of justice is no virtue."

It was the news system, thus, that was the first to break forward in pursuit of Richard Nixon; and since all systems are moved by individuals, if one had to choose a name with which to begin the story of the systems, it would be that of a pale-faced, hollow-eyed, debonair editor called Ben Bradlee —the executive editor of the Washington *Post*, crown-piece of a major publishing and communications empire threatened by the Nixon administration with reprisal and dismemberment.

Benjamin Crowninshield Bradlee, Boston-born, was a Back Bay Yankee (not, like Colson, a Swamp Yankee), of a family as traditional as the sacred Cod that hangs from the balcony of Bulfinch's Beacon Hill State House. Neither pious nor religious, he nursed beneath his apparent outer cynicism a particularly personal faith in America.

A Harvard man who had majored in Greek classics and American literature, Bradlee—both his friends and enemies agreed—had style. And just as the style of the Nixon administration led the Nixon team to its crime, so the style of Ben Bradlee governed his reportorial team.

Style was important to Bradlee. If any man belonged to that Establishment which Richard Nixon so hated, Bradlee did. His first wife had been a Boston Saltonstall; his second wife was a Pennsylvania Pinchot. He himself spoke impeccable French, and in his years in Europe had been a Sunday painter. At St. Marks, his preparatory school, he had loved reading in American history; his favorite book had been Otto Eisenschiml's *The Case of A.L.*, a study of the murder of Abraham Lincoln, which he remembered as "a marvelous combination of detective work, investigative reporting and good writing."

As for style—high style was something that John F. Kennedy had brought to Washington. Bradlee had known Kennedy since Kennedy was a junior Senator; loved him; when Kennedy became President, Bradlee visited the White House as if it were the home of a friend.

But as a journalist he could not resist puncturing even a Kennedy when his reporters came up with a good story—as when, for example, Bradlee, then Washington bureau chief of *Newsweek*, and his friends on the Boston *Globe* jointly foiled a Kennedy plan to place a totally unqualified old family crony, Francis X. Morrissey, on the Federal bench in New England. But Kennedy had equivalent style. He could be furious at Bradlee's stroke, accept it as part of the game President and press played with each other, and continue his friendship with Bradlee undismayed.

From the very beginning of the Nixon administration, it was the Nixon style that offended Bradlee most. "The man had no style, no style at all," said Bradlee. And as offensive as anything else in the Nixon non-style Bradlee found its lurid patriotism. Nixon, Haldeman, Mitchell, Ehrlichman, Finch, all the others of the White House team had seen military service and sported American flags in their lapels. Bradlee would rather be caught in a bordello on Saturday night than wearing an American flag in his lapel. But his patriotism was just as deep. In his freshman year at Harvard, Bradlee had marched down to the recruiting station of the Canadian Air Force in Boston with a companion— Archibald Cox's younger brother—and been rejected as a volunteer because he was too young. In 1942, as a junior, he had crammed seven courses into his schedule at Harvard so that he might, with nine other ardent volunteers of the class of 1943, get his degree without ceremony in August of 1942. On which day he carried off his diploma, married his Saltonstall and enlisted in the Navy. By fall of that year he was combat communications officer on his destroyer, and for twenty-one months his ship fought its way up "the slot" from Guadalcanal to Rabaul; until finally it was hit by shore batteries and put out of action in the bloody landing at Saipan. So that he considered himself as much a patriot as Messrs. Haldeman, Ehrlichman *et alii.* But his route to service in private life, or expression of it, was in journalism.

He had been named managing editor of the Washington *Post* by Katharine Graham, its publisher, in 1965. Since that time he had been building a personal team, just as Bob Haldeman was to do for Nixon. When Bradlee entered on his office, the night city editor was a man seventy-nine years old, the assistant night city editor was eighty-three years old, the night managing editor in his upper sixties. Bradlee was ruthless; he wanted only the best reporters in the game. And by 1974 he could look out from his glass-paned office over the acre-or-more space where his reporters sat and see a team that was his own. Gone were the old managing editor, the national editor, the world editor, the night managing editor, the sports editor, the women's-page editor. Of the twenty-four men on his national staff, only six had been on that staff when he came. His metropolitan staff was entirely of his own choosing. All feared Bradlee —but all found him at the same time the source of the gaiety and enthusiasm that made the Washington *Post* one of the most exhilarating papers in the East to work for. Brad-lee's lust for performance also made it one of the cruelest competitive shops in which any young reporter could fight for a toehold on the bottom rung of the ladder. But it was a team, as much as Nixon's White House was a team. Bradlee gave the team its direction, insisted on high performance—and the team excavated, wrote and printed the stories.

Among these young competitive reporters were Carl Bernstein and Bob Woodward (aged twenty-eight and twen-ty-nine), who, on Monday, June 19th, 1972, first traced the Watergate burglary to the White House. Bradlee had made his basic directive to them the same directive he had once received from an old Boston editor, Ralph Blagden: "If you can't find a woman in the story, look for the dough." Woodward's and Bernstein's search for the dough they have told with superlative skill in their own book.[1]

What astounded Bradlee was the reaction from the White House. "I knew," said Bradlee, "that they were contemp-tuous of people, but I never assumed they were dumb. I kept asking from June of 1972 on how could their con-tempt be so great as to think that Ben Bradlee would pub-licly destroy himself and the paper he loved by printing something not true. The only answer was that they *had* to attack us—for their own survival. You don't go on lying, and denying, and lying again, and dissembling unless you have to. No contempt could be big enough to embrace that much stupidity. Which led me to the conviction that we were right." And so, in the edition of October 25th, the Washington *Post* traced the money circuit of what later would be called cover-up directly to Bob Haldeman at the White House. Bradlee wrote the lead for the Woodward-Bernstein story himself; waited a day; then published it. And from then on, the reputation of Bradlee, his reporters, his publisher and all the properties of the Washington *Post-Newsweek* empire were at stake.

No story on the events of 1973–74 can avoid the use of that helpful administrative phrase, the "chemistry of groups." In small groups, in personal contact, there is al-ways a contagion of personalities—of courage, of fears, of brutalities, of gallantries, of meanness. In life at the Wash-

[1] *All the President's Men* (New York: Simon and Schuster, 1974).

ington *Post* the chemistry of its group—which ran from Messrs. Woodward and Bernstein through Bradlee to its proprietress, Katharine Graham—was a chemistry of courage and style that would lead them, once engaged in combat, to pursue their story to its end, at all risk and at all hazard. And the men and women of the *Post* have told and will retell their story so long as journalists remember their legends.

But it is impossible to understand the working of the news system without seeing the Washington *Post* as engaged in, or provoking, that competition which is of the essence of American journalism. Competition has been one of the engines of the news system since Joseph Pulitzer and William Randolph Hearst remade journalism in the 1890's. Though competition by the 1970's had changed from a competition for circulation into a competition for honor, if the team of the Washington *Post* had any secondary motive beyond the primary pursuit of the Nixon team which had pursued them so mercilessly, it was to lift the competitive honors from the *New York Times*.

For a generation, the *New York Times* had been, and is today, the most important paper in the nation. Its managing editor, A. M. Rosenthal, a contemporary and friend of Bradlee's, had for ten years been shaping news into more searching and more literary forms. Rosenthal punched hard. His team had not only outdone Bradlee's on scooping the Pentagon Papers from Daniel Ellsberg, but for a three-year period of competition to undermine the credibility of the Nixon administration, the *New York Times* had led with the facts. Now, however, with his own staff of new and ambitious reporters in place, covering a local police burglary, Bradlee with his advantage in manpower and place, was ahead and meant to stay ahead. Not until after the election could the *New York Times* catch up and Rosenthal's talented news team match the *Post*'s. But in the competition of the two newspapers, and with the reality of the immense story looming through the darkness, they had unleashed the pack instinct of all editors and reporters from coast to coast.

The Los Angeles *Times*, for example. The Los Angeles *Times* had been considered twenty years earlier one of the ten most reactionary papers in the nation. By a reverse of

Gresham's law, however, as more and more big-city newspapers died, the few that remained grew better—and of these, perhaps the Los Angeles *Times* was the best example. A family upheaval had made a new Chandler—Otis—publisher of the paper. A subsequent reshuffle had put in place a new national-affairs editor, Edwin O. Guthman. Guthman had been a reporter in Seattle in his youth; had later been public-affairs spokesman in Washington of Robert Kennedy at the Department of Justice; and loved Robert Kennedy as much as Bradlee loved John Kennedy. Guthman not only carried the Kennedys in his heart, but retained in his bowels a fear of what he had learned the agencies of American internal surveillance could do—and might, if unrestrained. Moreover, Guthman was as competitive as any editor in the nation and had enlarged his bureau in Washington to twenty reporters, led in size among out-of-town papers only by those of the *New York Times* and the *Wall Street Journal*.

If Bradlee, Guthman's old friend, was out front, Guthman would catch up. To his Washington news editor, Dennis Britton, and Britton's investigative team of Jack Nelson, Robert Jackson and Ronald Ostrow, Guthman gave the old police reporters' instruction: "Get out and knock on doors." By August the Los Angeles *Times* had come up with its first exclusive, the story of a specific intelligence fund at CREEP; and by October, the first precise details of how the Democratic headquarters at the Watergate had been monitored and tape-recorded.

The Los Angeles *Times* added a special flavor to the story. While the *New York Times* and the Washington *Post* managements both were publicly unembarrassed in their loathing of Richard Nixon, the Chandler family of the Los Angeles *Times* had been Nixon's original sponsors in California politics; and the chairman of the board of the *Times Mirror* corporation, Franklin D. Murphy, was Bob Haldeman's personal friend. If the Los Angeles *Times* dared, or felt itself compelled, to publish what its reporters were finding—why should others hang back?

At which point, then, in the fall of 1972, the action passed to the dominant delivery mechanism of the American news system, television. Or, specifically, CBS. Or, more specifically, within that broadcasting system, to Walter Cronkite, who on two evenings in October, 1972, highlighted his newscasts with an examination of the Watergate break-in. And with that, with the public authority of television insisting that the Watergate affair must be placed on the agenda to be explored, no politician could escape the insistence. It was as if the church had detected a heresy; the inquisition must pursue the suspects, extract the evidence and then turn the culprits over to the secular arm for punishment.

Until October of 1972, the Watergate story had been a detail in the grand strategies of the Presidential campaign, yet the only detail on which Democrats could hang their hopes. The Democrats sensed that this year's exercise in dirty tricks might be, in some way, more serious than the dirty tricks both sides had played on each other in the past. Now the press was providing them with information—and CBS was goading them.

The news system was doing no more than performing its normal function, and would do so over the next two years, with increasing relish. But it was sometime here, in the late fall of 1972, that the next system became engaged, as if one gear were clutching at another, locking into action the system of Congressional leadership by commanding the attention of Senator Mike Mansfield of Montana.

A onetime professor (of Asian history), a genuine man of honor, cherished by John F. Kennedy and trusted by Richard Nixon, Mansfield was wearing his politician's suit that fall as he campaigned in his home state in support of Montana's junior Senator, Lee Metcalf. Spurred by the news system's reports, with no bitterness for Richard Nixon personally, Mansfield made a simple political stump pledge to his people back home—as soon as this campaign was over, he would go back to Washington to "pave the way" for an investigation not only of the Watergate break-in, but of the whole practice, custom and financing of American elections.

In Montana, its senior Senator runs usually as plain old Mike. But in Washington, the senior Senator of Montana is the Majority Leader of the United States Senate, a man of immense authority. Mansfield is a laconic conversationalist, a "yup" and "nope" man; one must see him loping through the streets of, say, Helena, Montana, and hear him talking as he hand-shakes to realize how much plain talk is part of his background. Thus, in Mansfield's recounting of events as he moved the Congressional system into action, there are no flourishes.

He was embittered, he said, by the attacks on his old friends Hubert and Muskie, "those dirty letters people wrote about them," and disturbed by the Watergate break-in, "which went beyond the guidelines of American politics." He'd made his promise in Montana, he said, because "it was just plain wrong what happened."

Translated to Washington, Mansfield's campaign promise was a critical one. To investigate Watergate meant that Mansfield would have to move the investigation through the snares of internal Congressional politics. The proper vehicle was the Judiciary Committee of the Senate—but that was headed by Senator James O. Eastland, a man split by a total personal loyalty to Richard Nixon and a technical loyalty to his Democratic Party brethren. Thus, then, it would be Mansfield's problem to lift the action *out* of routine Senate channels and procedures, out of Eastland's established Judiciary Committee, and move it to what, eventually, became the most important Senate Select Committee ever chosen. Mansfield's personal choice for the investigation would be Senator Sam Ervin of North Carolina, and skillfully Mansfield moved to his goal.

A few days back from Montana, on November 17th, Mansfield wrote two letters, one to Eastland and one to Ervin, artfully sending each recipient a copy of the letter to the other.

To Eastland, his letter ran: "Dear Jim: With the election over, it seems to me that it is time to examine fully into the circumstances surrounding the so-called Watergate Affair. More is at stake than the impact which this episode may have had on one party or the other in the last election. Indeed, enough is already known of the facts to make clear that the matter is not to be dismissed as a 'political caper' or some sort of playful escapade. Watergate was not politics as usual. It was, to say the least, politics at its most unusual. It was not politics American-style.

"The Watergate incident contains implications of great gravity for all political activity in this nation. What may be involved is not only a question of federal crimes which are, properly, subject to juridical disposition but also a cynical and dangerous intrusion into the integrity of the electoral processes by which the people of the nation choose the trustees of federal office. . . . That other questionable electoral practices may have been pursued in this or past elections, in my judgment, does not diminish by one iota, the need for Senate inquiry into the Watergate affair."

He concluded by suggesting that Eastland turn an investigation over to his Sub-Committee on Constitutional Rights —headed by Sam Ervin.

To Ervin, Mansfield wrote a "Dear Sam letter" on the same day, explaining his suggestion to Eastland and continuing, ". . . I suggest that you and Senator Eastland discuss this matter and make a recommendation to the Senate for a single instrument of investigation. It seems to me imperative to concentrate the energy and resources of the Senate on an inquiry into the substance of the Watergate Affair. It has raised the very fundamental question of the right of every American to assurance from government of the integrity of the Federal electoral process. . . . In truth, the question is not political; it is Constitutional. At stake is the continued vitality of the electoral process in the governmental structure of the nation."

Mansfield received no reply to his letter to Eastland; except that a few days later, when meeting on the Senate floor, Eastland asked Mansfield, "Got your letter, what do you want me to do?" "Give it over to Sam Ervin," replied Mansfield.

A few days later came another Mansfield meeting, this time with Sam Ervin in the Senate Majority Leader's chambers—a short, private, un-dramatic chat between two old friends. "There was no need of us haranguing each other," recalled Mansfield. "I suggested a Select Committee, he agreed. We had no idea of the ramifications of what would come out. We wanted to avoid it, but we couldn't. We had a responsibility to lay it out, to preclude events like that from happening again. We drafted a resolution with me as co-sponsor. I told Sam I wanted no Democratic Presidential candidates on our side. This wasn't going to be a forum for a campaign. Sam agreed."

On February 5th, the resolution as drafted by Mansfield and Ervin reached debate on the floor of the Senate. Angrily, futilely, plaintively, Republicans argued that any investigation of Presidential elections should look into the elections of 1964 and 1968 and the allegations of wiretapping, fraud, eavesdropping that ran to Lyndon Johnson. Outnumbered, they saw their amendments voted down, and finally, on February 7th, they too joined in the language of the original resolution, voting by 77 to 0 for a Select Committe that would "conduct an investigation and study of the extent, if any, to which illegal, improper, or unethical activities were engaged in by any persons . . . in the presidential election of 1972. . . ." Further, the Select Committee would have the power to subpoena any persons "who the select committee believes have knowledge or information" about such activities. And, finally, it should bring back recommendations for any new legislation "necessary . . . to safeguard the electoral process by which the President of the United States is chosen."

One must regard the early history on the Ervin Committee, which the White House saw first as a PR menace, as something akin to the approach of a political hurricane—unpredictably slowing, then speeding, then erratically wheeling in course, then stalling in a twirl, then thundering in to shore to desolate all in its path at landfall.

Since the break-in at Watergate (and the "dirty tricks" shortly thereafter reported) had been the stimulus of the Ervin Committee, and since Watergate had been a crime of bugging and break-in, Ervin had hired as chief counsel and staff director a man he had never met—Samuel Dash, an expert on the legalities of wire-tapping, a civil-libertarian, chief of the Institute of Criminal Law and Procedure at Georgetown University, author of a book called *The Eavesdroppers*. Dash was a dogged and skilled investigator, but a political primitive, and he meant it as he described his forthcoming assignment as "the anatomy of a Presidential election." The committee recruited a Republican minority counsel, Fred D. Thompson; a Democratic deputy chief counsel, Rufus L. Edmiston; and another Democrat, Terry Lenzner, as assistant chief counsel. And then the staff grew into a thing of marvel. At its peak, the Ervin Committee staff numbered 97. Altogether, 157 people spent varying periods of time on the staff, including 25 lawyers,

20 investigators, 8 consultants, 6 administrators, 51 secretaries and clericals, 22 specialized research assistants for minority and majority committee members, 22 assistants specially assigned to computer work, and 3 volunteers.

For their operations they took over the auditorium in the basement of the New Senate Office Building. Here, crammed into cubicles partitioned by frosted glass, surrounded by safes flagged with red security stubs and seals, with tables, chairs, floors, safes piled and strewn with documents and papers, with the old projection room facing a Nixon poster with the face cut out, the investigators made their base. And by early March were off on their pursuit. Their crowning pride was their computer. So many men would be involved, so many contradictory statements, reports, files, conflicts in memory and date would be assembled that it would be impossible for any one man or group to keep them in mind, or even to keep them indexed. For this problem the computer provided the retrieval solution—press a button for any date, any name, any allegation, and the computer would instantly spit back as many as twenty variations of testimony or recollections of a given event. Against the computer, plus the Ervin staff, plus the auxiliary corps of the press, the White House began its defense with only two lawyers (a number later increased to six) and an information base which, from May 1st on, after the departure of Ehrlichman and Haldeman, could not begin to compare with the information base available to its besiegers.

"No one knew what the hell was going on when we started on the Watergate story," said Terry Lenzner. "If the President had come to testify in the early days of the hearings, he could have bowled the legs out from under us. But they were more disorganized than we were. It was events that took control of us. The basic decision was not to start with the top names, but to build the case from the bottom up. When we interviewed McCord, what he had to say was only hearsay evidence, he hadn't even heard of the Gemstone file. But we built names in satellite clusters—Haldeman's satellites, Mitchell's satellites, Ehrlichman's satellites, Magruder's. That's how we came up with Butterfield's name—a Haldeman satellite. And it was [Robert] Reisner's name that forced Magruder out. Once Reisner started talking, Magruder knew the ballgame was up—and he was off to the prosecutor. Reisner [a Magruder assistant at CREEP] was a good guy. He said, 'I've been waiting and waiting for someone to come call on me'—he had all this information bottled up and he was sitting there alone. People *wanted* to talk to us—assistants and secretaries. A secretary at CREEP called us and asked me to come out to her house and talk to her. We would talk to them in our offices if they wanted, or in offices we borrowed from other people, or even in the White House."

The experience disturbed Lenzner. It was like hunting prey. "I came to recognize a certain look in their eyes when we interviewed people," he said. "You'd talk to a bright young guy and hope he wasn't culpable, and then he'd turn to his lawyer with that look and you'd say to yourself, 'Oh my God!' I went out to the West Coast to ask Herb Kalmbach about his records. I got fifteen minutes before there was that look in his eyes—he asked to leave the room and went to talk to his lawyer, and came back and told us that some of the money he collected in 1972 went to support Hunt and Liddy. And he told us he'd shredded his records."

Even before the committee opened public hearings, one could perceive the dynamics of the three systems interacting—the news system, the Congressional system, the court system. On March 23rd, Judge John Sirica had squeezed out of his District Court into the embrace of the press and the Ervin Committee investigators the lesser guilty of Watergate—as beaters flail game into the range of the shooters. And as the game was flushed, the press would track it in public. James McCord unburdened himself to the Ervin Committee staff the day of Sirica's first admonition. On the 26th, he told his story to the committee itself in executive session—and within twenty-four hours of that testimony the first great hemorrhage of leaks gushed. The Los Angeles *Times,* first off the mark this time, reported the testimony as involving Dean and Magruder; and the *New York Times* and the Washington *Post* had the story the next day.

Press story fathered investigation, investigation fostered official discovery; discovery fostered more leaks; which fostered more investigation. Soon it was a game in which too many players were involved to list, and the rules were those of the Dodo in *Alice's Adventures in Wonderland,* who said, "Everybody has won, and all must have prizes." It was near the end of February that *Time* magazine's investigative reporter in Washington, Sandy Smith, uncovered the story of the official and authorized wire-tapping of the seventeen men in John Mitchell's first surveillance net. With Smith opening that story, others followed quickly, which brought to light the story of the illegal surveillance of Joseph Kraft. The *New York Times*, which had added an outstanding investigative reporter, Seymour Hersh, to counter the Washington *Post*'s team of Woodward and Bernstein, would top that in April by involving the President himself. And even before the Ervin Committee opened its hearings, *Newsweek* had persuaded John Dean to tell his story; and *Time* soon followed.

The pattern spread. For any given leak, there would be a counterleak. Lawyers for suspects would leak to the press —and rival lawyers for other clients who might be injured by the first leak would spring other leaks. Government officials, to clear themselves, would put out yet more leaks, insuring their defense by cooperation with a hungry press. And, most of all, the committee itself leaked. Some Senators out of simple ambition, and others out of outraged morality, began to view the committee's preliminary investigations as public, and their staffs would make available to privileged reporters Xeroxed copies of material which investigators were sure was still locked in their safes.

By the first week in May, the cascade of leaks had built up for the approaching hearings a national television audience—and any part of the public that missed the drama on television would not miss it elsewhere. The scandal was front-page on all newspapers across the nation—not since World War II had any single matter for so long and with such a grip on the emotions led editors to such display. In the *New York Times* alone, the story was front-page all through May, June and July, its editors dropping it from their front page only one day each month, as if to give their readership a breathing spell. And for those whom the daily press and television missed, there were the vivid poster covers of the news-weeklies, spread on 126,000 magazine stands across the nation, from corner drugstore to supermarket. For the news-weeklies, the entire affair was the choicest of opportunities to refresh their function of analysis and summary. From March of 1973 to July of 1973, *Time* magazine front-covered L. Patrick Gray, Sam Ervin, Nixon (twice), Mitchell (twice), Dean (twice), Ervin & Nixon, Nixon-Haldeman-Mitchell in a first montage, another montage of Haldeman-Ehrlichman-Dean-McCord-Liddy-Hunt. *Newsweek* front-covered Nixon four times, Dean once, Haldeman once, Mitchell once, Dean & Nixon, Haldeman & Ehrlichman, the White House, then the White House entwined in giant reels of tape. Whether one listened or one turned ear away, whether one passed news stands at airports, rail stations, subway stations, whether one preferred the morning paper headlines or the evening electronic news—the entire news system was announcing the Greatest Show on Earth.

And there was no doubt that it would be the Greatest Show in America—John Mitchell, John Ehrlichman, John Dean, H. R. Haldeman, all the President's men were scheduled to perform in public in the drama of how-the-mighty-have-fallen. No privacy would be inviolate from the interrogation of the committee, no curiosity about these men of power unsatisfied by the questioning to come. They would be scuttling across the screens like crabs without their carapaces, men of power stripped naked.

Along the way, of course, the Ervin Committee was to lose track of its broad mandate—to recommend to the Senate and nation how to improve its systems of Presidential election. It would call few witnesses who could cast light on how elections are or should be carried on, or could suggest ways of improving them; and it asked few questions of those it did call. It wound up recommending a highly technical law on campaign financing, ignoring the other substantive political realities of elections. But if it failed in its larger purpose, it did deliver an extraordinary exercise in American public education never matched in history—an examination of how a President conducted that office, what can happen in the White House, how far its power can extend, and how easily that power can be, and had been, abused in the administration of Richard Nixon.

The Greatest Show on Earth opened promptly in the Senate Caucus Room on May 17th, 1973, its mission still described at that point, correctly, by the *New York Times:* "The 1972 Presidential campaign went on trial today," and its staff still hoping that simple detective work and sworn testimony would lead them from the Watergate break-in and bugging to the answers and reforms necessary to safeguard the choice of a President. The committee hearings moved slowly at first, the witnesses led off by twenty-eight-year-old Robert Odle, manager of CREEP's office staff, and crawling along through John Bruce Barrett, one of the policemen who arrested the burglars at the Watergate, then through Messrs. McCord, Caulfield, Ulasewicz, Barker, Baldwin in the first week; then on, higher up the trail, to Messrs. Sloan, Porter, Stans and Magruder.

Magruder made the first peak—publicly, under oath, he said the authority to burglarize Democratic headquarters had been given him directly by the former Attorney General, John Mitchell.

The hearings peaked again ten days later as John Dean, speaking softly, reading continuously for a full day from a prepared statement, laid the responsibility at the door of the Presidency. "I left," said Dean, speaking of his meeting with Nixon on September 15th, 1972, "with the impression that the President was well aware of what had been going on regarding the success of keeping the White House out of the Watergate scandal, and I also had expressed to him my concern that I was not confident the cover-up could be maintained indefinitely." By now the plan of the committee's staff was operating with textbook results—working as a prosecution staff would work, closing a circle of irrefutable secondary evidence about the prime targets still to come, John Ehrlichman, John Mitchell, Bob Haldeman. And then on Monday, July 16th, matters split.

That day, while Richard Moore was testifying before television cameras and the nation in the Caucus Room of the Old Senate Office Building, several committee staff men were readying Alexander Butterfield in a small windowless room in the basement of the New Senate Office Building. They were preparing him for a private meeting with Sam Ervin and Howard Baker, the vice-chairman of the committee, at which the two Senators could hear directly from Butterfield what he had told the staff secretly the previous Friday—and was about to tell the nation openly on television that afternoon. Butterfield's was the only story that had not leaked in advance, and the staff was determined that this was one that would *not* leak until they made it public.

Tall, blue-suited, his eyes pouched dark, Alexander Butterfield began testimony at 2:00 in the afternoon with the normal identifying responses. Then minority counsel Fred Thompson asked, "Mr. Butterfield, are you aware of the installation of any listening devices in the Oval Office of the President?"

"I was aware of listening devices, yes, sir," replied Butterfield.

"Are you aware of any devices that were installed in the Executive Office Building office of the President?" continued Thompson.

"Yes sir," replied Butterfield.

The Butterfield testimony lasted no more than fifteen minutes—but the normally murmuring press benches went silent; reporters who had begun to accept the startling revelations of the two-month old hearing as commonplace stopped smoking, began scribbling. What had happened was almost too large to grasp for the moment. But the persistent questioning of Senator Howard Baker—"What did the President know, and when did he know it?"—now obviously had an answer somewhere.

The road to that somewhere would, within days, engage all the systems of the law—courts, judges, prosecutors—and ultimately reach to the Supreme Court in the pursuit of answers. That pursuit would acquire its own dynamics, the dynamics to be speeded by the pressure of public opinion until, ultimately, all Richard Nixon's privacy would be torn from him and his Presidency doomed. But for the moment, the public hearings of the committee still held national attention as the story of the President's men unfolded.

Butterfield was immediately followed on the stand by Herbert Kalmbach, writhing, conscience-stricken, already broken in spirit, a figure of pathos. On successive days, the committee moved through such lesser characters as Tony Ulasewicz (a second time), Robert Mardian, Gordon Strachan, and then, on Tuesday, July 24th, arrived at John Ehrlichman for five days of testimony.

The committee, by the day of John Ehrlichman's arrival, was in a mood of particular anger. Sam Ervin had written Richard Nixon, asking the White House for tapes of the President's conversations the day after Butterfield's testimony—on Tuesday, the 17th. On the 23rd, the President had rejected the request; immediately, that day, the Ervin Committee had issued two subpoenas, one for five separate taped Presidential conversations, the other for relevant documents. The next day, Tuesday, July 24th, John Ehrlichman took the stand.

Ehrlichman arrived with a counter-bitterness of his own, harassed, badgered, angered by the gauntlet of the press he had run that morning, infuriated by the leaks predicting his testimony. Ehrlichman's running line of defense before the committee sprang from several streams of loyalty—a personal loyalty to the President, a deeper loyalty to the country and the perfervid patriotism that had always blinded the men closest to Nixon to the consequences of their actions.

The President, argued Ehrlichman and his lawyers, had the inherent power, in the name of national security, to commit acts otherwise illegal.

By the next morning the testimony had been lifted to a colloquy of issues far beyond the level of election mechanics or break-in. Arguing with Ehrlichman's lawyer, John Wilson, early in the morning, Sam Ervin struck the keynote of the next two days. "I do not believe," said Ervin, "the President has any power at all except such as the Constitution expressly gives him or such as are necessarily inferred from the expression of those powers. I think the Constitution was written that way to keep the President and, of course, the Congress, from exercising tyrannical power."

Senator Herman Talmadge carried it from there half an hour later when it came his turn to question the witness directly.

"Now, if the President," asked Talmadge, "could authorize a covert break-in, and you do not know exactly what that power would be limited [to], you do not think it could include murder or other crimes beyond covert break-ins, do you?"

Ehrlichman: "I do not know where the line is, Senator."

Talmadge: "You are a lawyer, and I understand you are a good one."

Ehrlichman: "Well I am certainly not a constitutional lawyer, Senator. Far from it."

Talmadge: "Do you remember when we were in law school, we studied a famous principle of law that came from England and also is well known in this country, that no matter how humble a man's cottage is, that even the King of England cannot enter without his consent."

Ehrlichman: "I am afraid that has been considerably eroded over the years, has it not?"

Talmadge: "Down in my country we still think it is a pretty legitimate principle of law." (Applause.)

The hearings continued for the rest of the day, moving far beyond Watergate to the central Constitutional issue, until late in the afternoon Ervin tried to sum it all up in a statement sure to be a favorite of high school declamation contests for years to come:

"I do want to take this occasion to amplify the legal discussion and I want to mention a little of the Bible, a little of history and a little of law.

"The concept embodied in the phrase every man's home is his castle represents the realization of one of the most ancient and universal hungers of the human heart. One of the prophets described the mountain of the Lord as being a place where every man might dwell under his own vine and fig tree with none to make him afraid.

"And then this morning, Senator Talmadge talked about one of the greatest statements ever made by any statesman, that was William Pitt the Elder, and before this country revolted against the King of England he said this:

"'The poorest man in his cottage may bid defiance to all the forces of the crown. It may be frail, its roof may shake, the wind may blow through it, the storm may enter, the rain may enter, but the King of England cannot enter. All his force dares not cross the threshold of the ruined tenements.'

"And yet we are told here today, and yesterday, that what the King of England can't do, the President of the United States can."

And while Ervin was summing up, the President of the United States drew the line of the issue even more clearly. The President had received the two Senate Committee subpoenas on Monday of that week. On Wednesday, while Ehrlichman, Wilson, Talmadge and Ervin had been debating the limits of Presidential power, the President replied, promising as much cooperation as he could give, pointing out that he had waived executive privilege for the testimony of his onetime aides, but then concluding, "I cannot and will not consent to giving any investigatory body private Presidential papers." In effect, he had refused the subpoenas of the Senate.

And thus, Thursday morning, at the start of the third day of the Ehrlichman testimony, Ervin called for his committee to vote whether or not to pursue the President by law and bring him to court. The vote was unanimous and public. And Ervin capped it: "I think this litigation is essential if we are to determine whether the President is above the law and whether the President is immune from all of the duties and responsibilities in matters of this kind which devolve upon all the other mortals who dwell in this land."

With that statement, the committee was off again, twisting into, boring through, profiling the inner thinking of John Ehrlichman and through him the mentality of the team that had brought Richard Nixon to triumph and disaster.

The hearings were to wear on, week after week, month after month, fading finally from the major networks late in September. On July 12th, 1974, the committee released its final report, then liquidated itself entirely two months later, having recorded more than 7,000,000 words, published some, kept others secret, and having spent $1,500,000, or about one-third of what a great corporation is willing to spend for the television exposure of a single spectacular sure-fire movie to sell its automobiles, its soap, its investment programs.

There was no way to quantify the Ervin Committee's impact on the American mind. The President had stood under shadow when the hearings began; he stood under public indictment, and legal indictment seemed possible, when they ended. The ordinary television ratings could not measure the impact of the hearings—daytime television ratings are geared to measure housewife and homebody response to soap opera and the nonsense of the sunlit day before prime time gathers the rest of the nation in the evening. This rating system could not measure viewing by the working audience outside the home—the men who, in their offices, paused at coffee break to see what the Ervin Committee was doing; people who brought portable sets to the office; or the barflies who asked that the bar set be tuned to what was of public interest. Unable to measure this audience, the ratings were low—estimated at only 7 percent more than normal.

Yet there were other measures. The television stations of the Public Broadcasting Service re-ran the day's hearings for the nighttime audience and appended each evening an appeal for memberships and funds. And in response they counted 82,000 letters and $1,250,000 in new memberships and contributions. Then there was the response of people to the Ervin Committee offices. In the first two months of hearings, letters came in to the committee at a rate of 1,000 to 4,000 a day. From July 19th, after the Butterfield revelation, until Labor Day weekend, the daily count rose to 9,000. In November, the total topped one million, believed to be greater than the response to any other public hearing in the Senate's history. The responses, too, seemed to follow a pattern, and the pattern always seemed to profile an initially explosive reaction, then a thoughtful slow burn. First responses would come by telephone, jamming switchboards; then would come telegrams; then would come the letters, two days later; then more letters when the slow burn had reached incandescence. John Ehrlichman, for example, had tried to explain what he meant by "covert operations." "Information of this kind is obtainable," he said, speaking of Ellsberg's psychiatric file. "Insurance adjusters obtain it, investigators obtain it, attorneys obtain it, and they obtain it through nurses, through nurses' aides, through all kinds of sources." First in the pattern of response, telephone calls would come from indignant nurses; then letters from nurses about the honor of their profession; and then letters from some of the more thoughtful among them quoting the Nurses' Code of Ethics, which they held as binding on them as the Hippocratic Oath is on doctors. And by the time that wave of indignation was over would come the crest of the next wave.

But, finally, there was the response as measured by the public-opinion polls. Richard Nixon had stood at 68 percent in public approval of his Presidency in February of 1973. By July of 1973, only five months later, his public approval had slipped to 40 percent in the Gallup poll, and Harris interviewers found that 60 percent of those surveyed thought Nixon more wrong than right in refusing to turn over White House files to the Senate committee. In early

May, before the Ervin Committee opened its hearings, the Harris poll had registered public opinion against the President's resignation by a margin of 77 to 13. By June 17th, only six weeks later, the Gallup poll, hitting the target from another angle, recorded alarmingly that two of three respondents believed that Richard Nixon himself was involved in the Watergate cover-up, and half of them thought he had advance knowledge of the break-in.

By mid-August with the committee in recess, it had passed its high point of public attention. But the information had seeped down and was spreading. "When we began," said Terry Lenzner, "Archibald Cox was in the public mind just another bureaucrat. When we ended, he had authority." For the story could not stop where the Ervin Committee had left it; neither law nor public appetite could leave it suspended there; another system had been engaged that could not be stopped short of confrontation of the President at the bar. The White House had wasted its month of reprieve both in public sentiment and in fact. Months and months too late, it recognized that this was not just a battle of PR but the story of a crime, by whom yet unspecified, which demanded action by the state.

The polls of public reaction had always been important at Richard Nixon's White House, and remained so even after the old advance men had left. Nixon had had the courage to move against the polls as President when matters of state were involved, as in the Vietnam War. But in domestic politics, polls were critical, and, said Caspar Weinberger, Secretary of HEW, "I don't think Nixon began to take the matter seriously until the polls went down; then it became more serious than a PR matter. But, you see, they had no philosophical rudder to their administration to take them from there. They couldn't see the matter morally."

The new Nixon administration—for it was, in effect, a new Nixon administration that began in May of 1973—was, indeed, made up of men of morality. But morality was not enough to master the crisis they faced.

Strangers to each other, welded together neither by a common past nor by a common understanding of their leader, none knew the precise range of his mission at the White House, or had learned how far they could go in trusting each other. To the natural chaos of initiation to a defense line under overwhelming hostile fire had to be added the distortion of underlying reality—none knew the facts on which their defense line was based. Their leader was Alexander Haig, four-star general, a man bred in the military, trained to trust the word of the President, his Commander-in-Chief, in all circumstances, to obey orders, to execute command. And Haig had had only two days to think about the problems he faced from the Friday of his appointment in Key Biscayne until Sunday, May 6th, when he entered the large and sunlit office in the White House which only a week before had been Bob Haldeman's.

In Key Biscayne, the President had given his new Chief of Staff one overriding priority of duty—to get control of the bureaucracy, and bring the shattered White House staff together in a semblance of order. The task was immense.

"This government," said Haig one day a year later when his loyalty to Nixon still burned fiercely, "had operated like a three-legged stool—Haldeman, Ehrlichman, Colson. Now Haldeman and Ehrlichman had been flushed out and Colson was gone. On top of that was the style in which they'd operated. You had a situation through the bureaucracy that was calamitous; the old operation had sought to turn over the bureaucracy, replace the old Democrats, wipe out that philosophical resistance down below—they'd purged the bureaucracy."

The new Chief of Staff had discussed the problem of the bureaucracy with the President in Key Biscayne; and, in a single day, had persuaded the President that the old master plan for centralizing authority in the White House and King's Row could not work. Haig was an Army man who believed in dispersing full authority to field commands. He wanted a government run that way, too. And so, in the snap of a conversation, the Grand Plan of November, 1972, had evaporated.

But to plan a new way to control the bureaucracy and at the same time recruit new staff was much harder. "I came in with a hundred of the top five hundred posts in government unfilled," said Haig. "Either they'd quit or been fired. There was this system of vacuums; morale was shot. We had to find a new head of FBI, a new head of the SEC, a new Secretary of Defense, a new chief of CIA. We had to fill slots all the way down the line, and there's this tendency to get mediocrities when you put together a government under fire. It was a massive task. . . . It was time-consuming."

Haig had accepted his assignment in Key Biscayne with the thought that he was being invited to direct the White House staff in matters of government—and with the explicit understanding that the Watergate matter would be handled by the lawyers. But within days, Watergate had become a co-equal priority. "Only there was no strategy, no base of knowledge of what was coming up next, we needed a legal team and we had none," said Haig.

"And then," he continued, "I was here only a few weeks when Elliot Richardson . . . described to me the calamity of the Vice-President, and the Agnew calamity grew worse daily and hourly. By July, Elliot reported that it was a categorical open-and-shut case. We couldn't accept it; we told him to go back and re-assess. By September, Elliot said that he'd never seen a case with harder facts—and the President worried more about that than anything else. If Agnew chose the impeachment route and that merged with Watergate—! Arranging that cop-out was one of the greatest feats of bureaucratic skill in the history of the art."

As Haig first settled behind his desk as Chief of Staff in the gold-carpeted room through which the President's business flows, he could not escape Watergate, the crisis of authority and credibility. Thus, immediately, Haig had invited to join him a Pentagon lawyer, Fred Buzhardt, a West Point contemporary of his, who arrived on May 10th to be named President's special counsel on Watergate matters, while Garment shifted to prepare the defense before the Senate Committee. Yet two lawyers were not enough. What Haig wanted was a full legal team, led by someone of the eminence of a Supreme Court judge, to take overall charge of the case. The names suggested, however, simply did not suit the President's taste. "Their chemistry didn't work with his," said Haig. "He just never moved on the problem."

Meanwhile as Haig worried about the Watergate affair, he must worry about the White House itself, which he described as being on his arrival "a shambles." In a few days he had offered up the names of Schlesinger for Defense and Colby to head the CIA. On May 10th, John Connally was enlisted to come to Washington as "special adviser" to the

President. Haig recommended that the President reach out for his old colleague of Eisenhower days, Bryce Harlow. Harlow suggested that Melvin Laird be brought back also. By mid-June these major characters had been installed, too —but almost no one knew where he fitted into the new hierarchy, or the measure of either his access or his authority. "It was a staff that wasn't spawned naturally," said Haig, "and you had this uncertainty, with no one knowing exactly what he was supposed to do." Laird, for example, had been given the impression that he would be in charge of domestic affairs, as John Ehrlichman had been, and would be in charge of shepherding major programs through Congress, where his skills far surpassed those of the old team. Laird worked on government priorities, concentrating on moving the Agriculture bill through Congress, moving the Defense Department budget, moving the Manpower Retraining Act. He would, if he could, have moved on the Watergate matter; but the President forbade him privately to act in that area. Which Haig did not know, and so Haig accused Laird of not wanting to deal with the mess of Watergate, of sitting and carping from the sidelines.

If, under the old team, the White House had become the fourth unrecognized branch of government, the policy-making branch, now, under the second team, it relinquished all control over policy except for foreign affairs and defense programs. Nor could it even approach control over the central matter that bedeviled it, which was the faith and confidence of Americans in their government, because that was the Watergate affair—and in the Watergate affair they were stopped from making policy because the central character was Richard Nixon, who trusted no one. Much later, Fred Malek, deputy director of the Office of Management and Budget, was to say, "What Richard Nixon needs is a turnkey job. He needs to say to one person, 'you're in charge of the Watergate, you're in charge of the energy problem, you're in charge of the price problem.' Instead, he sits there for hours just bullshitting away with Haig and Ziegler, eating up their time, not letting them do their jobs, not putting anybody in full charge of the Watergate job."

It was already obvious now, however, in May and June, that the Watergate job was something that no PR strategy could handle. As news seeped out of every leak in the bureaucratic, investigative, and Senatorial systems, as the Ervin Committee's continuing testimony began to pile perjury on obvious perjury, the conflict between PR and truth was one of no-contest. It was no longer a question of who was lying, but how many were lying, and how soon the breakdown of the liars would reveal the truth. Too much was buried not to exude its stink—whatever it was had to be uncovered.

"It was," wrote William Greider of the Washington *Post* in an outstanding recapture of the mood of the time, "like the sour strains of two marching bands on the same field, but blaring different tunes. The press played the theme from 'Dragnet,' the White House played 'The Stars and Stripes Forever.' And they clashed brassily."

The White House press room, which had become a bear pit over the previous two years—with Ziegler the bear to be baited—now reached a state of macabre sadism and black humor. Ziegler became ever more elusive, and more and more often his deputy Gerald Warren filled in. "Can you tell us, Jerry, when we might expect a news conference or when the President plans to answer any questions in any form about some of these very serious charges of corruption?" Warren: "I have nothing to offer you on any of these subjects." Or— Q: "Are you aware of any new instructions going out to government public-relations officials on how to handle the press?" A: "I would welcome some myself." Was it true, one reporter asked of Warren, that the President would not hold another press conference until White House reporters stopped shouting at Ron Ziegler? "I think it would be nice if they did," replied the mild-mannered Warren. Q: "Would it be nice if we stopped shouting at you?" Warren: "You don't shout at me." Q: "I wonder if we could have a show of hands of people willing not to shout at the President if he would hold a press conference?" Warren: "I would be willing to accept the show of hands, too."

In June, the National Press Club, long past its days as a vital institution, shot off what was, for it, a blast of enormous daring. A committee headed by James McCartney of the Knight newspapers condemned Ziegler publicly: "The White House press secretary has been reduced to a totally programmed spokesman without independent authority or comprehensive background or knowledge of Administration policies. Rather than opening a window into the White House, the press secretary closes doors. Information about public business is supplied on a selective, self-serving basis. Legitimate questions about public affairs are not answered on a day-to-day basis; even worse, such questions are often not seriously considered." The nation was full of questions; nothing made sense; it was a time of chaos.

The chaos could all be traced to one man, the only one who knew the answers, Richard Nixon—and he was in flight. In the eight critical months as the crisis spread in public, Nixon was scrawling across the sky an outline of character beyond need of explanation—that of a man escaping from himself, escaping from what he cannot face, from his own inner thoughts. Even before May of 1973, Richard Nixon was the most peripatetic President in history. Now, starting in May of 1973, the flight path describes a White House that had become hateful to him, a place of anguish. And as Nixon flew, his new staff—still totally devoted to him—sought answers which only the absent President could provide.

Nixon's schedule, from the beginning of May, 1973, ran thus: he had let go Haldeman-Ehrlichman-Dean-Kleindienst on Monday, April 30th. Tuesday and Wednesday required his presence in Washington because Willy Brandt, the West German Chancellor, was there to negotiate with him. Then Thursday he was off to Key Biscayne for four days, returned to Washington for four days, off again to Key Biscayne for the weekend, and in and out of his White House, spending only thirteen full days there that month, chiefly to prepare his Watergate defense and speeches and receive foreign ministers. In June, he was to spend another ten days there (two to receive foreign potentates) before escaping on Friday, the 22nd, to San Clemente, where he stayed for two and a half weeks until July 9th.

But his problems pursued him to San Clemente. Melvin Laird, certainly the shrewdest politician on his new staff, flew out to see the President and told him abruptly, as is his manner, what he must do about Watergate: get the Ervin Committee in now, sit them around the Cabinet table, answer their questions, give out with information. Furious, Nixon responded that he didn't want to hear about Watergate, and ordered Laird never to bring up that subject with him again. Which injunction Laird obeyed.

Nixon was back in Washington in July for brief periods —seven days spent in the hospital with pneumonia, another five because the visits of various foreign ministers or chiefs of state required his presence (the foreign minister of West Germany, the Shah of Iran, the Australian Prime Minister and the Prime Minister of Japan, Kakuei Tanaka).

Then, in August, he was off again—to Key Biscayne in the mid-summer heat and to San Clemente, spending only five full days in Washington, one of them winding up his talks with Prime Minister Tanaka. September, of course, was the Agnew crisis month, which required that he spend almost all his time in Washington, during which he had to cope not only with Watergate but also the Agnew matter plus the visits on four separate days of such inescapable personalities as the Prime Minister of Pakistan, the Prime Minister of New Zealand, Soviet Foreign Minister Andrei Gromyko and Willy Brandt of West Germany again. And the Middle East crisis was approaching.

The bewilderment of the staff of Richard Nixon through the critical spring and summer months of 1973 is now, in retrospect, understandable. They were attempting to maintain and repair a Presidency, like a ground crew working over an airplane that will not fly because of defective mechanisms sealed from their sight. So they staggered each on his own path, each suspicious of the other, seeking a strategy to defend their chief in the belief they were defending the Presidency.

At the heart of their confusion lay the tapes. Without the tapes, there was no evidence against the President personally except John Dean's word. With the tapes, the chief witness against the President could be the President. But no one yet knew this, or had any sense of the extent of the tapes. Laird had heard a chance remark from the President that he had a tape of a telephone conversation with Senator Ervin. But Laird had become Secretary of Defense in 1969 and at Nixon's orders he had pulled the Johnson taping system out of the White House on February 15th, 1969, within one month of Nixon's first inauguration. It did not occur to Laird that the President might later have installed a taping system more elaborate than the one the Army Signal Corps had removed. Garment had not heard of the tapes until the end of June—when Lawrence Higby had told him and asked what he should say about the tapes if called to testify before the Ervin Committee. Haig, too, had heard about the tapes only in June. Had the President told his new staff about the taping when he appointed them, they might have had time to examine the tapes, destroy them or cope with them before the judicial system locked its authority over them as evidence.

Why Nixon, personally, did not order their destruction as matters moved toward climax can only remain a matter of speculation until Nixon speaks himself. From April 30th, 1973, on, the only man in the White House complex who knew of the tapes, except the President, was Higby— scarcely of enough stature for a President to seek counsel with on innermost matters. Richard Nixon was on his own. He took pride in his administration and achievements and may not have wanted those records lost. He may have thought of the tapes as entrapment for those who might denounce him. He may have thought of them as personal property, priceless historical treasure he could leave to his children. He may even have thought of himself as innocent. Or he may have considered them so absolutely guarded by executive privilege from all intrusion that he did not think at all—which is probably the case.

All speculation, however, becomes inoperative from the date of July 16th on—when Alexander Butterfield took the stand and made the existence of tapes known to the record and therefore evidence. From that day on, it was impossible legally to destroy such evidence. All that could be done was to interrupt their storytelling, and thus, on the advice of the two lawyers, Garment and Buzhardt, Haig on his own authority ripped the entire taping system out of the Oval Office, the Executive Office Building, the Cabinet Room and the telephones. And then proceeded to Bethesda Naval Hospital to visit Richard Nixon and tell him what he, as Chief of Staff, had just done. Nixon made no objection; and to Haig's recollection, muttered only that they should never have had a taping system in the first place.

But the spools, the words, the recordings did remain—in the basement of the EOB in four or five ordinary filing cases, mis-indexed and mis-filed, in a room electronically locked, guarded by the Secret Service.

"Nixon," said Fred Buzhardt, "could never have unlocked that room without the Secret Service, and even if he'd gotten in, he wouldn't have known how to work a recording device." Access to the tapes was by Nixon's permission only. Even though Garment was in charge of the defense before the Ervin Committee, he could not hear tapes —Haig relayed to Garment the President's refusal to allow him or anyone else to listen. The same message went to Buzhardt, then in charge of the President's technical legal defense; he could not listen to the first tape before October.

And no one wanted to press. Whenever one talked to a member of the inner circle at the White House, the phrase repeated over and over again about the tapes was that they were "radioactive." "You see," said Ron Ziegler, recalling the summer events to me, "up until October we'd made no decision whether to release those tapes, and anybody who did listen was subject to subpoena. The tapes were a danger to listen to."

Said Pat Buchanan, "The tapes were radioactive. We should have had a staff organized for defense; but unless you staffed up with lawyers, anybody else who listened could be taken to court. . . . We had no information base, you understand. The Ervin Committee, Cox, the press— they all knew more than we did. I don't want to listen to the tapes myself—I'm scared. There are people here I know who are entirely innocent, they're paying their life savings, five or ten thousand dollars a year, just to keep a lawyer on retainer; the lawyers are having a field day. I've got no lawyer."

Having no strategy, no open communication, no political leadership, the new men of the White House looked out in summer and fall and watched the authority of the Presidency dissolve. The new team had been jerry-built in a spasm, and time did not mend it. The feud between Haig and Laird became open. So did Laird's contempt for Ronald Ziegler. John Connally's disgust grew apparent. Harlow grew angry because he could not see the President. And yet other differences nagged. Buzhardt and Garment occupied adjacent offices, in the suite once occupied by John Dean. Buzhardt, a South Carolina conservative, and Garment, a Manhattan liberal, watched each other warily, not at all trusting each other until much later that year when they came to final and intimate friendship.

"There couldn't be a strategy," said Buzhardt much later. "The obvious thing would have been to get together and decide to destroy the tapes; but the whole issue was pinned on obstruction of justice; if we'd decided to destroy the tapes, that would have been real obstruction of justice, and we couldn't even talk about it."

Over all presided Haig—burdened with the still secret problem of Spiro T. Agnew, worried about the Middle East, trying to recruit staff from Cabinet level down to junior assistants, trusting the President, and totally inexperienced in any politics but that of the White House.

"Haig!" said Webster B. Todd, Jr., one of the best of the new young men on King's Row, trying to recapture in late 1973 the sequence of that summer's and fall's events. "Haig," he repeated, trying to be fair, "is a good guy. But when Ehrlichman and Haldeman left, there was this trauma of unquantifiable proportions. Al was brought in and given these baskets full of problems; he emptied all those baskets, and they were at least interfaced. But the worms were still there."

Todd went on, slowly losing his temper in a memorable outburst. "I've been dodging you, but I can talk today. I just wrote out my resignation this morning. I can't take it any longer. There's no rationale, no planning, no support system. They dump a whole basket of crap on us every morning and it's up to us to decide how to straighten it out. I'll do it once, I'll do it twice—but not as a daily diet. You can't believe how screwed up this place is. We had a whole summer to gear up to face the problem, but when the real blast of wind hit us, all Al Haig had was George Joulwan and General John Bennett to face it; that was the entire staff that replaced Haldeman and his bag of people.

"You had a bunch of guys in Al Haig's office whose crisis background was military, not political. You had Laird trying to do his bit, and he carried on the most open insurrection in the White House you ever saw. You had Bryce Harlow, and he couldn't get to see the President.

Then you had Buzhardt—Buzhardt's a guy of excellent reputation, a good lawyer, a solid guy. But he had no executive experience, no training, no staff. Buzhardt took everything they put on his plate—and that's not incompetence. He just felt he could do four day's work in two hours every morning with no staff. He didn't have time to listen to tapes. We tried to get Judge Sullivan to come down to take over the legal defense. So Sullivan asked who's he over, who's he under. Is he under Buzhardt or is he over Buzhardt? No one could tell him, so Sullivan says screw it and goes back to Chicago.

"Take any problem at all, it's all chaos. You know what Kettering said, 'Crooks I don't mind, but stupid crooks I can't abide.' It's unbelievable, it's so chaotic. I don't know who gets to the President and I don't think the people who do get to the President know how much trouble he's in.

"It goes all the way through the government. We've got an energy crisis on our hands, and Bill Anders of the Atomic Energy Commission comes in and says to me, 'Look, I can love fast-breeding reactors or I can love normal thermal reactors, I can love anything, but I can't do a goddamned thing until I'm told what the President wants, what the signal is.' I can't tell him what the signal is, and that's the situation all over the place."

Garment later described the scene, as the action passed from the Congressional system to the court system, in metaphors.

"There's this poem of James Dickey's that keeps coming back to me, I forget the lines. Of an airplane crash, and the parts and pieces are strewn all over the furrows of a Kansas cornfield—and there's the shed clothing over the trees, bodies, chunks of flesh on the cornstalks, and Dickey says that somewhere in the plane, one little piece of machinery must have gone wrong, one part, one valve—and all this happened. That's the way it's been—one piece in the machinery somewhere went wrong, and there are all these bodies around.

"We were afraid to find out facts. There was this wishful nonknowingness. We didn't want to get together and put all the pieces together, we were afraid of what we might find out.

"Then there was Richard Nixon—and I'm saying this

more in mystification than in anger—he had this weirdly paralyzing idea of fragmentation of his, of keeping it all in separate compartments so his friends and even his lawyers couldn't talk to each other. I came aboard the good ship Watergate on April 9th, and the President told me to find out the full story. I started and then I later found out that John Ehrlichman had told John Dean *not* to tell me the details. We were tiptoeing, all of us, through the tulips—only they weren't tulips, they were minefields. I wanted a full staff for the Ervin hearings, a staff that could get out refutation, contradiction, facts, instantly. But I couldn't get anybody to listen. The President said to me repeatedly, over and over again, that he was not involved, that he didn't know what had happened. But, God, what a jungle—you had the Plumbers, all those other operations, you had Watergate—and Watergate was the hole in the dike, the part that failed in the plane, the part that busted everything else loose.

"We were playing blindman's buff, stumbling around in a cloud. There was no information in here because the data custodians were gone, and their files were locked, and the President wouldn't let his tapes or information be made available. . . . There was this feeling that we could handle the tapes and the other information by remote control, without actually being contaminated by it. There was our not trusting each other, no one ever bringing it together, because we all knew if we got together, we'd probably decide to burn or degauss the tapes, which was the only smart thing to do—but that was illegal.

"The whole process operated in a self-destruct way. Here were persons of reasonable talent forced to push a stone uphill with their noses, and that situation will always produce mistakes. And that was the way we came into the Cox situation in September and October."

10

FIRESTORM:
FALL 1973

The "Cox situation" would have been inescapable no matter whom Attorney General Elliot Richardson might have named as Special Prosecutor on May 18th, 1973.

The same system of courts would have had to encourage any Special Prosecutor to go the same course once he decided to put the judicial system itself to public test. And if that course pointed logically to the White House, then led on into the Oval Office, the same rules of evidence would have had to clear the way. Inescapably, the courts would have had to hold that the President was bound as much by the law of the land as were all other Americans. But in the summer and fall of 1973, that course was to be an intricate, complicated and perilous route.

A resolution calling for a Special Prosecutor had been introduced by Republican Senator Charles Percy of Illinois, endorsed by a bipartisan group of Senators and passed on May 1st, the day after the liquidation of Richard Nixon's old White House staff. The action would endow the yet nameless nominee with sweeping power and responsibility. He would be required to investigate, subpoena, bring suit in court against anyone suspected of criminal wrongdoing in the campaign of 1972, up to and through the White House to the President himself. With such authority, any independent Special Prosecutor would sooner or later have ground his way to an ultimate "Cox situation." But the personality of Archibald Cox and his staff selections added a special political and cultural dimension.

The Cox group came of a generation of young lawyers whose attitudes reflected much of the social stirrings of the 1960's. Accident had trained most of them in those Ivy League universities which Nixon, Haldeman and Ehrlichman saw as the breeding ground of the elitists they loathed. The decade of the sixties had been churning out of these schools more and more lawyers who wanted to serve not great corporations or moneyed clients, but the causes of reform. A new ethos ran through thousands of such young lawyers, expressing itself in public-interest law firms and class-action suits. The esteem of their peers was to be won by dedication in bringing wrongdoers, whether of great corporations or high office, to the bar of increasingly sympathetic courts. And for this new breed, Archibald Cox, a professor at Harvard Law School, was a father type.

Over six feet, his hair brush-cut as was Bob Haldeman's, Cox had gone back and forth between government and classroom for more than thirty years. A man who lectured rather than spoke, given to pacing back and forth before almost any audience as a teacher paces back and forth before a classroom, Cox was above all a man of inflexible New England rectitude. His name had emerged late in the selection process. Haig had originally suggested that Richardson seek an unchallengeable Democrat for the new post—say, ex-Governor "Pat" Brown of California or ex-Governor Warren Hearnes of Missouri. Richardson had spurned those suggestions, had scouted and been turned down by at least five other nationally prominent jurists in the next two weeks; and then, just a few days before the Ervin Committee hearings were to open, had reached out for Archibald Cox in San Francisco by long-distance telephone and asked Cox to take the post.

Cox had been one of Richardson's law-school professors at Harvard; both had been Overseers of Harvard University; both were of Back Bay Yankee stock. And even though Richardson was genuinely fond of Richard Nixon, while Cox was even more deeply devoted to the Kennedy family, each was convinced of the other's complete integrity. If the Southern California team of Richard Nixon came from one distinct American sub-culture, Cox and Richardson came from another, equally distinct, but totally different in tradition and nature. Together, they represented all that Richard Nixon secretly respected and at the same time privately hated, for if anything stood as symbol of the "Establishment" that Richard Nixon scorned, it was Harvard.

Harvard, that brilliant collection of students and scholars in their brick-red, white-turreted colony by the Charles, has become one of the most competitive institutions in America since its control passed from the Establishment of ancestral gentry to the new control of rigid academicians. The new Harvard strains for rigorous quality; weaklings are crushed there as in a Marine training camp; and those who emerge —whatever their social origins—have a conviction of their own intellectual superiority, an unconscious arrogance that carries on for decades after their graduation.

When Richard Nixon spoke of the Establishment, he meant the entire self-selected aristocracy of the East Coast executive belt; but normally when he faced the Establishment personally, it bore a Harvard seal. Harvard was not an entirely bad word to Richard Nixon. He employed Harvard men in his first administration because their quality, like Kissinger's, was inescapable. But when, with his mandate of 1972, he attempted to reorganize his new administration and re-staff it, he said one day in conversation with Ehrlichman and Haldeman that they should give "ten points extra to anyone they could find from Oklahoma State University." Nonetheless, his respect for the Establishment and for Harvard persisted—and the Cabinet and staff of his second administration were more heavily dominated by Harvard men than those of any of the six Harvard men who had been Presidents of the United States (two Adamses, two Roosevelts, one Hayes, one Kennedy).

By late winter of 1973, though his inner personal staff was still of Southern California, his official Cabinet ran thus: Secretary of Defense, Richardson; Attorney General, Kleindienst; Secretary of HEW, Weinberger; Secretary of HUD, Lynn—all Harvard men. So was his new chief of CIA (James Schlesinger), who was a Harvard classmate of Henry Kissinger, about to become Secretary of State. So also were Director Roy Ash and Deputy Director Fred Malek of the Office of Management and Budget; and Nixon had appointed as Ambassador to India his favorite conversationalist, Harvard Professor Daniel P. Moynihan.

Nixon's ambivalence toward the Establishment—respect for its qualities, suspicion of its arrogant style—ran deep. The Cox-Richardson connection was only the last step on a long road. That road had begun with Nixon's first political trophy in his rise to fame, Harvard Law School graduate Alger Hiss—who had been the protégé of Supreme Court

Justice Oliver Wendell Holmes, also Harvard. Nixon's local team in Los Angeles County had been plagued by another Harvard man, County Republican Chairman Julius Leetham, now a California judge. On another level, that of history, Nixon considered his greatest rival to be Franklin D. Roosevelt, Harvard '04. It was the Roosevelt coalition Nixon hoped to replace in 1972 by the Nixon "new majority." But in his own time, in *mano-a-mano* disturbance of spirit, his real nemesis was John F. Kennedy, Harvard '40.

Now he had Archibald Cox as adversary. Not only was Cox a Harvard man—he was a devoted Kennedy Resurrectionist. Not only that: wherever Nixon looked out on the world in 1973, he was faced with Ivy League enemies. Sam Ervin of North Carolina looked and sounded the prototypical Southern courthouse philosopher, but Sam Ervin was a Harvard Law School man; as was his chief counsel, Sam Dash; as was Dash's assistant chief counsel, known at the White House as "Terrible Terry" Lenzner. The press was populated by Nixon's Ivy League enemies, the people who had scorned or misunderstood the Middle America expression of his triumph of 1972. There was Ben Bradlee of the Washington *Post*, a newspaper owned by the Grahams, a family of Harvard men. There was Osborn Elliott, Harvard, of *Newsweek*. CBS News was presided over by Richard Salant, another one of them. Nixon's polemic enemies bristled with Harvard men like Arthur Schlesinger, Jr. (author of a devastating book called *Kennedy or Nixon* in 1960), John Kenneth Galbraith and David Halberstam.

Nowhere, however, was Nixon's ambivalence about the Establishment more clearly expressed than in his attitude to the new Special Prosecutor's office. He had named Elliot Richardson as his Attorney General not only because Richardson was antiseptically honest, but because a genuine respect bound them together. Nixon expected total loyalty from Richardson as one of his own personal Harvard men, as he did from all his staff. But another code of honor bound Richardson to Cox, who, whatever their political differences, shared a sense of public responsibility which came down to them from their kindred pasts. Later, when Richardson resigned as Attorney General rather than fire Cox, James Doyle, Cox's remarkable public-affairs spokesman, explained it thus: "You see, I think at the bottom of it, if Elliot fired Archie, it meant that he could never walk down Beacon Street or across Harvard Yard again and hold his head high when he met friends." Doyle was, of course, a Boston Irishman who had observed the parochial breed of Yankees with as much detachment as he observed the parochial breed of Southern Californians whom Cox pursued; and understood them both.

If Cox could have invented a ceremony deliberately to make his background and political loyalties obnoxious to Richard Nixon, he could have done no better than by choosing the guests he did to witness his swearing-in ceremonies in the Solictor General's office at the Justice Department on May 25th, 1973. "I guess we were disenchanted with Archie Cox within eighteen minutes of his swearing in," said Pat Buchanan, recalling receipt of the news. For his swearing in, Cox had invited both Senator Edward Kennedy of Massachusetts and Ethel Kennedy, Robert Kennedy's widow. While the Senator relaxed on a couch in the room, Ethel stood proudly to be photographed as Cox swore to protect the Constitution of the United States. To the White House, the matter was clearly ominous—a Harvard law professor, a Kennedy man, surrounded by the Kennedy family, swearing to his mission to investigate "allegations involving the President, members of the White House staff, or Presidential appointees, and any other matters which he consents to have assigned to him by the Attorney General."

As if the ceremony were not enough, Cox proceeded to make the symbolism even clearer by selection of staff. On the day he had accepted his appointment from Richardson, Cox had asked two fellow Harvard Law School professors to join him as consultants—James Vorenberg and Philip Heymann. The three recruited the rest of the staff together; and since they felt speed was of the essence, they turned to the old-boy network—law professors who they knew could put them in touch with the best and brightest of recent Ivy League graduates. Selection was done largely by grades in school, clerkships and litigating experience. An occasional young bright might be a Republican—like Philip Lacovara, of Columbia Law School, a *summa cum laude* and campus manager there for Goldwater in the 1964 campaign. But

most were Democrats, decidedly Kennedy-oriented. Of the
five senior attorneys, all were Ivy Leaguers. All nine of the
Assistant Special Prosecutors were Ivy Leaguers. Of the administrative staff and staff lawyers, all but four out of twenty-
five were Ivy Leaguers. Of the total of thirty-seven lawyers
finally recruited, all but one were Ivy Leaguers, and of these,
no less than eighteen were young Harvards. Their age, from
senior staff to staff lawyers, averaged something less than
thirty-one. Two task-force leaders were aged twenty-seven
and thirty-two.

In Washington, at the beginning, the Cox team appeared
to be, as one reporter said, "a bunch of innocents about to
be hacked to pieces in a town of barracudas." Nor did their
initial action bode well—a skirmish with Ervin's committee,
Cox petitioning to stop publicly televised hearings as preju-
dicial to later fair trial. Ervin flatly turned Cox down. The
next action, a brush with Henry Petersen's original prosecution team of the Department of Justice, went better. Cox
neatly invited aboard the line prosecutors, Silbert, Glanzer
and Campbell; muzzled them; learned what they had to
give—and then accepted their resignations when, smarting
at being superseded in the case they had brought so far,
they wanted to leave. By mid-June, while the Ervin Committee still held the public spotlight, Cox was geared for action. His ninth-floor offices at 1425 K Street in downtown
Washington were as tightly guarded and security-sealed as
the inner fastness of the Pentagon. No sign marked the
metal door—simply a legend which read "PUSH BELL."
Closed-circuit television monitored the corridor; electronics
experts swept and cleared phones and walls; a newsman
was allowed in only by appointment; then he wore a little
red visitor's badge hung conspicuously around his neck as
he was escorted in and out of the office of the person with
whom he had an appointment.

By June, too, Cox had proved himself a somewhat erratic
but exceptionally effective executive. All administrative details were handled through the Deputy Special Prosecutor,
Henry S. Ruth, Jr. Five special task forces concentrated on
five specific areas: Watergate break-in and cover-up; the
financing of the 1972 campaign; the dirty-tricks team of
Donald Segretti; the ITT case; and the Plumbers' team,

which the President had hoped specifically to exclude from Cox's jurisdiction. And Cox reserved himself for grand strategy, which was soon to become the strategy of the tapes.

Richardson wanted no part of Cox's responsibilities; his time, his thinking were being absorbed by the approaching Agnew crisis. But the White House felt that since Richardson had appointed Cox, Richardson was responsible for him. If Cox's young brights poked at the Secret Service for more information about wire-taps, and then insisted on knowing all about the President's wire-tap of his own brother, Donald, the news came back instantly to the White House; which would result in a furious telephone call from the President to Richardson, and a second call from Richardson to Cox, Richardson urging Cox to restrain his boys. If the Los Angeles *Times* ran a loose-jointed story reporting a Cox investigation of the President's real estate, which was at that moment untrue, another Presidential telephone call would zap Richardson; and Richardson would have to call Cox for an explanation, which, sheepishly, came back that one of Cox's aides had simply assembled some press clippings and Cox was not, repeat not, investigating the President's personal finances.

If a perfect example of the internal dynamics of a subsystem were to be sought, the workings of the Cox team would serve well. Cox had lectured with such austerity over the years on the majesty of the law; had himself become so convinced of that majesty; and had surrounded himself with such dedicated young men who had learned law in its purity from textbooks, that nothing could deflect his team —not the press, not Congress, not the Attorney General, not even Cox himself if he had so chosen. What had to happen, by the dynamics of their charge, was that they must investigate a specifically alleged set of criminal acts. And the course they meant to go, though never run before, was textbook clear—even if it led to the White House.

They had, to the consternation of the White House, on July 23rd, 1973, drawn up their own subpoena to the President, requiring him to deliver nine specific tapes: two of June 20th, 1972, of a telephone call from Mitchell, and a meeting with Ehrlichman and Haldeman; one of June 30th; a tape of what would become the famous "containment" conversation between John Dean and the President on September 15th, 1972; the fifth, of March 13th, 1973; two tapes of the climax day of March 21st, 1973; another of March 22nd; and the ninth, of the President's meeting with John Dean on April 15th. Served at the Executive Office Building, received by Presidential Counsel Fred Buzhardt on Monday, July 23rd, the subpoena was rejected two days later.

From there, the action proceeded automatically: on Thursday, the 26th, the Special Prosecutor himself pleaded before Judge John Sirica, demanding that the President "show cause" why he rejected the subpoena. The threat was still of minor moment to the White House, now secretly preoccupied with the Agnew crisis and publicly riddled by the Ervin Committee. August was spent in an interchange of briefs between Cox and the President's new Constitutional lawyer, Charles Alan Wright, just summoned to White House service from the University of Texas.

Wright argued a grand Constitutional theme: that the President is sovereign; that his privacy is necessary to the proper leadership of the United States; that to deprive him of the candor and unrestrained opinions of his advisers by exposing their conversations was mortally to wound executive privilege. Sirica listened; weighed executive privilege against the demands of criminal evidence; then on August 29th rejected Wright's plea and ordered that the tapes be turned over to him so that he might himself review them and excise any privileged portions before handing them over to the grand jury.

Sirica's order, as the judicial system engaged, could be overturned only by a plea to the Court of Appeals in Washington; and there Wright, on September 10th, arguing for the President, made his case sharper: that the principle of executive privilege is inherent in the Constitution, overriding even in matters of criminal evidence. Only the Congress, he argued, by the impeachment process, could call a President to the bar of justice. Wright's arguments had framed the case politically and historically: If every one of the 400 District Court judges of the Federal bench across the country—most of them political appointees—could call on a President to expose his papers, files, documents, conversations and ruminations, then the Presidency was at the mercy of random barratry.

The panel of seven judges who considered the appeal was overwhelmingly liberal—largely Democrats appointed by Kennedy and Johnson in the previous decade. Yet it did not want to confront Richard Nixon head on. It urged that Wright, Buzhardt, Cox sit down together and try to work out some compromise that would satisfy Cox's need for evidence and the President's requirement of privacy. On three separate days the contending branches of the Executive arm —the President's Special Prosecutor and the President's Special Counsel—talked and argued. But they came to no compromise—putting the matter back to the Court of Appeals, which then pondered for three full weeks, from September 20th to October 12th.

It was six in the evening of Friday, October 12th, when the Court of Appeals handed out its decision from the clerk's office on the fifth floor. By a vote of five to two, it had upheld the District Court's order. And within five working days of the next week, it declared, the President must hand over to Judge Sirica the nine tapes sought by Archibald Cox. The rhetorical quality of the decision was unusual—sad, as if the judges shrank from the very action which they insisted: ". . . unfortunately, the court's order must run directly to the President, because he has taken the unusual step of assuming personal custody of the Government property sought by subpoena." Late as it was, the court voiced the hope that "Perhaps the President will find it possible to reach some agreement with the special prosecutor as to what portions of the subpoenaed evidence are necessary to the grand jury." But despite the sadness, the decision was firm: "Though the President is elected by nationwide ballot, and is often said to represent all the people, he does not embody the nation's sovereignty. He is not above the law's commands." It concluded, "The President's petition is denied. . . . The issuance of our mandate is stayed for five days to permit the seeking of Supreme Court review of the issues with which we have dealt in making our decision."

There were thus seven days of option left—from October 12th to October 19th—for the President to make his choice. He could seek further compromise with Archibald

Cox as the court had suggested; or he could go directly to the Supreme Court; or he could comply.

Or else—he could fire Archibald Cox. Cox was, after all, an appointee of Nixon's appointee Elliot Richardson—a subordinate in his Executive Branch who was carrying on an open insurrection against the President in that Executive Branch. Whether Nixon was defending himself or defending the principle of executive privilege, none of his lawyers could tell—and as they counseled together, in ignorance of what their President alone knew, they could come to no quick conclusion. The decision must be the President's.

One must remember now all the pressures interacting at this particular time in the mind of Richard Nixon, to understand the chaos in which he made his next set of critical decisions. Sixteen months earlier, in June of 1972, he had made the mistake of obstruction of justice. He had lost the opportunity to purge this crime by April of 1973 and compounded it. He had lied ever since. And had created a new command under him which would dissolve if he shared with it the full story of his action. And far greater Presidential responsibilities were pressing on his attention at this point than covering his own retreat to honor.

On this particular Friday evening of the Court of Appeals decision, October 12th, the Arab attack on Israel, the Yom Kippur war, was six days old—and that attack threatened world disaster. Thrown back in the first three days by overwhelming Arab-Soviet armor, the Israelis had retreated, then mobilized, then counter-attacked. By this Friday evening, having recaptured the Golan Heights, Israelis were within eighteen miles of Damascus, capital of Syria. But on the Sinai front, they were reeling under shock. The first four days of the war had cost them 100 planes of their 500-plane air force, and 650 tanks, a third of their armored force! The most sophisticated Soviet weapons, heat-seeking airborne missiles, hand-guided anti-tank missiles, were macerating their strike forces. Without re-supply, the Israelis were doomed—and only the United States could help. The Soviets has begun a massive aerial re-supply two days earlier—their Antonov 22's already unloading hundreds of tons of new weaponry at Cairo and Damascus. Thus, all day Friday, the Israelis had been pressing a plea for survival at both the Pentagon and the State Department; hours counted; but State and Pentagon were in disagreement and their quarrel was pressing its imperative way that afternoon and evening to the President's desk.

Not only that. Vice-President Agnew had resigned two days before, acknowledging himself a common crook. For two days the President had considered his choices for a new Vice-President; and now, this same Friday evening, with the critical decisions of the Israeli war upon him, on which hung war and peace, he had decided to announce the name of Agnew's successor, Republican House Minority Leader Gerald Ford. And so that same evening of the 12th, in a ceremony marked by a tasteless cheerfulness, he gathered his Cabinet and the nation's Congressional leaders in the East Room to present them a successor who might make them forget the squalor of his first Vice-President.

How much time Richard Nixon had to consider the implications of the Court of Appeals decision on that evening of multiple tensions, or whether he even had time to read it, is unknown. A Constitutional missile had been fired into outer space which would eventually explode in the Supreme Court. But so much more was pressing on him at that moment on Friday evening to divert his attention. No man can make more than a limited number of major decisions in one day without error. Moreover, he had been persuaded by his lawyers that no court in the land would violate the historic doctrine of executive privilege so far as to support Archibald Cox's plea for a violation of the President's private conversations. Given the torment of the Agnew affair, the ceremonial duty of announcing Gerald Ford that evening, the night-long crisis over Israel and Russia, the decision of the Court of Appeals must have seemed of lesser urgency.

And the troubled man was to be up late that night. The quarrel between the cautious Pentagon, reluctant to strip home forces of arms, and the furious State Department, led by Kissinger, who knew that America must act now or see the Arabs sweep the Middle East into the Soviet clutch, could be settled only by the President. He left the ceremonies for Gerald Ford; and then was locked with Kissinger until well after one o'clock in the morning, hearing Kissinger's plea for immediate, massive action, which meant that he must meet early the next morning with his war leaders; and at 10:30 on Saturday morning, after very little sleep, he presided over a meeting which included both Henry Kissinger and James Schlesinger of Defense, and made his critical decision: the Pentagon would move, must move by his direct order, to re-supply the Israelis that day. With that decision, and as the giant C-5's began to take off within hours, Nixon himself was off to Camp David to pause for breath and rest in the wooded hills.

Between that night of October 12th and October 23rd, eleven days later, all the paradoxes of the Nixon personality would be displayed for the record of history—both his greatness and his meanness, his capacity for bold, large decisions and for self-defeating, cheap manipulations. The sequence of events and overlaps of emotions, the strains of conflict in his own mind resulted thus in a week which in years to come may be read equally well as one of the great moments of Western world statesmanship or as the week in which he forced the United States Congress and the people to undertake his removal from office.

Only one man, perhaps, fully realized what was coming: Elliot Richardson. Richardson had been intermediary between the White House and Cox for months. As early as July 23rd, the day Cox had issued his subpoena on Nixon, Richardson had received a call from General Alexander Haig explaining that "the boss" was "uptight" about Cox's activities and "if we have to have a confrontation we will have it. . . . [The President wanted] a tight line drawn with no further mistakes" and "if Cox does not agree, we will get rid of Cox." In early October, as Richardson wound up the removal of Agnew, he met with the President again. "After we had finished our discussion about Mr. Agnew," recalled Richardson in an affidavit, "and as we were walking to the door, the President said in substance, 'Now that we have disposed of that matter we can go ahead and get rid of Cox.' There was nothing more said."

Thus, on Friday evening, October 12th, shortly after the Court of Appeals decision was issued and before he went to attend the announcement ceremonies for Gerald Ford, Richardson met Cox briefly in his office, Richardson holding out the hope that he might play a useful role in getting access to the tapes for the Special Prosecutor without confrontation. Then Richardson, exhausted by his direction of the Agnew excision, was off home to Boston for the weekend. He was not to see the President until a week later—and then only to tender his resignation.

The President, even more exhausted, had flown off on Saturday for the clean mountain air of Camp David; but felt well enough to helicopter back to Washington on Sunday morning for the first worship service in the White House in six months (he had stopped attending services after Easter Sunday of 1973, when he felt he had been criticized at Key Biscayne by the sermon of the local divine; but now, whether out of piety or relief or need, he wanted prayer again).

It was sometime on Sunday afternoon that Richardson, in Boston, received a telephone call from Alexander Haig. Could Richardson be in Washington Monday morning for an important meeting about the Middle East and the Court of Appeals problem? Haig asked. Richardson would meet the next morning first with Haig and Buzhardt, then with the President. And Richardson agreed, flying back to Washington that night.

When, however, the next morning, Richardson arrived at the White House for a two-and-a-half-hour conference (9:00 to 11:30 A.M.), it was with Haig and Buzhardt alone, not the President. Briefly they talked about the situation in the Middle East, Haig showing Richardson an ominous new message from Brezhnev, then explaining how urgent it was that the President's authority be maintained. Richardson had been both Secretary of Defense and Under Secretary of State, but sensed that was not the reason why he had been called to this conference. Facetiously, as he recalls it, he remarked that he was ready to go anywhere, that he was ready to pack his bags and take off, trying to urge them to their point. Their point was simple: Over the weekend, they had worked out an idea which they thought might satisfy the President and at the same time thread his case through the loophole the Court of Appeals decision had left. Nixon himself would prepare an authenticated "summary" of the nine subpoenaed tapes to satisfy the Court—and then they would fire Archibald Cox! To which, after hours of conversation, Richardson replied that, if so—he would resign. He, Richardson, was bound by oath—pledges he had made to Congress when he was confirmed, pledges signed and sealed in his chartering instructions to Cox. Cox could not be fired; he, Richardson, had promised the Senate that there would be no firing except for "extraordinary improperties," and Cox had committed none.

By Monday afternoon a fragile compromise had been worked out by the busy Haig. He had persuaded the President, still preoccupied with the Middle Eastern war, that an authenticated summary prepared by a figure he respected and trusted, such as Senator John Stennis of Mississippi, might satisfy Cox, and if so, Cox need not be fired; but the President felt "this was it" and Cox would get no further access to Presidential material. By mid-afternoon Haig had persuaded Stennis to undertake the task; and by late after noon Haig had persuaded Richardson to broach the matter to Cox as a satisfactory answer to his needs. But, like a good law professor, Cox responded that he wanted to see the proposal in writing.

Tuesday was a day of relatively slow movement in the crisis of the tapes. Melvin Laird had told reporters that day that he had warned the President he would face impeachment if he defied a Supreme Court order to produce the tapes. But the President's mind was on more important things.

In the Middle East, Nixon was directing the last and greatest gamble of his diplomacy. His Saturday decision, three days earlier, had had an electric effect on Israeli morale and, more important, on the combat situation. Within hours after that decision, the first U.S. Air Force plane was off from New Jersey; and by the time it arrived at Israel's Lod airport, thirteen flight hours away, seventeen other American cargo carriers were following. The Russian airlift was moving at a rate of 700 tons a day over secure flight routes. By Monday the first nine American C-141's had off-loaded 300 tons of cargo, the C-5's were winging in with 100 tons of cargo each, all of them threading around corridors of hostile or forbidden air; and by this Tuesday they were approaching peak rate of delivery of 1,000 tons a day. From Air Force bases all across the country—Ohio, California, Texas, Utah, Oklahoma—cargo was being relayed to bases in New Jersey and Delaware for the final airlift of 6,450 miles to Israel. And such cargo: fuselage parts, pal-

lets of ammunition, 24-ton helicopters, 25-ton howitzers,
50-ton tanks! In the month between October 13th and November 14th, the U.S. Air Force in 566 missions was to deliver 22,395 tons in a performance of technical virtuosity
surpassing even the performance of the men of the Hump
or the Berlin airlift. Other major systems in the country
might be set against the President, but the military system
still responded to his leadership. The airlift was, perhaps,
the last grand Presidential action in which Richard Nixon
could take pride. Internationally, his touch was still sure,
however palsied and uncertain it was at home.

By Wednesday, however, the domestic crisis had escalated, and was now rivaling the overseas crisis in intensity. Richardson had put Haig's compromise proposal in writing
for Cox. Richardson's original draft had included the sentence, "The proposed arrangement would undertake to cover
only the tapes heretofore subpoenaed by the Watergate
Grand Jury at the request of the special prosecutor." In
Richardson's mind, this sentence meant that only in this instance was Cox urged to accept compromise; for all other
investigations and records, Cox was free to pursue his
course as he would. Buzhardt redrafted Richardson's draft,
insisting that Richardson's key sentence was redundant, and
the final draft, omitting the sentence, was fired off to Cox as
"Proposal Submitted by Attorney General."

Cox's reply came back on Thursday; and was of scant
comfort. "The essential idea for establishing impartial but
non-judicial means for providing the special prosecutor . . . with an accurate record . . . of the tapes . . .
is not unacceptable. . . . There should be no avoidable
confrontation with the President, and I have not the
slightest desire to embarrass him," began Cox. But then
he went on—the verifiers must be "special masters" of the
court; moreover, if any case came to open trial, then the
actual tapes must be provided. Cox wanted the tapes not
now, not this week—but he did want a promise that, if necessary, the tapes would be produced in open court, for the
law cannot operate without evidence. "You appointed me,"
he wrote to Richardson, "and I pledged that I would not be
turned aside. Any solution I can accept must be such as to
command conviction that I am adhering to that pledge."

To consider the Cox reply, there gathered now in the

White House five men: Richardson, Haig, Buzhardt, of course; but two men, Garment and Wright, were called in from their compartments to be told for the first time of what had been happening since Monday on this matter for which they had been key legal counsel for months. To all except Richardson, it seemed that Cox had rejected a last attempt at conciliation and Cox must be fired. Richardson disagreed, and suggested that Wright now speak directly to Cox.

Wright reached Cox by telephone at his brother's home having dinner, and of their conversation there were only two auditors. Cox recalled the conversation as "decidedly nasty," "designed to elicit rejection." Wright remembered it as exploratory. But Wright followed this call with a letter concluding, "If you think that there is any purpose in our talking further, my associates and I stand ready to do so. If not, we will have to follow the course of action that we think in the best interest of the country. I will call you at 10 A.M. to ascertain your views." In international diplomacy, such a letter is called an ultimatum. Cox responded to the ultimatum not by phone but with a letter, recalling the conversation quite differently. Referring to a fourth point of the evening's unrecorded conversation, Cox said: "Point Four was that I must categorically agree not to subpoena any other White House tape, paper, or document. This would mean that my ability to secure evidence bearing upon criminal wrong-doing by high White House officials would be left to the discretion of White House counsel. . . . I could not conscientiously agree to your stipulations without unfaithfulness to the pledges which I gave the Senate prior to my appointment. . . . I categorically assured the Senate Judiciary Committee that I would challenge such claims as far as the law permitted. The Attorney General was confirmed on the strength of that assurance. I cannot break my promise now."

By Friday morning, however, even before the receipt of Cox's reply, the White House was off on a new strategy—a mixture of the old PR trickiness and sharp politics. The President would make his Stennis proposal public—and to buttress it, he would make it seem an act of generosity, a lordly waiver of executive privilege in deference to the Senate. Two days before, on Wednesday, Judge Sirica had dismissed the Ervin Committee's court action for the tapes. Thus, without being forced to do so by the court—or so it was hoped it would appear—the President would now extend the olive branch to Congress. Senator Ervin was in New Orleans, Senator Baker was in Chicago. Reached by telephone, provided with planes, both were in the Oval Office early that evening for a forty-minute conversation. Unaware of the separate trajectory of the Cox office or the ultimatums delivered by both the White House and the Special Prosecutor, Baker and Ervin considered the President's voluntary offer to have the tape summary verified by Senator Stennis, a man trusted by all, an excellent one. And thus, having conscripted Ervin, Baker and Stennis to stand behind him, the President could turn over to his aides the drafting of a bombshell statement.

Friday had been another day of exquisite world tension. The airlift to Israel was working smoothly. Assured of resupply, the Israelis were spending their stockpile of armor and weaponry; early in the week an Israeli strike force had crossed the Suez Canal and now, by Thursday, Israelis in full force were pouring into Egypt in a counter-attack that would, in a few more days, reach to within forty-five miles of Cairo. But the Russians, having armored the initial Arab attack, and seeing the war turned against their clients, were escalating, too. Three Russian airborne divisions had been placed on the alert, ready to move, ten days earlier. Did the Russians threaten world war to save their Egyptian clients? Moreover, Brezhnev on the hot line from Russia had asked that Kissinger fly to Moscow immediately. Armed confrontation between the Soviet Union and America hung in the balance. This Friday, thus, Kissinger was preparing for a post-midnight departure to Moscow to confer with the Soviet leaders, and Nixon was waiting the outcome.

Nixon had been in the same situation before in May of 1972, gambling in Vietnam, ordering the mining of Haiphong harbor, juggling international destinies while he juggled a Presidential campaign at home. Thus playing with fate brilliantly across the world, the President, still resolute, played the same gambler's game at home—but badly, mindlessly, totally miscalculating the consequences.

At 8:15 P.M., the White House released its statement: "For a number of months," began the President, "there has been a strain imposed on the American people by the aftermath of Watergate. . . ." Then to the central theme of all his politics—his need to control matters: "Our government, like our nation, must remain strong and effective. What matters most, in this critical hour, is our ability to act—and to act in a way that enables us to control events, not to be paralyzed and overwhelmed by them."

He then described what he was doing to resolve the domestic crisis. He reported that he had compromised with the courts and the Senate, that he was making summaries of required tapes available to Senator Stennis who would verify their accuracy, and that Senators Baker and Ervin agreed to this. And then: "I have felt it necessary to direct him [Cox], as an employee of the Executive Branch, to make no further attempts by judicial process to obtain tapes, notes or memoranda of Presidential conversations."

In conclusion, the President said, "Under the Constitution, it is the duty of the President to see that the laws of this nation are faithfully executed. My actions today are in accordance with that duty, and in that spirit of accommodation."

The statement was, in its own terms, a masterpiece of political art—it floated on a rhetoric of conciliation, compromise and earnest good will. What it left out, flatly, was the fact that the President was *not* complying with the order the Court of Appeals had issued the previous Friday.

Cox, having received from a friendly newspaper a text of the statement, responded by issuing one of his own which nailed the deceit: "In my judgment," said Cox's statement, "the President is refusing to comply with the Court decrees. . . . The instructions are in violation of the promises which the Attorney General made to the Senate when his nomination was confirmed. For me to comply to those instructions would violate my solemn pledge to the Senate and the country to invoke judicial process to challenge exaggerated claims of executive privilege. I shall not violate my promise." The next morning, the *New York Times* summarized the story in an eight-column two-deck headline which read: "NIXON TO KEEP TAPES DESPITE RULING; WILL

GIVE OWN SUMMARY; COX DEFIANT." The subhead read, "Israel Reports 10,000 Men and 200 Tanks Across Suez."

The next day, Saturday, October 20th, 1973, was the day that Alexander Haig was to call "the day of the firestorm," and if there was a vortex to the firestorm, it was the conscience of Elliot Richardson.

Since Thursday evening, Richardson had been preparing in his home, on a wooded knoll in McLean, Virginia, a memo to himself, called "Why I Must Resign." He had called Cox on Friday evening and told his old friend that he had just received a letter from the President instructing him as Attorney General to halt Archibald Cox from any further use of the courts to seek evidence against the President or the President's men. Richardson said he had made it "explicitly clear that I was not transmitting this instruction to Cox."

The ball, thus, was in Cox's court; a resignation by Cox would free Richardson from his conflict of loyalties. But a repudiation of the President's orders by Cox would make Richardson's behavior pivotal. Would he, as Attorney General, be bound by law and loyalty to obey the President? Or would he be bound by law and commitment to keep his pledge to the Senate—not to fire Cox except for "extraordinary improprieties"?

Cox triggered the Saturday action next day at one o'clock, in the ballroom on the thirteenth floor of the National Press Building. Gangling, gentle and firm, combining the qualities of old Mr. Chips and Joan of Arc, the Special Prosecutor opened at his best—and then proceeded to get better. "I am sorry to have had to bring you in on such a lovely day," he said. And it was a lovely day, autumn in Washington, the leaves yellowing, the sky blue and the barometer high, a cloud floating by occasionally.

"I am certainly not out to get the President of the United States," he said as the television cameras zoomed in close. "I am even worried, to put it in colloquial terms, that I am getting too big for my britches, that what I see as principle could be vanity. I hope not. In the end, I decided that I had to try to stick by what I thought was right." Then to his explanation of his oath and pledges. Then, "It is sort of embarrassing to be put in the position to say, well, I don't want the President of the United States to tell me what to do. I was brought up with the greatest respect for every President of the United States. But that isn't what is involved. It is that there is a basic change in the institutional arrangement that was established. . . ."

The first question to Cox was obvious: "Mr. Cox . . . Are you going to wait for the President to dismiss you?" Cox: "I am going to go about my duties on the terms on which I assumed them." A next question made it clearer: ". . . is not your intention in direct conflict with the President's order to you? And, if it is, and you are fired by the end of this news conference, what happens then?" Cox: ". . . I was appointed by the Attorney General. . . . I think there is a question whether anyone other than the Attorney General can give me any instructions that I have any legal obligation to obey." Q: ". . . how could you expect to succeed in this job?" Cox: "I thought it was worth a try. I thought it was important. If it could be done, I thought it would help the country, and if I lost, what the hell. . . ."

They were all watching the televised press conference—Richardson and his staff at the Department of Justice, the President's men, the Washington news system, the nation. Cox was defying the President outright. Cox insisted that only Elliot Richardson could fire him. Richardson was the executive arm of the President. He must do the President's bidding or leave.

At 2:20, Elliot Richardson was still in his office at the Department of Justice when Haig called, instructing him to fire Cox. Richardson, anticipating the call, had his answer ready. He would not, and demanded to see the President in order to resign. He waited almost an hour for a reply in his office with his putative successors, Deputy Attorney General William Ruckelshaus, Solicitor General Robert Bork. Republicans all, loyal all, they were a micro-spectrum of the civic strain that had run in that party for a century. Ruckelshaus had no doubt; if Richardson resigned, he also would refuse to fire Cox, and would resign too. Then it would be up to Bork, next in the line of succession. Bork said that, however much he hated it, somebody had to carry out a President's orders; he would do so, if it came to him; then he would resign immediately thereafter. Their talk was interrupted by another phone call at 3:20 from Haig—would Richardson come over immediately to see the President?

The President was a man caught by riptides. His Secretary of State was now in Moscow negotiating with Brezhnev. The world's news wires had carried the report of Cox's defiance to every capital overseas. Nixon's diplomatic leverage rested on the world's measure of his control of his own government. And that day at one o'clock he had been openly defied.

It had been the conviction of the President's inner counsel for weeks, as it had been the President's, that Cox would have to be fired. Now the world crisis gave him the occasion—but how could he fire Cox without losing Richardson, his administration's symbol of integrity? The President, as was his custom, balanced his choices with counsel while he waited for Richardson. He wanted to hear the opinion of his house liberal—Garment. The President was moody with Garment. He had been struggling with the bureaucracy for years; he had ordered the Pentagon to fly every cargo plane available to the Middle East. The bureaucracy, said the President, had resisted. The Pentagon felt that a single cargo of military equipment in one C-5 would be enough; Kissinger, said the President, was willing to go for a plane and a half; but he, the President, had commanded as he had done in the Hanoi crisis of Christmastime—everything that can fly and go, flies and goes. He had done that. But now here was open defiance by another branch of the bureaucracy. How would Brezhnev, in Moscow, read this open insurrection? He had to fire Cox, did he not? Even if it meant that Richardson would go? Yes, answered Garment, yes—after this afternoon's defiance, there was no other way except to fire Cox.

Having sought advice on his liberal flank, the President next called in Pat Buchanan, who monitored his conservative flank. He put it more sharply to Buchanan. You know, said the President, if Cox goes, Elliot and Ruckelshaus go, too. But with Kissinger in Moscow, what choice did he have? He had to show Brezhnev that the President of the United States controlled his own government. Buchanan replied as Garment had—that there was no choice, the President must fire Cox. And Buchanan remembers that as he left the Oval Office at about four, the next visitors coming in were Haig and Richardson.

"The President understood," said Richardson, "that my resignation was a 'given.' That I couldn't carry out his instructions to tell Cox not to seek documents. But he hoped I was not going to use this occasion as a means of creating any more difficulties than I could help.

"Then he shifted," recalled Richardson, "asking why I had to resign *now*. He was desperately concerned about the Middle East situation. From the perspective of Moscow . . . Brezhnev and his colleagues in Moscow could not conceivably understand the specific defiance of his orders by Cox in that afternoon's press conference. It was like the 1970 action in Cambodia—he wanted to show Moscow and Peking his determination; and to do that he would pay the necessary domestic price to do it."

Richardson, like Kissinger, Weinberger and Bush, had always been treated with special dignity and respect by the President. But Nixon's appeal to Richardson now was blunt. "He was concerned," said Richardson, "that my resignation would jeopardize his efforts in Moscow, jeopardize cease-fire in the Middle East. He really put it on me. He was really tough."

But Richardson saw no way to postpone his resignation. He could not carry out the President's orders on this day and fire Cox. Nor could he delay announcing his departure. "If I delayed my resignation for a week, it would be seen as a capitulation to public criticism."

For a long strained moment, the President looked Richardson steadily in the eye, and then Richardson repeated: he could not do it.

"Let it be on your head," said the President gravely, and went on bitterly to say that he was sorry Richardson did not put the nation's interest above his own concerns. At which point, Richardson said sharply, "Mr. President, what seems to be involved here is a perception of national interest. I'd like to feel that what I'm doing *is* in the national interest." There was an edge to his own voice, Richardson recalls, and the President responded more or less apologetically that there were different perspectives on the national interest.

Richardson rose, stood at Nixon's desk and made a ceremonial farewell, talking of the privilege of serving the President, acknowledging all his kindnesses and wishing him well.

With that, having made his resignation official, he left for his office—still convinced, as he recalled, that nothing he had learned from Archibald Cox's investigation or any other source varied from the President's public account of his involvement in the Watergate affair. At that moment, Richardson still believed the President was not guilty of an impeachable offense—only of a breach of political style and faith with which Richardson himself could no longer live.

By five Richardson was back in his office—only no longer as Attorney General, but counseling with Ruckelshaus and Bork as friends. At that moment, Haig called again— for Ruckelshaus, who left Richardson's office to take the call in his own office on the floor below. Haig, speaking for the President, asked Ruckelshaus to fire Cox. Ruckelshaus refused, said his only option, as Richardson's, was to resign and suggested that Haig call Bork. While Haig waited on the phone, Bork came down from Richardson's office, agreed to accept the odious duty. A car was sent to bring him to the White House to be named Acting Attorney General, where he then whipped off a quick two-paragraph note dismissing Cox. Bork's term as Acting Attorney General was to last seventy-six days.

At twenty-two minutes past eight that night, Ronald Ziegler announced to the news system that Archibald Cox had been dismissed, that Elliot Richardson and William Ruckelshaus had been discharged of further duties, that Cox had been notified of his dismissal by Bork, and that the Special Prosecutor's office had been abolished. And then, shortly after nine, the nation learned that FBI agents had arrived at the Special Prosecutor's office to seal it off from its staff members, close all files, patrol it in force; and, furthermore, that other FBI agents in the Department of Justice had moved to seal off the offices of the Attorney General and the Deputy Attorney General. At that point Haig's "firestorm" burst.

The reaction that evening was as near instantaneous as it had been at Pearl Harbor, or the day of John F. Kennedy's assassination—an explosion as unpredictable and as sweeping as mass hysteria.

It began within an hour of Ziegler's statement with the honking of cars outside the White House as protestors held up signs saying "HONK FOR IMPEACHMENT." NBC and CBS geared up for ninety-minute special shows which spread consternation nationwide. The telegraphic response began to spurt even before their shows were off air. By Tuesday morning Western Union had processed more than 150,000 telegrams ("the heaviest concentrated volume on record"); by Wednesday evening the volume had reached 220,000. At the end of ten days the total was 450,000. It was "as if a dam had broken," said one Congressman. Republican Senator Javits of New York reported that of the 1,150 messages he received, less than ten supported the President.

By Monday, as Veterans Day weekend closed, the political leaders began sounding off, Republicans as vehement as Democrats. A telephone survey by David Broder of the Washington *Post* brought these responses: from the Wyoming Republican Chairman, Jack Speight: "I just can't believe what's going on in that zoo. It's like 'tune in tomorrow for the next adventure.' " From Minnesota Republican National Committeeman Rudy Boschwitz: "You've heard of that play, *Stop the World, I Want to Get Off*. That's how I feel right now." From the liberal Republican Governor of Michigan, William Milliken: "I deplore what happened. It's a setback in efforts to restore public confidence in government. . . . Clearly we face a constitutional crisis."

The turmoil spread. Deans of seventeen law schools (including Harvard, Columbia, Yale, Stanford) joined in a petition that Congress "consider the necessity" of impeachment now. Churchmen inveighed. Students rallied—at Columbia, they heard one of their deans call the President "a paranoid egomaniac, a quintessentially hollow man." At Duke Law School, Nixon's alma mater, 350 students petitioned for the removal of Nixon's portrait from Duke's student courtroom.

And the news system flogged on. Perhaps unrecognized even by themselves, underneath the outburst of the men and women of the news system, lay their fury that Agnew, their chief public enemy, had been snatched from their reach, had been spared the shame and public guillotine of impeachment. Now their pent-up wrath focused on the President, and over the next few weeks, as stories of missing tapes and an unexplainable gap in one of the subpoenaed tapes mystified their readers or listeners, the wrath built to crescendo.

The Baltimore *Sun,* which had supported Nixon in 1972, declared that he had now "lost touch with truth and principle." The *New York Times* and the Washington *Post* disagreed in their responses. The *New York Times* favored immediate resignation, "The one last great service that Mr. Nixon can now perform for his country." But the Washington *Post* favored "exorcising" the President by the Constitutional process of impeachment and trial. The Detroit *News,* the Denver *Post,* the Atlanta *Journal* and other papers demanded resignation now—or else impeachment. The most respected columnist in Washington, the late Stewart Alsop, previously a judicious supporter of the President, wrote that in the last few weeks, Nixon had both acted the lion and played the fox, "But . . . there is in him something of still another symbol-animal: namely, the ass."

And, finally, *Time* magazine sounded off. Its history as the nation's leading news weekly had begun fifty years before with a cover portrait of Uncle Joe Cannon, and it had continued since as the voice of evermore civilized patriotism. Now it put to press the first editorial in its history: "The President Should Resign."

"Richard Nixon and the nation have passed a tragic point of no return," wrote managing editor Henry Grunwald. "It now seems likely that the President will have to give up his office; he has irredeemably lost his moral authority, the confidence of most of the country, and therefore his ability to govern effectively. . . . Despite ample instances of past government corruption, nothing can be found . . . even remotely approaching the skein of events that the word Watergate no longer defines or contains. . . . The whole White House pervaded by an atmosphere of aggressive amorality—amorality almost raised to a creed. . . . His [the President's] integrity and trustworthiness are perhaps the most important facts about him to his country and to the world. And these Nixon has destroyed. The nightmare of uncertainty must be ended. . . ."

The White House had defied the courts. If the law did

not bind the President to obedience in this instance, what laws could prevent him from other abuses of power, public or secret?

The question was now not one of burglary, break-in, cover-up, but of power itself—and the White House had been caught in a total misreading of the American mind. If there was anything that Richard Nixon prided himself on in his inner soul, it was his political instinct—that he understood the common people of America, in their precincts, with their fears, suspicions and aspirations, better than any of the wise men of the news system, the Establishment, the Ivy League schools. He had played skillfully on such fears and suspicions for twenty-seven years of active politics—and had won. But he had not understood how easily these same atavistic fears and suspicions of all power, of all government, could be turned against him. Willfully, for months, he had locked out of his mind what he knew of his administration's actions, his own actions, his own past impulses. He stood now doing the people's business, brilliantly, on the international scene. And in a single spasm on Saturday evening he had thrown away the enormous honor he might have gained for his world performance by a PR ploy. He was denying to the courts that evidence which the law insisted must be examined.

No less astounded were the men of his personal staff. Too preoccupied with the war, too compartmentalized to see the political picture whole, they had failed to recognize the question the President's act must raise. Isolated in their pockets, hardened by years of press hostility, they had for weeks and months ignored editorials, protests, denunciations, even appeals from within their own party. Now, as the firestorm burst, they could answer to no one the primitive question of everyone: What was the President hiding? Overwhelmed by public reaction, denied support by their party, stabbed by telephone calls from personal friends, wincing at letters from old companions, they realized too late what furies were at large. A letter to Ray Price, the President's speechwriter, from one of his oldest friends was typical. "I write," said the hand-scrawled letter, "because of an old respect and affection I have for you. . . . I know that it is your integrity and loyalty that keeps you from defecting from hopeless causes . . . but I do not believe that you will ever derive personal satisfaction from loyalty to a man who is at least venal, selfish and the worst traitor to our country in its history—at worst a felon."

Whether the hysteria was justified or not, it was real, it was a political fact. Within three days, Charles Alan Wright, the President's Constitutionalist, stood before Judge Sirica to capitulate, to announce that the President would yield the tapes demanded. "This President does not defy the law," said Wright, though his client three days before had done exactly that.

That was the heart of the matter. The President was part of the law, intricately interwoven into all its processes by the Constitution itself. But how far did that law control *him?* What right did the law and the courts have to invade the privacy which is absolutely essential to leadership?

That would be the issue for the next nine months, an issue above politics, to be written in the history of the government of free men for all time.

The President must have realized what now lay before him.

On Tuesday after the "Saturday Night Massacre," he had taken a second gracious farewell of Richardson, and told Richardson that "impeachment might be on the way." Nixon alone, of all the remaining team of the White House, knew what might be coming if pursuit of the tapes went further than Cox's request for nine. And there was no way out, as events soon made clear: of Cox's requested nine, two conversations had never been tape-recorded; and there was a critical gap of eighteen and a half minutes in the tape of his conversation with H. R. Haldeman on June 20th, three days after the break-in. No explanation of the gap made sense except, possibly, that he himself had erased the conversation.

Others, too, realized that the President was reaching the end of the road. In mid-November, Buzhardt telephoned Alexander Haig and said that he and Leonard Garment simply had to fly down to Key Biscayne and talk to the President about his problems. Buzhardt remembers that there were twenty-two problems on his list. Garment remembers that he had a list of fifteen subject matters to take up, coming on "like torpedoes." The President was bracketed, they felt, by matters like the tape erasure, by Bebe Rebozo's relations to the President's money affairs, by his tax problem, by Federal expenditures on his houses, and more and more. They could not function in his defense unless they got clear answers to the questions that plagued them.

They flew to Key Biscayne, but they could not see the President. They urged the President's resignation through Haig and Ziegler. "We spent a whole weekend discussing it," said Buzhardt; but Gerald Ford had not yet been confirmed by Congress as Vice-President, and so they decided simply to dig into "the trenches" and hold out until Ford made it. For Garment, it was the end of the road—"We had no access to our client, no access to the material. I wanted out." Leaving Key Biscayne, Garment decided to hand in his resignation as Counsel to the President, effective January 1st, 1974; and would not be in the crisis circle again until Buzhardt's heart attack, five and a half months later, brought him back to the defense of the undefendable President.

December, thus, was a gloomy month for Nixon—his two layers had urged that he resign; and his two closest aides, Haig and Ziegler, had considered the proposal seriously. December also saw the worsening of the gasoline crisis, as the Arabs continued their oil embargo. The fuel crisis was the sort of administrative matter where Nixon was at his best—he decided that the nation would refine what crude oil it could command into fuel for heating homes and factories so that ordinary people would not freeze. And balanced that by the decision that, where necessary, shortages at the refineries must squeeze down the high-fraction petrocarbons which move automobiles and airplanes. It was the only reasonable decision he could take, and it was ultimately successful—though, as usual, ignored by all his enemies. But PR required the President to set a national example by curbing his restless personal travel.

For most of the melancholy December days he stayed in his White House, PR-bound by the gas emergency, trying when time permitted to shore up loyalties. Some of those nearest and closest to him were murmuring about departure. Bryce Harlow had submitted his resignation, Ray Price had asked leave to resign, Barry Goldwater had been sounding off in print. Thus, just before Christmas, trying to cement his crumbling personal base, the President invited these three plus Pat Buchanan to join Rose Mary Woods and the family for dinner on Friday, December 21st. Their reports of the dinner are all different, but they agree that the main subject of discussion was still the PR dimension of the President's plans.

The President wanted to go to Key Biscayne for the year-end holidays—but that trip would publicly consume scarce gasoline for his private pleasure and the press would jump him. The group discussed whether a rail trip to Key Biscayne would look better—but it was pointed out that the Secret Service would have to guard every railhead, every bridge, every crossing, and would have to send a scout train ahead to clear the way, to spot mines or explosives, a very expensive proposition. The conversation rambled. Most of those present remember it as rather incoherent. Goldwater, characteristically, had a more human recollection—the President was drinking that night and relaxing with the few men he still trusted. Goldwater found him pleasant. "In all the years I've known him," said Goldwater, "I've seen him drunk only twice. He's really a wonderful fellow when he drinks. I wish he'd done more drinking when he was President." Nixon was to do much more drinking later—but by then to ease strain, not to relax with friends.

The President drove off the next day—in a Lincoln Continental instead of the usual helicopter, to save gas—to Camp David for two days. He was back in the White House by the 24th for Christmas dinner on the 25th; and then, having listened to all the advice he could bear, took off the next afternoon not for Key Biscayne, but for San Clemente —on a commercial flight, United Airlines Flight Number 55, with King Timahoe, the Irish setter that had replaced Checkers, at an extra cost of $24.00. He was to remain there two and a half weeks, until January 12th. In all the 254 days between May 3rd and January 12th, he had spent little more than one hundred full days at the White House.

I had missed the climax of the Cox-Richardson week, having taken one of those self-promised vacations abroad that all correspondents regret later when they are caught off-base. But the vacation was instructive, nonetheless, in what had become for me a question of power, of systems and state, for in some ways one could perceive American power and the action of its state best from overseas.

I had been wakened from sleep early Sunday morning at La Tour Vieille in St. Tropez by an almost hysterical French maid pounding at my door, calling, *"Il y avait un coup d'état aux Etats Unis, un coup d'état!"* Knowing that *"un coup d'état"* was impossible in America, I tried to de-code the French radio news bulletins, which cram all news into one minute every hour on the hour. Imagining from these snatches that the FBI had seized both the Department of Justice and the White House itself, I left for Paris, gath-ering up British newspapers at the Nice airport as I em-planed. With their flair for drama, the British newspapers were telling a story of complete chaos in America. One could almost hear tumbrels rolling over cobblestones, the click of jackboots in corridors, as British writers translated American news reports into cadenced doom with gleeful *Schadenfreude.*

From Paris I went to London, where it took a few days to re-orient to the continuing flow of news; but having been asked to appear on the BBC as an observer of American politics, I had to pull myself together. Was there any gov-ernment at all in Washington? the British were asking. If so, who was in control? Could they govern?

These seemed like strange questions for an American to be answering at that moment anywhere in Western Europe. Those were questions, I found, I could answer with pride. The governments of France and England, their state lead-ers, had capitulated totally and with shameful haste to the Arab and Russian threats—repudiating all pledges and commitments to the Israelis for arms, spare parts, necessi-ties. Total Arab victory would make Europe prey to what-ever the Arabs chose to extort from them for oil and ener-gy—or would make them beggars at the Kremlin for intercession. But no major European state had dared or had the will to act in the Middle East, though their survival as in-dustrial civilizations was at stake. America, if necessary, could survive without Arab oil. Yet only the American state had acted. If Western Europe still had a chance of survival, still retained an opportunity to negotiate terms with the Ar-abs in their undeclared economic war, it owed this chance to the United States, and to Nixon's use of its power. The

Europeans themselves and all their internal systems were powerless because their states were powerless. So they loathed America and delighted in the humiliation of its government.

From abroad it was quite clear: America remained the world's most powerful state, its power magnificently deployed.

But when I returned in a few weeks, I found all home politics changed, for all systems were now cocked against the President to challenge his leadership of the state. Not only the news system, as from the beginning, but the clergy, the labor system, the universities and scholars, too. The business system was divided; so was the Republican Party itself. Within the government, except for the Pentagon, the major systems there were also moving against Nixon's leadership—the courts, of course; the Senate, too; but, above all, the House of Representatives, where impeachment begins.

I had left for Europe still uncertain whether the criminality of his lieutenants touched the President himself, believing that his enemies must prove their charges against Richard Nixon, that he was a man to be presumed innocent, as all other Americans under charge were to be. In the new atmosphere, however, that attitude could no longer be maintained. Nixon now had to prove *his* innocence—for he had refused to yield the evidence which might trace alleged deeds to specific wrongdoers. He had acted blindly and brutally against Archibald Cox and Elliot Richardson, in violation of their commitment to Congress, on the pretext of the needs of power abroad; but now he had to demonstrate that it was truly for such needs and not for self-protection that he had so acted.

There was an issue beginning to come clear through the clash of drama and action at home and abroad in October. What did Richard Nixon actually mean by national security? All summer long, the Ervin Committee had exposed how his lieutenants had twisted that vital concept to their own political ends and personal ambitions. Another governing concept was now being pushed out of shape—"executive privilege" had been invoked against the tradition of due process of law. What was Nixon concealing? How far, in this concealment, was he justified in pressing his power?

How far had he already abused that power in the year just passed?

These were questions beyond the reach of all the adversary systems attacking him, or attempting to turn the state from his directions and purposes. By the Constitution, only the Federal state could seek such answers peacefully—and that power lay squarely in the House of Representatives of the United States.

By the time of my return, the Congress was gearing up to do just that—to ask those questions, to demand the answers, to impeach if necessary, and require the Senate to try for the first time in American history a man elected directly to the Presidency by the people. And the first step in this process had been entrusted to an obscure New Jersey Congressman, as close to being anonymous as a Congressman can be in Washington—Peter Rodino of Newark.

11

THE QUESTION PERIOD:
WINTER-SPRING 1974

The question that faced Peter Rodino of Newark as the year 1974 opened was very ancient but could, if one wanted to do so, be very simply stated:

What was the power of the sovereign?

But the complications of that question were now immense. For almost a thousand years the tradition on which American civilization rested had held that the power of all sovereigns, whether anointed kings or elected presidents, must have its limits. And for a thousand years those limits had changed with circumstances, defined and re-defined in each century. What lay before Peter Rodino and his companions of the House Judiciary Committee was the task of re-defining those limits once more in what was in fact a crisis of the political culture of the United States—a task of enormous drudgery and greater philosophical perplexity.

It is always a ruler's need—and hence his people's equal need—that the ruler command enough power to discharge his duties to them, both at home and abroad. But how far can he go in bending the established laws of his country to what he sees as needs? And how do men go about inquiring whether his use of his power injures the state itself? And what rights do citizens have which are immune from a ruler's power?

All summer and into late fall of 1973, Richard Nixon had been examined again and again—by a press corps which had never exercised political power and shared no sense of the loneliness, at times the agony, in which a solitary President must make decisions; he had been examined by a television system whose nature forces it to seek drama as much as truth; by a corps of lawyers in the Special Prosecutor's office, suspected of loathing his style as much as they did his deeds. Yet ever since the days of Magna Carta, which had first curbed the power of an English king, it had been written that every freeman would receive justice in a court of law before any action was taken against him. Nor would any baron go before a jury except of his peers. And none of his public adversaries could yet be thought of as peers of the President.

If there was such a body of peers, however, it was the House of Representatives of the United States, for it is truly representative not only of the people but of the calling of politics. Its members face the electorate every two years. Politicians all, knowing the limits of decency which politics both strains and imposes; compromisers and trimmers, most of them; most of their ablest drained off, decade after decade, to the Senate or to higher office elsewhere; reflecting all the country's ethnic communities, all their prejudices, all their interests; dominated by a center group of Middle Americans, flanked by racists of the right and wild men of the left—this House and its men and women include both louts and scholars, fine men and mediocrities. All together, however, they reflect all America's vices—and all its virtues, too.

With great wisdom, two hundred years before, the writers of the Constitution had chosen this body to initiate any action against the President, to inquire into the conduct of a President against whom charges of misuse of power might be brought—and if it judged the evidence against him sufficient, to draw up articles of impeachment to present to the Senate for the trial which that upper house must then conduct.

It was this body of ordinary men, swept by politics and passion, but tempered by experience and compromise, that had therefore, in the days after the firestorm, to begin the examination of Richard Nixon, a man very much like themselves—who had, indeed, begun his career as one of themselves.

The Speaker of the House was Carl Albert of Oklahoma, and it was he who had passed the task to Peter Rodino of New Jersey.

Carl Albert, the son of a coal miner and bred in poverty as stark as Richard Nixon's, looked very ordinary. Diminutive, booming of voice in public, soft-mannered in private, he was, however, quite extraordinary. A Rhodes scholar and a war veteran, he was a man who prowled the Library of Congress on days off; spent hours poring over old documents in the National Archives of the United States; knew and loved its history. Moreover, he was a master craftsman at the mechanics of House politics.

All summer in 1973, Albert had successfully beaten off the pressure to establish a special House Committee of Inquiry. He had deftly during summer pigeonholed several proposed early resolutions of impeachment. In the fall, he had skillfully outsmarted Spiro T. Agnew on Constitutional procedure and thrust Agnew to the mercy of the courts. Albert is a man of due process, criticized by many for the executive indecision that flows from his devotion to due process—but outraged when due process is violated.

"All summer," said Albert, "I was clinging to the belief that Nixon was the innocent victim of the men around him. But when they fired Cox, and Cox was only asking for evidence, they were denying us information." Due process had been violated on the weekend of the firestorm. "It was shoddy, such a shoddy show for men in high places to tell petty lies," said Albert, explaining why he had to act. He had met with the Democratic leaders of the House on Monday, October 22nd, two days after the dismissal of Cox and Richardson; for several hours they had surveyed together the chorus of impeachment demands rising from the floor, and then agreed that an inquiry must be set up immediately, to head off any stampede of floor resolutions which might, in the atmosphere of passion and street turbulence, cause impeachment to be voted instantly.

That evening, Albert summoned Rodino to his chambers alone. Albert could, if he wished, have taken the route of Senator Mike Mansfield to set up a special, or select, committee to conduct an impeachment inquiry. A century ago, in impeaching Andrew Johnson, House leadership had moved just such an impeachment through the House Reconstruction Committee. But Albert now, in 1973, chose process—the process which, over the years, without passion, had selected the House Judiciary Committee, a standing committee, and which had made Peter Rodino of Newark its chairman—a man publicly undistinguished but one in whom Albert saw special virtues. Several of the House

Democratic leaders, led by "Tip" O'Neill of Massachusetts, had questioned Rodino's ability to give the impeachment process the drive it required. But Albert was insistent.

"Pete," said Albert of Rodino, "is not the most aggressive member in the House. He's a little bit shy, but he runs a smooth, complete shop. I didn't want to go to one of the more spectacular members of the House, or someone who wanted to be a movie star." Thus, in his office that evening, Albert explained to Rodino what he sought of his committee—not an impeachment, but an inquiry. And all the resources that Rodino's committee would require for the inquiry would be at his disposal.

Rodino.

Each Congressman has several personalities. There is his street personality—the hand-shaking, baby-kissing, regular fellow, eager to be loved. Then there is his Congressional personality—austere, or sneaky, or imposing, or driven, or maverick.

Personally, Rodino was cherubic and charming. His speech could reach from the street guttural of Newark to the most precise literary and legal command of the English language, and almost unconsciously in private conversation he could let his speech slip back to the Italian dental "de" instead of the fricative "the" as he measured his listener. Rubicund of face, medium in height, his hair fringed with a ruff of white, he was at all times an amiable man and a bit of a dandy to boot—flashy gold cufflinks, flashy gold watch, a crimson handkerchief in the pocket of his neat blue jacket.

But, above all, as a Congressman, he was known as a man of the House. To be a man of the House is to be part of a special circle of loyalties. Committee chairmanships then still went by seniority, and chairmen may or may not be men of the House. Richard Bolling of Missouri, for example, holds no chairmanship; but he is a man of the House, as is John Brademas of Indiana, or "Tip" O'Neill of Massachusetts. These are men who can be counted on by the House leadership to give priority to legislative need over campaign rhetoric, to national interest when necessary over local interest. To be a man of the House requires not only that one understand its parliamentary trickeries but also that one love the House as an institution.

Rodino had been a man of the House since his arrival there in 1949. Twenty-five years earlier, when first elected, he had wistfully hoped to be appointed to the prestige-laden Foreign Affairs Committee; or failing that, to the Judiciary Committee; but he had been shunted off as a passing Italo-American big-city Congressman to the Veterans' Affairs Committee. He had then caught the attention of the leadership by a striking breach of House etiquette. Freshman Congressmen are expected to keep their mouths shut, but Rodino was too often gaveled to silence within his Veterans' Committee by its chairman, Congressman John Rankin of Mississippi, who did not like big-city foreigners anyway, and was pushing to the floor a bill calling for a $50 billion pension grab for returning veterans. "Jeezus," said Rodino, recalling, "we just came out of the war, that war meant so much to us, we didn't fight it to get rich." So, on the floor of the full House, he rose and in a fiery patriotic speech denounced the committee's pension grab. Rodino was young, but his military credentials were impeccable—a combat veteran of the First Armored Division, with a chestful of medals, he was the proper man to lead opposition to the grab, and so was chosen by the House leadership, within his first year, to be floor manager of the fight against the outrageous but popular cause. His success won Speaker Sam Rayburn's gratitude—and when the first vacancy on the Judiciary Committee opened, by the death of an Illinois Congressman, the House leadership saw to it that Rodino had his wish to fill that seat.

In 1973, twenty-four years later, with the defeat of Emanuel Celler in Brooklyn, seniority finally opened to Peter Rodino the chairmanship of the Judiciary Committee—and he became the only big-city Congressman to chair any major committee of the 93rd House. Years of service on the committee had won Rodino respect from other men of the House. He had jockeyed through the Immigration Act of 1965, which eliminated ethnic quotas. He had led the drive to make Columbus Day a national holiday, which pleased his Italian-American constituents. Liberals as well as his black constituents applauded his superb record in civil rights. For those of the right, Rodino could point to a record of patriotism, an anti-Communism almost as flamboyant as Richard Nixon's. And in any vote on foreign policy or military matters he could be counted on to support the President.

Rodino's new responsibility as chairman of the Judiciary Committee had thus rested easily on him as 1973 began, as did his comfortable routine of life. Four days a week he spent alone in a convenience flat in Washington; the other three days he went back to New Jersey to be with his family, doing political rounds, going to the opera, which he loved, whenever he could.

A loner, a grandfather type to his affectionate young staff, he cut no figure at fashionable Washington cocktail parties; but uncomfortable as he was at large dinner parties, he never missed any celebration at the Italian Embassy or any other event which touched on his Italian-American heritage. If he had any worries at the beginning of 1973, they lay back in Newark. A panic flight had driven tens of thousands of white citizens from Newark in a single decade; his district was now 52 percent black, 10 percent Puerto Rican; and his Italian-American voters were becoming furious at Rodino's Congressional defense of black causes. If he could not get his seat re-districted to the white suburbs in 1974, Rodino was almost sure to lose his seat to a black candidate in that fall's election.

This then had been Rodino's main concern until April 17th, 1973, the night when, sitting alone in his flat in Washington, he watched Richard Nixon first speak of the Watergate affair on television. "I was one of those guys who'd been saying we have to support him all the way on foreign policy. I wanted to believe him. I was waiting for him to say, By Golly, I'm going to make the guys who did this Watergate thing responsible. Even if he admitted his own failure, or that he misdirected things, the American people would have accepted it. That's what I wanted to hear." But he did not.

Then, said Rodino, his worry began. And it grew. By June he was reading all he could find about the role the Judiciary Committee might have to play in the still unimaginable case of impeachment. It was private reading mostly, but Rodino remembers when he realized he had crossed a line in his own thinking. On a plane from Washington to

Newark he was reading Michael Benedict's book on *The Impeachment and Trial of Andrew Johnson*. The man sitting next to him looked at the book and said, "That's an interesting book to be reading right now, isn't it?"—and Rodino hastily turned over a heavy manila Congressional envelope with his name franked on it, so the stranger could not recognize who he was. For Rodino, impeachment was no longer unimaginable.

Rodino had been at home in New Jersey when television reported on Saturday, October 20th, that Richard Nixon had decapitated the Department of Justice. The action infuriated him and he reached for the telephone to call Cox personally and congratulate him; then he watched the dramatic television reporting of the weekend, and was even more disturbed by the story of FBI agents sealing off both the Special Prosecutor's office and the Attorney General's office. When he returned to Washington on Monday, even before talking with Carl Albert, he telephoned the Acting Attorney General, Robert Bork, and as chairman of the House Judiciary Committee demanded assurance that "with all those people walking in and out," the security of all records and documents would be maintained. Bork reassured him. But to nail matters down, Rodino repeated his demand in writing, on the stationery of the chairman of the House Judiciary Committee—for he was now acting for a larger constituency than the black and Italian citizens of Newark.

The House Judiciary Committee, which was to perform with spectacular honor in the spring and summer of 1974, was in 1973 a committee whose mottled reputation had come down from the past. For years it had been considered a committee of Southern Democrats and Northern conservatives whose autocrat was Emanuel Celler of Brooklyn. Since the upheaval of the 1960's and the awakening of conscience in politics, the composition of the committee had been changing, but its reputation as a gathering of hacks lingered. There was little pressure on House leadership from young Congressmen to sit on this committee. But those few who *did* want to be on the committee, particularly on the Democratic side, were decidedly liberal. Here was where such powerful emotional issues as the rights of black people were shaped, where the civil rights of privacy, evidence, criminal jurisprudence, equality were drafted into laws, where behavior of judges and courts was considered. Liberals increasingly wanted a say. Thus, the reactionary committee of the past, where the chief brokerage had been suppression of black rights in return for special immigration bills for other ethnics, had been transformed in an unrecognized about-face. And a better cross-section of troubled Americans could not have been found, even by random selection.

This group, then, was the one which Peter Rodino had to guide to the resolution of a Constitutional crisis—thirty-eight men and women, twenty-one Democrats, seventeen Republicans. Few of them pure—at least sixteen had accepted election contributions from the same milk producers whose contributions to Richard Nixon's campaign they considered suspect. All of them lawyers. All of them politicians. Split by background, partisanship, ethnic heritage and prejudice. And they must decide how, in the millennia-old code of law of the English-speaking peoples, they could find authority to judge the man who had been elected little more than a year before by the greatest election margin of all time among free men and women.

Precedent, though much quoted, would be of little help. The only other impeachment of a President in American history had been that of Andrew Johnson in 1868—a Vice-President, a Democrat succeeding to the Presidency only by the tragedy of the assassination of Abraham Lincoln, a Republican. Andrew Johnson had been charged with violating a law passed specifically to curb him, the Tenure of Office Act of 1867. And despite that, a Republican Senate had refused, by a margin of one, to convict him because the known facts did not show he had violated that statutory law.

But Nixon was not charged with violating any specific act of Congress. Rodino and his committee, therefore, first had to establish the facts of the case, then seek the laws by which those facts could be judged.

There was to be a particular, gripping intellectual excitement about their exercise, because the peculiar nature of American law made that task extremely difficult. And one must pause over the intricate problem the committee faced initially. The United States, unlike its mother country, England, has a written constitution accepted as "the basic law" because it restricts what kinds of law legislatures, both state and Federal, can enact. Such legislative, or statutory, laws can be challenged as unconstitutional if they violate the "basic law." But the Constitution also lays down, as basic law, the frame of the Federal government, the powers given to each of its three branches, Legislative, Executive, Judicial. And provides only in the most general terms for punishment of a President by impeachment for exceeding his powers. Treason is, of course, clearly punishable by the Constitution and bribery by law. But what does "high crimes and misdemeanors" mean? Does that phrase mean a violation of a statutory law, a breach of a specific act of Congress—in the phrase of 1974's debate, the discovery of "a smoking gun"? Or does it mean a violation of the basic law—an abuse of the powers conferred on the office of President by the Constitution?

It mattered little that Rodino's committee was in the end overtaken by evidence of a statutory crime, the "smoking gun" of clear obstruction of justice. Abuse of power, violation of basic law, was where this particular committee had to begin. And that issue could be defined only after the facts had been established. Which required the appointment of a staff that not only could gather the facts, but could also define the kind of law by which those facts must be judged.

Which led to the appointment of John Doar.

John Doar had been a lifelong Republican—at least until he came to Washington from Wisconsin to serve in the Department of Justice in the time of Dwight D. Eisenhower with the recommendation of another Republican stalwart from Wisconsin, Melvin Laird. There he had become an apostle of civil rights, and was taken to the heart of Robert F. Kennedy when, in 1961, Kennedy became Attorney General and the black revolution began to gather speed.

Tall, curly-haired, soft-spoken, Doar was as dedicated to his cause as those men of Wisconsin who had gone off to fight for Union and Constitution against the slave states a century before. When he leveled his blue eyes at you, the quality of dedication that came through reminded one of the history of the fierce Wisconsin soldiers who had carved rings for themselves out of the bones of dead Confederate soldiers on the battlefield.

His performance in the South prying open black rights in the turbulent sixties had won him a national reputation. He was the law-bringer south of the Mason-Dixon Line, integrating the University of Mississippi, stalking quietly through streets of explosive Southern towns to bring justice, like a civil-rights Matt Dillon, aware that at any moment a bullet might pierce his back. The qualities that came to mind first when one thought of Doar were not flash or brilliance but courage, rectitude, doggedness, commitment, tenacity. And when Rodino began his search for chief counsel for his staff, these qualities brought Doar's name to the top of every list of lawyers suggested by the law schools and the legal establishment. Not a Constitutional expert, not a legal intellectual, but absolutely incorruptible, Doar was a man who could stand under fire.

"My task," said Doar later, "was to make the Constitution work, to make the process of impeachment work—whether to a trial or to a vindication didn't matter. I'd spent the last few years in Bedford-Stuyvesant [the largest black ghetto in New York], where I'd been communing with myself, the *New York Times* and the rooftops of Bedford-Stuyvesant. I'd seen only a little bit of the Ervin hearings on television. My concern was that the process work. I never saw myself as being the guy who would take the lead in this; yet the way it came out, I had to take the lead.

"I don't believe in participatory staffs," said Doar. "I ran that staff. I put it down that no one could be hired who had expressed an opinion or a judgment on Richard Nixon one way or another. No one could talk to the press. I divided them into task forces. They had to get the facts." The staff that Doar hired was almost leakproof. It was locked up on three floors of the Congressional Hotel, across the street from the Rayburn House Office Building, and scowling police challenged every intruder with security even tighter than at the Special Prosecutor's offices. Doar's staff was as rigidly compartmentalized as Richard Nxon's White House staff. Unlike the Ervin Committee staff, Doar's staff used no computers, only three-by-five filing cards to index information. Its job was to accumulate data—data from the Ervin hearings, data from the grand jury, data from the White House, fact upon fact upon fact—and compile them in six categories, coldly, clinically, without taking sides. And then to put those facts before the Judiciary Committee at whatever cost in time and patience it would take to put together the forty volumes of 2,000,000 words that eventually resulted.

The New Year of 1974 had begun with the emotions of the October firestorm at incandescence as the President's enemies demanded instant action—and then something seemed to stall.

Week after week, month after month, nothing apparently was happening. Doar would not talk, his staff would not talk. One could get a sense of movement only as if it were muffled by soundproofing; and then, if movement there was, it was an intellectual movement, a pursuit of an elusive concept; and to detect even such movement of thought, one had to beseech the Rodino office for shreds.

The Rodino office was a curious one, and, in its microcosm, made an interesting contrast with that of Richard Nixon. Men of high office are shaped, far more than they recognize, by their office staffs—their staffs are audience, echo boards, creators of the atmosphere of decision. In the White House, they talked of this interaction between leader and staff as "the chemistry" of personalities, and a similar chemistry was at work in the Rodino office. Rodino was no political virgin; he had grown up in the politics of Newark, New Jersey, and few political dirty tricks could astound him. But he had, by chance, early in the spring hired a young scholar of Oriental affairs who had left teaching to enter politics—Francis O'Brien. O'Brien, only thirty-one and looking five years younger than that, had served on John Lindsay's New York mayoral staff, assigned to community relations with the blacks. He had been recommended to Rodino as an assistant who could help him in the troubled race relations of Newark. Earnest, high-minded, cheerful, he was of that idealism one remembered in the young people of the Kennedy campaign of 1968 or the McGovern campaign of 1972. When to the bubbling idealism of O'Brien was added the dour idealism of Doar, plus Rodino's political know-how of House mechanics, an interaction of three personalities began of the same significance as the interaction of Nixon-Haldeman-Colson-Ehrlichman. O'Brien was a bachelor, and Rodino regarded him as a foster son; Doar, recently divorced, was passing through a personal crisis of loneliness; and Rodino had always lived a bachelor's life in Washington. Thus, night after night, all through January and into February, 1974, and beyond, the three men would gather late in the evening at Rodino's office, talking and talking about the case, sometimes until midnight, searching for a guide to thinking and a Constitutional frame to put over the developing facts.

Only by talking to Rodino could one begin to perceive what was happening in the mind of the chairman as these evening sessions shaped his thinking. He preferred to talk about other things to newsmen—about Newark, about his role in the Agnew case, about his role in the selection of Ford, about black-white problems in his home district. But when he was pressed hard, his attitude would come out with that characteristic weight and reverence which big-city politicians of polyglot constituencies give to the President. In Rodino, the characteristic was intensified by an Italian American patriotism, a conception of the President almost as a Civil Pope, a sacerdotal figure. Knowing ward and bloc politics as well as the deceptions of parliamentary tactics, he expected the President to be something larger than a Peter Rodino—much larger. He expected the President to be judged far beyond ordinary rules of law or political custom. Growing excited, he once burst out, "To me, 'high crimes and misdemeanors' were never precise. The way I read them, they aren't meant to spell out anything but a President's performance in office. I see it as the kind of conduct that brings the whole office into scandal and disrepute, the kind of abuse of power that subverts the system we live in, that brings about in and of itself a loss of confidence in this system. . . . I guess, all in all, it's behavior which in its totality is not good for the Presidency, nor any part of the system. I got to agree," he went on, "this is an effort to overturn the election . . . but if this country can't stand a crisis, something has happened I don't understand."

Thus, then, very early in the proceedings, the thinking of Peter Rodino and his staff flowed together to set the lines on which the great debate of July would be conducted. This inquiry would be steered away from Richard Nixon's conduct of national affairs to the conduct of his office, must be steered away from judgment on the public results of his leadership which the people had voted for to the inner quality of his administration which the people had no way of judging. How then to develop a legal frame in which whatever facts might be forthcoming could be properly judged? How to develop a frame of thinking which could preserve the Constitutional powers of the office, yet impeach the President if he deserved impeachment? On what grounds could an election of the people be overturned?

In this quest, men were dealing with the stuff of history, and making history, too. Despite whatever came later, the challenges and response in this quest to define the limits of a sovereign's power would illuminate forever Americans' concept of their Presidency. And of all the millions of words and scores of volumes written, and yet to be written, two brief documents published within eight days of each other set the issues most sharply. The first was the memorandum of the Doar staff to its committee on February 20th, 1974; the second was the reply of the President's staff a week later.

The argument of Doar's staff began by quoting the Constitution itself: "The President, Vice-President and all civil officers of the United States, shall be removed from Office on Impeachment for and Conviction of Treason, Bribery, or other High Crimes and Misdemeanors." The House, says the Constitution, impeaches; the Senate tries and convicts. So far, so good—clear.

But what did "high crimes and misdemeanors" mean? And what, indeed, did "impeachment" mean? The Doar staff chose to define them by describing the historical descent of the Constitutional phrases.

The phrase "high crimes and misdemeanors," they pointed out, had come out of the English background of the men who made the American Republic. So, too, had the word "impeachment."

Both phrases ran far back in time, to an age when America lay undiscovered and democracy was undreamed of—to the violent Middle Ages, when brutal French conquerors had tried to whip the stubborn English conquered into a manageable form of government. The Norman-Angevin kings, absent so often from their English dominion, had found they could govern most effectively by giving their

English vassals some sense of participation in that government, and had institutionalized their participation in a Parliament of Lords and Commons. Where the officers of the king did not act, or when they acted in a way of which Parliament disapproved, Parliament might "impeach" such officers. The word "impeachment" came from the old French "empescher"—to stop, to seize, to apprehend an officer of the king by action of Parliament in their judgment of right or wrong, with or without the cloak of statutory law. The first impeachment cited by the Doar staff was that of the Chancellor of Richard II, a certain Michael de la Pole, Earl of Suffolk, in 1386—impeached because he *failed* to act as he promised Parliament he would act. Other English impeachments had followed, slowly at first, then more swiftly, until the time of the religious wars when Oliver Cromwell moved to exercise first the power and then the tyranny of the Commons, and no less than 100 impeachments (according to Doar's account) were passed by Commons between 1620 and 1640.

A clear line ran through all these impeachments; they were not necessarily criminal trials; they were a way of getting at the men around the king, a way of cramping the sovereign by crippling his servants. And on occasion, when Parliament found a man guilty by impeachment, then, as with the Earl of Stafford—off with his head. This political logic broke down only when it reached its climax. When Parliament found the king himself guilty of wrongdoing against the state, then there could be no way out except off with his head, as happened to Charles I of England, in 1649. For if Parliament failed to behead the guilty king, obviously it would be off with their heads instead.

It was this drastic remedy of regicide that the writers of the American Constitution sought to avoid in their young republic. Experience led them to believe that a strong nation needs a strong national leader; yet, having just escaped from the tyranny of King George III, they felt that their new chief executive must be under some sort of control. So, in addition to other checks and balances, they wrote an ultimate check—removal of the President, not by beheading, but by impeachment and then trial for high crimes and misdemeanors, to be called by some scholars "the most powerful weapon in the political armory short of civil war," a weapon unsheathed only once before in the history of the American Presidency.

The early American politicians explored the meaning of impeachment and high crimes and misdemeanors with great earnestness in the debate over ratification of the Constitution. To those who argued that the new Constitution gave a President almost monarchical powers, the advocates of the Constitution responded: not so—every four years by vote of the people, or, in emergency, by action of Congress, he could be turned out of office. To those who felt impeachment weakened the Presidency too much, the counter-argument ran: not so—it made the President responsible for the acts of his subordinates and thus would strengthen his power and responsibility to see that the laws be faithfully executed. During this debate, James Wilson of Pennsylvania said, "Sir, we have a responsibility in the person of our President; he cannot act improperly, and hide either his negligence or inattention; he cannot roll upon any other person the weight of his criminality; no appointment can take place without his nomination; and he is responsible for every nomination he makes. . . ."

The logic of James Wilson had made much sense when Americans were only 4,000,000 people and the first Presidency was an office that could be staffed with four Cabinet members and a few secretaries, commanding an army and navy of 5,669 men in 1794. But by the time of Richard Nixon, 2,700,000 worked for the Federal government, and 2,000,000 more served in its armed forces. Was the President responsible for the actions of all of these people?

Obviously not. Else every President of the 200-year line might have been impeached for the action of some subordinate somewhere down the line of his appointments. There had been only twelve impeachments to reach the Senate in 200 years (not counting that of Andrew Johnson) and four convictions. The charges had run to personal behavior, to drunkenness, to "vindictive use of power." But none of those convictions had touched the President. Clearly, in the Nixon administration, breaches of the law had occurred. As the Ervin Committee had demonstrated, there had been indisputable instances of the "vindictive use of power." But could these be traced to the President himself? That was the core of the issue the Judiciary Committee faced.

The committee's staff thus argued that charges against the President need not be criminal in nature. Impeachment was not necessarily a personal punishment of the President, they said—it was a "remedial" measure. Its "function is primarily to maintain constitutional government," and "Unlike a criminal case, the cause for the removal of a President may be based on his entire course of conduct in office. . . ." Impeachment was "a constitutional safety valve." And then, in a coda, the staff acknowledged, "Not all Presidential misconduct is sufficient to constitute grounds for impeachment. There is a further requirement—substantiality."

Thus, then, the outline of the issues as Doar's staff presented them to the committee. The committee, on the basis of facts to be set forth, must find the President guilty of substantial misconduct, or acquit him; and it need not trace specific crime directly to the authority or command of the President.

The response of the President's legal advisers was equally noteworthy. It was more learned, semantically more exact, far more technical. The men who wrote the President's brief trusted their client, believed in his personal innocence. Thus, pinning all on the need that a crime—a breach of statutory law—be proven, their brief, ironically, might later have served as effectively and precisely to impeach the President as their opponents'. They argued the case of the office of the President, not the man.

They questioned, first, the history of the pivotal phrases "impeachment" and "high crimes and misdemeanors" which the Doar staff had outlined. What relevance, they asked, did the experience of the English kings of the thirteenth and fourteenth centuries have to the experience and power structure of Americans in 1974? They saw history differently.

Impeachment, they argued, was a phrase descended from a power struggle between an absolute monarch of England and the Parliament. Which would make the governing decisions of state? The legal history on the contest, they argued, began with the impeachment of Lord Latimer in 1376, when the phrase "high crimes and misdemeanors" first occurred. But the charge against Latimer was specifically criminal; and for all succeeding generations, until the great clash between Parliament and King in mid-seventeenth century, impeachments were bottomed on criminality. It is true, they continued, that in the years leading to the English Civil War, impeachments had become political—part of the ongoing power struggle between Executive and Parliament. But when Parliament triumphed in the Glorious Revolution of 1688, the old English power struggle was over.

Thus, argued the President's lawyers, by the time the Americans came to write their Constitution, the English had once again changed their view of impeachment—in the eighteenth century, impeachment was again simply punishment for crime. Contemporary impeachments in London, as the Americans were well aware, were apprehensions of men who had committed criminal acts. It was from this concept of impeachment that American thinking and experience took off. The great English political and constitutional struggle a century earlier had "centered on *who* should make governmental decisions." But "the American focus was on *how* these decisions should be made." It was clear, continued the President's brief, that the Americans had balanced parliamentary tyranny against monarchical tyranny, but the result was the conclusion that a President could be removed only for crime—not politics. By implication, they argued that what was happening now was a power struggle between President and Congress, a coarse political contest.

Then, squarely on to the defense of the Presidency: a President must not be at the mercy of a politically hostile Congress. The phrase "high crimes and misdemeanors" was indivisible: misdemeanor could not be separated out and interpreted to mean something other than criminal offense. The entire phrase had to be read as one—misdemeanor meant crime. "It is as ridiculous to say that 'misdemeanor' must mean something beyond 'crime,' " they wrote, "as it is to suggest that in the phrase 'bread-and-butter issues,' butter issues must be different from bread issues."

The President's staff supported his case with a review of American history. Judges of course could be impeached and, to be sure, ten had been, and four of them convicted. Judges, however, serve for life, not limited terns, and to restrain them the Constitution limited their tenure by "good behavior." Thus, judges had to be judged in impeachment cases on their overall behavior and conduct; but a President, no. A President can be removed only on evidence of "high crimes and misdemeanors" clear enough to justify a criminal indictment. To challenge a President for the pattern of his behavior was to usurp for Congress the right that belonged only to the people—an election. If this were to happen, a Congressional tyranny, a dislocation of the balance of powers, might result which would alter forever the American system of government.

There was no defense of the Nixon administration in the brief of the President's lawyers; not a trace of denial that somewhere, at sometime, some crime might have occurred. But the challenge to the Doar-Rodino theory of impeachment was clear: "If there is any doubt as to the gravity of an offense or as to a President's conduct or motives, the doubt should be resolved in his favor. This is the necessary price for having an independent Executive."

Somewhere between the two briefs, couched in their legal phrasing, echoing of history past and gone, was the root problem of modern America. How much power must its government and its President be granted in an ever more interlocked industrial civilization, an ever more volatile world of opinion?

The more often one visited Washington in the winter and spring months of 1974, the more confused one became.

The state still functioned mechanically—the Coast Guard patrolled the shores; the Weather Service daily predicted tomorrow's weather; Army, Navy and Air Force deployed and trained their men; the Internal Revenue Service collected the taxes with its usual zeal and efficiency.

The scenery was the same and a deaf-mute visiting Washington would notice no change. The winter crows cawed on Capitol Hill as ever; the oaks on Capitol Hill stood bare and beautiful as they always had in snow; the peppermint-striped flags at the base of the Washington Monument still snapped gay greeting to visitors driving in from the airport. The National Capital Parks Service presided routinely over its annual miracles. No city in the world cherishes its flowers more than Washington, except possibly Paris, and so, as winter gave way to spring, the custodians went about their work. The Japanese cherry trees put out their snow-pink blossoms on time. The oaks unfurled their green, and magnolias and dogwood flowered. Daffodils rose as they always had, and tulips, planted in the fall, made their show of color from the Capitol Slope to Lafayette Park. As one wandered in and out of Senate, House, committee hearings, White House, Executive Office Bulding, Washington displayed all its splendors unchanged. But if one were not a deaf-mute and asked questions, one could sense a change, like the change in an old friend apparently sound but whose wits and mind no longer connect.

The government purred and functioned like an engine turning over but going nowhere. There was a single exception to the general paralysis—its foreign affairs. If anyone threatened America by force from outside, the state could respond. But beyond that, one could detect no directions as one waited.

The winter of 1973-74, for example, would go down in folklore as the winter of the gasoline crisis. Though no one froze and industry still thrived, the two or three gallons metered out by harassed attendants to those who waited on line at gas stations took all pleasure out of driving—and suburban real-estate values were being wrecked. The gasoline crisis was, of course, to fade away by spring. But what underlay it was permanent—the energy crisis. Nixon, surfacing now and again, understanding the energy crisis, would make statements and propose plans. But Congress ignored his leadership as if he were a non-person; and as his authority diminished, the fuel-oil crisis worked its way through the economy and prices rose and kept on rising. A whole year would elapse before America could belatedly turn to face the economic crisis. The most gloomy of economists had predicted at the beginning of 1974 that prices might rise by as much as 10 percent. They would rise by 12 percent that year and keep on rising. The Arab world had discovered a new form of undeclared economic warfare and was waging it as purposefully as Hitler had waged his undeclared war in the blitzkrieg buildup of 1937–38. The West was as unprepared to face this new war as it had been to face Hitler's. The West was powerless to act because the United States was powerless to give leadership; and the United States was powerless to give this leadership because its President was in effect powerless himself.

Richard Nixon had disappeared from public view when he left Washington for San Clemente on December 26th. This, his next-to-last visit to the Western White House, had stretched out for seventeen days, and it had been unpleasant. It rained. It flooded. An extraordinary series of high tides washed up from the Pacific over his property, and there, finally, as for all the rest of his administration, he began to spiral in on himself in his fight for survival.

One could only assemble fragments of the Nixon of 1974, as if one were an archeologist trying to reconstruct an image from a broken sculpture.

He would fight—that came clear from San Clemente. He would finally recognize the impeachment process as real—and as his lawyer he appointed James St. Clair of Boston. He now had a new Attorney General, a neutral, Senator William Saxbe of Ohio. He would finally admit Buzhardt to full management of the tapes and appoint him special Counsel to the President, while Garment would become simply an "Assistant to the President." There would be an official survival group, called the "Defense Group." That group would meet every morning in the White House office of Dean Burch, who moved from his office as chairman of the Federal Communications Commission to the West Wing to direct strategy. And the strategy would be one of attack. As described by Ken Clawson, who had replaced Herbert Klein as chief of the Office of Communications, the strategy was simply, "Go get them." "For ten months," said Clawson, "the meekest, mildest Congressman could take us on and nothing would happen to him. It was a no-risk attack. Now we decided that if you open your mouth we'll knock your f—— teeth out." They were going to stop the leaks once and for all because, said Clawson, who had once been one of the abler leak-springers of the Washington *Post* team, "those bastards can rip a single page out of the Bible and if they play it right, they can make Jesus Christ sound like the devil."

But it was a directionless and moody team that returned from San Clemente. If there was official action to be taken, it fell to Alexander Haig. If there was a PR game still to be played, it lay with Clawson. If there was a legal battle, its command lay with St. Clair. And yet none of these men, except Haig, could see their leader at will, and what they saw of him disturbed them. There was something happening in the personality of the man. Even the Secret Service, normally so reticent, talked to reporters about his sudden whims at San Clemente "to drive somewhere, anywhere." He was restless. Sleep was difficult.

He teturned to Washington and the restlessness and aloofness grew through the spring. He could focus on foreign affairs and be imperative, keen, shrewd. But domestic matters bored him, details annoyed. His Director of Management and Budget, Roy Ash, had flown to San Clemente to discuss the impending new national budget with the President; but the President had not seen him, had channeled him to Haig. When Nixon escaped now to Camp David for the weekend, it was difficult even to establish his presence there—the reporters' normal telephones had been cut off from the communications booths inside the gates of the camp. He wanted privacy, craved it, required it to think his way through whatever lay ahead.

He had come back from San Clemente and then called for the tape recordings of the June 23rd episode, the obstruction-of-justice act, which his reflective mind early told him might lie at the heart of the technical charges of impeachment. None of his aides, not even the closest, was told until later that he had done so. But they could detect many changes in his personality now. His drinking bothered some of them. Some claimed that he would now have his first nip sometimes as early as eleven in the morning. Others insisted he was drinking only in the afternoon or late in the evening. But it was true that in the early morning he would sound hungover. And, more and more, the restlessness. He would waken Fred Buzhardt from sleep at four o'clock in the morning to discuss an obscure point in the tapes he had just listened to. The tapes preyed on him, and one had a sense of the man listening to himself in the afternoons or evenings, asking questions of himself, asking and asking and unable to satisfy himself about himself.

Questions were the only reality in the incoherent winter and spring of 1974. Yet no one knew what questions were essential until the Judiciary Committee might grind out the proper ones—and then if the facts warranted trial, and the House approved, the Senate would give the answers.

One could visit the hapless St. Clair, a white-collar lawyer, not a brass-knuckled criminal lawyer. He had hoped to serve the Presidency by defending Nixon on a Constitutional level—and if he succeeded, his name along with Nixon's would go down in history. But St. Clair was ignoring Rule One of his professional craft—he was defending a client of whom he could not ask the facts, from whom he could not expect true answers, whom he could see only at the client's will and hear from him only what the client chose to tell. The questions in St. Clair's mind, as he began his duties, were stark, and contradicted his sober conversation with a visitor about Constitutional verities. As he talked in his office on King's Row, one's eye could not fail to take in the huge blackboard beside St. Clair's desk with the wriggles and squiggles of tape-recording oscillations. St. Clair still believed that the erasure of eighteen and a half minutes of the President's conversation with Bob Haldeman on June 20th, the first recorded discussion of news of the break-in, was accidental. But a panel of experts had said that conversation had been deliberately erased. St. Clair's questions, as he began, were: Who had done it, and why?

Questions piled on questions. The Judiciary Committee of Peter Rodino had specific questions as well as Constitutional questions—and one could get lost following the intricate play of requests, subpoenas and rejections as the committee tried to find out what was on the tapes, then demanded tapes, then went to court to insist on its privilege of asking such questions.

The voters had questions. On February 5th, Democrats had captured a Republican House seat in Pennsylvania; on February 18th, Gerald Ford's old seat in the 5th Congressional District of Michigan was captured by a Democrat for the first time in sixty-four years. Three more special elections were held in the next two months, all in districts previously held by Republicans—in Ohio, California and Michigan. Two of the three were captured by Democrats, despite a personal salvage tour by the President himself of the Michigan 8th Congressional, Republican since Hoover's days. The one seat retained by a Republican replacement for a Republican incumbent was in a California farm district, where rising food prices were insulating food-producers from the discomfort of other Americans.

Each week brought partial answers to last week's questions which raised more questions and, in their confusion, they crashed on the mind, numbing it. In January had come the question of the tapes. In February there was the Rebozo question. What had Rebozo done with the campaign money he had received from Howard Hughes? And then the Don Nixon question again—where were the tapes of the President's eavesdropping on his brother? And if, as an official declared in California, the President's famous gift of his papers to the government had been falsely back-dated, what was the government going to do about that? The little men were pleading guilty or going to jail one by one, Krogh and Porter by the end of January, Kalmbach by the end of February, and they would be followed into court by Chapin, by Kleindienst, by Colson over the spring months. But when, when would the President himself come to judgment? That was the overriding question, and all other questions, each lurid and unthinkable a few months earlier, merged into the larger question: When?

March speeded the action. On the 1st, the grand jury had brought in indictments naming Haldeman, Ehrlichman, Colson, Mtchell, Parkinson, Mardian as co-conspirators in an obstruction of justice or as perjurers. In New York, the trial of Maurice Stans and John Mitchell was under way. On March 19th, Senator James Buckley of New York, a man absolutely devoted to the cause Nixon had led in 1972, who had, indeed, seconded Nixon's nomination in that year's Republican convention, declared, "It is my conviction that the President has been stripped of the ability to fulfill that mandate [of 1972]. . . . I propose an extraordinary act of statesmanship and courage. . . . That act is Richard Nixon's own voluntary resignation as President of the United States." (Responding that evening, the President said, "While it might be an act of courage to run away from a job that you were elected to do, it also takes courage to stand and fight for what you believe is right, and that's what I intend to do.")

April opened with both the Judiciary Committee and the Special Prosecutor's office still pounding away with fresh subpoenas for more tapes, but then on the 3rd came devastation once more. For three months the staff of the Joint

Committee on Internal Revenue Taxation had examined the President's tax returns covering four years. He had paid $72.682.09 in 1969 in income taxes—but only $792.81 in 1970. $878.03 in 1971, $4,298.17 in 1972. A steelworker, a schoolteacher, a hairdresser, any union man paid more than that in taxes—and the Joint Committee now determined that Richard Nixon owed the government $476,431 in back taxes and interest.

Richard Nixon himself, as President, had signed a new tax law at the end of 1969 which made all officials' papers —"letters, memoranda and similiar material"—ineligible for tax deduction as gifts after July 25th of that year. The stipulation had been inserted into the law in Christmas week of 1969 by Republican Senator John Williams of Delaware, who had been incensed by the tax deductions Lyndon Johnson had taken for such official papers when he had been President. And now Richard Nixon, so the committee said, was culpable not for fraud but for technical violation of the law he had signed. His Vice-Presidental papers, which had actually been delivered to the National Archives months before the deadline of July 25th, had not been deeded over to the government as a gift until well after that deadline. Moreover, whoever had signed the deed of gift in his name had back-dated the signature to make it appear as if it were on deadline; for that act, definitely fraudulent, one of Nixon's lawyers would ultimately, seven months later, plead guilty. But these fine points of tax law were lost on the public—the President had tried to get away with it, and must pay up. As a man of property, Richard Nixon was all but wiped out unless friends and mortgagees would help. The *New York Times* proclaimed the news with a three-deck front-page headline of the same visual impact as the headlines which had announced the Japanese attack on Pearl Harbor in 1941.

In the polls, Richard Nixon had been steadily dropping ever since the firestorm of October. The registers now plummeted again—in the Gallup poll to 26-percent approval, while in the Harris poll a slim plurality of 43 to 41 percent for the first time favored impeachment. Matters, it appeared, could not be worse. And yet they could. For the spring months were now about to come to climax with publication of the transcripts.

They had not been stupid at the White House all these months, nor unable to read the newspapers. Though they might be ignorant of what lay on the President's mind or how much he knew that he would not share with them, they recognized that there was, indeed, no way out except to face the reality of questions.

They had begun to face that reality at the end of February when the House Judiciary Committee requested tape recordings of forty-two conversations which it felt it must have in order to pass judgment. They were not about to repeat the blunder of October and let the Judiciary Committee carry its request to the courts by subpoena (which eventually it would and did). They could not once more defy the courts and then surrender under compulsion. They had met in Key Biscayne, where the President had flown in the second weekend of March for a four-day stay, and taken a bold-stroke decision. They would voluntarily release the transcripts of the critical conversations demanded by the Judiciary Committee, and there, before all the American people, would be the answers—the President's own words, mottled, scarred by profanity, ugly in indecision, but sufficient, as they thought, to prove their case: no statutory crime had been ordered or committed by the President sufficient to warrant impeachment.

The White House staff had begun transcription on return from Key Biscayne. The quality of the tapes was bad. The originals of the nine initial recordings claimed by Archibald Cox were in the possession of Judge Sirica. Of those tapes the White House still possessed only mechanical, flat-tone, difficult-to-decipher, secondary reproductions. There were internal disputes about what should or should not be released. All were convinced that whatever was relevant must be published, if any transcripts were published at all. The lawyers, led by Buzhardt, felt even the profanity and the vulgarity should be published. But Ziegler was against publishing the profanity, and preferred "expletive deleted." It was an evolving decision over the weeks, said Buzhardt. "The tapes had to be located, and I located them. Then they went to the secretaries. Then the transcripts had to go to him. Then they came back to me."

And then, on April 29th, the President was ready to make his stroke. "He really thought he was innocent," said

Buzhardt later. "He didn't think he had done anything of a criminal nature or an impeachable nature. That was the problem. And no one then had listened to all the tapes to find out differently."

And so, on the evening of April 29th, one year less one day from the evening on which he had explained to the nation why he was dismissing his palace guard, the President took to the air. Hs manner and voice were composed; he wore an Oxford-gray suit and gray tie. His hair showed a silvering at the temples. It was one of the most impressive of all his countless public appearances in the twenty-two years since he had carried his appeal by television to the nation over the hostility of the liberal press and Dwight Eisenhower's palace guard.

A year before, he had said precisely, "I was determined that we should get to the bottom of the matter and that the truth should be fully brought out—no matter who was involved. . . . [the] responsibility therefore belongs here in this office, I accept it."

Now, with a stage setting of thirty-eight bound volumes piled on a table beside him, one for each member of the House Judiciary Committee, he was not only accepting that responsibility but letting the nation, as well as the committee, judge how he had met it. As the camera panned to the volumes, he said:

"They include all the relevant portions of all the subpoenaed conversations that were recorded, that is, all portions that relate to the question of what I knew about Watergate or the cover-up and what I did about it. . . . everything that is relevant is included—the rough as well as the smooth, the strategy sessions, the exploration of alternatives, the weighing of human and political costs. . . . I want there to be no question remaining about the fact that the President has nothing to hide in this matter. . . ."

But he had lost track of the truth—about himself, about the facts, about the nature of the crime charged to him. He was, whether he realized it or not, lying—lying by abstraction and by necessity. His composure, it seemed to anyone who had watched him for twenty years, was real—he had persuaded himself of what he was doing, that by letting the nation read even the dirty conversations of his inner counsel he could clear himself of penalty for what he and they had escalated into Constitutional crisis.

And with the release, what remained of Richard Nixon's public support crumbled. The tapes spoke for themselves. They spoke in a vulgarity of language, an indecision of tone and a profanity of such commonness as to make the imaginative level of Lyndon Johnson's obscenities seem artful by comparison. Liberal moralists and conservative traditionalists could only compete in adjectives of denunciation. Hugh Scott, the Republican Senate Minority Leader, ran off the first string—"deplorable," "disgusting," "shabby," "immoral." John Rhodes, the Republican Minority Leader of the House, said the President should consider resigning. Elliot Richardson sounded off, warning that for any Republican to support the President in the coming fall election would be "a prescription for suicide."

"I'm embarrassed to have our kids read this and think it's part of the life I'm in," said Robert Strauss, the Democratic National Committee chairman. "If this is what he thought he *could* release," said Democrat William Hungate of Missouri, "I'd like to hear what else is on those tapes." Republican Representative John Anderson described himself as "dismayed and disheartened." John Ashbrook of Ohio, a hard-core Goldwater conservative, said, "I listened to him on television last Monday night and for the first time in a year I believed him. Then I read the March 21st transcript and it was incredible, unbelievable."

It was worse than the firestorm of October. That had burst overnight. This time it took the *New York Times* four days to publish the text of the full 1,308 pages of transcript the White House had released. In a week, paperback publishers had chugged out by plane, truck and rail 3,000,000 copies of what must have been history's largest instant best-seller. It took days to read the transcripts, but by the following week, from coast to coast the editorialists of even those newspapers which had supported Richard Nixon for so long were volleying, one after the other, with calls for the President's resignation. The Chicago *Tribune*, the century-old bible of Republicans of the Midwest, was off with its call within nine days. So, too, were the Omaha *World Herald*, the Kansas City *Times*, the Hearst newspapers, the

Cleveland *Plain Dealer*—the organs of the heartland, the spokesmen of Middle America.

A running public-opinion survey by *Time* magazine had been under way before the release of the transcripts. At the height of public attention to the Ervin hearings in August, 1973, it had found 60 percent of those polled still favoring Richard Nixon's continuance in office, 20 percent for resignation, 10 percent for impeachment. In November, 1973, after the Cox-Richardson firestorm, the figures had shifted to 49 percent for continuance, 29 percent for resignation, 10 percent for impeachment. In April, just before the latest upheaval, it had found only 37 percent for continuance, 38 percent for resignation, 17 percent for impeachment. And now, within two weeks of the release of the transcripts, a Louis Harris poll found the nation 49 to 41 percent for Nixon's impeachment and removal; and majorities of 3 to 1 and 2 to 1 judging him guilty of one crime or another.

Yet outrage is not evidence; outrage is political. Nor are style and profanity evidence either. To impeach a President required still that one specify the nature of his crime and the nature of the laws under which he could be charged. Which brought one back once more to the Committee on the Judiciary, which at this point of turbulence disappeared entirely into closed session to hear the evidence which John Doar, at Rodino's direction, had been compiling.

12

JUDGMENT:
SUMMER 1974

If there were any coherence at all to events in the numbing months of late spring and early summer of 1974, it rested on the strategy and tactics of Peter Rodino.

His strategy was clear: to force his committee to vote not on a matter of crime, but on a matter of principle–the use and abuse of power. There would later, in retrospect, be a futility about that strategy, for the resignation of Richard Nixon would rob the committee of the opportunity to have its resolutions added to the formal law of the land.

But the tactics of Peter Rodino required secrecy—a secrecy that baffled and befuddled both the news system and the public waiting for judgment. Secrecy was necessary so that his committee would not be split prematurely on party lines. On the substance of whatever final judgment the committee made, Americans must see it as a judgment beyond political prejudice or partisan affiliation. Thus, week after week, month after month, committee members must deliberate in secrecy, pounded by evidence however dreary, however repetitious, however tedious, without being polarized, without being frozen in public positions that later they might not be able to abandon.

It was impossible to demean or be cynical about Peter Rodino. However amiable, dilatory or indecisive he might seem in public, he was in private a man acting beyond himself and beyond all pressure. And one could not but admire his skills. He must buy time for Doar and his staff to assemble the evidence that would erase party lines. To buy time, he would yield to the Republicans on his committee on every procedural point; he would soothe his left-wing Democrats by every guile and flattery he could conceive. He would use his authority only when he must, from time

to time, and then he would act as the autocrat of conciliation, compromise, delay.

Winter thus passed into spring with, apparently, no
movement; and in spring one could observe the committee
going even further underground on May 9th to hear Doar's
evidence; to remain underground for eleven weeks of sessions in Room 2141 of the Rayburn Office Building until
July 24th. Days with earphones clamped over members'
heads as Congressmen listened to tapes, emerging excited or
perplexed; other days emerging with frustration and exasperation at John Doar, who droned on and on and on,
reading fact, buttressing fact with testimony, suffocating
committee members with his dry voice; other days emerging with views so contradictory as to make one wonder
whether the members had been sitting in the same room
hearing the same testimony, as they talked to the news system: "TAPE PROVIDES NO NIXON LINK TO MILK FUNDS,"
front-paged the Washington *Post* on June 6th; and on the
same day in the *New York Times,* "NIXON TAPE IS SAID TO
LINK MILK PRICE TO POLITICAL GIFT."

It was at all times possible, even behind the uncertainty
and secrecy, to identify a hard-core Democratic vote
against the President and a hard-core Republican vote for
the President. But even when one spoke to such hard-core
men, one found a quality of concern rare on Capitol Hill.

Sarbanes, for example. There had never been any doubt
that Congressman Paul Sarbanes of Baltimore would vote
against the President. Tough, learned, a hard-knuckled
street campaigner, he would talk like this in June:

"What this relates to," he said over a quick sandwich in
his office between sessions, "is something fundamental.
We've gradually been losing our perception in this country
between substance and process.

"I'm really worried about the American political system
—how successfully we use this system to meet the fundamental problems of our people. The problems aren't simple
and I'm afraid of simplistic solutions . . . my apprehension
runs to what is fundamental to the process. The democratic
process is founded on the premise that you'll have disagree-
ments on fundamental policy, and so it's a way of resolving

these differences. Take Nixon—he's entitled to veto anything under the Constitution, even though I disagree.

"But the real problem here is a process that undercuts both the laws and that system. The essential distinction of our system is this open process, that's what lets us gain power or lose it. The Nixon people have another point of view—of a plebiscite, of a vote being a license to do whatever you want to do. I feel we've got to get back to a system of Cabinet government resting on institutions; these institutions protect us; not even a Pat Gray could twist those institutions out of shape; you can only bend them just so far, then they snap back or they leak to the press.

"But supposing you had one thousand people on Herb Kalmbach's private payroll, what then? Supposing you got a thousand of them, and none of them are law-enforcement officials, none governed by the rules and regulations of the FBI or the CIA, a whole operation of irregulars. If Ulasewicz didn't have the Ehrlichman connection, it would only be a private activity; but with the Ehrlichman connection, that activity has the cloak of authority.

"No one has yet made up his mind," he continued, trying to explain how his own mind was working, "but I'm for looking at the pattern of behavior; and then, if it's dangerous, the preamble to the impeachment has to formulate it into an historic charge. And this decision has to be so firm, so fair, that when people start poking at it ten or fifteen years from now, it stands. You don't want this to become an American Dreyfus case—that could destroy the whole American political system."

Or Wiggins of California, for example. There was no doubt that Wiggins would vote for the president, until months later he, too, found he had been deceived by Richard Nixon. Wiggins was at once spokesman for the cause of law and spokesman against what he saw as a push against the Presidency by a partisan Congress which might alter the Constitutional balance. "My feeling is still that this committee will produce one of these twenty-five-thousand-page encyclopedic books indicting Richard Nixon and the Republican Party for everything under the sun, and then . . . indict him on two hundred pages of this evidence. . . . When the record is published it will contain thousands of words which will be used for years to come to damage and

smear the whole Republican Party. But the issue is relevance
—relevance to an impeachable offense. My first mission is
to see if I can persuade them all to act like lawyers. It's a
goddamned weak circumstantial case. . . . The committee
has avoided any kind of standard on what is an impeachable offense." For Wiggins, the issue was judgment to be
made on a man by his deeds despite the style or the language of the transcripts; a right conferred on everyone by
the Constitution, and one which he would fight to maintain
for the President, too.

But between Sarbanes on the one hand and Wiggins on
the other, both moved by conscience to unshakable votes,
one could find others whose consciences unsettled them.

William Cohen of Maine, for example, a first-term Republican Congressman with a shaky base back home. "I'd
like to come back to Washington," said Cohen, "but this issue is too important. I'm staying up until two A.M. reading,
trying to reflect, to place in context eight or nine thousand
pages of evidence and testimony . . . and see if it stacks up
to the meager phrases of the Constitution. . . . I don't care
how other Republicans vote. I make my own decision. . . .
I think we're in a dangerous time. We're at the point where
nobody trusts anyone any more. . . . we see a distrust of
the President, of Congress, of business. . . . There's no
sense of . . . credibility. . . . It's crucial that the public accept the verdict of the committee and of Congress, and perceive it as fair and non-partisan, whether the decision is to
impeach or not."

In a Cohen one could begin to see the Rodino-Doar
strategy working—to crack party line and conscience as
evidence crushed down. And the strategy was working because there was no counter-strategy. No direction of defense, except on legalitics, from the White House; and no
liaison between White House and Republicans on the committee. Nixon loyalists looked to their ranking minority
member, Edward Hutchinson of Michigan, for leadership.
But Hutchinson, as fresh in his post as minority leader of
the Judiciary Committee as was Rodino as committee chairman, was less wise in parliamentary tactics; and aging.
Hutchinson would assemble his Republicans on the committee to caucus but rarely—and then only under prodding
by the members. So that not until July 11th, when Hutchin-

son finally, still in secrecy, assembled committee Republicans in caucus to discuss the drafting of a minority report to counter the Democratic majority report, did the orchestration of concern which Rodino had been cultivating for so long become apparent for the first time.

As Congressman Tom Railsback of Illinois recalls the meeting, he had demurred at the outset. He had agreed that a minority report was required, but he felt it should not be made public.

"Why not?" asked Hutchinson, according to Railsback.

"Because there may be some of us that may not agree with the minority position," said Railsback.

"Well," said Hutchinson, "I think it's about time that we find out where we stand and we find out if there are Republicans that are going to want to vote to impeach a Republican President."

"Ed, that's what I'm trying to tell you," Railsback said, "I may vote to impeach the President." And with that, it was quite clear the Rodino-Doar strategy had worked.

The crack-up had been occurring in different ways in different minds for weeks—the needs of the underlying political process pressing against the inclination of partisan purpose. At least three Democrats on the committee, Southerners who had come from conservative constituencies that had given Nixon some of his most spectacular majorities of 1972, were being torn. At least six Republicans of the committee, later to vote against Nixon, were weighing, with equal disturbance of spirit, the causes for which Nixon spoke against the means by which his men had pursued such causes of their hearts.

Congressman Hamilton Fish of New York, for example. Fish was a conservative of pedigree. Not only had his father, the previous Congressman Hamilton Fish, been one of the more flamboyant reactionaries of his time, but the line ran back to one of the founders of the Republican Party, the original Hamilton Fish, who had served as Ulysses S. Grant's Secretary of State. To discover young Hamilton Fish wavering was astonishing. But he had had, he said, an entirely open mind until some time in May, when the evidence and the facts and testimony began to build and build in a pattern of lawlessness that somehow went to the heart of what the conservative philosophy was all about—law and order.

For M. Caldwell Butler, a Virginia Republican who, in his House roll-call votes in 1973, had voted with Nixon 75 percent of the time, the moment of self-question had come when, with earphones over his head in closed session of the committee, he had found "this absence of surprise or remorse" in the live tapes. Said Butler, "It was obvious that the President, not Haldeman, was in charge."

For James Mann, a conservative Democrat from South Carolina, a state that had given Richard Nixon a 71-percent majority in 1972, decision had come slowly. Smooth, gentle, melancholy of voice, almost clerical in manner, Mann considered that the issue had become Constitutional for him when the committee in early July had called live witnesses, to put flesh and voice to the documentary evidence. The testimony of Butterfield had moved him to the thought of overall Presidential responsibility, "this question of accountability—to what extent can a President stay behind closed doors and run this country and wash his hands of the responsibility for the action of his men."

For Walter Flowers, a Democrat of Alabama, a Nixon man in spirit, in whose Congressional office hung a portrait affectionately inscribed to him by George Wallace, evidence shaped into issue at two points: "The March 21st tape was devastating . . . the general lack of morality by people in the Oval Office, when the President talked about paying off —a crime of obstruction of justice in everyday, chit-chat terms." And then had come the live testimony of Henry Petersen. Petersen had been obedient to the President in reporting grand-jury testimony at the President's request. But the President had then passed the information on to Haldeman and Ehrlichman, "not with the view of finding out what was going on," said Flowers, "but to help them prepare their own defenses." Flowers had been bored by Doar's tedious readings of fact and evidence. Only later would he recall that "Nobody really saw where we were going until we got there."

But however they were getting there was not to be judged from the outside. From the outside, the question was, as it had been since early in the year, not how the Judiciary Committee got there—but when. For it was clear that the committee's decision would be only Act One in a three-act drama. It would take the House weeks to debate the articles of impeachment offered by the Judiciary Committee. And if the House voted them up, that would be only Act Two, on which the curtain could not fall before the end of August. Then it would move to the Senate for Act Three sometime in September. Thus, the high trial in the Senate could overlap the national elections in November. And if the trial spun on beyond that time, it might run beyond the legal term of this 93rd Congress—and could the next Congress, the 94th, Constitutionally convict a President impeached by its predecessor?

It was a time that reminded this reporter of his days as a war correspondent. In a war, all the best dispatches are written from the winning side, because headquarters of the winners knows where its troops are, where they are moving, what the plans are. At losing headquarters, no one ever knows quite what is going on, where the divisions are, where the next thrust may come, the next breakthrough be reported. Victors know and may or may not choose to tell; the losers ask questions.

At the White House, the losers were more hospitable than ever to reporters who dropped in. Each morning, there gathered as usual in Dean Burch's second-floor office in the White House the Defense Group, the President's men of strategy. But they had no strategy. Like men in a fortress watching the enemy slowly move his siege machinery into place, they waited with no relief in sight from over the horizon and every sortie futile. Their explanations of strategy limped. They had, indeed, expected the explosion following the publication of the transcripts April 30th. The most intelligent of the Defense Group adjusted to the reaction—but their new gloss on the transcripts was fascinating. They no longer denied that the President had committed a small crime on March 21st in authorizing payment of blackmail. But, as one of them put it to this reporter: there was Nixon on March 21st with this new information from Dean; and, yes, he had agreed to pay blackmail on the spur of the moment. But would you have done differently had you been President and been surprised by totally new charges and needed to buy time to find out, yea or nay, whether your dearest friends, your most trusted officials, were guilty or not? The small crime of March 21st, as revealed in the transcripts, was no longer denied by the end of May. But, asked the Defense Group, was it an impeachable offense?

Other questions at losers' headquarters were even more disconcerting. I visited one official, an old friend, who for twelve years had been one of Nixon's most devoted lieutenants. And then, as if he feared being overheard, he leaned forward and asked softly, "Tell me the truth—do *you* think he's guilty?" And I, startled by his question, could not answer before he continued, "You know, Teddy, if Haldeman knew and Ehrlichman knew, he must have known, too. If they're guilty, he's guilty—they were just that close." Or another official, "I ask myself every day what I am doing here that will make a difference ten years hence. Should I go on with it? Can I go on with it?"

But when one pried to get at the personality and mood of the President, the curtain fell. Yes, he was not feeling well. Yes, there were health problems. Basically, he was exhausted. And, yes, it was true that when he went off to Key Biscayne in May he was so tired he fell asleep on the short helicopter ride from Key Biscayne to the Grand Cay home of his friend Robert Abplanalp, as the *Times* reported. Overwhelmingly, those at the defense command were protective of the President. Though he could not lead, they would try to follow. He was irascible, testy, and even among themselves they did not want to gossip about him; those in his favor for the day or the evening would pass his commands to those out of favor for that day, wryly, without comment, sometimes with bemusement, sometimes with alarm. One memorandum I was able to see was dated June 3rd, 1974, as the President prepared to go off on that month's voyages of foreign affairs. He had ordered his military aide, Lieutenant Colonel John Brennan, to pass his command to Ronald Ziegler. From Brennan to Ziegler, the memo read thus:

"Last night, 2 June 1974, the President very emphatically related to me his views regarding press pools. I am instructed to inform you, in very forceful terms, that *never*, under *any* circumstances on *any* leg of *any* trip, will a representative from the following be allowed on the press pool:

"New York Times, Washington Post, Time Magazine, Newsweek, CBS, Richard Lerner of UPI.

"The President also emphatically stated that this is not appealable—do not appeal to General Haig and do not bring the subject up to the President as he wants to hear no more about it. This is a direct command from the President.

"The President directed that since the Office of the Military Assistant to the President is responsible for the aircraft, he is holding us responsible to make sure none of the above are allowed on aircraft as part of a press pool. The President also said he wants you to continue submitting press pools to him in advance of a trip.

"Being tunnel-visioned, narrow-minded Military people, we in this office intend to carry out fully the instructions of our Commander-in-Chief."

All the proscribed publications and reporters, except for Lerner of UPI, did of course make the trips abroad that the President scheduled for the month of June—if not in the press pool itself, somewhere in the press entourage. The staff knew better than the President how much he needed press coverage—foreign affairs was his strength, and his defenders could defend him best when he was displayed overseas. But they scheduled him as managers of an aging singer schedule her to repeat her familiar triumphs, like Judy Garland singing "Over the Rainbow" once more. And the audience watched in the same way—not paying attention to the actual performance so much as listening for the cracks in the voice, wondering whether the performer could make it safely through to the curtain.

In this last extravaganza overseas, Nixon proved himself once again a master as chief-of-state. Henry Kissinger had just pulled off in May the latest of his major diplomatic coups, negotiating a truce between Israel and Syria; and with this as springboard, the President took off. Compared to other heads of government in the Western world, Nixon was huge. One government of England had fallen in spring, and the new shaky majority of Harold Wilson was approaching its second test. Willy Brandt of Germany, his friend, had recently been unseated by a domestic spy-scandal in Bonn. In Japan, another friend, Prime Minister Kakuei Tanaka, was about to be driven from office by an Oriental Watergate affair. France was approaching an election that would give it a presidency balanced on knife edge. Italy was in dissolution; and even in Canada, the government of Pierre Trudeau was in trouble. The aging Golda Meir had submitted her resignation in Israel, and leadership there had been taken over by the yet untested Yitzhak Rabin. Troubled as he was, Nixon still led a state with a clear foreign policy.

The President's trip abroad in June cheered his Defense Group even though the anticipated flip-up in his public-opinion registers was minimal and spotty. But the pattern of his last travels, as in his previous years' journeying, spoke louder than explanation of his mood. He had left for the Middle East on June 10th and visited, in the presence of television, the great sights—the Sphinx and the pyramids and Jerusalem as he had visited the Great Wall of China in the glory of early 1972. He spent nine days on his trip to the Middle East, then came back and apparently spent four days at Camp David. Then two nights and a day at the White House and off to Moscow on June 25th. From which he returned eight days later—to Key Biscayne, where he lingered for four days. He was back in the White House for only four days thereafter and then on the 12th of July he was off to San Clemente for sixteen days, not returning until the Judiciary Committee had adopted its first article of impeachment of the President. All in all, he was in the White House of the President of the United States for only six days of the last six weeks of his effective authority.

Those reporters who followed him to San Clemente on his last three weeks there reported him sadly. He was no longer reported as waking at night, restless, playing the piano, disappearing on long motor drives with Bebe Rebozo, as he had been in January. Rebozo was not even there. The President rarely left his compound. His staff was more friendly to reporters now at the end—Haig being host to several press parties at one of the villas, Clawson making available whatever officials could be persuaded to appear. But the President was solitary. The debilitating phlebitis which had pained him on his June trips abroad was reported as subsiding. He would stroll, usually alone, on the beach within his compound, occasionally accompanied by Haig. He saw few.

And all about was the smell of decay. When a President habitually travels to the same places, a small commerce grows up about those places. Now, in July, even before the verdict of Washington had been rendered, the merchants and hoteliers of the area had cast their judgment. "To the San Clemente Inn," wrote Lou Cannon of the Washington *Post* in a lovely dispatch at once evocative and premonitory, "there is no more White House and to the White House, there is no more San Clemente Inn." The pleasant hotel had summarily evicted all White House staff aides and the Secret Service ten days earlier. The White House press had enjoyed the Laguna Beach Motel for the years of the Nixon administration; his trips to the West Coast produced little obligatory news and the Laguna Beach Motel had given rest with a sea view fifteen miles north of the Western White House. On this last trip, the motel's management began to evict the press from its quarters. The Surf and Sand Hotel in Laguna Beach, which had provided press-conference headquarters for the traveling White House, was liquidating the facility. The literature of the restaurant that replaced the old press room was elegiac: "Our private meeting and banquet room is named the Press Corps Room in recognition of the members of the fourth estate," said its brochure. But, wrote Cannon twelve days before the end, "At Laguna Beach, as at San Clemente, both the Nixon administration and the press corps that covered it have already passed into history."

For reporters left behind on the East Coast during those days, the outcome was less clear. I flew from Washington to New York each week; only twelve years earlier, the same shuttle service had made the flight in an hour and twenty minutes at a cost of $15. Now one could make the trip in half the time, but at twice the cost. Was it worth it, one asked, to move twice as fast at twice the cost? That had been Richard Nixon's problem—to move as fast as possible to where he wanted his government to go, at much more than twice the cost.

How fast, how much, at what cost?—that was one of the central problems of American politics, and the face of the beautiful capital underscored the question.

The face of the city had changed since I first came there in the summer of 1941 from Asia. That first interview with a State Department official, who told me that war was coming with Japan, had taken place on King's Row of what was now called the Executive Office Building.

Now, as I visited Washington, I could not help but match the present with memory. The bloat of the state and the bloat of aspirations had changed Washington. The temporary shacks on the Mall which, on my first visit, had still housed World War I spillover from the armed services had been removed. The Mall was beautiful and clean. But the Pentagon had been built since then, a monster occupying thirty-four acres, directing 1,214 American generals and admirals who could strike terror or spread devastation around the entire world. An enormous building was being finished on the north side of Pennsylvania Avenue, called the J. Edgar Hoover Building, to concentrate the FBI, whose offices had once been dispersed from top to basement of the Justice Department building. Buildings proliferated—new museums all to the south of Pennsylvania Avenue. A State Department building of eight stories and ten acres and more than 1,000 rooms rose on what once was swampland.

The country had grown, to be sure, since I had first visited Washington in 1941; but the structure of government had by far outgrown real growth. It was all there in concrete and marble as one drove. Washington traffic had always been bad—ever since John Adams had complained about it almost two centuries before. It had been even more impossible when I got there for the first time. I had hoped that when Washington built its subway system, going about would become convenient. But the subway project, which had seemed a temporary annoyance to this visitor in 1969, had become by 1974 a permanent blight. It would not be finished in 1980, as planned a few years before. It might possibly be finished by 1985; or perhaps even years later, when I would be too old to take advantage of a subway.

So one was reduced to the shuffle again, the hustling of cabs in the heat or in the rain, the circuit back and forth between the empty White House and the crowded Rayburn Office Building, where headquarters of the victors lay. At the Rayburn Building, one wormed through tourists, gawkers, fellow journalists, and the stake-out of cameras and television, to squeeze out of the reluctant Congressmen who gathered in Room 2141 just what it was they were doing, or thinking, about the faith with which a handful of people, two centuries before, had inspirited the society that had thrust up these overpowering buildings to shelter the faith.

It was now mid-July, a time of restrained hysteria. The mind could no longer absorb all the facts, all the documents, all the variorums, all the testimony coating the crisis. There were too many facts—"Like pieces of popcorn that form a decorative Christmas tree chain only when someone strings a thread through them," in the memorable phrase of James Naughton of the *New York Times*.

And this, in essence, was what Peter Rodino was saying when, angry with John Doar for the first time, he confronted him in the chairman's cubbyhole office just off Hearing Room 2141, on the morning of July 19th, 1974. For months Rodino had been protecting Doar, giving him time to do the job that strategy required, to pile the evidence up so as to split those Republicans and Southern conservatives who, bound by policy to Nixon, might conceivably find themselves more bound by the law against him. Doar had now been droning for months. He had won for himself the title of "chief archivist" of the impeachment hearings, had so absented his personality from his presentation that once his flat monotone had put even James St. Clair, the President's chief counsel, to sleep. Now, said Rodino, *now* this morning, Doar must lay it on the line. Under pressure from the House leadership, Rodino insisted that Doar must thread the string through the popcorn at once—and give analysis to the evidence, shape the facts into issues. And with that ultimatum Rodino stalked off in operatic anger, leaving Doar with his Wisconsin-Irish temper at a slow boil.

Doar's formal analysis had already been written—a Summary of Information 306 pages long, distributed to the committee before he entered the room, shaping the testimony delivered into an indictment of the President as derelict. But Doar had spent the previous night in his apartment on New Jersey Avenue working on notes for an oral introduction to this summary, and he now proceeded to make the case of his staff, ad-libbing from his notes, still smarting from Rodino's outburst of temper.

And with that, the thread was going through the popcorn. Doar was trying to make himself clear, and for ninety minutes he talked. He would not let his case pivot on the events of March 21st, because, he said, referring to the volume he had just submitted, the evidence could not let the case pivot on a single episode. They were discussing here, and had been discussing for months, he went on, not an episode, or two or three unrelated episodes, but a pattern of conduct, a President's image of his own authority. "I think everyone wants to believe our President. I wanted to believe that he had nothing to do with Watergate." But the evidence would not permit it. There was something in this President that had allowed him to authorize a whole series of interrelated crimes, mounting to an obstruction of justice. There was, said Doar, the President's personal dictabelt of the evening of March 21st—the President had told himself of the charges which disturbed him; but the next day he had told the Attorney General nothing of that, only of political necessity: "he would like him to give Senator Baker some guidance, he would like him to hold Baker's hand, to babysit him starting like in the next ten minutes." There was, said Doar, "that remarkable ten days between the 15th and 25th of April 1973 when he had discussed the case of law with Henry Petersen against suspected criminals—and then turned Petersen's private information over to two of the suspected criminals." Doar reached back, stringing his thread through the recorded conversation of March 21st, 1973, when the President congratulated John Dean: ". . . you had the right plan, let me say, I have no doubts about the right plan for the election. . . . You contained it. Now, after the election, we've got to have another plan, because we can't have, for four years, we can't have this thing—you are going to be eaten away. We can't do it."

Doar roved back and forth over the dates, trying to reduce the March 21st episode, on which the President's stalwarts hung their defense, to a detail in his accusation: "what we have tried to do, in the best way we can in this book is . . . to summarize, to quote, to cite, to pull together fairly, objectively, forcefully if we believe that force is required, in a way that would be helpful to you in making your decision." This was not a matter of deciding whether a smoking gun—a direct contact between the President, personally, and an illegally ordered action—could be found. It was a question of how a President governed. Reading from his notes and then lifting himself to a bitterness that contrasted sharply with the monotone of his earlier recitals, he extemporized, "When you get into the proof, and try to find the proof of the means, you find yourself down in the labyrinth of the White House in that Byzantine Empire where 'yes' meant 'no,' and 'go' was 'stop' and 'maybe' was 'certainly,' and it is confusing, perplexing and puzzling and difficult for any group of people to sort out. But, that is just the very nature of the crime, that in executing the means, everything will be done to confuse and to fool, to misconstrue so that the purpose of the decision is concealed."

Doar had dictated the night before to his secretary the paragraphs that he thought made his case best: "The critical question the Committee must decide is whether, as he claimed in his statement of April 30th . . . the President was, in fact, constantly deceived by his closest political associates or whether those associates were in fact carrying out his policies and decisions. This question must be decided one way or the other." And then the committee had to decide whether "that statement was part of a pattern of conduct designed not to take care that the laws be faithfully executed, but to impede their faithful execution, in his political interest and on his behalf."

With that, Doar submitted his Summary of Information. And then deposited with the committee the drafts of possible impeachment articles, composed by his staff over the previous six weeks, that ranged from the outrageous and unreal to the most somber and concrete, to suit the tastes of those who had always hated Richard Nixon or who had always supported his government yet had come to fear it. The staff had called its drafts "suggestions," from which the committee might choose its indictments: for bombing of Cambodia, for enriching his personal estates at government expense, for cheating the government of taxes due it, for failing to enforce the anti-trust laws in dealing with ITT, for flouting Congress' authority over the purse by impounding funds which Congress had ordered spent. A penumbra of lesser charges floated through the staff drafts, in flamboyant and overblown language, all surrounding the heart issue: that Richard Nixon through his men and his administration had frustrated the operation of justice against wrongdoers and abused the power of state against a number of free citizens, and, thus, against all citizens.

It was characteristic at all times in the crisis of 1973–74 that no straight roads converged on the central story. Each road of investigation opened byroads, and byroads opened on chambers, from which opened other roads of story, and each deserved a book in itself. No one would read all the books, all the documents, all the testimony ever again. The minimum necessary compendia—the Ervin hearings, the tax committee report, Judiciary Committee hearings, administration responses—totaled seventy-four volumes; beyond that were trial transcripts, other related Congressional hearings, still further unrevealed or unpublished jury testimony and tape transcripts yet to come; and beyond that the words of the press, and the memories of the participants. One man would never, certainly, come to know it all.

There were, thus, in the five days between Doar's Summary of Information on July 19th and the debates of the committee televised for America more stories than one could catalogue: of leadership caucuses in the Speaker's Chamber urging speed; of Republican caucuses of loyalists both within and without the committee; of ideological caucuses of the revanchists of the Democratic left trying to mobilize the necessary votes for articles of impeachment of Richard Nixon on Cambodia, on impounding, on his tax record. All were coagulating in opinion, in shifting majorities on the half-dozen issues which the President had brought to a point of judgment. But of all such coagulations, the most important certainly was the coagulation of opinion that brought seven uncertain and self-questioning Congressmen to Republican Tom Railsback's office at eight in the morning of July 23rd, the day before public proceedings were to begin.

The meeting had come about both accidentally and by design. The previous evening had ended the second of two free-wheeling, unstructured and secret sessions of the committee in which all had tossed their ideas and impressions back and forth. It was now quite clear that at least eighteen of the twenty-one Democrats would go all the way to impeach Richard Nixon on any charge; and that ten Republicans would go all the way to the end, on the then-known evidence, to clear him on any charge; but that in between were ten men whose minds reflected a non-partisan conscientious doubt. And of those in doubt, all ten came from that area of Middle America whose swing-shift opinion had affirmed Richard Nixon's policies in 1972 by a majority of 18,000,000. Rodino had asked Walter Flowers, Alabama Democrat, if he could gather some of these swing members together, to give him that base in the political center without which the conclusions of the committee might go down as those of an Inquisition seeking heretics. Flowers had strolled down the corridor on the evening of the 22nd with his friend Tom Railsback, Republican of Illinois, two men of almost the same age who had formed a friendship in the House gymnasium, where they played paddleball together. Flowers, stimulated by Rodino, suggested that he collect a few undecided Democrats, and Railsback a few undecided Republicans, to work ideas out with the dominating straight-line Democratic liberals who were already drafting their articles of impeachment. Flowers could bring Mann of South Carolina and Ray Thornton of Arkansas (two other troubled Democrats), and suggested that perhaps Railsback could bring some of the troubled Republicans—men like Fish, Cohen, Butler.

They met, thus, the next morning in Railsback's office, Room 218 of the Cannon House Office Building, eating Danish pastry and sipping coffee under the unseeing eye of a mounted blue sailfish. The Cannon Building is one of the three office buildings of the House. The Rayburn Building is for senior men and committee chairmen. The Longworth Building, the shabbiest office building, with the occasional raunchy atmosphere of a college dormitory, holds mostly junior Congressmen. But the Cannon Building, where they met, is tenanted largely by men of middle rank. And these were seven men of middle rank, middle mind, middle perplexity who met, three Democrats of the South, substantially more conservative than their fellow Democrats of the North, and four Republicans, substantially more troubled than their fellow Republicans of the committee. All of them, though, came from rural or small-city districts, where a certain amount of political independence is considered a virtue and where people know what their Congressman is and does because the mass news system does not come be-

tween. Said Cohen later of the group: ". . . they're basically reasonable people, and the whole object of getting a
small group together is that you expel the extremes. . . .
Just those who say, 'Well, what about this? Do you think
the evidence is there on this issue?' " Jerome Waldie and
Charles Wiggins, both of California, both cuttingly intelligent, both leaders on one side or another of the partisan
divide, were not going to help these troubled people make
up their minds.

It was with relief they met. Each, except Cohen perhaps,
had felt originally that he should vote for Nixon. But all,
over the previous half-year of hearing and studying and listening, had come to believe that final judgment must go
against their original preference. "We were all amazed,"
said Flowers later, "at how close we were as to the . . .
gravity of the evidence . . . and I said, 'It's nice to discuss
these legislative details. But we ought to discuss whether we
are willing to discuss to impeach the President of the United States.' "

To their astonishment, they were willing—seven men
who, without questioning each other, knew they had voted
for Richard Nixon as President two years before. And who
felt now that he must be removed. They would stand together and throw out the lesser charges of the draft impeachment—on Cambodia (Cohen: "How could we vote to
impeach when we had all voted funds for continuing the
bombardment?"); on ITT—it was the President's duty to
have a policy on conglomerates, largeness and size of business. And thus down the line, until Thornton of Arkansas,
who had come in late, made his point. "I think," he said
later, "the only contribution I made was to state the
thought that the offense was a continuing offense . . . it
was the continuation of the threat that was really of concern to me."

The threat of Richard Nixon lay clearly there, as Thornton expressed it—not so much in the accumulated evidence,
damning as it was, but in what lay ahead. That threat, not
motivated by cupidity, unstirred by treachery as in the case
of Charles, King of England, who conspired against the
cause of his state with enemies abroad, lay to the future of
the Presidency—the threat of where the power of some future President might reach if not checked now. Of Nixon's

misuse of power, these seven Congressmen of Middle America, small-town America, were convinced: it was dangerous. With their support, Rodino would have a cause in history to present to the House; without them, he would be a partisan Democrat overturning by partisan votes the man whom the people had voted for only twenty months earlier.

Railsback referred to his group as "the fragile coalition." But that, wrote James Wieghart of the New York *Daily News,* "was a misnomer. It was not a group held together by baling wire and spit, but a coalition of seven like-minded men who had decided after long deliberation and much soul-searching that Richard Nixon, the President of the United States, had committed offenses against the office of the Presidency serious enough to warrant his impeachment and removal from that high office. . . . It was a coalition of conscience and there was nothing fragile about it." With their approval the meaning of the Constitution could be stretched all the way down the generations of American independence to the indescribable complexity of American life and its diverse heritages in 1974.

The next day, July 24th, the Supreme Court of the Unites States would give its reading on Presidential power; and the next evening, the proceedings of the Judiciary Committee, in its search for definition of power, would unroll before camera for all Americans to see.

One could see it all there as the full thirty-eight members of the Judiciary Committee gathered on the night of July 24th in the high-ceilinged chamber of Room 2141.

Sitting in their two-tiered benches, no longer dressed in the shirt sleeves or simple dresses they had worn in untelevised sessions, but groomed for the cameras and the nation, they were immensely impressive. On the upper tier were the elders who had sat on the Judiciary Committee of the past —all except Rodino, Conyers, Eilberg and Donohue of old-stock white descent, respectable and serious men. The lower tier held the juniors, those who had actively sought entry through this committee over the previous eight years into the working of American justice. Their names read like a roll-call in a scene from a Grade-B World War II movie, when the sergeant calls the roll of his ethnically all-inclusive platoon. The names read, from left to right, Mezvin-

JUDGMENT: SUMMER 1974 399

sky, Jordan (black and female), Rangel (black), Father Drinan, Seiberling, Sarbanes (Greek), Holtzman (female), Hogan, Cohen, Froehlich, Maraziti and Latta. All alike committed to interpret a Constitution written two centuries before for a small nation of farmers and merchants, most of them English by descent and Protestant in faith—a Constitution which had now been stretched across a nation which reached across one-fourth of the earth's circumference; a Constitution stretched to cover the most tightly interlocked, advanced industrial civilization in the world, in a nation in which the children of the pioneers, and descendants of those who wrote the Constitution, were but one among many minorities and the children of slaves.

It was at 7:45 that proceedings began, as the gavel came down and Peter Rodino said, ". . . I as the chairman have been guided by a simple principle . . . that the law must deal fairly with every man. . . . It is now almost fifteen centuries since the Emperor Justinian . . . established this principle for the free citizens of Rome. Seven centuries have now passed since the English barons proclaimed the same principle by compelling King John, at the point of the sword, to accept a great doctrine of Magna Carta, the doctrine that the king, like each of his subjects, was under God and the law. . . . We have reached the moment when we are ready to debate resolutions whether or not the Committee of the Judiciary should recommend that the House of Representatives adopt articles calling for the impeachment of Richard M. Nixon. Make no mistake about it. This is a turning point, whatever we decide. Our judgment is not concerned with an individual but with a system of Constitutional government. . . ."

And they were off, each member allowed fifteen minutes to make a statement, in order of seniority, and one began to follow the debate intent on the occasion rather than the substance, bemused by the faces and sounds of voices: Hutchinson, white-haired, clean-mannered, dogged, pleading for a delay. Donohue of Massachusetts, his speech obviously written by an aide, his voice hoarse, with the rasp of old-time Massachusetts Democratic politicians. Then McClory, Republican of Illinois, his skull gleaming, his voice vigorous, midwestern. And with McClory, suddenly one detected a political wobble—a trouble in his mind: the

President's rejection of House subpoenas bothered Mc-Clory, bothered him more than anything else. Then Brooks, Democrat of Texas, violence in his voice: "This committee has heard evidence of governmental corruption unequaled in the history of the United States, the cover-up of crimes, obstructing the prosecution of criminals, surreptitious entries, wiretapping. . . . Never in our 198 years have we had evidence of such rampant corruption in government."

No particular distinction marked the discourse until the call came to Robert Kastenmeier, Democrat of Wisconsin, a soft-voiced man, starting with a soothing conversational tone and then picking up an intensity that held the room in hush.

"Impeachment is the one way in which the American people can say to themselves that they care enough about their institutions, their own freedom and their own claim to self-government, their own national honor, to purge from the Presidency anyone who has dishonored that office . . . Justice Brandeis," went on Kastenmeier, "warned Americans of the dangers of illegality of official conduct. 'In a government of laws,' he wrote, 'the existence of the government will be imperiled if it fails to observe the law scrupulously. Our government is the potent, the omnipresent teacher. For good or for ill, it teaches the whole people by its example. Crime is contagious. If government becomes a law breaker, it breeds contempt for the law. It invites every man to become a law unto himself. It invites anarchy.' Mr. Chairman, in my view Richard Nixon has shown disrespect for the citizens of this nation and he has violated their Constitution and their laws, engaging in official wrongdoing. Society, through its elected representatives, must condemn this conduct. Otherwise we will cease to have a government of laws. I will, therefore, vote for the impeachment of Richard M. Nixon and I do this with the belief that the House of Representatives will agree and that his trial in the Senate will result in his conviction and removal from office."

A pause. Sandman of New Jersey, his voice a snarl reminiscent of Joe McCarthy's twenty years before, rasping a tight defense of the President. Don Edwards of California, following, and predictable. By now the heat of the bodies in the audience jammed on little folding chairs was beginning to overcome the air-conditioning, warming up the room uncomfortably, smoke eddying toward the vents. Then Railsback spoke.

A tall man, speaking in pensive tones, his hair thinning, there was, even as Railsback began, a melancholy, a suppressed anguish as his voice spoke in the upper tenor register: ". . . I have agonized over this particular inquiry. . . . I regard it as an awesome responsibility, one that I did not relish at all, one that is particularly difficult for me because we are considering a man, Richard Nixon, who has twice been in my district campaigning for me, that I regard as a friend, that he only treated me kindly whenever I had occasion to be with him. . . . (who) has done many wonderful things for this country . . . and someday the historians are going to realize the contributions that he has made. . . ."

Railsback leaned forward into the camera, and it was obvious he was talking to his own people back home in his own district, who had voted for Richard Nixon by a majority of 62 percent, and he was explaining how he had come to his conclusions, explaining to them as if he were explaining to himself, dismissing all other charges, ITT, or contributions from dairymen, or bombings in Cambodia. His problems were those he wanted to share with his constituents, he said.

"They relate to what I would call abuse of power. I cannot think of any area where a conservative or a moderate or a liberal should be more concerned about the state of our government." And Railsback continued in the devastating narrative style Sam Ervin had introduced a year before. He cited the abuse of the Internal Revenue Service on September 11th, 1972; and the fact the President had encouraged John Dean to use the IRS against political opponents four days later and had called George Shultz a "candyass" for not cracking down on political opponents. He continued through the President's use of the CIA to halt the investigation of the FBI into the break-in; rhetorically questioning and answering himself, he alternately peered at camera and looked down to the transcripts and his notes: The events of March 21st, and the President's accession to blackmail— "Well, for Christ's sake, get it"; on from there to the President's conversations with Henry Petersen; and the fact that in this process of justice, having promised Petersen to keep grand-jury information secret, Nixon had immediately shared it with those under suspicion. And on to the problem of the subpoenas, the President concealing information, and then, concluding, "Some of my friends from Illinois . . . some of my people say that the country cannot afford to impeach a President. Let me say to these people . . . I have spoken to countless others including many, many young people, and if the young people in this country think that we are not going to really try to get to the truth, you are going to see the most frustrated people, the most turned-off people, the most disillusioned people, and it is going to make the period of LBJ in 1968, 1967 look tame."

Railsback was not just an ordinary Congressman; he was of importance; a member of the conservative Chowder-and-Marching Society of Republicans on the Hill; a man whose impact on House Republicans could be sweeping. No junior Republican like Cohen, or Butler, or Hogan could match him in influence.

It was not until shortly after ten the next morning that the President received his first real defense, from Wiggins of California, a man with silver hair, broad forehead, burly shoulders, his voice slow, masculine, full of pauses and the absolute mastery of a good lawyer over the facts of his client's case.

"I cannot express adequately the depth of my feeling," he said, "that this case must be decided according to the law, and on no other basis. The law, you see, establishes a common metric for judging human behavior. . . . If we were, ladies and gentlemen, to decide this case on any other basis than the law, and the evidence applicable thereto, it occurs to me, my colleagues, that we would be doing a greater violence to the Constitution than any misconduct alleged to Richard Nixon. . . . In the context of the law . . . personalities become irrelevant. . . . I am not going to attempt to state the law of this case in any great detail within the time allotted to me now, but I think that it probably can be characterized in the one word, fairness. Fairness is the fundamental law of these proceedings."

Wiggins was rocking back and forth now, his voice booming.

"We would be doing violence to that fundamental principle, it seems to me, if we approach these proceedings with

any preconceived notions of the guilt of the President. . . .
he is entitled to a presumption of innocence. . . . The law
requires that we decide the case on the evidence. . . . It
must trouble you, Mr. Doar . . . to consider the evidence
as distinguished from the material. . . . Thirty-eight books
of material. My guess, Mr. Doar, (is) you can put all of
the admissible evidence in half of one book. . . . Simple
theories . . . are inadequate. That is not evidence. A suppo-
sition, however persuasive, is not evidence. A bare possibility
that something might have happened is not evidence. . . ."

Wiggins was now off, speaking in the narrative style that
came to dominate the hearings. "I pick two issues because
it is evident that some members here are concerned." Then,
in a passage of forensic brilliance, Wiggins discoursed on
how the CIA had been misused. Like St. Clair, the President's lawyer, Wiggins would not deny wrongdoing within
the administration; admitted that there were "misdeeds" by
others, specifically John Dean and John Ehrlichman. ". . .
That was a wrongful act," he said, but "There is not a
word, not a word, ladies and gentlemen, of Presidential
knowledge of awareness or involvement in that wrongful
act."

He had made his point just as his time ran out. On this
point, and others like it, he would build the ablest defense
of the President until, only eight days later, he would learn
that the pivot point of his entire defense was false, because
the President had been false to his defenders.

Thursday's session ran on through noon, resumed at
1:30, resumed again in the evening and closed at 10:45.
Friday's sessions began in the morning, continued for a full
afternoon and through the evening, closing at almost midnight. The hearings resumed in the early afternoon of Saturday and again at four o'clock. All day Wednesday and
Thursday, Congressmen had made their statements; on Friday, the hard-core Nixon men had lashed the majority, pin-
ioning their counter-attack on "specificity," the need of
specific charges to remove a President. On Friday evening,
the Democrats reorganized, and all through that long session and into the next day they joined as a chorus, with
Waldie of California as chorus master, taking up the broken thread of narrative, hour after hour, in five-minute

snatches, talking not to each other but to the television audience, spinning the long story out.

It was a hot and muggy week, and yet tired reporters and even more weary committeemen clung to the thread of argument in the chamber, almost careless of events outside. On Thursday, the Supreme Court affirmed one of the great theses of Richard Nixon's administration, one of the underpinnings of his 1972 landslide—that the compulsory busing of schoolchildren could indeed be limited, and that forced busing must not wipe out local governments' jurisdiction over the children of their communities. But this week it seemed like a story of secondary magnitude. On Friday, the newspapers reported that 1,160 men had been killed in South Vietnam in a battle at Danang—but these were no longer American troops being killed; Nixon had pulled them out. The Washington *Star* ran the story on page two. Other papers buried it.

Inside the chamber, the hearings pulsed with a life of their own, unknown Congressmen or -women suddenly making themselves into distinct personalities—like Congresswoman Holtzman of Brooklyn, young, slight, frail, beginning in a quavering, uncertain voice, then through the days acquiring timbre and stab and self-confidence. There were stars, like Barbara Jordan of Texas, a large black woman sitting either with arms folded, leaning forward, or slouched far back on her seat, suddenly loosing a flow of Churchillian eloquence, of resonance, boom and grip so compelling as to make one forget to take notes—and remind oneself that here was a new force to be reckoned with in years to come.

There were jokesters—Hungate of Missouri, in particular, telling Missouri stories, and replying to the Republican challenge for direct proof by remarking that if an elephant walked into the room, his adversaries would demand proof that it wasn't a mouse with a glandular disorder. And Cohen, topping that with a Maine parable about circumstantial evidence—that if you went to bed at night with the ground bare and woke in the morning to see it covered with snow, then it was a reasonable presumption that snow had fallen at night. There were the low blows—of Latta of Ohio attempting a smear of Minority Counsel Albert Jenner for having defended the civil rights of prostitutes. There were the hard, mind-wrenching politics of some Presidential defenders. Mayne, Republican of Iowa, recalled a reality Democrats preferred to ignore: he pointed out that the Senate had spent more than $2,000,000 investigating Watergate, the House another $1,500,000, countless lawyers and hundreds of investigative reporters had been engaged in tracking down the irregularities of this President. But no one had ever investigated Lyndon Johnson, who had arrived in Congress, stone poor, at a Congressional salary of $10,000, had never been paid more than $22,500 a year until he became Vice-President in 1961, and yet had "acquired a multi-million dollar empire based on monopolistic licenses granted by the Federal government in the lucrative teleivision and radio industry." There was the punctuation of a bomb threat the first night as the chamber was cleared of people; there were young protesters another night, screaming and being thrown out; there were the hasty lunches and gobbled dinners between sessions—but nothing could divert those involved from the grip of the proceedings.

The moment of decision came early Saturday evening, after a long day of parliamentary maneuver. The maneuvers, the courtesies, the votes on amendments, and amendments to amendments to strike or substitute were all confusing. But, listening, one realized that these sterile courtesies were in themselves part of the grace of the process, the inherited wisdom of the past requiring that a President be removed not by beheading in Whitehall, as was Charles of England, or in the Place de la Révolution, as was Louis XVI of France—but just this way, by meticulous procedure.

The roll-calls all day Saturday had been difficult to follow. But just before seven in the evening, with the penultimate roll-call, technical as it was, came the crucial question: to substitute the text of Paul Sarbanes for that of Harold Donohue as Article I, Obstruction of Justice. The Donohue resolution had been a partisan Democratic resolution. The Sarbanes substitute had been worked out during the week by Republicans, Southern conservatives and liberal Democrats.

The last Congressman officially allotted time before this climax roll-call was Walter Flowers of Alabama. And it was obvious, as one listened, that this Southern conservative was lifting the story to another level—from the present case against Richard Nixon to the judgment of the future, when others might weigh what he and his companions of this committee had done. For Flowers was talking of power in this last allotted five minutes.

"Make no mistake, my friends, one of the effects of our action here will be to reduce the influence and the power of the Office of the President. To what extent will be determined only by future action in the House or in the Senate. . . . That is what we are doing here. But we will and should be judged by our willingness to share in the many hard choices that must be made for our nation. . . . In the weeks and months ahead I want my friends to know that I will be around to remind them when some of these hard choices are up, and we will be able to judge then how responsible we can be with our newly found Congressional power."

A short intervention then by Fish of New York. An attempted intervention by McClory of Illinois. Then, Rodino, speaking as chairman: "The question is before us and . . . I am going to put the question." A voice vote first, the ayes booming in a majority, the nays loud but decidedly fewer. Rodino: "The clerk will call the roll."

Each knew that the television camera was on him as he spoke his aye or no. There was no glee, no exultation, as each voted. First, the roster of the Democrats, a cascade of ayes—Sarbanes downcast, Jordan's arms folded in judgment, Holtzman frowning, Mezvinsky's face down and inscrutable, Rangel keeping score, head down also. Then to the Republicans, to Rodino's left, and the resounding no of Hutchinson, the first mark of vigor from the aging gentleman in the entire proceedings. Then McClory, followed by Smith and Sandman, "No." Then the "Aye" of Railsback, first Republican to vote against the President; followed by two more nos; and one aye from Hamilton Fish. Then a no from Wiley Mayne, and three successive ayes as the call moved to the younger Republicans on the lower tier. Aye from Hogan, from Butler, from Cohen, and the rest was perfunctory except for a surprising aye from Froehlich of Wisconsin, who had taken little part in the proceedings. The last vote from Rodino himself—in a very hoarse voice, his face staring directly at camera: "Aye." A hush. Then Rodino saying, "The clerk will report" and the clerk: "Twenty-seven members have voted aye, eleven members have voted no." Five minutes past seven, Saturday evening, July 27th, 1974.[1]

This session was now about to break up, and the reporters and cameramen were on tiptoe to rush from their seats and catch the last wisp of wisdom or last chance quote for history, but there must be another roll-call, a technical one, to accept the Sarbanes text not as a substitute but as the operative first article of impeachment. That was over in moments by the same vote, 27 to 11. And one saw Doar getting out of his seat stiffly, as if his back ached, creaking as he rose; and then he was overwhelmed by the rush of press to the benches.

James Naughton of the *New York Times* best summed up the end in his superb dispatch on the hearings. Rodino had cleared the room very swiftly after the proceedings had closed—he had been told that a Kamikaze plane had just taken off from the National Airport on a mission to crash into the Rayburn Building. Rodino then went, wrote Naughton, "to his cubbyhole office to look out the window for the Kamikaze plane. No plane appeared. Mr. Rodino sat, as if at the wake of a friend, speaking of inconsequential things with Mr. Doar. Suddenly he rose without a word and walked from the office. And cried."

Neither tears nor Kamikazes could alter or affect what had happened to America in the previous two years.

The committee suspended its sessions on Sunday. Proceeded to pass (by 28 to 10) an impeachment article, II, for Abuse of Power on Monday, setting forth the limits of authority on which a Congress was prepared to stand and fight, stating in essence that this Congress could not trust this President. And on Tuesday, it passed (by 21 to 17) a third article of impeachment, with little debate, summoning Nixon to trial for refusing to obey the subpoenas of Congress necessary to an inquiry on his fitness for leadership. It rejected all other charges and suspended hearings. But by

[1] See Appendix A for texts of the Articles of Impeachment.

then the hidden tapes of June 23rd had been heard at the White House by the President's own inner guard of last defense; and they, too, had rejected him.[2]

What had happened, as Flowers pointed out, was that the action of this committee was a passing of powers in the American Constitutional system. The powers of all future Presidents might be reduced because Richard Nixon had abused them. Much of that power would pass to Congress —but Congress had yet to prove its fitness to govern the nation. Much would pass elsewhere—to the press and to the bureaucracy. The United States government was entering on a period when it must re-think all of its political processes, measure its old myths against its new realities; and there was no confidence that it could do so in time to meet crises at home and abroad.

[2] See Chapter One.

13

BREACH OF FAITH

The true crime of Richard Nixon was simple: he destroyed the myth that binds America together, and for this he was driven from power.

The myth he broke was critical that somewhere in American life there is at least one man who stands for law, the President. That faith surmounts all daily cynicism, all evidence or suspicion of wrongdoing by lesser leaders, all corruptions, all vulgarities, all the ugly compromises of daily striving and ambition. That faith holds that all men are equal before the law and protected by it; and that no matter how the faith may be betrayed elsewhere, at one particular point—the Presidency—justice will be done beyond prejudice, beyond rancor, beyond the possibility of a fix. It was that faith that Richard Nixon broke, betraying those who voted for him even more than those who voted against him.

All civilizations rest on myths, but in America myths have exceptional meaning. A myth is a way of pulling together the raw and contradictory evidence of life as it is known in any age. It lets people make patterns in their own lives, within the larger patterns. Primitive people saw the forces at work as sun gods, moon gods, war gods, and prayed to them. Judaic civilization rested on the belief in the One Almighty, and Roman civilization on the myth of the Republic. So, too, did later states and civilizations rest on myths—whether of the mandate of Heaven (as in China), or on the divinity of kings (as in medieval Europe), or on the Hegelian dialectic (as in the Marxist states of our times).

There is, however, an absolutely vital political difference between the mythology of other nations and the mythology of America. Other states may fall or endure; they may change or refresh their governing myths. But Frenchmen will always remain Frenchmen, Russians will be Russians, Germans remain Germans, and Englishmen—Englishmen. Nationhood descends from ancestral loins. One can easily contemplate the British Royal Navy becoming the People's Royal Navy, its remaining salts cheering alike for Comrades Horatio Nelson, Francis Drake and Wat Tyler. But America is different. It is the only peaceful multi-racial civilization in the world. Its people come of such diverse heritages of religion, tongue, habit, fatherhood, color and folk song that if America did not exist it would be impossible to imagine that such a gathering of alien strains could ever behave like a nation. Such a stewpot civilization might be possible for city-states—a Tangier, a Singapore, a Trieste. But for so mixed a society to extend over a continent, to master the most complicated industrial structure the world has ever known, to create a state that has spread its power all around the globe—that would be impossible unless its people were bound together by a common faith. Take away that faith, and America would be a sad geographical expression where whites killed blacks, blacks killed whites; where Protestants, Catholics, Jews made of their cities a constellation of Belfasts; where each community within the whole would harden into jangling, clashing contentions of prejudices and interests that could be governed only by police.

Politics in America is the binding secular religion; and that religion begins with the founding faith of the Declaration of Independence, "We hold these truths to be self-evident, that all men are created equal, that they are endowed by their creator with certain unalienable rights, that among these are life, liberty, and the pursuit of happiness."

These words were written by men who had taken the best ideas of their English-speaking heritage and made them universal. Such language was almost incomprehensible to the non-English-speaking peoples who were drawn to America later in ever growing numbers seeking the promise. But the ideas were compelling, and still compel. The ideas could be couched in inflammatory political phrases: "No taxation without representation" or "Give me liberty or give me death." They could be robed in legal phrases, or juridical admonitions against illegal search and seizure; guarantees of right to trial; guarantees of freedom of assembly, free speech, free press and, for the first time in history, the guarantee that the state would support no "establishment of religion." Most important of all, the original political myths promised "equal justice under law" and its consort, "due process of law." Though the millions of strangers who came here to become Americans could not read the notes, the melody of those phrases gripped them.

Of all the political myths out of which the Republic was born, however, none was more hopeful than the crowning myth of the Presidency—that the people, in their shared wisdom, would be able to choose the best man to lead them. From this came a derivative myth—that the Presidency, the supreme office, would make noble any man who held its responsibility. The office would burn the dross from his character; his duties would, by their very weight, make him a superior man, fit to sustain the burden of the law, wise and enduring enough to resist the clash of all selfish interests.

That myth held for almost two centuries. A man of limited experience like George Washington was transformed, almost magically, into one of the great creative architects of politics, fashioning a state and an administration out of nothing, a work of governmental art equal to that of a Lenin or a Mao. An ambitious politician like Abraham Lincoln of Illinois could, in the crucible of the Presidency, be refined to a nobility of purpose and a compassion that hallow his name. A snob like Franklin D. Roosevelt and his missionary wife, Eleanor, could find in themselves and give to their country a warmth, a humanity, a charity that make them universal symbols of mercy and strength.

Within all the myths, thus, the myth of the Presidency was crucial in the action against Richard Nixon. Many stupid, hypocritical and limited men had reached that office. But all, when publicly summoned to give witness, chose to honor the legends—or, if they had to break with them, broke only to meet a national emergency.

Richard Nixon behaved otherwise. His lawlessness exploded the legends. He left a nation, approaching the 200th anniversary of its glorious independence, with a President and a Vice-President neither of whom had been chosen by the people. The faith was shattered; and being shattered, it was to leave American politics more fluid and confused than ever since the Civil War.

Richard Nixon's legacy is best understood as a set of questions—questions that reach back for years, that reach forward for decades, questions about ourselves and what we seek from government.

The simplest set of questions can be embraced and answered in the formula of popular detective stories: Who did it?

Like any popular detective story, this is a story of bungling criminals. It begins with the circumstance, very difficult for Richard Nixon's enemies to accept, that most of the top men involved were devout patriots, convinced that what they were doing was best for their country. Men like Ehrlichman, Haldeman, Krogh were true believers in the purpose of America as they saw it, and sought nothing for themselves. Indeed, their self-righteousness made them far more frightening than men like John Mitchell, who was a rogue of a recognizable type, a cynic of fading health and energy who saw the crimes coming and failed to act. Beneath came all the others, men of little patriotism and no principle, as self-seeking as their enemies saw them—the hustlers, the bullies and all the crawling creatures of the underground, men set in motion by nothing more than ambition, and whose authority came from the self-righteous moralists at the top.

They entered into government, all of them, with no greater knowledge of how power works than the intrigues of the political antechambers and the folklore of advance men—and were quickly off into a dark land.

They were tantalized by the temptations of power, particularly the abuses of it they had found in Washington after the departure of Lyndon Johnson. Too many of the subordinate instruments of intelligence of the American government —the CIA, the FBI, the defense intelligence agencies—had crossed the threshold of law years before. They were there to be used. The clumsy break-in at Democratic headquarters in 1972 by Nixon men was technically criminal but of no uglier morality than the spying at Barry Goldwater's headquarters which Howard Hunt of the CIA had supervised for Lyndon Johnson in 1964. Their penchant for wire-tapping must certainly have been stimulated by the wire-tapping authorized by Johnson against the Nixon campaign of 1968. Their little early illegalities must have come naturally—and must have seemed only a step beyond those of their predecessors.

Still, there was nothing inevitable about the ultimate Nixon tragedy as the affiar took root in early 1969 and 1970. But the political leaders of the Nixon administration, though they were experts at administration and professionals in politics, were amateurs in government.

They could not understand the essential balance there must always be in large affairs between cynicism and suspicion on the one hand and faith and trust on the other. A naïve politician gets nowhere he flounders in passion, manipulation, prejudice, greed, interests. A successful politician must, inescapably, be something of a hypocrite, promising all to all, knowing that, if elected, he must inevitably sacrifice the interests of some for others. But a man in government must know when to choose trust and faith over political need. If exposure of his acts threatens to contradict his words, he must renounce his acts and keep his word, because the people must trust his words at whatever cost—or he cannot govern. In the Presidency, *a fortiori*, where the words are the words of the High Priest, it is essential to recognize the moment for truth.

That moment came first, for Richard Nixon, on June 20th, 1972, when he and Haldeman discussed the lawless break-in at Watergate during the previous weekend. The lost clue in the detective-story "whodunit" still remains the deliberate erasure of eighteen and a half minutes of that morning's conversation. Did they recognize the difference between what the partisan politics of the campaign required and what the responsibility of the Presidency required? Did they measure the extent of their gamble? No one but Nixon can know who erased that tape later, or for what reason. But the two top men of the administration—Nixon and Haldeman—must at least have exchanged surmises as to how the break-in came about and what they should do about it. The extent, if any, of their first recognition of responsibility is forever lost. By June 23rd, however, three days later, came a clear act of obstruction of justice—the attempt to use the CIA to halt the FBI's investigation of the crime. Straining as hard as imagination permitted, and if one drew on no other evidence, one could persuade one's self from the transcript of that conversation that here were two malicious politicians simply playing dirty tricks without any awareness of what government is supposed to mean.

There was as yet nothing inevitable about the great explosion to come. For the first weeks after the burglary, it was possible for the President to purge himself simply by calling for or permitting the indictment of two men, John Mitchell and Jeb Magruder. Nixon would have had to butcher these two aides; this would have been painful. But as President he would have been faithfully executing the law and so would have retained his Presidency—and with it the power, as a politician, to pardon later those who had served him fervently but neither wisely nor well. Indeed, in those early weeks, before John Mitchell committed perjury, it would have been difficult for even the most effective prosecutor to have persuaded a District of Columbia jury that the nodding acquiescence of the faltering old man was in fact complicity in crime, or participation in a conspiracy. But Mitchell's reputation would have had to be sacrificed and with it his dignity, for he would then have been exposed as a fool. And Magruder's freedom would have had to be sacrificed, for he was then already a criminal.

By the time of the election of 1972, however, too much more had happened, with or without the President's knowledge, for him to have satisfied the law without sacrificing not only Mitchell and Magruder but also his personal lawyer, Kalmbach, his official lawyer, John Dean, and probably his personal aides, Haldeman and Ehrlichman. Of their precise complicities in cover-up the President was either unwitting or could make himself appear to have been unwitting. His lying had already begun—tentatively but undeniably.

By early April of 1973, he could no longer even make himself appear unwitting. In March he had come under blackmail and had begun to learn all the details of the bungled cover-up. This pained his neat mind, for the cover-up was grotesquely mismanaged, hilariously inefficient, his white-collar managers proving themselves hideously incompetent at what Mafiosi could do skillfully. Not only that: by April, 1973, the news system had the story in raw outline, by May in detail, and by midsummer the Ervin Committee had put face, flesh and voice to the drama in public. Yet Nixon persisted in concealment. And it was his persistence in the cover-up that gave the motor energy to the charges of obstruction of justice, Article I of impeachment.

This persistence in the cover-up led, however, to drama of a greater order—the search for evidence. And when the evidence, the tapes and the internal White House memoranda began to unfold, they revealed a more shattering hidden story: that of abuse of power. In that story, quickly or slowly, everyone interested in American politics began to see the fundamental threat—the threat to the future, the threat that moved the most thoughtful members of the Judiciary Committee to vote for Nixon's impeachment. If such practices had occurred before, they had occurred secretly. Now they were public. If they were to be accepted publicly and not repudiated, then all future Presidents would be free to break the same laws Nixon had broken.

The challenge to the myth was open. If the Judiciary Committee did not act, the office of the Presidency would be transformed. And then there would be no faith, no real strength in America, no compelling reason for men to stand and fight or die in jungles or in air, nor even to behave decently to one another as law-abiding citizens.

From mid-April of 1973 to his end in 1974, the President lied; lied again; continued to lie; and his lying not only fueled the anger of those who were on his trail, but slowly, irreversibly, corroded the faith of Americans in that President's honor. He knew what he was doing, for he consciously relied on the mystique of the Presidency to carry him through what lay ahead. Very little in all the transcripts of his conversations is more poignant than an interchange in one of the last recorded with Bob Haldeman—a telephone conversation on April 25th, 1973, when their front of deception was being broken, but hope still lived. "Bring it out and fight it out and it'll be a bloody goddamned thing," said Nixon to Haldeman that day as they recognized how damning John Dean's testimony might be. But, admitting that the fight would be "rough as a cob," Nixon continued, "we'll survive. . . . Despite all the polls and all the rest, I think there's still a hell of lot of people out there, and from what I've seen they're—you know, they, they want to believe, that's the point, isn't it?"

If Nixon had committed a historic crime—treason, or accepting graft, or knowingly warping American national policy for personal or partisan ends—the detective story would suffice. Its answer to the question is that the criminals were caught because they were bunglers.

But the initial crime was so commonplace; and Nixon might have erased it so easily by acting as Presidents must act against lawbreakers; and he compounded that crime so casually into the cover-up and disaster, that another set of questions presses on—not how the criminals were caught, but why Nixon did what he was caught doing.

"Why?" is a political question and one that will overhang American politics for years to come. Nixon was not a stupid man. What did he think he was defending beyond his own skin and reputation?

To get at the political answer, on must discard the criminal-story approach and approach the facts as a political detective story.

Many clues mislead or confuse, as in all detective stories. There is, for example, the almost absurd love of money which underlay so much of Richard Nixon's behavior—his use, for example, of government purse and government facilities to give him the comforts which many poor men can only imagine. But other Presidents—Eisenhower and Johnson, too—had shared this absurd love of money. Nixon's personal avarice turned out to be irrelevant—no one bought, bribed or paid either the President or any of those closest to him for favors which personally enriched them. There is the bizarre shakedown of great corporations and industrialists organized by his campaign financers—but his operators were acting not out of personal greed but out of managerial zeal and competitive instinct, tracking down the same big game of fat cats their rivals hunted, only with more enthusiasm, lawlessness and efficiency than ever before. And there is no record of any such corporation or contributors' group, from ITT to the milk producers, having succeeded in buying favor from the Nixon administration or its agencies remotely comparable to the secret lease in 1922 of Naval oil reserves at Elk Hills and Teapot Dome by Edward

L. Doheny and Harry F. Sinclair, who "loaned" or paid $100,000 and $223,000 respectively to Secretary of the Interior Albert B. Fall. There are all sorts of other clues and facts, from the bloody (like the bombing of Cambodia) to the technical (like the impoundment of funds). But they, too, lead one off the trail.

To trace the answers to the question of "Why?" one must accept the political reality that Richard Nixon and his men were, for the first time in American politics since 1860, carrying on an ideological war. Because they felt their purpose was high and necessary and the purpose of their enemies dangerous or immoral, he and his men believed that the laws did not bind them—or that the laws could legitimately be bent.

Again one must go back to a set of American myths to explain the intensity of the ideological war that began in the decade of the sixties—the war simplifiers see as the struggle over "government controls."

Wrapped around the original political myths of America —of liberty, of equality, of a government-of-laws-not-men —had been a culture, long since demolished, with a set of social myths now twisted by time and Talmudic exegesis into the rigid political dogmas of today.

The old social myths rested on the underbracing belief that a free citizen was able to control his own future by his own efforts. In the original American community of farmers 200 years ago, when rich and fertile lands spread unplowed beyond the Alleghenies, it was considered a matter of gumption and go, of thrift and diligence and planning, whether a man made it or did not. Accident, or drought, or a bad harvest might prevent him from reaping what he sowed—but next year might bring better luck. Government was the town meeting, which built roads to the city to sell the harvest or, on a Federal scale, opened roads over the Alleghenies to the fertile loam of the Midwest. But in corporate America, since the turn of the twentieth century, fewer and fewer men have been able to control their own future by their own efforts—except lucky speculators or the very rich who controlled their family future by wisely sheltering the fortunes that came down to them from their fathers. Now, in a present-day America, everyone was locked up—in corporations, in unions, in organizations, in schools, in draft boards, in the tax net—and group leverage was the thing. Nixon and his men believed in the old social myths and the old culture; his adversaries believed in mobilizing group leverage to compel the Federal government to do their will or protect their future. Nixon and his men believed in no free rides. His adversaries believed that government must provide the ride. Translated into practical politics, the old social myths gave no guidance on how you provided jobs or security for all in an industrial society, how you made sure the paycheck would stretch with inflationary prices, how you protected people in old age when there was no hearth to warm them, no village green where they could sit and sun, no family to nurse them.

The old myths extolled self-government. In a beautiful political symmetry, the states and the Federal government originally agreed that each had separate responsibilities, and after that, the states worked out the powers of counties, villages, towns, cities, giving them large subordinate responsibilities. But in practice, by the 1960's, the heart of the problem lay in the cities and suburbs—how you moved resources down to local governments so they could meet their local responsibilities; and secondly, whether the Federal government would or should insist that local governments adjust to the national cultural requirements of the day.

But the most deceptive inherited social myth was of American power. The virulence of that myth was fresh—and rested on the fleeting dominance of American arms as they spread triumphant over the entire globe in 1945, when, from the Golden Gate to Karachi, from the rim of the Atlantic all the way to the Middle East, no plane flew the globe except under the surveillance or with the permission of American might. Americans fight their wars with a singular moral ferocity that is the terror of their enemies; strangers who see the American planes winging in overhead must regard them as the Christian world regarded the Arab horsemen of the seventh and eighth centuries. Not only that —Americans were accustomed to carry this moral ferocity into home politics while they fought their wars, ostracizing entire social groups, choking free discussion at home, seeking enemies hidden among themselves, granting autocratic powers to the President who must command the war effort.

What had happened, however, by the sixties, was that the myth of American power had been substantially eroded by the revolutions of the post-war world. Americans were confronted with a new reality—they were engaged in the first major war that they would not win. By the time Nixon came to power, that realization had split the country at every level, and resentment at the waste and killing in Vietnam had spilled out into the street in sputtering violence and frightening bloodshed.

Nixon had, to be sure, recognized the erosion of American power abroad. As soon as he was inaugurated in 1969, he had begun to liquidate the war in Vietnam, the first strategic retreat of American arms since George Washington yielded the cities of the Atlantic seaboard to the British. But he clung to the old doctrine that the President must command this retreat, that the President alone could make the decisions and arrange the timing for a withdrawal from Asia that would bring peace with honor. Those who opposed him, whether in the streets or in the news system, he would treat with the moral ferocity of previously sanctioned wars. He had come out of one war a veteran; moved up in politics at the time of the Korean War, at the height of the anti-Red hysteria of the late forties and early fifties. He had won his first national fame by trapping Alger Hiss. Hiss, a trusted officer of the State Department, had been dealing with Whittaker Chambers, a member of the Communist conspiracy. Of his role in that case Nixon made the first chapter of his book, *Six Crises*—and he would never forget, nor let his closest aides forget, about Alger Hiss. For him and for them, the enemies of America were present as much within the government as overseas. His distrust of the servants of government began then, and continued to the end. The idea of ever present conspiracy blurred and merged always in his political thinking with the political issues which his ideological enemies thrust at him.

The real domestic political issues had been growing increasingly divisive for years before Nixon came to power: How could the cities be helped to meet their responsibilities? How far should the Federal government go in support of education? At what price to the whites must the needs of the blacks be met? How should the government go about making a national welfare system reasonable? What price must be paid to clean the environment of a pollution that all recognized as a menace? Here, in modern politics, very few of the old social myths helped either explain or shape the new realities that demanded confrontation.

And one divisive question above all was tearing at America when Nixon came to power: What right did the government have to conscript American men to kill people in other countries in order to save those countries?

The political detective story of Nixon's crime begins there—with his belief that he, as President, was sole custodian of America's power. The Nixon men saw themselves as waging war in Vietnam to make peace. They had no doubt that national security required them to carry on that war by all means possible until peace with honor had been won. If the end was good, then the means, however brutal, must also be good. And from this concept of the President's authority came most of the early illegalities, the buggings, the wire-taps, the surveillances, the minor crimes. Until finally the President's men saw no distinction between ends and means, and they were making war not just in Vietnam but all across the home front, too. All the disputes over home issues, as well as foreign issues, were sucked into the vortex of ideological war; and, as in war, victory became the only goal and the means savage.

But the political story does not quite answer the "Why?" or explain the particular ferocity of behavior of the men at the White House.

To explain the venom and hatred of their struggle, one must add one more condition—the change of culture that was taking place all over America of the sixties. All great political conflicts, everywhere, are underlain by a struggle of cultures, as men begin to see their places in the world differently, as their "consciousness" is "raised" to new perceptions and indignations. And the political struggle of the sixties and the early seventies was taking place at just such a moment of cultural upheaval. The Nixon men were men of the embattled old culture. As such, they believed the new culture was not only undermining the authority of their President to make war-and-peace, but striking into their homes, families and schools, too. It was undermining the values with which they had grown up and still held dear.

The beardies and the long-hairs, the bikini-clad and mini-skirted merged in their minds with the rioters, the street demonstrators, the draft-card burners, the sex revolutionaries. They had no great literate spokesmen to speak for their side; but as politicians and manipulators they could fight back by the code of the jungle.

This conflict of the two cultures far surpassed in emotion the traditional American political struggle between "conservatives" and "liberals." Both cultures now shared only one word, "freedom," which came down from the original political myths. But that word, as it always had, concealed the practical conundrum—one man's total freedom meant curtailing some other man's freedom. The prosperity of the sixties had incubated so many experiments, so many dreams, had opened so many avenues for self-exploration that now the concept of individual liberty or community responsibility carried totally different meanings on different lips. There were the people of the old culture who still felt no one should be allowed to threaten close-knit family life; who felt a choke in their throats when the flag passed by; who felt the Bible was an eternally true code of morals which teachers ought to be free to read in class; who felt that neatness in dress, diligence in work, neighborliness were visible indexes of good citizenship. But others of the new culture, just as sincere, believed that good family life required free choice in or out of wedlock, that the responsibility of parenthood or personal behavior patterns was theirs alone to decide. A new babbitry of permissiveness confronted an old babbitry of conformity.

The two cultures clashed in every form of expression—in language, in costume, in slogans. They clashed, as political issues between them hardened, over such trivia as pornography and homosexuality. They clashed over much more important matters—civil rights, "law-and-order," safety in the streets, drug abuse, the dignity of women.

Claiming for themselves the undeniable right to lead their own lives and to direct their children's lives as they wanted, the spokesmen of the new culture paradoxically insisted on ever widening intervention by the government in other people's lives—to tell other people where to send their children to school, where and how to build their homes, where and how to dispose of their wastes. The old

culture insisted that such social controls were dangerous—
but it also insisted, as paradoxically as its adversaries, that
government must have the right to send men to die in an illegal war, that police must have the right to raid without
court warrant the homes of anyone suspected of hiding narcotics.

The line of clash between the two cultures ran through
families as well as communities. Fathers against sons, mothers against daughters, students against teachers, arguing
over such matters as dress and manners and morals and sex
and drugs and rioting. Bob Haldeman wore his hair crew-
cut, his son wore his hair shoulder-length. Within families,
within communities, much of the clash could be translated
as the natural clash between generations—most fathers and
mothers have revolted at some point against their own parents. Long-hairs and short-hairs, beardless and bearded
have succeeded each other in those generations of American heroes whose portraits hang in schoolrooms and the
corridors of the Capital. But now this clash of culture and
personal values was taking place at the same time as the political clash over the hard issues. And the two multiplied
each other emotionally and politically, to conceal the intricate, complex, true problems of American government—
What must be changed in this industrial society where the
old social myths no longer held? How fast the change? How
much control was needed? Who would control? Who must
pay? Who must get hurt?

One must see all three wars—the war abroad, the ideological war, the cultural war—as intersecting in the agony
of an unstable personality in order to answer the personal
"Why?" of Richard Nixon's collapse.

Unless one is satisfied that Nixon is a total hypocrite, a
man of unrelieved brutishness, one must ask how he could
stomach what he authorized and learned about his administration and its underground. And the answer can come only
by imagining that here was a man who could not, in his
waking moments, acknowledge the man he recognized in
his own nightmares—the outsider, the loner, the loser.

Throughout his career, except for a few brief years in
1971 and 1972, that had been his inner role—the outsider,
the loser. "They" were against him, always, from the rich

boys of Whittier College to the hostile establishment that sneered at his Presidency. His authority as President was being challenged by the news system, the rioters, the Congress, the intellectuals. The culture, the manners, the credos of his lonely life of striving were being wiped out by the fashions of the new culture. Nixon could deal masterfully with Russians, Chinese, Arabs of the Middle East by the old set rules of power. But at home the rules were being changed against him, and he was losing. Losers play dirty; he, too, would change the rules. His ruthlessness, vengefulness, nastiness were the characteristics of a man who has seen himself as underdog for so long that he cannot distinguish between real and fancied enemies, a man who does not really care whom he slashes or hurts when pressed, who cannot accept or understand when or what he has won. Thus, then, the portrait of a man who saw himself at Thermopylae or Masada.

Over and over again, as one reads the transcripts of his inner thoughts from the tape recordings, one sees he did consider such matters as honor and faith, and even thought of himself as honorable and faithful. But then he came down, knowingly, against honor, against faith. Cornered by history, he seemed to be defending all at once the authority of the Presidency, his cultural values, his confederates— and his own skin.

And always, in the crisis, he reacted as the cornered loser. He could not shake that characteristic—which made of the election of 1972 not only a political paradox but a personal paradox: the loser had won—and won by such a margin as to unsettle even more stable personalities. He had won so largely that he could misread his victory. It was a victory for his ideas and politics. But he saw it as personal, as a loner. It was not simply an election he had won; he had conquered a land; its citizens were the occupied and he could toy with law as he wished, however much a hostile Congress, the news system or intellectuals protested.

Yet even those who had voted for him in 1972 thought otherwise.

The election of 1972 is one of the great illuminations of American politics. Richard Nixon, unloved and unlovable as he knew himself to be, had won by the greatest margin of all time. Enormous manipulative skill, it is true, had gone into his victory—but the break-ins and lying had contributed nothing to it. Nixon had forced issues to popular clarity better than any President since Roosevelt; McGovern had sharpened them; and on the issues, Nixon won.

Nixon and McGovern had made clear the central cleavage line between them—their differences over the reach of government control, over the meanings of freedom, over how much change the people wanted and how fast. Those differences had been growing ever since Nixon had entered on the national scene. The succession of Democratic candidates whom Nixon fought traces that growth. First, Stevenson, the most eloquent liberal of his time, but a man who now, in retrospect, can be seen as the last of the great civilized conservatives. Next, John F. Kennedy, marginally more liberal than Stevenson, a man of the center, personally elegant, a persuasive advocate of a powerful Presidency. Then Lyndon B. Johnson, a quantum jump in populist liberalism and racial tolerance. Then the candidates of 1968 —Humphrey, Robert Kennedy, McCarthy—another escalation by the Democrats on the liberal scale. And then, in 1972, McGovern, the supreme political moralist who married the liberal idea to the fashion of the new culture. The progression is inescapable—the more liberal the Democratic candidate, the better Nixon did against him until, finally, in 1972, the margin was overwhelming, his mandate real.

Nixon had promised peace and was delivering it. He had promised to free the young men from the twenty-five-year-old draft, and was doing that, too. He had launched the most advanced environmental program in American history, and both air and water were being rid of filth. He had pushed through Congress his historic revenue-sharing plan, and in the small cities and towns of America, where such marginal help could still make a difference, he was a political Santa Claus. On all the major ideological issues between himself and his rival he placed himself against the extension of Federal power, pledging to diminish control, to go slow, to curb the intrusion of law, regulation and Federal dictate in private lives and local communities.

One can single out one issue, at once symbolic, stylistic and crushingly real, to characterize Nixon's campaign of 1972—the school problem that divided black and white communities in the great metropolitan areas of the United States. In one of his finest state papers, Nixon had, in 1970, defined ideologically exactly where he stood on community ways of life in the big cities. No other President had ever done so before; it is worth recalling. "We cannot be free," he said, "and at the same time be required to fit our lives into prescribed places on a racial grid—whether . . . by some mathematical formula or by automatic assignment. . . . An open society does not have to be homogeneous, or even fully integrated. There is room within it for communities. . . . it is natural and right that members of those communities feel a sense of group identity and group pride. In terms of an open society, what matters is mobility: the right and the ability of each person to decide for himself where and how he wants to live, whether as part of the ethnic enclave or as part of the larger society— or, as many do, share the life of both. . . . As we strive to make our schools places of equal educational opportunity, we should keep our eye fixed on this goal; to achieve a set of conditions in which neither the laws nor the institutions supported by law any longer draw an invidious distinction based on race. . . ."

In the jargon of his political technicians, Nixon was wooing "the peripheral urban ethnic vote." But in the common talk of ordinary voters, Richard Nixon was the man who came out flatly against "forced busing" of children out of home neighborhoods to neighborhoods their parents thought dangerous. McGovern's position on busing, on community life, on welfare was never at any moment throughout his campaign really clear. McGovern was for morality. But however sweet and gentle a person he was, no one could be sure he would not push his interpretation of what was moral down to the grass roots, at whatever cost, at whatever liquidation of settled ways of life by anonymous regulators in Washington.

It was on such issues, as much as by his performance abroad, that Nixon engineered his final triumph over his old enemies.

But there was to be no generosity in his victory, no reconciliation. His war went on—to a madness of hubris, to a denial of his own promises. To protect his 1972 victory, in which he had fought for freedom from government control, he proposed to substitute personal control—and he was to use every device, every instrument of power, within or without the law, to sustain it. He deceived both the public and his advisers. He obstructed the working of law. Above all—instead of the disturbing web of ideological controls McGovern threatened to write into law, he tried to impose his own illegal controls, inspired by vindictiveness and self-righteousness. He blasted the fundamental faith that bound ordinary Americans of whatever origin, including his own constituents, to each other and to the country—and destroyed the myth which held that they made the laws and the President they elected would faithfully execute them.

Thus, he gutted his true mandate. Suspicion of government is instinctive in human nature—and healthy, if not carried too far. In a democracy like America, the folklore of this atavistic suspicion has set up the Constitutional safeguards against government's abuse of power. But among Nixon's constituents particularly, this suspicion remains morbid. What they do achieve, they think they achieve on their own. And government, they believe, is the conspiracy that takes away from them what they have earned. They fear and hate the imagined conspiracies of men in government. What Richard Nixon did was to convince them they were right in their suspicion.

And as it all came out—the use of spies, the use of revenue harassment, the blacklists, the cheating, the menace of the self-righteous, the toleration of thuggery—the revolt against Richard Nixon swept those who had voted for him as certainly as those who had always voted against him.

If, at the most charitable interpretation, Richard Nixon's agony of 1973–74 was a defense of the Presidency as well as of himself, then he betrayed that great office, too—for if power was taken from the Presidency of Richard Nixon, as it had to be, it was taken at a moment in American history when a powerful President was more important, more necessary than ever before. He had thus left America with possible tragedy—desperately needing a strong President in a hostile world, yet with all the winds of fashionable opinion blowing against the office, reducing it, risking America's direction on the chancy outcome of a debaters' quarrel of the news system, the Congress and the judiciary.

So much, then, for the simple questions of who, how,

why. The crime was clear at the end. And so was the peril: that government might become free to move against any American, personally, with or without the law.

But then there has to follow a set of questions without answers, for Richard Nixon's legacy, in addition to the peace he left behind, is questions. Where are Americans going? And how will they get there? Those questions, if anyone can find answers to them, are the scenario of the future.

The grab bag of questions starts, of course, with politics. Will Nixon's "new majority" of 1972 endure? That majority was as genuine an expression of will as the Johnson majority of 1964. Johnson blew his majority apart by the Vietnam War. Has Nixon blown apart his majority by breach of faith? Will anyone on the conservative side of the political divide ever again be able honorably to debate those underlying issues of control and freedom without being mocked by the memory of the man who betrayed them? Will he be the Hoover of his time, haunting Republicans for the next twenty years? How much disgrace will the prevailing ideas of 1972 bear in the future because Nixon has disgraced them?

Nixon provoked the new campaign-financing law of 1974. Its new rules will change the nature of American campaigning. They all but eliminate the possibility of new national parties ever again rising from a limited base of opinion; in this sense, they restrict the arena of politics to established parties. But they are primarily designed to throttle the flow of money to the politics of the manipulators. This may be very healthy if the law works—but will it then leave the two great parties to be swept by the hot-eyed, intemperate issue men whose techniques for sweeping a party were tested and proven in the Republican struggle of 1964 and the Democratic struggle of 1972? Will the professionals of the ideological wars replace the bony old regulars of the remote past, or the more skillful professionals of manipulation of the Nixon era? And will these new professionals of ideology prove as unforgiving and vindictive as Nixon's warriors showed themselves to be in their moment of power?

Nixon has left behind a news system more powerful than

ever—made so by its successful struggle with him. His hatred of the news system and his unrelenting effort to crip ple, manipulate, deceive and coerce the leadership of that news system have provoked a counter-hatred which now has a life of its own. Will its suspicion of Richard Nixon be translated into a permanent suspicion of the Presidency itself? The pursuit of Richard Nixon has made folk heroes of investigative reporters. But how much will the folklore of their triumphs inspire a new generation of editors and reporters to consider not only the Presidency but all government as a conspiracy against the people, to be ripped apart perhaps irresponsibly, for years to come? If Nixon has bequeathed to his Presidential successors a permanently hostile news system, he has cursed them all. And he has cursed all the men of House and Senate who might be found, by the press, of insufficient zeal in frustrating a President, any President, whether he merit it or not.

Such questions lead on to the relationship of President and Congress. The Nixon disaster has ushered in the new 94th Congress—overwhelmingly Democratic, refreshingly vigorous, more determined than any Congress since 1866 to curb Presidential authority. This Congress has taken the opportunity of general questioning provoked by Nixon to question the antique machinery of Congress itself. The new Congress has astounded and delighted all observers by its first efforts to make the Congress responsible to the changing needs of a new generation of Americans. But the role of Congress is defined not so much by the Constitution as by the voters. A Congressman is supposed to represent his constituents, not the nation at large. It is his duty to protect the specific interests of the people who elect him, whether they want farm supports, aid to Italy, the defense of Israel, quotas or no quotas, cross-busing or no busing, high milk prices, guaranteed wages, or secure jobs for workers of the arms and aerospace industries. In moments of great crisis, Congress can act and has acted in the large national interest. But normally, and over the long run, each Congressman must behave like a toy wound up by his constituents to go their pointed way. A Congressman must make claims on the whole nation; but only the President can decide for the whole, when the conflicting demands come to his desk. And since all demands cannot be met, because reality and resources set limits on total demand, the President must decide. That, among other things, is his duty. *"Gouverner,"* said a great French leader, Pierre Mendès-France, *"c'est choisir"*—to govern is to choose. The President still has to do it.

There, Nixon leaves another question. How does a man go about being President? Of his major duties—chief executive, policy-maker, High Priest—which is the most important?

That was the question that most plagued the leaders of the Nixon administration. And what they learned should not be discarded, throwing out the baby with the bath.

The Presidency, they learned, has to be reorganized; and their view of the office's problems should not be rejected in its entirety simply because their President saw politics as war and pursued politics above and beyond the law.

It was odd that Robert Finch and John Ehrlichman, far apart in philosophy and ethics, both of them thoughtful men, internal rivals from the first weeks of the Nixon administration, saw the problem and much of its solution in the same way. The plan for reorganization of the Presidency that evolved from their conversations with the President shared a central recognition: that the office has become the administrative center of too many conflicting interests. Congress has, over generations, solved too many problems by establishing special bureaus, special commissions, special agencies—and then dumped them all on the President for resolution of conflicts. Bureaus, commissions and agencies have become so numerous, so captive to the interests they were set up to guide, so fossilized in statutes, that their supervision by a solitary individual executive is impossible. The thought of the Nixon-Haldeman-Ehrlichman-Finch reorganization plan was, then, that the executive burden of the Presidency was of lesser importance than its policy-making responsibility, and must be subordinated to it. The plan collapsed because policy, as it flowed from Nixon, embraced lawlessness also. There, in his role as High Priest, Nixon failed most—and thus, all else in his planning came to naught. But the problem of the Presidency, the near-impossibility of one man being both policy-maker and executive at once, remains.

Even if the purest and noblest man had sat in the White

House in the Nixon years, he would have had to recognize this challenge, created by the simultaneous inflation of Presidential authority and the shortfall of any President's personal reach. No single Cabinet officer can supervise the energy problem, for example—not Interior, not Commerce, not Defense, not Agriculture, not State. Only the President can put it all together. No single office can make policy on the clash of American races—not HEW, not HUD, not the Department of Justice, not the Labor Department, not the Civil Rights Commission. Only the President can make national policy which is at once moral, wise and workable. No single Federal agency can master wages, prices, inflation— not Treasury, not the Federal Reserve Board, not the Labor Department, not the Council of Economic Advisers, not Agriculture. Only the President can.

All of which means that the office has become one in which greater and greater power has to be concentrated. And so the power to set policy has to be simplified—even, if necessary, by surrounding the President with what in John Ehrlichman's six-point plan was an Executive Council that would leave the President free to concentrate on policy. Some such reorganization must take place—whether by elevating the Constitutional Vice-President to Executive Vice-President, or by repackaging all agencies and departments into groups linked by function, or by some means yet to be devised.

But—and here is another of Nixon's legacies of questions —how can such expanded power be given a President whom the people do not trust? Or to a man who, like Nixon, may be ignorant of his priestly function as custodian of the faith? How does one choose a man who understands the priestly function?

The questions lead on and on, at this moment when the tradition of American politics has been ripped open. No one who, like this reporter, has followed the campaign trails for twenty years can fail to be haunted by the changes he has seen and the dangers that grow. In all matters except trust, the Presidency has been an experimental office since George Washington first held it in 1789. The entire electoral process has been left by the Constitution to the trial and error of succeeding generations. But now, as the parties split and tear at each other and within themselves, one is more troubled than ever. Can the election of a President be meaningful if the Twelfth Amendment is invoked, as in the next election it may be? What may happen if, in a close election like that of 1960 or 1968, the election is thrown into the House and the antique and explosive clauses of that amendment deny the nation a President of any credibility at all? And how long will the crazy-quilt pattern of primaries, ever more important in instructing people, be left as they confuse in their bewildering variety? How long before a long overdue Federal law makes sense of that vital national exercise by reasonable national legislation? How, and by what judgment, must standards be set for the fair use and reporting of television, which has changed American politics forever? And other questions—of survival of the Republican Party, of the fratricide in the Democratic Party—go on endlessly.

But these are long-range questions, and there is one last set of questions that Richard Nixon leaves behind as his immediate legacy to the next few years.

How much has his betrayal weakened the vital office he held?

Or has the episode been a purifying one, making the office more trustworthy and thus stronger?

In a time of crisis, 2,000 years ago, in 52 B.C., when the Roman Republic was dying, when decades of turbulence had caused its citizens to question their institutions, the last great plea for political civility came from a man who had been Consul only eleven years before—Marcus Tullius Cicero. Cicero was a tough, selfish and scheming politician who had executed supposed conspirators without trial when in power. But now, as he aged, he rose above his earlier self to write a book on the Republic, *De Republica,* urging a renewal of faith by trying to redefine the tradition that once had bound Romans to each other. "A commonwealth," he wrote, "is the property of a people. But a people is not any collection of human beings brought together in any sort of way, but an assemblage of people associated in an agreement with respect to justice and partnership for common good." Yet he was too late. His fellow citizens could no longer agree on what they meant by "justice" or "partnership for common good"; nor could the handful of politicians who soon brought about a revolution. First they killed Caesar, the man whom Cicero thought to be the greatest enemy of justice and the common good. And when they beheaded Cicero a year after, it was for the same reason. Vindictiveness, passion, killing ruled Rome; the people stood apart from assassination and execution alike because they no longer knew what to believe, and recognized that their leaders believed nothing. By then the Republic was dead, for the myths of law that had bound the Romans in the beginning had been stripped of meaning, reduced to decorative phrases carved on the marbled walls of the Empire, and the palaces of the tyrants who followed.

The Nixon crisis has been a similar test of faith and law, bloodless but no less threatening. If his humiliation can heal the breach of faith in government which he provoked and make way for the election of a trusted President in 1976, then his resignation may go down as the last, best act of his career—tragic, haunting, but necessary for the Republic.

But if his acts make all future Presidents suspect, to sink or bob in waves of emotion and popular opinion, subject to the shifting political winds, he will have diminished unforgivably the powers of the central office about which the Constitution revolves.

If he has indeed destroyed the power of a President to lead, he has destroyed all. And that will end in disaster worse than sin or crime.

The story deserves a Victorian coda, a farewell to the actors.

The little men—the burglars, the spymasters, the paymasters—were indicted and pleaded or were found guilty. Some were set free at once, while another handful was imprisoned but set free in very short order. Magruder and Colson; Dean and Kalmbach; Krogh and Segretti; and other, lesser creatures, having acknowledged their crimes, received as their fee for confession the mercy of the court—and many were writing books or lecturing about sin and redemption, or thinking about it, to repair fortune or reputation. Only Gordon Liddy, with a strange integrity, still refused to plead for mercy—Nixon's mistake, said Liddy, was that he had been "insufficiently ruthless." Liddy had no criticism for Sirica, the sentencing judge, because "John and I think alike. I mean that he believes the end justifies the means." Liddy recognized that he had been fighting a war and asked no quarter. But there were also many decent men who had served worthy causes in the Nixon administration and they would earn no honor for service to their country; their lives may be forever injured.

Of the larger men, the general staff of the conspiracy—Mitchell, Haldeman and Ehrlichman—all had been found guilty by a District of Columbia jury. They had gathered in the august ceremonial chamber of the U.S. Courthouse, under the frieze of Hammurabi, Justinian, Solon and Moses, and as they rose and turned, on October 1st, 1974, to face the first panel of 155 prospective jurors, 90 percent of them black, one could read in their downcast faces the doom they foresaw.

Their trial was anticlimax as it wound on for the next thirteen weeks in the stark but crowded second-floor chamber where common criminals are tried. But, stripped of power, they were what they had been in the beginning—the flotsam of politics, now left behind on the beach by the wave that had carried them so high, scavengers' trophies, their sadness gloated over by most of those who came to watch. They fought hopelessly against the sound of their own voices played back on tapes. They tried futilely to make it seem as if accident, not purpose, had entrapped them. But the crimes for which they were being tried all seemed to have happened long ago; they were exhausted and impoverished, and their own memories were now confused. Even at the end they did not know what had gone wrong; they had entered into power ignorant, and power had further blinded them. Of them all, the saddest was John Ehrlichman, who had tried as hard as he could to make America a better place to live in and yet had injured it. He traced his guilt to faith in Richard Nixon, but since Nixon did not know what he had done wrong, Ehrlichman could not know either. Ehrlichman sought to plead his own case before the jury, and was refused. Like Haldeman and Mitchell, he was sentenced to two-and-a-half to eight years in jail.

As for Richard Nixon—he had left for San Clemente. A Vietnam veteran on the lawn who saw him board his helicopter caught the moment best: "I watched," he said, "and it was just like the war. He was one of those people we put in plastic sacks and sent off. He'd had it, a shot right between the eyes; he was dead before he knew it. But we had to go on." Those who make a war of American politics must suffer war's consequences.

For several days, the current of power still coursed in Nixon. He would telephone the White House switchboard from San Clemente to question old aides; but then, one day, trying to reach one of those once closest to him, he found that he was put on the hold button—his call no longer commanded priority. And then, some time later, calling another loyalist still working at the White House complex, he was told: "Those who served you best hate you most."

Thus, he retreated into himself at San Clemente. His staff, by spring, had dwindled to four ladies, paid for out of a government allowance of $45,000. But that allowance would end on June 30, 1975. Already almost a million pieces of unanswered mail had piled up in his offices; and when, finally, he would be reduced to his allotted pension of $60,000 a year, he would be pinched. His take-home pay, if California and Federal taxes were both imposed on his pension, would come to about $500 a week. His travel, telephone bills, living expenses would all have to come out of that. But he is deep in debt, owing more than $460,000 in back taxes plus interest to the state and Federal tax systems. His legal bills will amount to hundreds of thousands more; his medical bills are substantial; these deductions may so shelter his full pension as to let him live in modest comfort.

Tourist, strollers and surfers have begun again to use his beachfront at San Clemente, as they did in the days before he was President. Weeds are beginning to grow over the four-hole golf course his admirers built for him. The bougainvillaea over the adobe walls of his six-acre estate grows ragged. The Secret Service still protects him, but soon, unless he makes money again, there may be no personal staff except Manolo Sanchez and his wife, if he can afford them. Graying, ill, conspicuously diminished in weight, he works several hours a day in his office, and sits with his phlebitis-pained leg propped up on a chair when he relaxes. Occasionally he receives friends and rambles in alternate bursts of nostalgia and hope; rarely does he leave the compound for visits outside.

Only his memoirs can restore his fortunes, and he is impatient to tell his story. But Congress has denied him possession of his papers, letters, documents, tapes. He is permitted personal access to copies of them, but no other President of the past has been subject to such deprivation of what has always been considered personal property. The records, Congress felt, should remain in government custody, available to courts, Congress and "historians." All his privacy was thus certain to be riddled, if not immediately, eventually. He was, he said of himself, to be picked over "like a carcass." But he had brought it on himself. The Foundation and Library which he once hoped to build as the ultimate repository of the damning tapes, the most complete record ever of a President's thinking, have been liquidated. No one can guess where the famous tapes will finally come to rest, or how their full publication will weigh his name in history—the Peacemaker or the Betrayer of the Faith.

In his memoirs he will have to judge himself finally as a man and a President. They will certainly be the most fascinating of all those written by members of his team. But the real end of his political story came in the statement by which he accepted the pardon given him by his successor, Gerald Ford, on September 8th, 1974, a month after he announced his resignation.

It was issued from San Clemente, only seventy-two miles from Whittier, where he had grown up.

Since he left Whittier, he had been all around the world and triumphed brilliantly in its great capitals. All the way from Whittier, however, he had been trying to understand How Things Work. His successes rested on how much understanding he had gained. But so did his crime and his disaster. He did not know how faith worked, or why it was so important for a President of the United States to understand. His final statement made that perfectly clear:

". . . one thing I can see clearly now," he said, in accepting his pardon, "is that I was wrong in not acting more decisively and more forthrightly in dealing with Watergate, particularly when it reached the stage of judicial proceedings. . . .

"No words can describe the depths of my regret and pain at the anguish my mistakes over Watergate have caused the nation and the Presidency. . . .

"I know that many fair-minded people believe that my motivation and actions . . . were intentionally self-serving and illegal. I now understand how my own mistakes and misjudgments have contributed to that belief and seemed to support it. . . .

"That the way I tried to deal with Watergate was the wrong way is a burden I shall bear for every day of the life that is left to me."

Thus the last official pronouncement of the 37th President of the United States.

He still had not really learned the way America works.

APPENDIX A

THE ARTICLES OF IMPEACHMENT

The articles of impeachment voted by the Committee on the Judiciary of the House of Representatives and submitted to the House in its report of August 20, 1974, read:

RESOLUTION

Impeaching Richard M. Nixon, President of the United States, of high crimes and misdemeanors.

Resolved, That Richard M. Nixon, President of the United States, is impeached for high crimes and misdemeanors, and that the following articles of impeachment be exhibited to the Senate:

Articles of impeachment exhibited by the House of Representatives of the United States of America in the name of itself and of all of the people of the United States of America, against Richard M. Nixon, President of the United States of America, in maintenance and support of its impeachment against him for high crimes and misdemeanors.

ARTICLE I

In his conduct of the office of President of the United States, Richard M. Nixon, in violation of his constitutional oath faithfully to execute the office of President of the United States and, to the best of his ability, preserve, protect, and defend the Constitution of the United States, and in violation of his constitutional duty to take care that the laws be faithfully executed, has prevented, obstructed, and impeded the administration of justice, in that:

On June 17, 1972, and prior thereto, agents of the Committee for the Re-election of the President committed unlawful entry of the headquarters of the Democratic National Committee in Washington, District of Columbia, for the purpose of securing political intelligence. Subsequent thereto, Richard M. Nixon, using the powers of his high office, engaged personally and through his subordinates and agents, in a course of conduct or plan designed to delay, impede, and obstruct the investigation of such unlawful entry; to cover up, conceal and protect those responsible; and to conceal the existence and scope of other unlawful covert activities.

The means used to implement this course of conduct or plan included one or more of the following:

(1) making or causing to be made false or misleading statements to lawfully authorized investigative officers and employees of the United States;

(2) withhlding relevant and material evidence or information from lawfully authorized investigative officers and employees of the United States;

(3) approving, condoning, acquiescing in, and counseling witnesses with respect to the giving of false or misleading statements to lawfully authorized investigative officers and employees of the United States and false or misleading testimony in duly instituted judicial and congressional proceedings;

(4) interfering or endeavoring to interfere with the conduct of investigations by the Department of Justice of the United States, the Federal Bureau of Investigation, the Office of Watergate Special Prosecution Force, and Congressional Committees;

(5) approving, condoning, and acquiescing in the surreptitious payment of substantial sums of money for the purpose of obtaining the silence or influencing the testimony of witnesses, potential witnesses or individuals who participated in such unlawful entry and other illegal activities;

(6) endeavoring to misuse the Central Intelligence Agency, an agency of the United States;

(7) disseminating information received from officers of the Department of Justice of the United States to subjects of investigations conducted by lawfully authorized investigative officers and employees of the United States, for the purpose of aiding and assisting such subjects in their attempts to avoid criminal liability;

(8) making false or misleading public statements for the purpose of deceiving the people of the United States into believing that a thorough and complete investigation had been conducted with respect to allegations of miscon-

duct on the part of personnel of the executive branch of the United States and personnel of the Committee for the Re-election of the President, and that there was no involvement of such personnel in such misconduct; or

(9) endeavoring to cause prospective defendants, and individuals duly tried and convicted, to expect favored treatment and consideration in return for their silence or false testimony, or rewarding individuals for their silence or false testimony.

In all of this, Richard M. Nixon has acted in a manner contrary to his trust as President and subversive of constitutional government, to the great prejudice of the cause of law and justice and to the manifest injury of the people of the United States.

Wherefore Richard M. Nixon, by such conduct, warrants impeachment and trial, and removal from office.

ARTICLE II

Using the powers of the office of President of the United States, Richard M. Nixon, in violation of his constitutional oath faithfully to execute the office of President of the United States and, to the best of his ability, preserve, protect, and defend the Constitution of the United States, and in disregard of his constitutional duty to take care that the laws be faithfully executed, has repeatedly engaged in conduct violating the constitutional rights of citizens, impairing the due and proper administration of justice and the conduct of lawful inquiries, or contravening the laws governing agencies of the executive branch and the purposes of these agencies.

This conduct has included one or more of the following:

(1) He has, acting personally and through his subordinates and agents, endeavored to obtain from the Internal Revenue Service, in violation of the constitutional rights of citizens, confidential information contained in income tax returns for purposes not authorized by law, and to cause, in violation of the constitutional rights of citizens, income tax audits or other income tax investigations to be initiated or conducted in a discriminatory manner.

(2) He misused the Federal Bureau of Investigation, the Secret Service, and other executive personnel, in violation or disregard of the constitutional rights of citizens, by directing or authorizing such agencies or personnel to conduct or continue electronic surveillance or other investiga-

tions for purposes unrelated to national security, the enforcement of laws, or any other lawful function of his office; he did direct, authorize, or permit the use of information obtained thereby for purposes unrelated to national security, the enforcement of laws, or any other lawful function of his office; and he did direct the concealment of certain records made by the Federal Bureau of Investigation of electronic surveillance.

(3) He has, acting personally and through his subordinates and agents, in violation or disregard of the constitutional rights of citizens, authorized and permitted to be maintained a secret investigative unit within the office of the President, financed in part with money derived from campaign contributions, which unlawfully utilized the resources of the Central Intelligence Agency, engaged in covert and unlawful activities, and attempted to prejudice the constitutional right of an accused to a fair trial.

(4) He has failed to take care that the laws were faithfully executed by failing to act when he knew or had reason to know that his close subordinates endeavored to impede and frustrate lawful inquiries by duly constituted executive, judicial, and legislative entities concerning the unlawful entry into the headquarters of the Democratic National Committee, and the cover-up thereof, and concerning other unlawful activities, including those relating to the confirmation of Richard Kleindienst as Attorney General of the United States, the electronic surveillance of private citizens, the break-in into the offices of Dr. Lewis Fielding, and the campaign financing practices of the Committee to Re-elect the President.

(5) In disregard of the rule of law, he knowingly misused the executive power by interfering with agencies of the executive branch, including the Federal Bureau of Investigation, the Criminal Division, and the Office of Watergate Special Prosecution Force, of the Department of Justice, and the Central Intelligence Agency, in violation of his duty to take care that the laws be faithfully executed.

In all of this, Richard M. Nixon has acted in a manner contrary to his trust as President and subversive of constitutional government, to the great prejudice of the cause of law and justice and to the manifest injury of the people of the United States.

Wherefore Richard M. Nixon, by such conduct, warrants impeachment and trial, and removal from office.

ARTICLE III

In his conduct of the office of President of the United States, Richard M. Nixon, contrary to his oath faithfully to execute the office of President of the United States and, to the best of his ability, preserve, protect, and defend the Constitution of the United States, and in violation of his constitutional duty to take care that the laws be faithfully executed, has failed without lawful cause or excuse to produce papers and things as directed by duly authorized subpoenas issued by the Committee on the Judiciary of the House of Representatives on April 11, 1974, May 15, 1974, May 30, 1974, and June 24, 1974, and willfully disobeyed such subpoenas. The subpoenaed papers and things were deemed necessary by the Committee in order to resolve by direct evidence fundamental, factual questions relating to Presidential direction, knowledge, or approval of actions demonstrated by other evidence to be substantial grounds for impeachment of the President. In refusing to produce these papers and things, Richard M. Nixon, substituting his judgment as to what materials were necessary for the inquiry, interposed the powers of the Presidency against the lawful subpoenas of the House of Representatives, thereby assuming to himself functions and judgments necessary to the exercise of the sole power of impeachment vested by the Constitution in the House of Representatives.

In all of this, Richard M. Nixon has acted in a manner contrary to his trust as President and subversive of constitutional government, to the great prejudice of the cause of law and justice, and to the manifest injury of the people of the United States.

Wherefore Richard M. Nixon, by such conduct, warrants impeachment and trial, and removal from office.

APPENDIX B

THE RESIGNATION SPEECH

President Nixon announced his resignation from office in a tele-vised address at 9 o'clock on the evening of August 8, 1974. This is the text.

Good evening.

This is the thirty-seventh time I have spoken to you from this office, where so many decisions have been made that shaped the history of this Nation. Each time I have done so to discuss with you some matter that I believe affected the national interest.

In all the decisions I have made in my public life, I have always tried to do what was best for the Nation. Throughout the long and difficult period of Watergate, I have felt it was my duty to persevere, to make every possible effort to complete the term of office to which you elected me.

In the past few days, however, it has become evident to me that I no longer have a strong enough political base in the Congress to justify continuing that effort. As long as there was a base, I felt strongly that it was necessary to see the constitutional process through to its conclusion, that to do otherwise would be unfaithful to the spirit of that deliberately difficult process, and a dangerously destabilizing precedent for the future.

But with the disappearance of that base, I now believe that the constitutional purpose has been served, and there is no longer a need for the process to be prolonged.

I would have preferred to carry through to the finish whatever the personal agony it would have involved, and my family unanimously urged me to do so. But the interests of the Nation must always come before any personal considerations.

From the discussions I have had with Congressional and other leaders, I have concluded that because of the Watergate matter I might not have the support of the Congress that I would consider necessary to back the very difficult decisions and carry out the duties of this office in the way the interests of the Nation would require.

I have never been a quitter. To leave office before my term is completed is abhorrent to every instinct in my body. But as President, I must put the interest of America first. America needs a full-time President and a full-time Congress, particularly at this time with the problems we face at home and abroad.

To continue to fight through the months ahead for my personal vindication would almost totally absorb the time and attention of both the President and the Congress in a period when our entire focus should be on the great issues of peace abroad and prosperity without inflation at home.

Therefore, I shall resign the Presidency effective at noon tomorrow. Vice President Ford will be sworn in as President at that hour in this office.

As I recall the high hopes for America with which we began this second term, I feel a great sadness that I will not be here in this office working on your behalf to achieve those hopes in the next two and one-half years. But in turning over direction of the Government to Vice President Ford, I know, as I told the Nation when I nominated him for that office ten months ago, that the leadership of America will be in good hands.

In passing this office to the Vice President, I also do so with the profound sense of the weight of responsibility that will fall on his shoulders tomorrow and, therefore, of the understanding, the patience, the cooperation he will need from all Americans.

As he assumes that responsibility, he will deserve the help and support of all of us. As we look to the future, the first essential is to begin healing the wounds of this Nation; to put the bitterness and the divisions of the recent past behind us and to rediscover those shared ideals that lie at the heart of our strength and unity as a great and as a free people.

By taking this action, I hope that I will have hastened the start of that process of healing which is so desperately needed in America.

I regret deeply any injuries that may have been done in the course of the events that led to this decision. I would say only that if some of my judgments were wrong, and some were wrong, they were made in what I believed at the time to be the best interest of the Nation.

To those who have stood with me during these past difficult months, to my family, my friends, to many others who joined in supporting my cause because they believed it was right, I will be eternally grateful for your support.

And to those who have not felt able to give me your support, let me say I leave with no bitterness toward those who have opposed me, because all of us, in the final analysis, have been concerned with the good of the country however our judgments might differ.

So, let us all now join together in affirming that common commitment and in helping our new President succeed for the benefit of all Americans.

I shall leave this office with regret at not completing my term, but with gratitude for the privilege of serving as your President for the past five and one-half years. These years have been a momentous time in the history of our Nation and the world. They have been a time of achievement in which we can all be proud, achievements that represent the shared efforts of the Administration, the Congress and the people.

But the challenges ahead are equally great and they, too, will require the support and the efforts of the Congress and the people working in cooperation with the new Administration.

We have ended America's longest war, but in the work of securing a lasting peace in the world, the goals ahead are even more far-reaching and more difficult. We must complete a structure of peace so that it will be said of this generation, our generation, of Americans, by the people of all nations, not only that we ended one war, but that we prevented future wars.

We have unlocked the doors that for a quarter of a century stood between the United States and the People's Republic of China.

We must now ensure that the one quarter of the world's people who live in the People's Republic of China will be and remain not our enemies but our friends.

In the Middle East, 100 million people in the Arab countries, many of whom have considered us their enemy for nearly twenty years, now look on us as their friends. We must continue to build on that friendship so that peace can settle at last over the Middle East and so that the cradle of civilization will not become its grave.

Together with the Soviet Union we have made the crucial breakthroughs that have begun the process of limiting nuclear arms. But we must set as our goal not just limiting, but reducing and finally destroying these terrible weapons so that they cannot destroy civilization and so that the threat of nuclear war will no longer hang over the world and the people.

We have opened the new relation with the Soviet Union. We must continue to develop and expand that new relationship so that the two strongest nations of the world will live together in cooperation rather than confrontation.

Around the world, in Asia, in Africa, in Latin America, in the Middle East, there are millions of people who live in terrible poverty, even starvation. We must keep as our goal turning away from production for war and expanding production for peace so that people everywhere on this earth can at least look forward in their children's time, if not in our own time, to having the necessities for a decent life.

Here in America, we are fortunate that most of our people have not only the blessings of liberty, but also the means to live full and good and, by the world's standards, even abundant lives. We must press on, however, to a goal of not only more and better jobs, but of full opportunity for every American, and of what we are striving so hard right now to achieve, prosperity without inflation.

For more than a quarter of a century in public life I have shared in the turbulent history of this era. I have fought for what I believed in. I have tried to the best of my ability to discharge those duties and meet those responsibilities that were entrusted to me.

Sometimes I have succeeded and sometimes I have failed, but always I have taken heart from what Theodore Roosevelt once said about the man in the arena, "whose face is marred by dust and sweat and blood, who strives valiantly, who errs and comes short again and again because there is not effort without error and shortcoming, but who does actually strive to do the deeds, who knows the great enthusiasms, the great devotions, who spends himself in a worthy cause, who at the best knows in the end the triumphs of high achievements and who at the worst, if he fails, at least fails while daring greatly."

I pledge to you tonight that as long as I have a breath of life in my body, I shall continue in that spirit. I shall continue to work for the great causes to which I have been dedicated throughout my years as a Congressman, a Senator, a Vice President and President; the cause of peace not just for America but among all nations, prosperity, justice and opportunity for all of our people.

There is one cause above all to which I have been devoted and to which I shall always be devoted for as long as I live.

When I first took the oath of office as President five and one-half years ago, I made this sacred commitment: "To consecrate my office, my energies and all the wisdom I can summon to the cause of peace among nations."

I have done my very best in all the days since to be true to that pledge. As a result of these efforts, I am confident that the world is a safer place today, not only for the people of America, but for the people of all nations, and that all of our children have a better chance than before of living in peace rather than dying in war.

This, more than anything, is what I hoped to achieve when I

sought the Presidency. This, more than anything, is what I hope will be my legacy to you, to our country, as I leave the Presidency.

To have served in this office is to have felt a very personal sense of kinship with each and every American. In leaving it, I do so with this prayer: May God's grace be with you in all the days ahead.

ACKNOWLEDGMENTS

First come my personal thanks to those "without whom," literally, this book could not have been written.

Foremost among them, Hedva Hadas Glickenhaus, who has given me all of the mind, spirit, and devotion that anyone could ask of a companion on the line. Then my wife, Beatrice Kevitt Hofstadter, whose tenderness sustained the writer and whose knowledge of American history contributed so much to this book. Next, Simon Michael Bessie, much more friend than publisher, who has been the silent and fostering partner of my writing for more years than either of us cares to remember. Edward T. Thompson, managing editor of the *Reader's Digest*, was the forceful inspirer of this book and its most encouraging drillmaster. Jane Smith, of the *Reader's Digest*, provided not only meticulous research, but a unique knowledge of how one presses the levers in the nation's capital. To William Schulz and Ann Dear, of the *Reader's Digest*, goes my gratitude for constant help. To Tom Hyman, Paul Hirschman, Barbara Campo and Lisa Morrill, of Atheneum, my thanks for critical professional contribution.

Several outstanding journalists generously took from their personal time enough energy to add reporting that I sought of them, for which I am particularly grateful: James Wieghart and Frank Van Riper of the New York *Daily News;* Martin Plissner of CBS; and Eugene Methvin of the *Reader's Digest*.

Beyond that, there are men who shared with me their understanding of the Nixon years, their insights being more important than fact or story in illuminating what I have written: Leonard Garment, Robert Finch, Charles McWhorter, Terry Lenzner, Charles Wardell, Patrick Buchanan, Raymond Price, Fred Buzhardt, William Safire, Elliot Richardson, John Whitaker, Webster Todd, Jr., Taft Schreiber, Carl Greenberg, James Bassett, Julius Leetham, Tom Evans, Franklin D. Murphy, Daniel P. Moynihan, Melvin Laird, Charles Schumer, Richard Allen, Herbert Klein, Peter Peterson. None of these men is responsible for my opinions—or conclusions; and many of them will disagree with me. But I owe them thanks.

A small seminar that meets in New York from time to time has provoked me continuously to confusion and political resolution. To the members of that seminar my thanks: Richard Clurman, A. M. Rosenthal, Arthur Gelb, William F. Buckley, Osborn Elliott, and Irving Kristol.

Then there are the men and women of the official Washington information services, so seldom recognized, but who perform, for all of us, a vital function. Among these, first, James Doyle, press officer of the Special Prosecutor; then, Diane Sawyer, once of the White House press office; David Holmes, Superintendent of the House Periodical Press Gallery; Roy McGhee of the Senate Periodical Press Gallery; Helen Starr of Congressman Rodino's office. Then Francis O'Brien's name should be mentioned as one of the most helpful, though he fits into no known category—an observant scholar, plunged into events, forced to explain them on the run. All of these good people extended themselves for this book beyond what duty called for.

The most important acknowledgment that must be made is, however, a collective one—to the men and women of the national press corps. It was a time for heroes and the news system made the most of it. Whether its new-found power will end in excess worries me deeply. But—as we used to say in World War II—it was better to win the war than lose it; and time enough to worry about the news system's use of power, or abuse of it, after the victory.

My own reporting in this book has been amplified by the reporting of so many others that only a catalogue would contain all the names. No future historian will be able to write of the Nixon crisis without poring over the dispatches of the great news teams. I have tried to acknowledge directly in the text the names of those from whom I have specifically drawn. But at the Washington *Post*, in addition to those already acknowledged in the story, I should add the names of Carroll Kilpatrick and Haynes Johnson. The *New York Times* news team provided the foundation for my understanding, as it has for many others. In addition to Seymour Hersh, I would like to express my thanks to Johnny Apple, and above all, to Jim Naughton for a literary quality he brought to reporting, whenever given time, that will make his high style enduring. There are so many others, not acknowledged in text. The news team of the *New Republic*— John Osborne and Walter Pincus—matched the best. The Los Angeles *Times* news team moved in for the first time to the center of national events. All reconstructions of the past few years must include the records they have left.

Television network reporting is erased from the record as soon as the dial is flicked. In addition to the recognized performance of Walter Cronkite, John Chancellor, and Howard K. Smith, which helped all of us to keep track, I want to add personal thanks to Donald Hewitt and Mike Wallace of CBS for shared confidence or reminiscence.

The news-weeklies, *Time, Newsweek, U.S. News & World Report,* shaped American understanding during recent years. But of their news teams, I have a particular personal obligation of thanks to Murray Gart, *Time's* chief of news-gathering; and also to Stanley Cloud.

In this collective time of American life, it was the powerful news teams against the Nixon government team. But there were half-a-dozen loners following the story, from whose dispatches I have learned so much. As a loner myself, I should mention outstanding reporting by other loners on which I have drawn. Timothy Crouse, of *Rolling Stone,* for example, provided the best reporting of the conspiracy trial of 1974. Anthony Lukas published in the *New York Times Magazine* two articles, under enormous pressure of deadline, which no future historian can ignore. Richard Reeves and Aaron Latham of *New York* magazine and Nina Totenberg of *New Times* did their thing in their respective magazines with little support other than professional commitment. Elizabeth Drew wrote a series of articles in *The New Yorker* that are not only singular in quality, but indispensable as reference. I should add other loners whose work is also indispensable as source material: Adam Clymer in his exploration of Richard Nixon's tax returns; Nick Thimmesch; Mary McGrory.

I write these acknowledgments naming some very close to me, and some whom I have never met. It would be derelict of me not to mention one institution and one man who would think of themselves as oddly bracketed: the *Congressional Quarterly* and the late Steward Alsop. The *Congressional Quarterly* is the best technical reference work for those who write about official America. I acknowledge my dependence on their source material. Stewart Alsop was the political compass of Washington in these years of turmoil; he knew what was right, what was wrong. I wrote this book hoping he would like it, because I took so much from his thinking.

An acknowledgment must be made to the U.S. Government Printing Office, the official publishing service of the United States, which makes available the transactions of our times. Even though the volume of its publications overwhelms any man's capacity to read it all, the publications are absolutely essential. No other government does it as well.

Then, finally, should come a confession of forgetfulness. All writers unconsciously plagiarize. So have I, I am sure. I have talked to so many people. Some of the most valuable I may have overlooked in these acknowledgments. Even more valuable are those who have talked to me in the fading tradition of I'll-tell-you-how-it-happened-if-you-don't-ever-quote-me-by-name. If I have left out the names of those who wanted to be remembered, or quoted the names of those who wanted to be left out, I nonetheless want to thank them all. As a recent President of the United States said, "you win some, you lose some." But you can't win them all.

My acknowledgments thus go to all who have helped, mentioned or not. No book such as this is ever a one-man job.

INDEX

Daily Worker, 162

Dairy industry, campaign contributions by 68, 416; investigation of, 381, 401

Daley, Richard, 52, 58

Dancing Bear: An Inside Look at California Politics (Hill), 74 n.

Dash, Samuel, 264, 297, 323

Dawson, William L., 64

Dean, John W., III, 19, 50, 97, 109, 126, 165, 319, 414; background and career of, 183–184; campaign intelligence duties of, 184, 201, 208; "cancer on the Presidency" phrase, 258, 260; as Counsel to the President, 150, 183, 184, 189, 193; disclosures to prosecutors by, 268–269, 271, 275; dismissal of, 283–284; and enemies list, 198; and hush-money demands of Hunt, 256–257, 259, 273; imprisonment of, 432; implication of Nixon by, 280–281, 314; Liddy suggested by, for CREEP, 202; and Liddy-plan, 203, 208; McCord accusations against, 264; and Mitchell, 183, 184; and Nixon's financial affairs, 99; question of immunity for, 281; his resignation demanded, 277; sacrificed, 272, 273, 277; "screw our enemies" memo of, 198; in tape of March 13, 1973, 253; in tape of March 17, 254–255; in tape of March 20, 257; in tape of March 21, 257–259, 278–279; in tape of March 22, 261–262; in tax crackdown operations against political enemies, 196–198; his voice on tapes, 249 n.; Watergate Committee investigation of, 299; Watergate Committee testimony of, 300, 301, 302; in Watergate cover-up, 21, 209, 210, 212, 214, 215–218, 251, 252–256, 268–269, 403; Watergate investigation "contained" by 217–218, 251, 326–327, 393; written Watergate report assignment, 262, 267

De Antonio, Emile, 196

Declassification of documents, 192, 194

Defense Department, 309; and arms supplies to Israel, 330–331; under Laird, 138, 152, 314–315; during Nixon resignation crisis, 35, 49–50; Nixon's search for a Secretary, 136, 138; Richardson appointed Secretary, 228, 232–233, 322; under Schlesinger, 35, 310; wiretap at, 161. See also Pentagon

Defense Intelligence Agency, 174

DeLoach, Cartha, 252

DeMarco, Frank, 100

Democratic National Committee (at Watergate), break-in, 206–207

Democratic National Convention of 1952, 52, 57–59

Democratic National Convention of 1968, demonstrations at, 166

Democratic Party, 431; basic governmental philosophy, 69; in California, 71, 72, 73, 77; Colson strategy against, 185–186; Congressional special elections won by, 373; increasing liberalism of candidates of, 424; labor unions and, 67; majority base in Roosevelt coalition, 286; members on House Judiciary Committee, 380, 381, 384, 395–396, 403–404; in Nixon crisis, 287; politics after 1952, 59; reaction to Watergate, in 1972 campaign, 294

Dent, Frederick B., 36

Denver Post, 344

Detroit News, 344

Dewey, Thomas, 172

Dickerson, Nancy, 172

Direct-mail programs in political campaigns, 75, 116–117

"Dirty tricks": Dick Tuck, 201; in 1960 campaign, 95, 199; in 1964 campaign, 131–132, 412; in 1968 campaign, 132, 252, 412–413; in 1972 campaign, 199–201, 202, 205–207, 251, 254–255, 294, 297; Special

Have you read these bestsellers by

JOSEPH WAMBAUGH

☐ The Blue Knight

A hard-hitting, tough talking, realistic novel that provides a cop's-eye view of police brutality. The entertaining and exciting story of Bumper Morgan, a Los Angeles cop, on which the popular TV series is based. $1.75 (0607-07)

☐ The Onion Field

"Wambaugh's account of a true-life cop killing and its aftermath reveals the intensity of a police investigation when one of their own has been gunned down."
—*King Features* $1.75 (7350-01)

☐ The New Centurions

The big nationwide bestseller about cops by a cop— Joseph Wambaugh who spent 10 years with the Los Angeles Police Department. $1.75 (6417-04)

DECEMBER 11, 1944 ... U.S.S. *Candlefish*, submarine on wartime patrol, mysteriously lost at Latitude 30 in the Pacific. All hands perish, except for one survivor.

OCTOBER 5, 1974 . . . Six hundred miles northwest of Pearl Harbor, a submarine surfaces in front of a Japanese freighter. It is the *Candlefish*, in perfect working order fully outfitted down to steaks in the freezer yet without a trace of life aboard.

In Washington, D.C., a naval intelligence officer is convinced that the *Candlefish* was the victim of another Devil's Triangle, and convinces his superiors to send it on a voyage retracing her route of thirty years before in the hope of uncovering whatever fearful force lies in wait at Latitude 30.

Only when the sub is well out to sea, with no turning back, do he and the rest of the crew begin to suspect why the *Candlefish* has come back from a watery grave, and what that means to every living soul aboard.

GHOSTBOAT

by George E. Simpson and Neal R. Burger